The Creation of Kindness

By

CORA E. CYPSER

Published by

KIM PATHWAYS

Inquiries regarding requests to print all of part of *The Creation of Kindness* should be addressed to KIM PATHWAYS.

To order directly from the publisher add $3.00 to the price for the first copy and $.50 for each additional copy. Send check or money order to KIM PATHWAYS.

Opinions expressed in this book are not necessarily the views of the publisher.

291

More information from:
KIM PATHWAYS
16 Young Road
Katonah NY 10536

Contents

Contents (continued)

Contents (continued)

v

Contents (continued)

Contents (continued)

Charts

*Dedicated to all those human beings
down through the ages
who thought kindly
of those who would come after them
and who diligently took care of the earth.*

Prologue
THE PROCESS OF BECOMING
by Rudy Cypser

One Vast Process. We, all peoples of the earth, and the entire earth itself are participants in a vast process of becoming. It is a single process, with many parts, all playing a role in the process that leads to our becoming. Our process extends over hundreds of millions of years, and it involves all beings all over the earth. We all constitute a single body that ever so slowly becomes what our creator has destined us to become. We each, individually, play our part in that process, more or less contributing to that process, for we humans have been given free will– a freedom to contribute more or less, or even to oppose that becoming.

Consciousness. In the very beginning, before living beings, there was the beginning of relationships and cooperation among basic elements. Atoms and then ever larger molecules were formed. These cooperating relationships were the building blocks out of which higher and higher forms of cooperating relationships evolved. With the passage of hundreds of millions of years, living forms and ever more complex life was formed. After the cells and the primitive fish, ever more complex creatures of the sea and the land and the air became. Consciousness, the ever more complex practice of cooperative relationships thus began in a most elemental fashion, and grew to its present capabilities. Teilhard de Chardin beautifully explained this growth of consciousness from inanimate, to animate, and then to reflective beings. The highest forms of consciousness today are expressed in empathy, caring, kindness, unselfish (agape) love, compassion, understanding, forgiveness, and the willingness to give of oneself for the benefit of another. This consciousness defined the very essence of each being– from the most elemental to the most complex. Each had an identity– its capability for consciousness– its very soul.

Tribal Movements. In our history, our earth has undergone massive changes. Continents have shifted many thousands of miles relative to each other. There have been: a long series of ice ages that swept the earth, cataclysmic volcanic eruptions that darkened the earth, floods that covered much if not all of the earth, droughts, and even massive impacts of meteors from outer space. In all of this, the evolving human race was constantly adjusting to changing living conditions. Mass migrations of tribes flowed across the face of the earth, seeking survival and better living conditions. If it wasn't the geologic or climatic changes, it was the predator tribes that forced great movements of peoples.

The Common Search. Our knowledge of the exercise of human consciousness goes back only about ten thousand years. This is a relatively short interval in the time span of our becoming. Still, in this last ten thousand years, great advances have been made. With the amazing capacity for reflective thought, humankind in all parts of the earth have been inspired to seek the fruits of consciousness. Moreover, thoughtful people in every corner of the globe have sought the meaning and purpose of life itself. In this, they have tried to understand the grand process of becoming, and the mind or spirit that wills it, which many call God.

The Great Crescent. A vast ferment of searching the mysteries of our creation and our fulfillment has occurred. In our part of the globe, we have been particularly affected by the religious thought in the long arc extending from India to Egypt. This arc particularly includes the Indus valley in India, the Arabian peninsula, Mesopotamia, the upper reaches of the Tigris and Euphrates into present day Iran and Turkey, Palestine, and the great civilizations of the Nile River in Egypt. Trade routes crisscrossed this area. Ideas and counter ideas were carried and distributed in every direction. Countless military invasions, this way and later, that way, added to the interchange.

Thus one finds vestiges of the Harrapan civilization of the Indus valley in Arabia and Mesopotamia. The people of the Arabian peninsula, in turn, mingled their heritage with those further up the Tigris and Euphrates rivers all the way to the Iranian and Turkish regions. The Hittites from Turkey, and the Sumerians and Semites from Mesopotamia, in turn, carried their culture through Palestine and all the way into Egypt, where an advanced civilization and a complex theocracy was flourishing. The Egyptians, for a time, took control of Palestine and as far East as present day Iraq. Greeks impressed their ideas across the entire arc under the banner of Alexander. The Romans then did likewise. Jews from Palestine spread across the region as a result of the Roman conquests and the Jewish Diaspora. The Christian movement took root in much of this same land as its apostles spread the Christian gospel. The Turks and Iranians later on preached Islam throughout the Persian empire, extending this teaching from Spain to the Indus valley, and also well into Europe. The Europeans, notably England and France, later impressed some of their cultures on the land.

Cultural Absorption. In all of this, thoughtful persons in every land absorbed the ideas of all the cultures they were exposed to. The result is that each of our cultures benefited from all the others. The roots of our ideas are sometimes obscure– even hidden. However, we all are more interrelated and indebted to each other than we usually realize.

Throughout the earth, various groups have tried to assemble the wisdom and practice that had been handed down to them. In particular, sacred scriptures appeared in Egypt, Palestine, India, China, and elsewhere. These scriptures often combined rules for practical living with theories about our human relationships to the creator and provider of the earth, our God. One finds a common thread in much of these writings, extolling the value of consciousness and its practice in human relationships. For example, whether it be the Hindu, Buddhist, Zoroastrian, Jewish, Christian, or Moslem writings, one finds almost the identical golden rule, "Do unto others what you would have them do unto you."

Common Inspiration. One can readily assent, therefore, to a common heritage of ideas in many peoples of the earth. Somewhat more surprising is the existence of these common threads of understanding even among peoples who have been greatly isolated from the other tribes of humanity. It has been the experience of many persons that their yearning to practice the virtues of consciousness is strong even with a very minimum of earlier interaction with other peoples from whom they might have drawn these inclinations. Accordingly, it has become a commonly accepted theory that more than the interchange of ideas is at work here. It is as if each one of us is somehow inspired and motivated to follow the way of increasing consciousness and to practice it despite pressures to the contrary. In the terminology of the religious, we are inspired by a holy spirit to go that way. All the sacred writings of the major religious faiths of the world reflect this.

Thoughtful persons in many tribes and other groups opened their minds and hearts to the inner voice, and tried to listen to the spirit of God within. Almost universally, the concepts of a loving and providential God resulted. It is not surprising that many listeners focused on the needs of their people and their time, and the possibilities of a loving response. Hence, it is natural that a loving, providential God would indicate to all peoples the ultimate satisfaction of needs such as security, freedom, and a peaceful, bountiful land.

The Hebrew Bible. In the later part of this last ten thousand year period, a scant three thousand years ago, the Jewish people were becoming a kingdom under the leadership of King David. The formation of this kingdom was a unique event in its combination of political, military, and theological unions. A major attempt was made to collect the wisdom, political laws, and theological ideas that had filtered down through the ages to these peoples.

All this was, understandably, an aggregate of the flow of ideas that had crisscrossed Palestine, which was between the great Egyptian civilization on one side and the civilizations of Mesopotamia, Arabia, and India on the other side. All this was particularly influenced by the hundreds of years that tribes from Palestine had spent in Egypt, before their exodus back to Palestine. The sifting, selecting, interpreting and writing of all this material was a huge undertaking. It is understandable that, as it was done for David who was bent on kingdom formation, that the selection and interpretation would be influenced by the needs of such formation. A short time later, another updating of these Jewish records was done during the seventy odd years that much of Israel had spent in the Babylonian captivity. Again, the shape of these records would naturally serve the yearning for a return and a reconstruction of the Jewish state. Despite the apparent parochialism, the Bible stands as a monumental expression of the world's striving to appreciate and practice its gifts of consciousness.

Utilizing Myth. Many of the sacred scriptures written by different religious groups had a purpose– to convey ideas and principles, rather than to be an accurate history of prior events. Writers of these scriptures therefore frequently were at liberty to aggregate earlier myths and semi-historical stories into a new story which served to convey the religious ideas and principles. Most of us have only recently stopped associating myth with untruth. Even though the stories are not literally true, we have begun to appreciate the marvelous ways in which myths from many cultures have, over the millennia, carried fundamental truths to our shores.

Still Becoming. Having spent hundreds of millions of years to date, we find ourselves still in a relatively primitive state of consciousness. We, the people of earth, still experience hatred, jealousies, and rage, which certainly are not the fulfillment of consciousness. Despite our relatively great capability for consciousness, we, the peoples of earth, still practice great violence to each other, including pogroms, holocausts, and devastating wars against each other. It would seem that millions of years still may be needed for our full becoming.

We might do better, and speed up the process of becoming, if we all understood the reality of our common, cross-cultural heritage, the similarity of our basic principles, and the fact that we all are united in one process guided by our common creator and providential God. That process, called here "The Creation of Kindness," extends over all time and all worldly space, to which we are all related. It is our hope that this book will, in at least a small way, encourage that understanding.

The Creation of Kindness

I

Creation

Where have we come from?
Where are we going?

In the beginning, we were only a dream of God.
God dreamed of star dust and atoms and of love.
Planets, rocks, waters, algae, dinosaurs, gave way
to smaller creatures playing among tall trees.
Voices were heard calling to one another.
Houses were made, for those alive
and then for those who died,
and houses were raised up to worship God.
The earth was plundered for her shining wealth.
Trade routes criss-crossed the land
and soldiers marched along the routes
enslaving some, and killing some
and carrying tales of heroes and of gods.
The soldiers still are marching on
still boasting of their power and their gods.

1.1 On Direction

If you are planning a journey, it is a good idea to know where you are and where you have come from. Only then can you plot a wise course.

If you are caught in a trap, in order to get out, you must think back to the circumstances that caused you to become entrapped. Then you can escape without making the same mistakes, and encountering a similar misfortune.

If your society, your culture, your world situation is stifling your group, your community, the whole world population, how carefully you must note where you are, and where you have come from! How heedful you must be when contemplating your future movements! How diligently you must carry out your plans, so that the future will be radiant.

For this reason, for the people of the future, let us consider our past. Has humankind made any progress in the things that matter most? Have we been understanding of one another? Have we borne our share of the burden? Have we been accepting of our responsibilities as well as enjoying the resources of our abundant earth? If we and the earth are to have a future, we must be kind to one another, tender-hearted and forgiving.

Truck driver, you must be kind, or the earth will perish! Lawyer, you must be honest, or the earth will perish! Mother, you must be drug-free, or the earth will perish! Politician, you must be just! Government, you must listen to the people!

1.2 The Beginning

In the eternal sustaining now of God, there was star dust. We come from God by way of star dust.

When there was only star dust, there were no human beings to acknowledge God's goodness and wisdom. There was no communication. God had no other being to love, only a dream of what there was to be (out of star dust).

A whirling mass in the void became our earth. Parts of this rotating and liquid mass were flung off and trapped by pulls from the earth and the sun. Some of these tremendous blobs of matter may have become the moon and the planet Mars. Mars escaped from earth only to fall into the force field of the sun. The moon never made it far enough away from earth to circle the sun on its own. God made the heavens this way that we might enjoy a full moon rising. As this, our twirling earth, cooled, compacted rocks in its interior expanded and rose up through the warm ocean, and we do not know if there was any other being there to praise God for all this.

Eras. Scientists have made up names to help us keep track of human development and the age of the earth. We talk about eras and ages and cultures, and for such as myself, it is easy to become confused. Let's take a few examples. The earliest and beginning time of the earth is called the *Archaean*. From the Greek, *arch* means *ancient* and an *eon* is an indefinitely long period of time. This particular period of time is calculated at 4.6 <u>billion</u> years to 2.6 <u>billion</u> years back, and is the first part of a longer period called the Pre-Cambrian. In the Pre-Cambrian Era (dated from 4.6 billion years to 570 million years before the present) basic rocks were surfacing on the earth and sea life began in the vast ocean (3.5 billion years *Before the Present* or *BP*). There are three other giant eras. After the Pre-Cambrian Era comes the Paleozoic Era (570 million years through 230 million years BP), then the Mesozoic (230 million years through 65 million years BP), and then the present or Cenozoic Era (dated at 65 million BP to the present). These eras describe the times when different forms of life were developing on earth. As *zoe* is Greek for life, *Paleozoic* means *remote life* or *life in older times*; *Mesozoic* means *middle life*; *Cenozoic* means *recent life*. The Cenozoic Era refers to the Age of Mammals, or creatures who are warm blooded and with hair. These creatures, which include us, developed partially in response to the cold ice ages.

This recent giant era, the Cenozoic, is further divided into periods of epochs that have names which all end as the word Cenozoic begins, with the Greek word *ceno* (or *cene*), meaning recent. These epochs or time periods all describe which portion of the Cenozoic they represent and are as follows:

Paleocene	(means old part of most recent)	65 - 54 million BP
Eocene	(dawn of most recent)	54 - 38 million BP
Oligocene	(scanty or few of most recent)	38 - 22.5 million BP
Miocene	(less recent)	22.5 - 5 million BP
Pliocene	(more recent)	5 - 1.8 million BP
Pleistocene	(most recent, a glacial epoch)	1.8 million - 10,000 BP
Holocene	(including all up to the present)	10,000 BP - present

We are living in the Holocene Epoch, which is the time of civilization. Each epoch signals the starting point of a new development in life forms. If we were all fluent in Greek and Latin, we would have less trouble understanding what the scientists are writing about.

The Pleistocene Epoch is further subdivided into the ages and stages of <u>human</u> development. These are sometimes described in English. *Paleolithic* refers to *Old Stone Age* customs and tools; *neolithic* refers to the *New Stone Age* with improved stone tool techniques. When the sections of time are described in English, such as the *Bronze Age*, those of us who speak in English continue to have trouble with our visualization. The *Bronze Age* is when the common use of bronze weapons in civilized societies took place. In our inability to visualize we might think that the *Bronze Age* and the term *neolithic* go together as belonging to early civilization, but the Bronze Age is back in the past and won't return (hopefully). However, we can still perform in a *neolithic* (or *New Stone Age*) manner in solving world problems. Neolithic pottery is a pottery type from early civilizations, but there are people today that use the same pottery making method. Neolithic treatment of fellow humans, such as barbarism, can also take place today, and in that case "neolithic" can mean powerful people lacking in consideration for others. However, not all early neolithic people were inconsiderate or abusers of power.

Scientists use these designations to help us locate the placement of events. Millions of years can be very confusing to us with time bound lives of less than a hundred years, so we give names to these vast sections of time. Names and signs increase our ability to act. It is convenient to use road signs when taking a journey. Such signs help us to direct our footsteps. We give names to what we do not totally understand, and it helps us to relate and respond. We name the animals and then we can control them. We name each other, and when we call each other by name, we can become friends. We give names to God to help us to relate to God.

Back in the Archaean our earth's early covering was mainly water vapor (H_2O), ammonia (NH_3), and methane (CH_4). This swirling mantle of the earth and stormy electrical charges combined to form the first quiet movement of life in the deep sea. There was no human there to look out over the fitful reaches at the wonders being created or to understand the formation of amino acids, nucleic acids, or carbohydrates. There was only God and God's anticipation. We do not know how God did this great work. We look back from where we are and ponder and marvel. We do not know how God will similarly propel our future.

Fossil algae in the rocks of Rhodesia have been dated at 3.4 billion years old, and algae in the rocks at Warrawoona, Australia at 3.5 billion. From those Archaean times it took 3 billion years for the algae to multiply sufficiently to cause an oxygen revolution (about 400 million years back). The earth had been lifeless deserts, but due to the action of the algae in the ocean, the oxygen content of the air became sufficient to support life on land. These multitudinous marine plants created a layer of ozone that enabled life to exist on land by encouraging the production of free oxygen (O_2) and ozone (O_3). This raised ozone level made a protective layer that kept out the ultraviolet rays from the sun which are destructive to life. As more photosynthetic plants developed, they absorbed the carbon dioxide (CO_2) and gave off oxygen into the atmosphere. With a lower level of CO_2, the atmosphere no longer retained the infra-red radiation received from the sun, and thus the earth lost heat. With the removal of this CO_2 heat-capturing mechanism, the climate became more extreme, with possibilities of glaciers and ice caps. **Ice Ages.** Remarkably, the earth maintains optimal conditions for its kind of life. Multicellular animal life became possible when there was enough free oxygen in the atmosphere to sustain rapid metabolism, and plants and animals developed on earth's outer crust. Our earth continued to go through many phases of warming and cooling. In the later part of the Paleozoic Era (between 280 and 230 million years BP), the earth was a violent place with much mountain building. There was a severe ice buildup over Africa, Australia, and South America. Drying seas produced deserts and tremendous salt deposits in Russia, Germany, and Kansas. Near the end of the Mesozoic Era and during the Age of Dinosaurs (about 100 million years BP), the earth was very hot with a temperature range of 6 to 12 degrees above average. There are fossils of alligators on Greenland from this time period. Cycles of cold and warm repeated themselves. Scientists have been able to record that 3 million years ago when early human types may have been around, ice accumulated in the Arctic. Since then there have been 20 or more advances of cold polar waters and ice sheets with in between periods of warmth. A recent maximum glaciation was 400,000 years ago when the ice sheet reached the area which is now London. Then it warmed again, and 125,000 years ago there were hyenas and hippopotami in the London area. A mere 75,000 years ago the ice returned. Sea levels dropped as water became stored in the ice cap. The Adriatic was a vast plain. One could walk from Italy to Africa and from England to France. This last glaciation petered out 10,000 years ago. When the ice melted, the sea levels rose again, destroying the land bridges.

These ice sheets are a very important part of earth's geology, and have drastically influenced our physical world and our genetic make up. Scientists have been able to give us information about ice ages using a method that

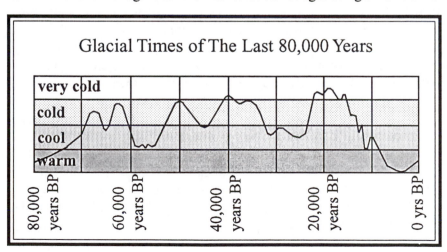

Glacial Times of The Last 80,000 Years

measures the temperatures of water at the bottom of the ocean for many millions of years back. Water decreased in temperature from 70°F at the end of the era of dinosaurs (65 million years back), to 36°F at one million years back. The method used was to measure oxygen isotopes in fossil sea shells. It was calculated that in the last 300,000 years, there has been a warm and cold temperature change in shells corresponding to the ebb and flow of glaciers. This checks out with the measurements of other scientists who propose that due to the earth's rotational wobbles and other circumstances, there have been cycles of cool summers and mild snowy winters, which contributed to snow build up. The actual cycle depends on many factors. Models have forecast ice peaking approximately at 19,500 years, 24,000 years, 43,000 years, and 100,000 years BP. These cycles have significantly affected the migrations and evolution of animals and human beings.

There are many variables that can cause glaciation and warming. One Ice Age formation theory involves algae and changes in our atmosphere. The hot earth produced algae which eventually triggered the oxygen revolution which allowed the development of trees and dinosaurs. However, these forests died and stored large amounts of carbon dioxide (CO_2) from the atmosphere as coal. Perhaps this CO_2 trapped under the ground allowed for an over abundance of free oxygen in the atmosphere which prevented the sun's rays from getting through. Less CO_2 can cause cooling.

If there is volcanic activity or other prolific burning which produces dust from CO_2 and other gases, these particles may prevent the sun's rays from getting to the earth and may offset the heat trapping effect of the CO_2. We know that the eruption of Tambora in Indonesia in 1815 put so many haze particles in the air, that the lack of sunlight caused lower temperatures and less plant growth. Even a seemingly minor factor like the location of the volcanic activity north or south of the equator has much to do with how the haze particles spread across the earth. Radiation that is scattered sideways helps to keep the earth warm. Too much CO_2 in the atmosphere prevents the escape of heat from the earth. Dust in the tropics traps heat. Clouds and haze can keep the heat out. Many factors combine to give the final result. If the result is coolness, and there is snow cover, once the snow buildup starts, it builds on itself. This is because the white surface reflects the sun's rays back instead of absorbing heat to itself like rocks and dark vegetation would.

Our earth may get hotter in the next hundred years due to high atmospheric CO_2 levels. If Arctic melt caused sea levels to rise only twelve feet, it would drown many coastal cities. Increased evaporation rates due to warmer temperatures threaten us with massive forest fires. But haze from such fires and volcanoes may form cloud cover that will block sunlight and keep the earth cool. The ocean warms more slowly and may also keep us cool. At present, Antarctica is trapped in place and is a fairly dependable cooler. Loss of forests through burning and cutting, brings desert land, and desert land reflects the sunlight back into space, another cooling factor. It may be possible to have a stable earth.[1] On the other side of the problem, an ice sheet cycle is due back in about 8000 years, and enough CO_2 pollution with green house warming might keep our civilized earth warm and help to counteract the formation of ice.

Other factors that may help to trigger ice ages are the tilt of the earth's axis and the earth's orbital motion. We know that the 23.5 degrees tilt of the earth, as it rotates around the sun, causes us to have summer and winter. This tilt can increase 1.5 degrees either way from 22 degrees to 25 degrees which can cause summer and winter temperature extremes.

The earth's orbital motion can vary from almost a circle to an ellipse, with the sun at one focus of the ellipse. In the elliptical case the earth is nearer to the sun in one part of its journey, and further away at the opposite part of its journey. Presently this near approach to the sun occurs in January, so those in the southern hemisphere feel the extra summer heat.[2] This cycle takes many years. When this near approach comes in June, then we in the northern hemisphere will have warmer summers.

Actions of the sun can also result in warmings or glaciations. Sun spots or lack of them may affect the temperature of the earth. Low sunspot activity such as in 1645 to 1715 AD can cause colder weather. The period of the sun's rotation is 27 days. When the sun has a deep coronal hole which is larger than the ordinary sunspot, pointed right at us, we get the effects of magnetic storms and direct beams of whatever other particles the sun gives off. As the interior of the sun is hotter than its exterior, the earth gets more heat from such radiation.

The journey of the sun with its solar system as it spirals the galaxy every 200 million years can also have dramatic effects on its planets. Its cycle may take it through asteroid belts that may be disturbed by its passage. Asteroids may collide with the earth and cause continental and climatic disturbances. Other stars may fling off material or exert gravitational pulls.

Plate Tectonics. The temperature changes that take place on our globe can lead to further changes in the earth's surface. There is the phenomenon of continental shift. Glaciation may cause continental shift, and continental shift can cause glaciation. When ice builds up to a thickness of two miles high, it is very heavy. This weight can start cracks that widen as glaciers melt, their frozen flowing causing land masses to split apart. The weight may even cause the earth to have rotational wobbles.

The melting of glacial ice caps can cause land areas to become flooded, with portions remaining above sea level isolated from each other. Today, melting of our ice caps could raise present water levels 200 to 300 feet and disrupt our civilization. Given enough centuries of time, the land would re-emerge. All that extra shiny surface of the water would reflect the sun's rays back from the earth, and eventually have a cooling effect after thousands of years, which would once again encourage ice storage and lower sea levels.

Placement of continents and circulation of the oceans cause temperature changes. There is a theory that continental shift could have blocked major circulation routes in the ocean and disturbed warming and cooling mechanisms, thus causing an ice age. The early continent *Gondwana* in the southern hemisphere, made up of South America, Antarctica, Australia, Africa, and India, may have blocked ocean flow. Gondwana got its name from the present day Gondwana, a province in India whose distinctive combination of geological features and plant fossils were later found on other continents. Fossils of the primitive fern, Glossopteris, are common to southern Africa, Brazil, India, Australia, and Antarctica. There are fossil sites of a mammal-like reptile, Lystrosaurus, in southern Africa, India, and Antarctica. Lystrosaurus lived 160 million years ago when Antarctica was a land bridge between the southern tip of South America and Australia. South America left this grouping over 100 million years ago, and India, Australia, and Antarctica departed 65 million years back.

In the northern hemisphere between 1.4 billion years BP and 335 million years BP, the land masses resting unsteadily on the earth's mantle closed together and burst apart several times. There was much mountain building, first with what was known as the Red Sandstone Continent (Europe, Greenland, and North America), and then with the land mass of Laurasia (the Sandstone continent plus Siberia). These were rocky, stormy, volcanic times, but there were sea animals with shells in the offshore waters of what has been called the Iapetus Sea. 650 million years ago, the land mass in the northern hemisphere split apart again. In 575 million BP North America was tilted sideways south of the equator bumping into Africa, and in the next drifting apart, some coastal areas were exchanged. Scientists believe that the land where Boston, Massachusetts exists, was once a continental section of northwest Africa as their rocks are identical. Parts of Scotland share similar shoreline edges with formations in Connecticut. Their coastal waters have similar sea forms. When the continents broke apart, they were not particular about which gorges had come from where. Various pieces slid on to the continental plates and rode off in haphazard directions. Their land cover went with them. Similar vegetative processes

One Possible Scenario for Plate Tectonics

1.4-1.0 billion years ago	Europe, Greenland, & North America join together in Red Sandstone Continent & split.
800-600 million years ago	They join & split again. Baltic Shield to Scandinavia, Grenville Rocks to eastern North America, only life was in shallow coastal waters, Iapetus Ocean.
575 million years ago	N. America and Siberia lie on equator.
400 million years ago	Collision of Africa and N. America, coastal pieces exchanged, beginning of Appalachian Mountains.
290 million years ago	Africa heads south & collides to form the super continent Gondwana south of the equator with S. America, India, Australia, Antarctica, & Florida.
250 million years ago	Collision of Europe and Asia, beginning of Urals.
230 million years ago	Ice covered Gondwana.
250-180 million yrs. ago	All continents together called Pangaea, sea called Panthalassa. There were forests, early dinosaurs.
145 million years ago	Start of opening up of present Atlantic.
120-80 million years ago	North America parts from Europe. South America parts from Africa.
70-60 million years ago	South America joined to North America, but parted again temporarily.
65 million years ago	Rocky mountain uplift, west coast of N. America.
65 million years ago	India, Australia, and Antarctica leave Africa.
50 million years ago	Collision of India & Asia, beginning of Himalayas, Australia parted from Antarctica.
40 million years ago	Collision of Africa & Europe. Beginning of Alps, Atlas, Pyrenees, and Carpathian Mountains.
40-20 million years ago	Ancient Tethys Seaway narrowed and became Caspian, Black, and Mediterranean Seas.
30 million years ago	Japanese islands rose from the sea.
15 million years ago	Antarctica is glaciated.
10 million years ago	Beginning of Andes.
5 million years ago	Arctic glaciation begins.
4 million years ago	Pre-humans (Some may have developed separately on separated land masses.)
2 million years ago	Glacial episode in northern hemisphere.
900,000 years ago	Alaska & Siberia joined by frozen tundra.
100,000 years ago	Another glacial episode in the north.

were in place in both areas.

The northern continents drifted together again 380 million years back, and pressed onto the southern continents, so that in 250 million BP, one massive landform existed, called Pangaea, and one large ocean, Panthalassa. The continent of Pangaea in its turn fell apart. About 65 million years back India slid off Africa and rotated upwards on it tectonic plate to its present position on southern Asia.

Meteorites. No one has come up with a good explanation of why continents decide to drift. There is a theory that molten material flowing inside the mantle impels the continents in a fairly leisurely manner. Tectonic plates also could be disturbed from outside forces. If a large meteorite landed on Gondwana, it could send portions of continent helter-skelter in different directions. Such a meteor could easily have split into pieces and had other falling sections whose craters are now under the sea. The southern Indian Ocean has a large crater type formation where the mid-ocean ridge divides into the south west ridge and the south east ridge. Between these two ridges is a large round depression. This may be the bed of an ancient meteorite.

If such a meteorite fell, it would leave tell-tale signs behind. The dust and debris from the impact of such an outer space visitor could cause darkness at noon. Necessary photosynthesis would be halted. The phyto-plankton near the surface of the ocean would be eliminated by the darkness causing harm to our atmosphere. A layer of dust would accumulate on the earth. Such a questionable layer of dust has been found between rock specimens dated about 65 million BP. This dust layer may confirm that a large meteorite collided with the earth causing continental plate movement.

Diamonds are sometimes the result of a meteoritic fall. Diamonds are found on the earth in regions which have undergone great pressure, from either inward or outward forces. When a meteorite falls, much of it may vaporize going through the atmosphere or vaporize on impact. If any substantive elements such as nickel, iron, and carbon, are left when the meteorite strikes earth, appropriate particles may be pressurized into diamonds. Often there may be tiny diamonds spread around a meteoritic rock-fall. It is speculated that the hole that is Hudson's Bay in Canada is a meteorite crater. Diamonds have been found south of this location. Their travel south from the place of impact probably took place on a ride of glacial ice. Winslow Crater in Arizona is a more recent example of what can happen when a meteorite strikes. It is only 22,000 years old, 1 mile wide, 600 feet deep. The object that caused this depression vaporized upon impact.

Diamonds may be formed from veins that rise up from the innards of the earth. These veins are under tremendous pressure and squeeze the carbon they contain into diamonds. It may be that meteorites in crashing down, plow deeply into the earth piercing its mantle, engendering such heat in their vaporization that molten stuff forcibly rising from the bowels of the earth changes into diamonds.

If the continent of India were resting quietly united with Africa, the push from a meteorite could cause it to move northward at a fairly rapid pace. Greenland was at one time attached to the North American plate. It may have separated when a meteorite crash caused the Hudson Bay depression. Similarly, from the land mass of Pangaea, the North American continent may have headed north and west, and South America may have headed south and west, if a large meteorite fell in what is now the Gulf of Mexico about 100 million BP. A very large meteorite hurtling to earth breaking into several tremendous pieces about 65 million BP would be a great enough force to cause India to head north, Australia to head east, and Antarctica to head south. Pieces of meteorite would vaporize, leaving nothing behind but holes and diamonds. One piece could have landed in Kimberly, Africa. One piece could have landed west of Madagascar. A chunk could have landed in the Indian Ocean splitting the oceanic ridge. A piece could have landed in India, which had many diamonds for export until the more prolific nine-teenth century diamond strike at Kimberly in Africa. The pieces of tectonic plate would be nudged like billiard balls by an eight ball. Perhaps even one hit that penetrated a tectonic plate, such as the Kimberly location, would be enough to knock the plate apart and send pieces floating in various directions. A body in motion will continue in motion until it is acted upon by an outside force. A tectonic plate will drift until stopped. India floated on until it collided with Asia.

Other continental movements involved the Tethys Seaway between Eurasia and Africa which started to narrow 50 million years back, and was almost closed about 20 million years ago. This may also have been caused by the same meteoritic push in the environs of South Africa. The Tethys Seaway became the Mediterranean, the Caspian, and the Black Seas. This closing raised the Alps, the Pyrenees, the Atlas, and the Carpathian Mountains.

Continental Biological Evolution. Similar animals evolved on the different continents. North America and Europe continued in separated but wonderful states of formation. There is no reason to think that one continent stopped in its evolutionary progress, while the other raced on ahead. Neither side of the Atlantic was quiet or sterile. The earth was working its work in both hemispheres. Ancient camel types have been found in North America. Although we have no camels now, a small early camel was in North America

32 million years ago; its remains were found at the Brule Formation in Wyoming. A giraffe-like large camel was in North America in the Early Pleistocene, 2 million years back with remains at Broadwater Formation, Nebraska. A camel, Camelops, perhaps the last to survive in North America, a relative of the llamas, was here from 40 to 12 thousand years ago. Its remains were found at Rancho La Brea in California. Even the rhinoceros lived in North America but became extinct there 6 million years ago. When the Mexican land bridge surfaced, North America and South America exchanged some of their animals. We acquired the armadillo from South America at that time.

The odd life forms evolved similarly in Australia. 100 million years ago Australia was joined to Asia. Lystrosaurus and similar animals ranged across Gondwana. They migrated down under (or it may have not been down under at that time, but near the equator). When the continents separated, these animals evolved in a different manner, in their closed systems, into the Australian animals that we know today.

Some of this change also involved New Guinea which was accessible to Australia by the Taurus Straight, a land bridge exposed because of ice buildup at the poles. The wallaby lived both places. The bats in New Guinea developed from those in Australia. There is a wide variety of birds which have developed on each land mass from common ancestors. There is an imaginary line running between the Philippine islands of Mindanao and Sangihe, between the Indonesian islands of Borneo and Celebes, and between Bali and Lombok. On the north side are Asian life forms, while on the south side are Australian types. This is called the Wallace line after Alfred Russel Wallace who proposed a theory about how species develop in isolation.

Different types of animals will evolve from common ancestors if subjected to different environmental influences. As we look around the world, we are impressed with the marvelous diversity of species. The ice ages seemed to trigger a hardier type of animal such as warm blooded animals with fur and larger brains. White haired animals evolved in areas of snow. Dark brown animals crept through the shadowy jungle. Wolves and polar bears represent the northern climes. Brown bears live in temperate zones. Koala bears live on the eucalyptus trees in Australia. Think of the varieties in color of fur of the dog, cat, and horse population!

Consider the Yeti or Big Foot creatures of which we hear rumors. Those reported in West China have red hair. The hair color on monkey species ranges from tan to red to brown to black. What variety in the cat family! These life forms seem to have been challenged out of adversity. They had to adapt to strange circumstances in order to survive. God must have had such fun creating the animals. She must have particularly enjoyed creating us humans. God seems to like diversity.

Was there anyone there watching when God formed the twisting gene chains in the different species? Was the human being watching when the animals roamed from area to area, seeking better pastures, and the different gene pools mixed, giving even more variety? Were there improvements and failures? We were not there with supervising knowledge, but we can look back today and marvel at the way God works.

Where animals traveled, people also found their way. One method of tracing possible human evolution and migrations is through investigating the extinct animal remains at prehistoric sites. What kind of animal life was around when Gondwana split up? Were there pre-monkeys on Gondwana? Different conditions and predators in Africa, India, and South America led to different types of monkeys. In Africa there were animals which are now extinct such as the dinotherium, perhaps a link between a dinosaur type and the modern elephant. These were hunted by the early humans one million years ago.

Let's look at the development of monkeys, apes, baboons, and human beings. In South America the two main types of monkey are the Hapalidae, like lemurs with weak tails, and the Cebidae with strong tails that can curl around branches. The Old World monkeys (the Cercopithecidae) of Asia and Africa are superior in intelligence to those from South America. When jungle turned into grassland, they had to come down from the trees and be quick to grab their food and make a getaway. Indian monkeys are represented by the Hindu sacred monkey, the proboscis monkey, and the negro monkey. The gibbon is the tailless ape of the East Indies allied to the orangutan and the chimpanzees. African monkeys are the guenons, green monkeys, and the mangabeys. Australia has a rain forest, but no monkeys. Madagascar has lemurs, but no monkeys. If a species is comfortable in a place, it will expand and utilize that space, and there is little need for a new species.

Ancient primates were Oreopithecus (25 million years BP), Pliopithecus (22 million years BP), ProConsul (21 million years BP), and Dryopithecus (16 million years BP in Europe, China, and India). These animals thrived in certain areas where they could live comfortably. They remained the same, and did not have to change. The lowland gorilla lives in Africa today with the same level of intelligence that was necessary for his ancestors many millions of years back. If things go well for you, there is no need to change. It is not necessary to expand the brain size of members of your group. The human species today may see no need to change or expand its capabilities.

1.3 The Human Being

All of us are curious about where the human came from. Where did she make her first home? Did she travel great distances on her prehistoric feet? How long have human beings lived all over the world? Why are we so similar, and yet so different? When God created our marvelous gene structure, did she build in similar aspirations, like a desire for a peaceful world, and the inner knowledge of how to acquire it? Do we have to make war-like mistakes in order to learn of the necessity for peace? Will we naturally evolve to peace and order, or will we always be in process?

In trying to answer the above deluge of questions, we must realize and admit our ignorance. Research can confirm or dismiss some of our suppositions, but we can never really know for sure. Different groups propose theories that they would like to believe are the final word for the question, "Where did we come from?" One group is for total evolution of humans from some common ancestor of the apes. If the ape can evolve, why not a related more intelligent type? Another group believes in instantaneous creation. As God is all powerful, God can make the human in the blink of an eye by simply wanting the human to be made. Still others like to think of astronauts from some other creation dropping by our earth and leaving a matched pair of crew members behind. Not one of us can claim with certainty that we know what kind of help God had, or that we understand God's method.

There is the possibility that different primates slowly evolved from early lemur types on separated continents. Archaeologists tell us that in the Miocene Epoch (22.5 through 5 million years BP) there was the development of a number of types of ape-like creatures. One of these, which they named Ramapithecus, was an animal who had man-like teeth rather than fangs, and who may have been an ancestor of either the ape or the human. *Rama* is one of the Hindu trinity, and *pithecus* means *ape like*. His remains which have been found in Africa, Asia, and India, have been dated between 14 and 8 million years back.

Evolutionary development in mammals may have been accelerated due to changes in climate. In this Miocene Epoch, the time when some creatures learned to walk on two feet, the earth went through interglacial periods when it was a green garden. At other times the poles were covered with ice, fierce winds were blowing, and deserts were forming. Areas near the equator that were once warm and lush, dried out into savannas. The fossil remains of many species of early monkey types from such a varying climate are found at Fayum Oasis in what is now Egyptian desert. The tails of these grassland African monkeys degenerated. In South America there continued to be jungle, and the monkeys needed their tails for swinging through the trees. Their species could function effectively as they were. There was not much impetus to change.

There was a period from about 10 million to 5 million years BP when we don't have much information. Early in our present century, miners in South Africa discovered the most primitive human type ever found. They called her Lucy, but scientists tagged her as *Australopithecus afarensis*. She was dated as being 5 million years old.

The next big events in human generation were dated to Africa approximately 2 million years ago. One, scientists called *Paranthropus*, a pre-human type animal that used tools. It could heave rocks and throw sticks. By looking at fossil teeth we can tell that Paranthropus was a vegetarian browser. The second upright animal, *Australopithecus*, was related to Lucy and was a hunter of small game. Both Paranthropus and Australopithecus co-existed in the same territory. The vegetarian Paranthropus did not need improved tools to grub for roots. She was a tool user, but the hunter Australopithecus had to be more alert to get her dinner. She was a tool maker. Instead of bashing small animals with handy sticks and stones, the tool making primate sharpened these tools to make them more effective. Both creatures walked upright, but Australopithecus had a larger brain capacity. It is likely that Paranthropus met an evolutionary dead end, while Australopithecus apparently roamed forth and developed further. Fossilized tracks of Australopithecus were discovered in the rocks of Olduvai Gorge in Tanzania, Africa. Due to the many lava layers in the area, fairly precise dating of these tracks is available. These footprints tell us that our predecessors were walking upright almost 2 million years back. This early rung on the evolutionary ladder is given the further designation of *Homo habilis* which means *man of ability*.

Because fossils of both these early primates were found in Africa, many anthropologists say that Africa is where the human race had its beginnings. There is also the possibility that Australopithecus developed on the continent of India as it floated across the Indian Ocean. Paranthropus may have developed from African primates in Africa, while in the same period of separation, Australopithecus formed in India. When India ground to a halt and attached itself to Asia about 50 million BP, the population of Australopithecus emerged, enlarged, and moved north to Russia, east to China, and west to Africa and Europe. On reaching Africa, Australopithecus mingled and fought with the slower moving Paranthropus. The more agile species became the dominant group. The two species may have together generated other species such as the *Homo erectus* primates who were eventually found from China to Spain.

Homo Erectus. We rise up the evolutionary ladder still higher with *Homo erectus*, known in some quarters as *Pithecanthropus* (a noun that combines the words for *ape* and *man*). Can we suppose that *Homo erectus* thought about the future and retained memories of the past? Did she have instinctual knowledge that enabled her to desist from eating poisonous plants? How did she communicate with others of her kind? Could she heal herself by drawing on inner strengths? Were certain members of this community in balanced harmony with the earth and its processes?

Homo erectus bands ranged widely over Europe 500,000 to 300,000 years ago, and existed at Verteszollos in Hungary. They hunted an early species of elephant in the Ambrona Valley northeast of Madrid, Spain. They used fire to frighten these animals into swamps and over cliffs, and wooden spear tips sharpened and hardened in fire to make the kill. The *Homo erectus* human also used an improved style of stone tool making which is called *Acheulian*. This toolmaking style is named after a town in France, Saint Acheul, where many such tools were found. This doesn't mean that it was confined to that particular area, or that it originated there. This type of toolmaking lasted from 500,000 to 75,000 years back, and was wide spread over Africa, Europe, and Asia.

From the rather haphazard chopping of rocks by Australopithecus, this advanced tool maker progressed to the chipping of slender blades from hand-ax stones. *Pithecanthropus* survived and thrived and covered the globe. From tool specimens we know that she was also present in India, and skeletal remains of *Homo erectus* have been found on Java dated to 800,000 years back.

An interesting thing about the tool making by *Homo erectus* individuals is that the *hand ax* industry is found in Africa, Europe, the Mid-east and India, while *pebble tools* or smaller choppers are found in north Asia, China, and also in India. Some hand axes were quite large, usually pear shaped or pointed on one end. They may have been thrown at herds of wild animals browsing at water holes. Pebble tools were chopping stones with edges, some as small as pingpong balls, others as large as billiard balls. India played host to both tool making populations. China may have been a fringe population that didn't get the cultural word on hand axes.

The formal name of the Peking human is *Pithecanthropus pekinensis*. In China parts of 45 individuals have been found in a well-stratified cave in which the deposits go down 160 feet deep. Each foot of cave debris

The Making of The Human Being

70 million years back	Evolution theorists believe that our antecedents looked like squirrels.
30 million years back	Monkey type remains at Fayum, Egypt.
20 million years back	*ProConsul*, pre-ape of Africa, not human line.
14 million years back	*Ramapithecus* in Africa, Asia, India, early man-like primate, probably not human line.
5 million years back	*Australopithecus afarensis*, Lucy, most primitive human type ever found.
2 million years back	*Australopithecus africanus, (Homo habilis)*, tool maker, first certain human, larger brain, South Africa and Olduvai Gorge in Tanzania.
2 - .8 million yrs back	*Paranthropus (Australopithecus boisei*, East Africa and *Australopithecus robustus*, South Africa), tool users, may not be human line.
.8 million years back	Possible *Homo erectus* (erect man), Java.
.7 million years back	*Homo erectus*, Pithecanthropus pekinensis.
.7 million years back	*Homo erectus,* Lantian Man, Shaanxi, China.
.5 million years back	*Homo erectus*, (true human), Olduvai.
.6 - .3 million back	*Homo erectus* Spain, Hungary, Heidelberg.
60,000 years back	Late *Homo erectus* specimen, Ethiopia.
300,000 through now	Early *Homo sapiens* (wise man), Swanscombe(London), Steinheim(Germany).
250,000 years back	E. Africa, Olduvai Gorge, early *Homo sapien*.
110,000 through 35,000 years back	Neanderthal Man, early *Homo sapiens*, all over Europe, around the Mediterranean.
100,000 through 80,000 years back	Neanderthal relatives, Solo Man in Java, Rhodesian Man in Africa.
85,000 years back	*Homo sapiens*, Dordogne Valley SW France.
60,000 years back	Early *Cro-Magnon,,* Ethiopia.
44,000 years back	Modern type Neanderthal, Shanidar Cave in Iraq, Tabun woman in Israel.
35,000 years back	*Cro-Magnon*, Stone Age people from Mid East, made cave paintings in Europe.
10,000 years back	Civilized human

contained the dust of 2500 years of occupation. These ancient cave occupants had an 800 to 1300 cubic centimeter brain capacity which may have been large enough to support language (twice the brain size of *Australopithecus*). Some people think there is a correlation between brain size and being considered true humans. The brain of an ape is not large enough to support a speech center. Modern man's cranial capacity is 1200-1500 cubic centimeters. These *Homo erectus* individuals or true humans may have been around even earlier than 800,000 years ago, but their remains may be too scarce for us to find. In Britain flint instruments found with a sabre tooth cat were dated 450,000 BP. A campfire site at Terra Amata in southern France has been dated at 400,000 BP.

Homo Sapiens. *Homo erectus* persons seem to have been replaced 300,000 years back by the more modern early *Homo sapien* types. Examples of early *Homo sapiens* are Swanscombe Man, found near London, dated at 250,000 years back, and Steinheim Man from Germany, about the same date. The most prolific remains of early *Homo sapiens* are those of the now extinct Neanderthals, who lived in Europe, Asia, and Africa between 110,000 BC and 35,000 BC. They were rugged hunters, dwelling in community groups, and probably speaking basic language. About 35,000 BC the Neanderthals mysteriously disappeared. To some extent, they may have been flooded out. A cave site in Spain has been uncovered where a mud slide archaeologically preserved the remains of twelve people.

In Combe Grenal, France, archaeologists have uncovered at least 75,000 years of Neanderthal habitation. Monte Circeo Man from an Italian cave is dated at 40,000 BC. Shanidar Cave in northern Iraq (250 miles north of Baghdad in the Zagros Mountains on a branch of the Tigris) was host to Neanderthals for 60,000 years. A Spanish caveman 30,000 years old was measured to be as tall as a modern European. They used improved Acheulian tools. In some caves which contain Neanderthal remains there is a sterile layer without tools or bones, before the times and remains of later advanced *Homo sapien* types such as *Cro-Magnon*. This denotes lack of habitation due to flooding or desertification. Formal names for the tool cultures of Europe are Oldowan or Australopithecine (beginning about 500,000 BP), Acheulian (150,000-75,000 BP), Mousterian (around 45,000 BP), Aurignacian (40,000 BP), Perigordian (30,000 BP), Solutrian (20,000 BP), and Magdalenian (15,000 BP).

After the disappearance of the Neanderthal, a more advanced cave culture developed. *Homo sapien* cave culture with use of *Aurignacian* type tools developed in Europe and Asia as far east as Afghanistan. In France this advanced cave culture was called *Gravettian*. France has cave paintings depicting hunting scenes. Cave art developed between 25,000 and 10,000 BP. This art was practiced by the mammoth hunters of southern Russia, the Pushkari, who shifted from caves to living in tents of skins. These early people had housing units with floors scooped out, each with its fire place. Cave art was also practiced in India. Beads and clothes made out of skins are part of the Gravettian culture. India, as the first maker of cotton cloth, may have used cotton as a substance cooler than animal skin. Sungir, Russia has a burial with beads dated to 24,500 BP.

There were early cave sites that were flooded out due to rising waters from glacial melt. For example at 25,000 BP the Adriatic was dry land. There may have been manifold cave culture sites on the Adriatic floor, or around the bases of islands such as Sri Lanka and Indonesia.

There are many questions still to be answered about the entrance of the *Cro-Magnon* cultures into Europe and Asia and the passing of the Neanderthal. Did one kill off the other? Did *Cro-Magnons* bring new diseases that the Neanderthals had no immunity to withstand? Did melting of the Ice Cap and subsequent flooding of Neanderthal cave sites cause population shifts and wars over territory? Between 35,000 BC and 10,000 BC the *Cro-Magnon* people multiplied and became successful. It is believed that they entered Europe through the Near East land cross-over. The Near East lying in a temperate area, and accessible from all points of the compass became the meeting and melding point for early peoples and cultures. It also became a center for trade and an area to be fought over. Jerusalem's geographic location may have given rise to the notion that it was the center of the earth, and thus somehow representative of the whole earth.

Some tribal groups would find a relatively safe spot and stay there. Others who depended on hunting or herding would have to keep on the move. Those peopling Tibet did not have a very fertile homeland, but they could defend their territory easily. They domesticated the yak, and they and the yak lived in happy symbiosis. They ate yak meat, drank yak-butter tea,

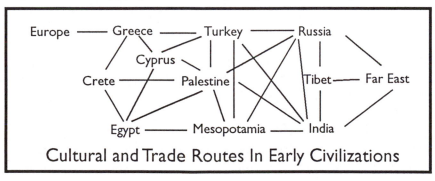

Cultural and Trade Routes In Early Civilizations

had fuel from yak dung, made rope from yak hair, and wore clothes of yak hide. They became yak herders, and developed social and cultural customs built around taking yak herds to pasture. One of the customs of these highland people was similar to the levirate obligation of the Hebrews. A Tibetan woman married not only her husband, but her husband's brothers. Other mountain people were those in the Zagros Mountains of Iraq, and the Basques in Spain. They managed to stay fairly aloof from the changing and argumentative cultures in the plains.

Mysteries confront anyone trying to unravel the beginnings and the trails of the different modern-day races. Africa contained ancestors of the Bush people, but not the modern African. We do not know the genetic history of the present-day negro. We do not know where the light skinned human type arose. There are albinos, or Negroes who genetically have no pigmentation. Perhaps the Ice Ages with weaker rays from the sun, encouraged less pigmentation in the skin.

We admire the muscular build of athletes, and we know that some of our predecessors must have been very muscular in order to be able to chase mammoths over cliffs, and run, spear in hand, after wounded animals. There were no flabby stomachs in that crew. Facial features would also be expected to change down the centuries. Someone who ate raw meat from off the hoof, so to speak, would have strong jaws and wide mouths. Giraffes developed long necks because those individuals who could reach higher on the trees, could get more to eat and thus were more likely to survive and produce offspring. If a gene pool developed fine knife type tools, and for thousands of years, all members of the group cut up their food delicately before eating, the gene pool would have the opportunity to develop a smaller mouth.

We know from our discoveries of tool deposits that about 35,000 BC the species Homo sapiens was present everywhere, even in Australia and North America, but perhaps later in South America. It is believed this species crossed to America from Siberia about 40,000 years back, following the migration trails of the large animals. Perhaps they hunted those animals to extinction. At about 11,000 years back, the mammoth was no more.

Archaeological remains in eastern Siberia have been dated at 30,000 BP. North America's oldest known skull, 17,000 years old, was found at Laguna Beach, California. Remains at Meadowcroft Rock Shelter in Pennsylvania are dated 14,000 BC. Well preserved tools at Monte Verde, Chile are dated 11,000 BC. Stone spear points at Clovis, New Mexico are 9500 BC. Human travel may have been facilitated by land bridges which were exposed due to storage of water in the polar ice caps and by ice free corridors. There was also the possibility of boats. The South Americans may have arrived by boat from Pacific Islands or boats down the west coast of America 30,000 BC. They could have walked the corridor east of the Rockies before 28,000 BC, but it closed with ice, and that and the Siberian land bridge didn't open again until about 10,000 BC.[3] Early settlers on Tierra del Fuego may have come from the northern Siberian exchange, or from a southern Pacific exchange by boating plus island hopping using land exposed during ice build-up. Early Americans, Eskimos, and Australian aborigines used a similar weapon, the spear thrower. The wooden boomerang was used in Australia in 9000 BC. Humankind covered all available territory, multiplied, depleted resources, and was forced to move on. We do not know where this spread of Homo sapiens originated.

Today we are confronted with five main Homo sapien Cro-Magnon types– Capoids, Caucasoids, Mongoloids, Congoloids, and Australoids. 80,000 years ago there were distinct strains of humanity centered in Siberia, China, India, Australia, the Caucasus, Europe (the Neanderthals), North Africa, and South Africa. Some of these territories still display modern groups with the same characteristics as way back when, such as the natives of New Guinea. If you have a working model that gets along with its environment, there is no need to change. Some early people did not need to wander, but were able to survive in the same place. Others wore out the soil and the game and had to migrate. Still others were forced to become nomads with a fairly regular pattern of travel.

Humans in The Ice Ages. It would be very interesting if we could coordinate the movements of people and animals with the glacial periods of the earth. Between 230 million years back and 65 million back, the earth was warm. There were dinosaurs. At 65 million back, the poles got colder and the dinosaurs disappeared. Between 65 million and 1 million years back was a generally cool period.

At 30 million years back, Antarctica experienced its first heavy glacial.

At 15 million years back, Antarctica had its second strong glacial. About this time there may have been early human types coming onto the scene in India, Africa, and Asia.

At 4 million years back, ice was forming in the Arctic. The remains of the very early *Australopithecus* named Lucy date just before this time.

At 2.4 million back the diatoms in the sea disappeared. There is the theory that so much floating ice shaded the ocean, sun light could not get through to help them live.

At 2 million back, there was the first serious glacial in the Northern hemisphere. This was also the time when *Australopithecus* roamed South Asia and South Africa. *Paranthropus* was also in Africa.

At 500,000 BP there was a maximum glaciation. There have been nine full ice age cycles in the past million years. There is such a cycle of glaciations about every 100,000 years. *Homo erectus* people were living on Java and in China with knowledge of fire.

At 200,000 BP there was a glacial cycle and examples of *Homo sapiens*.

At 100,000 BP there was the beginning of the most recent glacial cycle.

At 80,000 years back, the earth was fairly warm.

At 70,000 years back, it cooled again.

At 40,000 years back, ice build-up at the poles had made land bridges available. Humans arrived in Australia by land bridges that passed through Indonesia. The Pacific was lower by several hundred feet.

About 37,000 years back, there was a warming with melting of polar ice and flooding, at which time the Neanderthals disappeared.

The last glacial maximum was around 20,000 BP. This peak ice period forced the people out of the northern regions towards the Caspian area and Europe. In North America the ice was two miles thick in places, down as far as New York and Oregon.

From 15,000 to 10,000 BP there was melting of ice and rising of ocean waters. Areas such as the Sahara and Arabia, which were tropical in 14,000 BC, suffered a rise in temperature at 12,500 BC, began drying out, and underwent desertification (9000-8000 BC). The sea encroached upon other areas.

From 10,000 BP to the present we have been enjoying an interglacial. 8,000 years from now the ice build-up should begin again with sea levels lowering, unless global warmings from pollutants change the pattern.

Between 80,000 and 10,000 years back, world temperatures were generally colder due to ice piled up at the poles. This made the sea level low enough so that there was free passage by foot between some land masses. England and Europe were connected. Asians could walk to Java and to Australia. Island hopping Indonesians may have gone boating as far east as South America. If the Arctic ice wasn't reaching too far south to bar the way, northern Asia had access to North America. The Bering land bridge between the two continents was a very broad piece of land jutting far down into the Pacific and warmed by the Pacific waters. It carried animal life between Asia and America for many millions of years. It is speculated that about 40,000 years ago, bison, caribou, musk ox, lion, mountain sheep, and even *Homo sapiens* may have crossed to North America from Asia.

This cooler climate of the last 80,000 years pushed humankind into the warmer regions, such as the lowlands off southern Asia or into what is now the dry Sahara, which was moist and lush 50,000 years ago. When the ice melted, land bridges would close, but those nomad types in the equatorial belt could spread out to the north, and live off migrating herd animals. Thus we see that the ice ages could have resulted in the migrations of peoples and animals. Ice ages had definite effects on population spread.

Ice ages and the movements of continents not only affected the wanderings of ancestral people and pre-people, but also influenced changes in their genetic structure and increased their intellectual capabilities. There is the theory of the survival of the fittest.

Where did *Homo sapiens* begin her wanderings? Did she start from Africa? If she were prolific in the lowlands off the coast of India, the rising seas of 10,000 BC would bury all traces of her presence twenty miles out to sea, or hundreds of meters deep in silted river beds.

65 million years ago, the dinosaurs were fading away, and the mammals were coming into prominence. For some reason about this same time, the land mass of India separated itself from its position on South Africa and slid across what is now the Indian Ocean to settle on southern Asia. This may have been a normal tectonic plate movement, or there may have been a catastrophic collision of the earth with another heavenly body.

If we speculate that India's movement was due to a meteorite, and if we consider what may have been the magnitude of such a meteoritic collision and how it seems to have fortuitously influenced the preparedness of our earth for humankind, we must marvel at the work of the creator. God can use meteorites to influence the flow of love on earth. She timed the removal of the selfish and greedy dinosaurs. She encouraged the evolution of the human by pushing Africa and India apart. If our present attitudes prove to be a problem for earth's continued existence, God will surely find means to encourage her earth into loving directions. God is able to raise up from the stones a people who will praise her.

God's Part in This. Our God is an orderly God who sees the overall picture and knows the results she wishes to achieve. "The movement of the earth's crust, volcanoes and air currents follow laws, whether fully understood by man or not. An unpredicted earthquake, though the cause of vast human suffering, is still an outward expression of terrestrial order and fidelity."[4] At our stage of evolution, we must accept our inabilities and our tendencies to kill each other, but we must work past these upsetting deficiencies. We have been programmed to compete. Our orderly creator will help us past our violence to greater spiritual understandings and to a peaceful well-run society. All will be fed; all will have opportunity for fulfillment; even the fear of death will be diminished.

Surely, a God who can form an earth can create circumstances that encourage those earth forms created, into more positive directions. Such a God could send a meteor which would raise clouds of dust that could suffocate life that was proliferating in brainless and ravaging directions. If we do God's will and act in accord with what is good for the earth, God will surely send the necessary environmental support in our direction.

God promises that a remnant shall be saved (Isaiah 37:31-32). Our God is a remnant God, the God who builds up the remnant, the meek, the gentle, and allows them to inherit the earth. 65 million years ago, some little meek creatures hid in caves while the dust settled on and caused the destruction of the giant dinosaurs.

Life on The Indian Plate. Coming back to the tectonic motion of India and the little early monkey types on India and Africa, they didn't know enough to wave "good bye" to each other when their land masses parted. They didn't notice the gradual separation. It could have taken ten or twenty million years. If the parting were due to meteoritic impact, there may have been thick clouds and smoke for several years after. Random winds could have blown these around to affect life in different areas. Circumstances may have been rough, but the adaptable models would have survived.

After the effects of the explosion died down, those early mammals who were left on Africa continued on as they were. There was no further need to change. If things are going well for you and food is plentiful, you will not elect a new president. You will conservatively go with things as they are.

But if your president has lost touch with the poor, you will go for a change, even allowing new tax burdens to be placed on your shoulders. Consequently, the early mammals on Africa continued to eat wild onions in the fields, as the lowland gorilla does to this day. If they were at the stone throwing, tool-using stage, these pre-human types continued on with their method of slugging small game with stones in order to get their dinner. As Africa was in the warm belt of the earth, we assume that small game, berries, and roots were plentiful enough to support a large population of pre-human specimens.

The story of how the population of pre-humans on their Indian island continent ride to Asia, made out, is probably about the same. The survivors were on a warm spot. Their jungle growth was similar to what was left behind on Africa. There may have been climatic changes to savannah and plain, but they were able to handle that. Life was comfortable, but there may have been the need for certain adaptions.

It was a different situation when the Indian plate slid into the plate of Asia. When two plates collide, mountains are formed. When one plate overrides another, there is volcanic activity. When two plates slide past one

Marvelous Events
Having To Do With Earth

Happening	Time (approximate)
Birth of Earth	6 - 4.6 billion years ago
Acquisition of Moon	6 - 4.6 billion years ago
Formation of Sea & Continents	6 - 4.6 billion years ago
Movement of Continents	4.6 billion years ago - present
Life on Earth	3.5 billion years ago
Invertebrates	2.5 billion years ago
Green plants (plankton)	2 billion years ago
Sexual reproduction	600 million years ago
Vertebrates (primitive fish)	450 million years ago
Forests	350 million years ago
Paleolithic Ice Ages	280-250 million years ago
Dinosaurs	225 - 65 million years ago
All continents together	250-180 million years ago
Birds with feathers, first mammals	150 million years ago
N & S continental masses part	80 million years ago
India and Asia together	40 million years ago
Manlike primate	14 million years ago
First Hominids (primitive tools)	2 million years ago
Recent Ice Ages (possible land bridges)	1.8 million - 10,000 years ago
Homo erectus (used fire)	500,000 years ago
Homo sapiens	300,000 years ago
Religious Behavior	50,000 years ago
Civilization	10,000 years ago

another, there are earth quakes. There did not seem to be any vents in that portion of the continental plates, so there was no volcanic activity in that particular area. With the India collision, great mountains were thrown up. This happened very gradually, but there must have been tremendous earthquakes. The large island of India docked on Asia approximately 50 million years ago. For awhile there was water between the continent and subcontinent that had to be crossed over. What are now valleys of rivers flowing down from high mountains may have been fairly inviting low lying plains or islands. The passengers on this giant boat had had in the neighborhood of 15 million years to change genetically. So had their relatives in Africa. Perhaps there were no changes. We cannot be sure of this. Perhaps their changes did produce a "missing link."

250,000 years back, archaeologists found the men and beasts of East Africa to be gigantic. Specimens at Olduvai Gorge carried hand axes, but wore no clothes. It was a warm climate. Those species developing on India were lighter weight and smaller boned. Perhaps speech developed on this floating continent, but it is more likely that in both Africa and India, the hunting and gathering life style continued on pretty much as before. The land was green. They accommodated to their turbulent everydays. However, we must note that India has a different type of elephant than the African elephant. The Indian elephant has smaller ears, eyes, and tusks, and is more easily tamed. Also, India has species of monkey that are similar to, but different from African monkeys. Interesting evolutionary threads can be seen in the variation of monkey species. Cranial capacity and other genetic enhancements doubtless increased among the primates on the floating continent through the process of natural selection.

As the Noah's Ark of the Indian subcontinent docked and the crunching and grinding of plates commenced, the more intelligent of the travelers may have explored ways to leave the situation. Many may have drowned as a result of the tsunami, or great waves due to earthquakes. Many may have had the roofs of their caves collapse on them. Was there need for speech? Did those communities who could signal and explain dangers, survive better?

Some of those ancestors (who may have had patches of red hair) climbed over the forming Himalayas and headed north. This exodus took a long period of time. It covered several ice age cycles with their accompanying interglacial periods. This battle with the elements sharpened the wits of those fleeing the earthquake region. As they went between glacial and interglacial, their hair had changes in quantity to accommodate. Their brains became larger. Their skin which needed protection in the hot climates, lost its color in colder regions. We still have genetically related processes that can make dark people lighter in color.[5]

After India docked, humans gradually penetrated north, northeast, and northwest as far as the ice would let them. There were primitive pre-men in the Far East and China over a million years back. In 1.7 million years before the present there was an individual we call Yuan-mou Man. His ancestors may have stepped off the Indian continent when it arrived on Asia. In the 900,000 BP glacial build-up, sea levels were low, and *Homo erectus* could travel between continents. In this period, much of the available land space turned into windy desert. *Homo erectus* might have been on the march looking for better land. The Chinese Lantian ape-man is dated 800,000 BC. Peking Man is 500,000 BC. Due to ice and melt cycles in the last 500,000 years, the Siberian land bridge may have been exposed twenty times. In warm times, the Peking human had the opportunity to follow the bears to Alaska and down the American coast.

Migrations. Some groups remained in India. Picture the family communities striking out in various directions, gradually moving to hunting grounds when the ice receded, and then migrating southward again as the ice came back. The racial divide may have occurred during this period of fluctuation when groups became trapped in areas apart from each other. Groups in the north managed to exist above the glacial line, in an interglacial age. Those arriving in the Gobi area of China about 50,000 BP became a localized genetic group that possessed Mongolian traits. Some group was able to thrive in the Caucasus area, and members of this group also penetrated northern Europe when the ice belt lifted. Those in Europe localized and may have become the sturdy Neanderthals. Some flowed back into southeast Asia, Malaysia, Indonesia, and even to Australia when the land bridge was available.

Around 80,000 years ago when there was a warm interglacial, people were plentiful. They expanded across the areas where the ice had kept them out, such as northern Russia and Greenland. Many of them continued to thrive even when the ice came back. Our relatives (not necessarily our ancestors), the Neanderthals, peopled Europe. At the ice melt, flood, and time of rain about 37,000 BP which could have ushered in a time of easy living for the human being, the Neanderthals in Europe disappeared. They may have been flooded out of their caves. They may have been killed by plague. Genetically, they may just not have been adaptable enough. Changes in diet can cause changes in human disposition. As Mother Nature produced less that was free for the taking, the gatherers of berries and the hunters were forced into cultivating grasses and inventing better tools with which to pursue the faster animals. When caves became overcrowded, the human had to invent houses and tents. Perhaps the Neanderthal could not adjust to new ways or new diets or new germs.

With the migration of peoples another change that took place was the necessity for greater communication. Very basic meaningful communication between humans may have begun to assist with their material needs. Perhaps the Neanderthal was not a skilled communicator. We know the Neanderthals thought about God, for burial sites have been found which show they had an awareness of death, and had emotions about parting from a fellow human being. They had progressed from cannibalistic appetites to ties of friendship. Did this give them new notions of God? Was God a friend as well as a power who threw lightning bolts? Did they feel God watching? Did they think God expected a response from them? Did they communicate these yearnings after the eternal to other human types that lived back then? There may have been some kind of spiritual communication transferred in the thought layer (similar to extra sensory perception), as researchers have observed in human and animal today. Are we of the present able to communicate our yearnings for all the world to live in friendship, either spiritually or by word of mouth?

Some areas would be more inducive to colonization than others. The Caspian area today is home to an amazing variety of cultures. It is a large body of water with accompanying rivers that could be used as travel routes. At one time in its geological history it was part of the ocean, but mountain building 20 million years ago sealed it off. While the north Caspian waters can be frozen solid in the winter today, the southern part is open. Scientists have studied the Caspian in our present time as they fear a rise in its sea level that will threaten those who live on its shores. They have studied sediments that tell them about climate changes and lake levels for the past 400,000 years. Melting of the polar ice caps 10,000 years back did not flood the Caspian, but caused desertification in that area, and produced the exact opposite result. The sea level fell 100 meters.[6] This may be the reason for settlers from the north penetrating south to found cities such as Jericho, and to build in the Mesopotamian plain.

Other cultural conveniences went along with the human migration trails. We know that food conservation and production were not of European or African origin. The ancestors of sheep, goats, pigs, and cattle did not come from Europe but from the Near East. Before 8000 BC sheep were domesticated in the Zagros Mountains between Iraq and Iran, also herds of goats are archaeologically documented in 7500 BC. In 7000 BC pigs were domesticated in Turkey, and in 6000 BC, cattle. The plant ancestors of wheat and barley come from the natural habitats that existed between

Anatolia to Afghanistan. Pottery seems to have developed in the Far East and traveled westward. Many religious beliefs also seem to have traveled east to west.

Travels of migrant bands across continents seem to follow a logical pattern. In North America those who landed on the west coast, headed east. Those who landed on the east coast, headed west. If a group is relatively unopposed and reaches a coastline barrier, they may thrive inventively in the coastline situation, such as the early Joman peoples on Japan. If when reaching the opposite coast, your group has multiplied sufficiently, you try to cross the waters, or descendants of your group try to make the return journey bringing inventive innovations with them.

Fishers and herders who multiplied in the temperate belt in the unpredictable regions around the Caspian Sea, could follow the animal herds east or west until they were stopped by the oceans. We know that western Europe had an influx of people spreading in from the Caucasus and reaching to the British Isles which were accessible by land bridge. When the ice melted, rains and high waves destroyed land bridges and flooded out those living on the lowlands. Later traders had to use boats to ferry the valuable tin that was found in Britain.

The Japanese were traders as early as 13,000 BC. Most of Japan rose from the sea in the last 30 million years as volcanic islands. This may have been a side effect from the knitting of the Indian-Asian tectonic plates. The Japanese became very accustomed to earthquakes. In Japanese mythology the world rides on the back of a giant catfish, whose movements cause the earth to tremble. There was a community of Caucasians on early Japan which was still accessible by land bridge about 20,000 BC. These Caucasians showed some Neanderthal features. This community of Joman hunter-gatherers made the earliest pottery recorded about 11,000 BC. These Caucasian groups may have been squeezed out by later Mongoloid population pressures from the Gobi area. There are descendants of these Caucasians on the island of Hokkaido, Japan, even today. This racial group has been there for 20,000 years. Japan became insular with the world ocean level rising, sometime between 16,000 and 10,000 BC. They had water craft in 18,000 BC.

Signs of visitation in the Americas, such as rock carvings and tools were available only after the date of 20,000 BP as people had bigger brains and could communicate their presence. The 20,000 BP glacial cresting point with land cross-overs may have been the start of the human being's latest search for the safe land where she could dwell in peace. Unfortunately, the hoped for land is usually claimed by others who have similar needs and aspirations. The land continues to be a source of conflict.

1.4 Selection in Species

We can get information about genetic traits from looking at the results. We can examine what kind of people live in different areas of the earth. Of course, as human beings we are all related and all similar, but there must be a rational and land-related way to explain the races. If a group of mammalians live on the edge of their group in relative seclusion, they develop distinct differences. There are Asian elephants, and there are Indian elephants, and there are mammoths. Each has similarities and differences. The Neanderthals in northern Europe had their distinct characteristics. The Chinese far to the west in their private enclave developed Mongoloid characteristics. It is believed that Mongoloids originated in the seclusion of the Gobi region. The Asian Indian seems to be in the middle of all these developments, and their territory is located amid all the main travel routes between the separated areas. It is possible to see the structure of the Indian face mingling with that of the Chinese in the Vietnamese features. Those in Tibet have similar facial structures to the Australian aborigines. One can see many genetic similarities between those living in India and the Capoid race in Africa. One can see Indian features mingling with the European in the Mesopotamian plain. Analyzing blood types and other genetic peculiarities (such as blood vessel endings and nerve ganglions where the tail used to be) can suggest where racial groups originated.[7] Blood type B is high in the Mongoloid and low in the American Indian, although their common ancestor may have come from the same area near the Siberian land bridge.

When thinking of racial differences, we should not neglect what myths tell us, such as the story of the twins Romulus and Remus who supposedly founded the city of Rome. They were left on a hillside to die, and taken care of by a friendly mother wolf who nursed them as if they were her cubs. What kind of people would develop from children left to the care of a wolf? Having language capabilities, they would invent their own language to make known to each other their needs. We notice in some children today, particularly if they are rather isolated, the ability to make up some of their language.

A Korean legend states that one of their country's ancestors was a bear. Some early peoples lived in caves near bear populations, and occasionally killed one for eating, with appropriate religious apologies. They believed that the killed bear would remarkably return as a new born bear, so this animal harvesting was logical and allowable. If adults in a caveman family were destroyed leaving infant children to be brought up by a nursing mother bear, these adopted children would certainly have interesting language and behavior adaptions.

When a population is confronted with an ice age, it seems that those who are more alert and inventive live through the challenging situation and thus the species develops bigger brains. The ice age created temporary pockets in which evolutionary change seemed to go faster. Some areas such as Africa didn't experience as much variation, as food was often plentiful during times of mild change. The lowland gorilla still exists today much like his ancestors existed.

When bigger brained species of prehumans formed in isolated areas, they could make better use of resources than the smaller brained. With the general rule of one similar species per niche, the bigger brained would take over the territory of previous species. The back and forth variations of the ice ages amplified the effect of processes of natural selection that take place in frontier populations.[8]

The main population stock may exist comfortably in its area, and face no particular challenges. In its comfort, it may find nothing more entertaining than sex and games and trading, and its young may reproduce rapidly, so that there are children having children, the immature producing less mature infants by giving them less nurturing care. The older more mature members of the group will be having less of the children, and the main population stock will not develop any new and enabling characteristics.

Off on the sidelines, an isolated population group may be facing more challenges. They may be thinning out from starvation, working harder to grow new strains of food crops, building better boats to fish from, making sturdier nets. They don't have time for leisure. The children see the need for tribal cooperation and work diligently. Marriage and sex is a reward for industrious conduct. Few children are produced, as the group realizes they would be extra mouths to feed. The indigenous tribes in Peru have no more than two children as three would be too many to carry if a starvation trek became necessary. If a third child is born, it will be left to die. Each child that is accepted is treated as a gift to be treasured, and receives attentive care.

In the time when the main population group was made up of the Neanderthals, they seemed to be rather intelligent, hardy, and doing very well in their environment. Some disaster overtook them, perhaps due to disease, or a children-having-children population, and they disappeared from the scene. A sub group of Cro-Magnons that had been developing off on the Ice Age sidelines, moved in and filled up the vacuum.

We know today that excessive radiation, sea sickness pills, and even diseases like German measles can cause genetic changes, and therefore birth defects. Early human beings were exposed to different levels of radiation from the sun, to strange medicines in the plants they must have tried, and diseases have always been with us. As we talk about birth defects in human beings, we also should talk about birth enhancements. If a large meteorite brought strange radiation in its wake, there might be a variety of both birth enhancements and birth defects produced. The enhancements would be better equipped to struggle on; the defects would die out. If there were no need to change, the dominant gene pool would continue on as before. If the dominant group died out due to environmental changes, the enhancements would assume the dominant position.

One example of a genetic variation due to location is the case of robins in Sweden. Because there is more daylight to gather food for their young, robins lay more eggs in Sweden than they do in countries to the south. Can humans be falling into similar ways? Is our electric lighting causing greater production of humans by humans?

Many factors affect gene development, but genetic changes occur slowly. In experimenting with flies, which reproduce rapidly, and should be able to show up differences, it has been possible to grow only a few extra hairs. Perhaps hair is one of the genetic clues that God has given us with which to trace our origins. God has lots of time to make genetic changes, millions of years. Hairless dinosaurs were able to evolve into hairy mammals. These creatures could better withstand the shifting temperatures of glacial and interglacial stages.

If we think about hair, we notice that the lowland gorilla in Africa has a marvelous patch of red hair on the top of his head. Genghis Khan was a red head. *Cheaper By The Dozen* by Galbraith is a recent story about a whole family of red heads. We accept people and animals with red hair. We do not insist that they all live together in one section of a city. We allow them to freely live out their differences in their chosen territories. We don't worry about their origins particularly. Red hair is noticeable, but not too dramatic, other characteristics being equal. We accept this sample of diversity.

We also are very accepting if other people have black hair, but when people have black skin, we have been trained to find this characteristic more noticeable. The color of skin seems to be very important to people in recent times. Though they come out of many different languages, cultures, and countries, people with black skins respectfully call each other "brother" or "sister." They recognize a common genetic and prehistoric bond.

Among Caucasians there are other minor differences that many of us find unsettling. We accept the ability to speak as the right of all human beings, but some do not have this power. We class them as autistic. Caucasians, blacks, and all other racial divisions have unusual gene combinations which produce humans that are retarded, unhealthy, dwarf, giant, bisexual, or otherwise not approved by the general population. Models like these may have been among our ancestors. God made them, so they must be viable and "good."

If all of us would accept our differences as enhancements necessary at some point in the evolutionary process, and admit that we are children from the same creative beginnings, we would be able to live more peacefully in this wonderful world that sustains us. We are a successful group existing productively. Our greatest enemy is our fear of each other.

Creative Survival. Three million years ago in what may have been an early paradise, the continents were green woodlands and vegetative plains. In a step up from eagles grabbing chipmunks, early hominids using stones could catch small game. One million years ago, in comparison, the ice was built up all across Siberia, the seas were lower, the jungles dried out into grasslands and deserts. Other forces continued to work in the world. There were volcanic eruptions, earthquakes, torrential winds and rains, changes in the patterns of ocean currents. As the glaciers came and went, barriers were put before migrating groups. In the melt of an interglacial, sea levels would rise, and people would form isolated gene pools. Land bridges disappeared, and folk like the Australians were trapped on Australia. Contrarily, when the glaciers came, hunting activity and human habitation were forced to a belt around the middle of the earth. The game became scarcer and harder to catch. The slow moving mammoths were hunted to extinction. Early tool using creatures had to be more inventive to capture the speedier animals that survived by evolving to run faster. The tool users became tool makers and came up with better bows and arrows, better arrow points, sharper axes, so that they could acquire their food supply. God's challenge of an ice age, made it necessary for the early human to sharpen her wits. If her descendants were going to thrive, they would have to evolve to be craftier. The genes of those more able to get along, were the genes that were passed down. We often grow from our challenges.

Now that we have proved ourselves to be a successful and brainy bunch, is the same fate as the Neanderthals, awaiting us? When ethical values are such that children produce children, those infants produced by the very young have nervous system disorders such as Attention Deficit Disease. When free sex is practiced among the young, many babies are born with AIDS. On the whole, babies produced by the young are given inadequate parenting. Our whole population will gradually become more susceptible to disease, and not be stimulated to produce more capable brains.

We may be seeing this happen before our very eyes, and we can also see the opposite occurring in a secondary population. We have observed from educational testing that our students are getting lower and lower test scores. In China where individuals are not allowed to marry and mate until the sum of their ages is fifty years, there is less disease, less Attention Deficit Disorder, and more ability for the children to absorb the educational feast offered to them.

We can act responsibly in this situation. Our creative God will help us today, as this good God has helped our ancestors to survive through countless ages. Surely God was there when the early human roamed through the fields searching for roots and berries to feed her little son. Surely God's spirit was near when she stood on the hilltop and gazed at other far off hills. Friendly and comforting spirits must have spoken in her ear. It may have been more easy to hear God's instructive voice without the roar of motor cars, television, and jets. Were our forebears closer to God's love and care, than we are?

God was somehow present in this marvelous creation. God was certainly visible as power in the earthquake, but God was also a provider, a mothering nature who sent herds of animals upon the vegetated plains. All the human had to do was reproduce, pick berries, dig roots, and stone to death animals which she could roast as food. Did she thank God for all God's bounty? She had some notion of a great provider who had given her life, and as she roasted the flesh of animals, she may have watched the smoke rise up to heaven with curiosity and reverence.

1.5 Events of Religious Significance

As era followed era, we must not assume that early people either worshiped God or had no thought of God. Perhaps they did not know or care about their origins, as they were so caught up in the business of everyday. We of today often seem to be following the same pattern. We think of God and our beginnings and endings only when faced with dramatic situations.

Life in early times must have been very dramatic. There were many reasons to speculate on one's possible end, and why people were on the earth in the first place. Consider the petrified footprints of the two *Australopithecus* of two million years back, walking together across the African landscape that was soon to be covered with molten lava.[9] They may have had only a 400 to 600 cubic centimeter brain size, but one was supporting and guiding the other. In these early brains there was concern for the other. They may not have had the gift of language, but they could look into each others' faces and communicate with their spirits.

The brain may have enlarged partially in response to this desire to do a good job of caring for the other. If we exist by ourselves, we may get discouraged. Caring for a supportive community, causes us to put out a little more effort. Evolution selects those who care for others as they are inclined to live longer and produce more children. Those who trust in providence are under less stress and less subject to heart disease than those who live in fear.

Other aspects of living also influence our genes and the principle of selection of the fittest. We have the expression, "You are what you eat." Drinking alcohol warps our minds. Beef fattens us with cholesterol. Hunters and gatherers had different eating habits, depending on where they lived. Some ate cereal grasses. Some tamed cows, dogs, and sheep. Some dined on mammoth or bear. Some ingested each other. Being more in touch with and more dependent on nature, they respected the spirits in the grasses and bears. They observed that bounteous Mother Nature replenished what they took, and they believed that if they took a bear's life for their food, his spirit would be released into the spiritual home. The bear would then enjoy Bear Heaven for awhile, or he could come back as another newborn bear ready to again sacrifice his body for human food. The same was felt to be true about the human. His spirit would return. A bear might come back in a human body, and vice versa. In death the various spirits were released to a more noble sphere. There are graves in Mesopotamia and China which confirm that people believed in this release of spirit. There is the Indian practice of *suttee*, which allows the wife's spirit to follow that of her husband by her being burned with him on his funeral pyre. Hindus believe in the return of a soul into another animal or human. There is still theological discussion on the transmigration of souls today.

Food Taboos. Whatever made the Neanderthals disappear must have been very traumatic for the Neanderthals. With their approximately 800 cubic centimeter brain size, they must have thought deeply about their existence. One possible reason why the Neanderthal disappeared may have had to do with her eating habits. Eating can be both a physical necessity and a religious experience. The Neanderthal survived in the cold glacial environment, because her community was able to pursue woolly mammoths and force them over cliffs. In the cold they could eat meat year round. When the earth warmed, the mammoth kill could feed a group over the winter, but with spring would come the maggots, and your meat was no longer refrigerated. Perhaps *Cro-Magnons* had developed resistance to warm weather diseases and were hardened to plague. If observing *Cro-Magnons* watched Neanderthals die after eating spring time meat, they may have decided that God did not approve of meat eaten after a certain date in the spring. Shortly before the spring full moon, they would throw a big party to consume all that was left of the winter kill. Then would come their season of fresh fish and of eating whatever greens and berries the land produced. They would eat grains, nuts, roots, and roasted migrating birds and herds in the fall. These seasonal diets fitted in with Mother Nature enabling the spring migrants to reproduce in their time, the fish to reproduce in their time, and the plants to bloom and seed, and it all worked very well. The Bible tells us that in the Hebrew tribe's walking through the desert, the migrating birds were not to be eaten for health reasons. The birds would eat the raw meat of decaying animals, and thus they would carry poisons to the humans who ate them. The Neanderthals couldn't refrigerate their mammoth or bears or other large game over the winter in the warm interglacial period. The stuff got gamey. When the community group ate thereof, people became poisoned. If, in your hunger, you turned to the migrating birds, and they had feasted on rotting animals, you had the same sickening result. Food taboos doubtless developed very early.

Such seemingly unexplainable sicknesses and deaths must have made the Neanderthals question God's care, and seek for whatever advice they could get. Neanderthals and non-Neanderthals prove by their early burial customs that they had beliefs in the spiritual. They buried their dead in special positions with food for an afterlife. They believed there was something after death for those they loved. They must have had similar notions about a caring God or Mother Nature for those still alive. In primitive societies today, there are shamans and medicine men who mediate God to the community. Even in advanced civilizations, we often accord superstitious reverence to those who practice medicine. Religious specialists of back then, prescribed diets for their constituents that seemed to meet with God's approval. Herders would be advised to kill one sheep, and eat it all at once as in the Exodus. When wandering in the desert, they would be instructed to eat only what was produced fresh from the land— no unclean animals such as pigs, no birds, and no holding a substance over to the second day.

Much later on the North American continent we have the example of the Indians showing pilgrims how the Great Spirit liked them to celebrate Thanksgiving by eating fall birds roasted. The proper harvest festival procedures seem to require that you eat all your perishables before the first frost, because the frost does them in. Gather your grains with proper prayer and bury your roots acknowledging God's goodness. We follow our early ancestors' leadings by having our hunting seasons in the winter. We have Lent in the spring. On Mardi Gras we eat all the meat and grease before it starts to rot. Then our religious directives advise fresh caught fish.

Pockets of this method of living, which depended on refrigeration or air temperature too cold for flies, survived far to the north with the Eskimo and also in the more temperate areas with mountain dwellers such as Tibetans. They could manage pretty well up on the high plateaus where it was colder, and live off their yaks, killing them when it was convenient, and eating them all at once. Early Koreans managed to dwell near bears and to live off fresh bear meat. However, the bears were not as easy to tame as yaks or oxen. There were bear cults at Drachenloch in the Swiss Alps, also in Siberia and with the Ainus of north Japan. These cults were associated with an extinct bear similar to the Kodiak bear of Alaska.

Liturgies. The Neanderthal thought of the dead as going on a journey and supplied the corpse with food and flowers. Natufians in the Jordan Valley area had a ceremonial burial of the deceased. The earlier *Pithecanthropus pekinensis* did not bury, but perhaps ate the corpse as a matter of conservation or as uniting herself with the spirit of the dead and acquiring his power.

Cave art as drawn by cave dwellers from Spain to India seemed to have religious significance. When Australian aborigines of the present practice cave art, they combine it with dancing and the recitation of legends. Ancient French cave art seemed to be concerned with luck in the hunt. Indian customs of today would lead us to believe that women drew these cave designs. Women artists in the Mithila area of northeast India today, paint scenes of Hindu gods on canvas material. Formerly, they drew on walls. This painting craft has passed over the centuries from mother to daughter. They paint with vegetable or mineral pigments applied with twigs. When the Aryans arrived in India 1700 BC, they accepted the gods of the land. The cave paintings probably helped them to visualize the aspects of the creator which were being worshiped.

Both Indian and French prehistoric cave art have some seemingly pornographic scenes. Indian phallic representations may have to do with the search for god-given energy. The male worshippers of Siva honor the phallic image as representative of godly energy. In Genesis 24 Abraham made his servant take a phallic pledge, when he sent him off to find a wife for his son Isaac. Another example of a phallic pledge was when Jacob had Joseph promise to bury him in Palestine (Genesis 47:29).

Other religious symbolism had to do with circumcision which was practiced worldwide from Australia to America. Today in Africa some tribes use circumcision as a rite for entering manhood. This basic action of circumcision leads one to believe in communication among early religious human beings or descent from a common practicing ancestor.

Our ancestors and their relatives must have had a hard time during the latest series of ice ages from 1.8 million to 10,000 BP with its fluctuations in temperature, but there was always a belt of vegetation across the Sahara and Arabian deserts where there were rivers that have since disappeared, or now flow deep underground. Animal life flourished, and in 10,000 BP, as far north as southern Russia, there were communities that knew about farming, and built houses out of trees and animal skins, with stone fireplaces, and holes in the roof for smoke to escape.

Hunting and gathering populations had penetrated across the land bridges to Britain. Between 15,000 and 8,000 BC we find small farming being done there. Hunting instruments had improved markedly since the first appearance of homo sapiens. In Denmark and northern Germany trees were cut down for boats and oars. There wasn't much pottery, and crops were not cultivated, but merely harvested if they appeared. Early community dwellers were also present on the American continent. Descendants of these folk have stories about the world being destroyed by water and by fire. Our Bible talks of human kind being flooded out and of being kept from a beautiful garden by a *flaming* sword. All these peoples had cultural and religious speculations that helped them to survive and interpret their environment. Human everyday happenings were being related to god-like forces.

1.6 Beginnings of The Human Soul

God created us in God's image; God created us to be somehow like God. If we accept either evolution or instantaneous creation, we can confess that God made this a very interesting world with a very complicated human shape to walk upon it. This human fitted nicely into the world God had started on its way.

We haven't been able to say too much about the evolution of the soul until we have first talked about the evolution of the earth and of the human. A soul is rather difficult to define. We cannot see it; it is a spiritual entity. A human soul is evident when there is animation and life. It has something to do with our mind, with our conscious willing and believing. It also has something to do with our subconscious. The soul seems to be attached to our physical body, though in religious beliefs the soul is regarded as something that lives on, separate from the body, when the body is no longer animate.

God as grand designer must have had a reason for gifting the human with a soul. Perhaps God made the soul as the meeting place of God and human. Only because we have such a meeting place, can we have a knowledge of God, and the consequent urge to be god-like.

Scientists have long been searching for the *missing link*, the genetic carrier between the human and the pre-human. Some people believe that in our journey from ape to human, there was an instant when the creature became human, that God stepped in at a point in time and gave the human a soul. Some geneticists would term this genome the Genesis Gene.[10] Conversely, there are many who believe that all the universe is insouled, that animals have souls, that trees possess inner energy, and that the soul is an expression of God's love for her creation.

Let us think about the development of soul. If we look at a human being, can we observe her soul? We observe trees, and because they do not seem to have a brain, we do not credit them with having souls. Perhaps all living things, no matter what their size, have something spiritual attached to their mass of material, that is connected to God or to the unseen part of our material universe. The earth, having mass, could have spiritual components to accompany that mass. A tree, having mass, may likewise have a spiritual component. The high voltage Kirlian photographic process shows that leaves have associated energy particles. Our bodies are permeated with energy fields. Can these unseen energy particles be connected with the concept of *soul*?

People and their souls have come from somewhere through a strange and wonderful process. If we call that unknown cause or process, "God," we may feel that we are being guided to some great end, by that unknown. As we come from God, to God we naturally return. If you were God, what would you do with the spiritual part of the human you had created, when the material part could no longer carry it around? Anaximander of Greece (about 600 BC) felt that there was one "indestructible eternal substance out of which everything arises, and into which everything once more returns."

Where was God when the earth was torn from its parent star and hurled across the heavens? God somehow placed the moon in the sky and gave us countless stars. From earth we safely enjoy their twinkling light, but, close up, we would not be able to bear their ferocity. There is the theory of the Nemesis Star, a sister star to our sun, that will return every 26 million years and cause meteorite disturbance. What kind of hands did God use when she formed the stars? How did she mold the earth into high mountains and low lying seas? God did not use our human hands or our human abilities. God used a spiritual control. Spiritual control can cause mountains to be moved and to cast themselves into the sea (Matthew 21:21).

In the Book of Job 38:4 God asks, "Where were you when I laid the earth's foundations?" Were we there to decide the earth's dimensions, "when all the stars of the morning were singing with joy?" Were we in touch with this vast process of the boundless God? Yes, our thoughts were somehow there, as we can send our minds back and imagine what it was like. The part of us that contains a tiny spark of God's knowledge, can be with God's spirit, back at mountain forming time. This wonderful spirit of God is still working through water, stone, and metal to make a more complex material world, to make plants, to make animals, to make of us a still more special creation with many unimaginable future abilities and talents. We who move on the earth may be able to help in our own creation.

We do not know what spiritual yearnings were in our pre-historical forebears, or when they obtained the gift of speech to communicate their feelings to each other or to praise their unknown God. To make speech possible they needed both a large enough brain and the proper throat formation or hyoid bone. Alpine yodeling may be an unrestrained cry from the throat of early man that sounded his delight across the mountains. There were also comforting whirrings and clickings, as well as shrieking challenges. Through the gift of speech, the early humans were able to reinforce their spiritual capabilities.

We have seen that there were several types of early human being. Even today there are humanoid types around that amaze us. We have giants, and we have dwarfs. We have athletes and inventors. We have women, and we have men. Yet we all have in common that we were made by God. Being made by God, we each must have some spiritual part of that creator in our material nature (as we can know something about an artist by looking at his art work). We all have an inner something that we define as soul. This soul has something spiritual of God connected with it.

If we agree that plants and trees have some sort of energy particles that dwell with their physical substance, surely we can admit that the early biped possessed a soul. As she roamed through this environment wherein she had appropriately evolved to exist, she doubtless had a feeling of a loving providence. Even as humankind today can sense that something is expected of us in our world, the early human could sense that she should reproduce her kind and thank the whole of nature for supporting her in the garden in which she existed. She gradually came to understand that she could love or harm the other creatures that were in her environment.

The words *love* and *harm* can have a wide range of meanings. We must be careful how we define the quality of love. Our definition of *love* might include the wish for fulfillment for both ourselves and others. *Harm* might connote the unnecessary exercising of power due to an inner fear. When we evaluate this long and dangerous journey that the human has taken over time, we are surprised by the fact that the human being loves herself and loves other human beings in spite of inner fears and lack of trust. The quality of love seems to keep rising to the surface.

Learning from The Dinosaurs. We have heard about the dinosaurs. They stalked around chomping on lush vegetation and each other, about 230 million to 65 million years ago. They, too, were creatures of God's making. Why didn't they evolve into more able specimens? Tyrannosaurus Rex stood on his two back feet, and waved his arms around. Surely with two free arms, he could have become a stone thrower or a tool maker.

Dinosaurs may have been so healthy and profuse that they ate themselves right out of a stable home. Today we worry about keeping enough trees in our environment in order to protect our ozone layer. The dinosaurs did not have the intelligence to worry about their future, so they were denied a future. They ate up their environment thoughtlessly in their greed. The eco-system reacted with ice-ages and other protective built-in mechanisms. We hope that this same fate does not overtake our species. Dinosaurs could die from extreme heat as well as from extreme cold. Perhaps our physical bodies have evolved to be more adaptable than those of the dinosaurs.

Perhaps the dinosaurs were too big. Many of these large animals could demolish a whole forest and destroy the green layer that preserves the earth. A comparatively treeless earth might bring on an ice age. We do not know why ice ages came and went, why winters would get longer and longer, but it may have been triggered by a lack of trees. We need trees to absorb CO_2 and to create a protective ozone layer. However, many tiny humans cavorting around the globe might have been just as serious a threat to the eco-system as giant mastodons. Human beings may have unwittingly endangered their ecology by their group hunting habits, in which fire was used to burn off an area to force the prey into swamps or rivers. As the population increased and as more fires were used to roast meat and keep warm, humans may have destroyed the earth and air that nourished them. The Neanderthals may have hastened their own end by encouraging a warm interglacial age. A sudden warming might have flooded the low lying plain that was the Adriatic. We may not be the first generation to disturb the atmosphere and eco-layers. An ice age may be the earth's natural protective response to over-population by human or animal.

Learning from Pollution. We worry about similar upheavals today being wrought by too much smoke filtering out the sun, or too much CO_2 with its heat trapping effect. Ozone, formed when gas vapors and other hydrocarbons mix with heat and sunlight, creates breathing problems by damaging lungs. Paradoxically, while ozone near the earth's surface is a health concern, ozone at greater altitudes is beneficial because it helps block dangerous rays from the sun. Because of competition from other pollutants, ozone is being depleted in the upper reaches of the atmosphere where it is helpful. Worldwide pollution may be creating a "greenhouse effect" in the stratosphere with other noxious gases which don't allow the sun's heat-rays to escape the earth and which contribute to ozone production close to the earth. The helpful far-up ozone layer may be undergoing destruction from propellants in spray cans. Besides carbon dioxide, greenhouse gases are methane, nitrous oxide, and chloro-fluoro carbons. These gases cause the earth's surface to warm by trapping the infrared radiation that otherwise would be reflected back into space. Our wasteful life style contributes to ecological disaster. Sulfur dioxide from industry causes acid rain. Even perfumes may be poisoning the systems of those who use them. Poisonous gases of various sorts may have been abundant in dinosaur days from plentiful volcanic eruptions, but the dinosaurs had no way of knowing or of controlling their future. Supposedly, we have the caring, the knowledge, and the ability to redirect our efforts. More importantly, we have a belief in a loving overseeing providence. We have minds and spiritual components that can respond to this providence. Dinosaurs did not seem to possess our kind of soul.

Reflective Thought. If it is granted that the human does have a quantity called a soul, at what point in time, at what place in earth, did the human soul first become responsive to her God? The historical moment when the human became reflective is an important event in the history of humankind. The Bible speaks of this moment by using symbolic ancestors (the man and the mother of all the living) in the Garden of Eden, somewhere to the east of Palestine. It relates that the human beings recognized their nakedness before God (Genesis 3:10). They ceased to accept their likeness to the animal kingdom and observed their own behavior. They could reflect on their actions instead of reacting instinctively. The human had capacities to contain the spiritual. She could stand off to one side and look at herself and think creatively about her behavior. She could empathize with other human beings who were having difficulties. There are those who would like to place this reflective event in the Caucasus, and there are anthropologists who would like to have it in Africa with that continent's plentiful archaeological remains. India may have claim to being the place of earliest religious reflection. It may have represented such a challenge to the early bi-ped, that she responded by having to plan her future in order to survive. When she faced danger and death, and found unseen hands helping her in her calamities, she formulated an idea of spirits which accompanied her material situation. These ideas were reinforced from generation to generation, until they could be written down. As one place where we derive early religious writings, India may be where reflective thought came into being.

The antiquity of the Hindu beliefs also argue for the antiquity of the human race in that area. Looking back to earlier times when India floated onto Asia (50 million BP), and seeing the variable life forms from Australia, it seems possible that the gene changes in the India-Australia-New Guinea area might have produced a lively pre-human. Australopithecus may have developed on the floating continent, extended herself (on its arrival on Asia) back to Africa and Europe, and in traveling north and doing battle with the Ice Ages, become a more reflective individual who could talk about those reflections with another.

God's providing love has made for us a very durable earth. When we behold the folding and unfolding of the continents, when we realize that there have been explosions that have shaken the whole earth, placed the moon in the heavens, sent suns colliding and meteors falling, we see the puniness of our neutron bombs and our political power plays. We must confess that all things are in God's control, that God has knowledge of how to make a world, and that God will lead us gently to fulfillment. Each era has its own types of fulfillment, yet we are fundamentally the same kind of people. We possess souls that have a component that began before we existed and extends beyond our present.

The offspring of viable communities would have greater chances for survival. This survival of the fittest would gradually increase physical brain size and ability to think. It would also encourage growth of soul, that part of us that can stand outside ourself and make judgments and decisions about the self. The soul is also that quality within us that can communicate with the other and with God. God uses our souls to communicate with us. God gives us the freedom to respond as we will. God needs our souls for the development of the qualities of love and empathy in God's creation.

God made and insouled the early human being. A God who can create a universe, can certainly make spiritual yearnings to counteract and control our physical yearnings. We can see through all humanity this thread of spiritual guidance or inner sensitivity to something better that seems a part of our created nature. The individual is allowed an awareness of her own situation, and can foresee the possible results of different courses of action. Not only is her own gratification or self-fulfillment considered, but she also has the ability to consider the fulfillment of those around her. God seems to have built into us and this creation, a quality of altruism and the freedom to go after it. The human can plan for the future and can make choices which affect that future!

Having the capability of reflective thought, the ability to know ourselves and have empathy for others, we credit ourselves with inner feelings, sensations, or mysterious inner knowledge, and name this quantity *soul*. Does the soul exist in our mind? Is it associated with our flow of inner energy? Or is it the spiritual accompaniment to our material being? We have lived on this earth for so long a time, and we still cannot define what this very important concept is!

There is a tremendous lack of knowledge about the characteristics and abilities of the individual soul. There is even greater confusion when we speak of the union of two or more souls. What happens in a group when the energy waves emanating from our individual consciousnesses reinforce each other? "When a group of people become more closely united in a common cause (even the temporary unity in fighting a fire) there is an expansion of consciousness."[11] Where there is the unity of many, miracles can be accomplished. The next step in our evolution may have to do with the further collaboration of souls.

Footnotes

1 If there is to be melting of the ice caps, and drying out of interior temperate lands, we could divert the melting ice through giant pipelines to irrigate interior farm lands. If we can build oil pipe lines for investors to make money, we should be able to build water pipe lines in order to keep our earth habitable.

2 "The Earth's orbit stretches from nearly circular to elliptical and back again in about 100,000 years, making the Earth's distance from the Sun vary by about 11 million miles." When a circle, the earth is 93 million miles distant during all seasons. Today it's elliptical, and it's closest to the Sun in January; farthest, in July. *Ice Ages, Past and Present*, Jon Erickson, Tab Books, Blue Ridge Summit, PA, 1990.

3 William Calvin, *The Ascent of Mind*, Bantam Books, New York, 1990, p.112.

4 Albert Fritsch, *A Theology of The Earth*, Center for Science in The Public Interest, Washington DC, 1972, p. 2.5.

5 A living specimen is Michael *Heal-The-World* Jackson, the singer. Vitiligo is caused by a gene that disrupts the movement and storage of proteins within the pigment cells. Some of the lepers in the Bible may have been accused of having contagious leprosy when they displayed this uncontagious affliction.

6 Christopher Leahy, *Earthwatch*, "Waves of The Future," June 1991, p. 26.

7 A "Mongolian Patch" is visible on some new-born Mongoloid and Negroid infants.

8 William Calvin, *loc. cit.*

9 Display in Natural Museum of History, New York City.

10 The Genesis Gene would be a human gene (a) critical to the development of the central nervous system, (b) playing a modifying role in general human development (i.e. lesser hairiness, upright posture), and (c) one which was "too perfect," (i.e. free of non-coding sections called introns, and/or had a unique promoter sequence). Information from J.R. Cypser.

11 Albert Fritsch, *loc. cit.*, p. 3.7.

II

The Growth of Communication

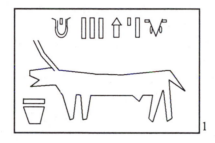

2.1 Language

Before they could write things down, human beings had to have a language. Some of our human development was due to a superior ability to communicate which apes didn't have. The more they talked, the better people became at talking. Speech is a social activity. The word is imaged in the mind of the giver, articulated through her muscles, and sent across a space to a receiver. The receiver has to activate her muscles through hearing and using nerve cells. She transmits what has been sent to her mind and images the word there against the back drop of her individual personality. Surely God is behind such a complicated process. Surely God wants us to communicate that which will enable and enhance the minds on both the giving and receiving ends of our spoken messages. A word is not just a physical thing; it has meaningful spiritual components, both good and bad.

Some language specialists group languages according to ethnic and national headings. The roots of language are difficult to pursue, but some languages have more in common than other languages, although we are all children of the same earth. Some languages are like some peoples in that they become insular and build up their own specialties without foreign influence. Some tribes would marry only within their own tribe. Other tribes were forced to accept the language of an outside conqueror. Some countries that are host to refugees today expect the refugees to use the language of the host country.

Language Divisions. Three main language groupings are the Semitic, the Aryan, and the Turanian (which contains the language groups that are left over). Others divisions add the Hamitic languages and the Chinese languages. More specialized groupings could be made, but would make an explanation much more complicated.

The Semitic languages are spoken by those people who consider Noah's son Shem to be their common ancestor. The actual members of the Semitic language group are not necessarily the descendants of Shem as recorded in Genesis 10. This group contains political and tribal alliances that were set in place and respected through countless centuries. Slave women would take their language, religion, and customs with them and further the language through their children.

The northern Semitic language is carried by the wandering Arameans. The middle branch contains the Canaanite, Moabite, Ammonite, Edomite, and Phoenician dialects. The southern grouping is the Arabic languages. Early Semites came in waves from southeast of Mesopotamia. Among their numbers were the Arameans, some of whom may have claimed Abraham as their ancestor. These Arameans are mentioned in the Tell el-Amarna letters and in inscriptions of Assyrian kings of the 14th century BC.[2] They settled in upper Mesopotamia between the Euphrates and the Khabur Rivers. At some point the Arameans passed over the Euphrates and occupied Syria driving out the Hittites. Arameans are connected with the cities of Damascus, Zobah, Maakah, Beth Rehob, Hamath (Syria) and Haran (northern Mesopotamia). Their ancestral land was Aram Naharayim or Padam Aram.

The Aryan language is the Indo-European family of languages. It was first seen in Central Asia, east of the Caspian, and north of the Indian Cush. It spread northwest where it became the base language of the Celts in Europe, and later the Italians, the Greeks and the Teutonic people. It also is found in Persia and southeast to the Ganges. It is the language of the Fire Worshipers of Persia and of the Gypsies. Some consider Sanskrit, the ancient language of the Brahmins in India, to be the root of the Aryan tongues.[3] In the early Sanskrit writing, the *Veda*, the Hindus call themselves *Aryas*, the word meaning *excellent*, or *honorable*, or *lord of the soil*.

The Turanian class of languages comprises the not necessarily related languages of Chinese, Sumerian, Tungusic, Mongolic, Turkic, Finnic, Acadian, Basque, North American Indian, and the Dravidian tongues (Tamil, Siamese, Malayic, Polynesian, and Tibetan). The name *Turanian* comes from the Tura, a river in Siberia, where some of these tribes had origins.

The Dravidians lived in India before the Aryans arrived there. The family of Dravidian languages contains about twenty tongues unrelated to other known languages. These may be the remnant of the mother tongue of our earliest speaking peoples. These languages exist primarily in South and Central India and in Northern Sri Lanka. Tamil is such a language. It is derived from a language spoken in India prior to the Aryan invasion that took place about 1500 BC. An earlier Indus Valley civilization (2500-1500 BC) had steatite (made of soap stone) seals with pictures and script. This script is structurally related to the Dravidian languages. Another early language is the Basque tongue used in the Spanish Pyrenees.

If we wanted to consider just three main language streams, we might consider the first stream to be the Turanian hunter-fisher-gatherers going north along the Tura to Siberia and south down the Indus and Ganges. Some of these groups may have become very insular, and developed language peculiarities. They might have started a new language development or intermixed with European early peoples such as Neanderthals and evolved as a different language type, such as Aryan. Next we would have the Aryans as agriculturalists pooling in the Caspian region and as the land wore out, searching for more fertile soil by going south to Mesopotamia, by traversing west along the Danube, or by retracing their steps to India. Some language groups were meat eaters, and were accustomed to tracking wild animals. They eventually learned how to domesticate animals, but this required guiding the animals to good pastures. These may have developed into the Semitic branch who drove herds between India and Egypt, searching for a safe and hospitable land. As they were less insular, their language developed more rapidly, acquiring new words from territories they passed through.

In considering further subdivisions, the Hamitic languages are ancient Egyptian, Coptic, Berber, and some small groups in Abyssinia. Chinese is the very basic language of an isolated people, which was fixed very early in time, by writing. It did not change much, although many dialects are spoken in China today. Japanese may be grouped with the Turkish, Ural, and Korean tongues. There can also be found a relationship between Japanese and Aryan, even though Japan borrowed the Chinese method of character writing. The early Yamato dialect, still used by the Japanese Shinto religion, has similarities with both Aryan and Hebrew-Semitic.

Mergers. Between 4000 and 3000 BC, the Sumerian (Turanian) language became combined with the Semitic language in Mesopotamia, as the two populations merged. The Sumerian language system contained two dialects which language specialists have termed the Emeku, more formal and harsh, and the Emesal, to be used in the family and with children. There were many voice tones employed for the same sounds in Sumerian, as in present day Chinese. A high-toned *baw* could mean one thing, and a low toned *baw* could mean something totally different. One had to be very careful about the tone of one's voice. Nowadays we have developed more mouthing sounds so we don't have to be as careful about pitch.

The Chinese language tones and those of Sumer may have descended from a flowering, inter-glacial Siberian tundra. China has a Yangshao culture dated at 5000 BC. It is conceivable that people fleeing the glaciating tundra went as far east as China and southwest to Mesopotamia, taking both language and writing ability. On the religious side, Yu-Huang is the Taoist Lord of Heaven. Is there any relation between this Yu-Huang (pronounced Yu-Wang) and the later day Hebrew Yahweh? The God of Heaven of the Khaldeans could be the same Lord of Heaven proclaimed by the Chinese. The Moon festival of China gives thanks to the gods of soil, rain, and wind. New Moon festivals of the Hebrews are mentioned in I Samuel 20:5a,6b, Isaiah 1:13, Ezekiel 45:17 and 46:1. Language and religious feasts traveled hand in hand.

2.2 Dating

In order to properly understand history, we must locate ourselves through the use of dates. We feel the need of proper BP (*Before the Present*) dates for Ice Ages, and we would like to have uncontroversial BC (*Before Christian Era*) dates for early kings. Ice cores can give us some reliable dates. From the dust they contain, they tell us that 10,000 years back there was a lot of volcanic activity, and that 16,000 years back, ice sheets had begun to melt. Observing the changes in magnetic designs in rock layers, can also give us scientific dates as reversals in the magnetic field over the last 150 million years have become fossilized.

It is difficult to give anything but very approximate dates for the reigns of early kings. An error that is frequently made when dating kingdoms, is to believe that the ancients had the same notions of historic and evolutionary time that we have. Early peoples did not have weeks or months or calendars like we do today. They timed events by sun or moon or stars and by important occurrences. Our seven day week may have arisen from a convenient division of full moon appearances or from a sexual rhythm. Our months come from moon rises and from constellation placements. The sun has its yearly maximum and minimum distances north and south that signalled the seasons. Herders would count the length of a migration as a unit of time.

When considering dates, we should make allowance for the importance of the early ruler in the lives of his subjects. When he began to reign, that was the year one. When he died after a reign of thirty years, that would be considered the thirtieth year of his reign. With the next ruler, would start a new counting unrelated to the old. If this successor didn't like his predecessor, he could blot out the predecessor's name from the oral records, or chip it off the temple walls, and succeeding generations might not hear about the previous reign at all. If we simplistically add up the lengths of all known kings' reigns to find out how much time has passed, we may be omitting many years of rule.

Genealogical listings can help with dating. Young men in Korea today are expected to be able to recite the names of their ancestors for one hundred generations back. This recitation was very important for early humans who did not have writing abilities. When an ancestor did something disgraceful, you simply dropped his name from the record. If you were at the stage of writing down these ancestor lists, you blotted the offender's name off the paper (Psalm 109:13).

The art of writing added considerably to our ability to date events. The names of certain important or notorious rulers would be mentioned in the court records of various countries. We could add up the lengths of the reigns of the various kings in the different countries and see if the outcome agreed. For instance the court correspondence of Akhenaten in Egypt to the Hittites and Babylonians helped to align and confirm the dates for Hittite, Babylonian, and Egyptian rulers. Even with this extra source of confirmation, we might miss out on a few dynasties from the different areas.

Another omission of early writers is the use of vowels. Today we are faced with the problem of inserting e, a, i, o, or u sounds to go with the ancient consonants. We also have to decide if there is a vowel between consonants or if the two consonants are to be voiced together.

Having written records was a great help to our knowledge of the course of history. What did people do when they wanted to describe events that took place before writing became common? They told and retold stories that had been told to them by their ancestors, of situations that had taken place thousands of years before. Some of these events we can confirm through archaeological records. Some tribal migrations we can trace through a trail of pottery. Of course many tribal migratory events took place pre-pottery.

Dates before 2000 BC are very unreliable. Results of carbon dating can have variations of plus or minus 200 years. The carbon sample may be contaminated. Artifacts can fall into an earlier or later archaeological layer or can be intentionally misplaced into a later layer by ancient antique buffs. Most scientists who venture to establish dates are very conservative, and will stick with the most recent dates. Many unrecorded events can upset the time scheme by sliding in and taking up space between noticeable happenings, so that as much as 500 years could be lost in times of famine or disorder. The more ancient dates may be the most reasonable. The human being has been capable of creativity for a very long time, and religious thinking and powerful leaders have been on earth longer than we realize.

When I set down a list of kings and their dates, I am usually succumbing to someone else's valued opinion. However, I am very suspicious of any dates before 2000 BC, unless they are verified by hard scientific evidence. I use dates in an attempt to keep a sequence in the correct order. If there is a datable event that goes along with a given king, then we can give credit to that date, and date other events from it.

Explosion of Thera. A specific event that can be dated scientifically was the volcanic explosion of the Island of Santorini in the Aegean Sea east of Greece and north of Crete. One thing we have to be aware of, is that one place can go by many different names, according to who is talking about it, what they want to tell you about it, and from what point of history or language they are viewing it. Place names can confuse our ability to date events. Akrotiri was one of the ancient names for the island of Santorini. It was once called Stronggyle because of its round form. Later, for its beauty, it was called Kalliste. Thera is our name for the post-explosion city on the island. The name of Thera (or renaming) came years after the explosion, when people had forgotten some of the danger and horror that occurred when the eruption brought an end to the flourishing Cycladic culture. Long before the approximate date of 1200 BC for the Trojan war, the Phoenicians led by Cadmus had taken possession of the ruined island. They built a community and named it after a chieftain, *Theras*. Akro means *summit*, so *Akro-Thera* becomes *Akrotiri* and means the *Summit of Theras*.

This cataclysmic explosion of Santorini may have been spoken of by Plato in his writing, *Timaes*, when he told about the lost continent of Atlantis. The number that he set down as the date of Atlantis' disappearance many interpret as a time interval of 9000 years before. It would be very difficult for Plato to date an event that had no written documents to verify it. To add to complications with dating, at some point in numerical figuring, it was difficult to determine whether a number was to designate one hundred or one thousand. If we assume Plato's figure was intended to be of the hundreds, then 900 years back from his lifetime of 400 BC, would give 1300 BC for the Atlantis destruction. If we conclude that Plato couldn't really know exactly, but gave his best educated guess for the time of this event in his far distant past, we are probably closest to the truth.

Three methods have been used by scientists to fix a fairly reliable date for this shock that shook the early Mediterranean world. Carbon dating gives an approximate date of no later than 1600 BC. Dendrochronologists who date happenings by observing tree ring growth, observed that after the explosion, trees had smaller growth, and thus smaller rings for several years due to less sunshine getting through the volcanic smog. By comparing trees in the bogs of Ireland, they found that years of smaller tree growth occurred after 1628 BC. Other scientists who take cores of polar ice, found excessive volcanic dust in their core samples for 1645 BC plus or minus 20 years.[4] Rather than taking Plato's word, we can be fairly certain that an approximate scientific date for this event is 1628 BC.

Relying on king lists can throw off the correct timing of events. With a cataclysmic happening like a volcanic explosion, whole populations are undergoing suffering. Poisonous gases are floating around the earth. People are dying from mysterious lung ailments. Even kings succumb to plagues and governments fall. There is often no one to replace the king effectively, and the city enters into a period of disorder. With dust darkening the air, farming is hindered because of less sun getting through to crops. Famine stalks after plague. The remnants of the village dwellers leave their homes for any port in a storm. There may be a period of 200 years where nothing much is recorded, because of so much death and unsettlement.

There are ancient Iberian villages near Borja, Spain. One of these Bronze Age sites, Majaladares, shows evidence of being abandoned about 4000 years ago. Could cities as far away as Spain have suffered a decline due to the explosion of Thera? Was the earth covered with a belt of poisonous soot? If the winds come from the west, it seems likely that Egypt and Sumer were affected much more seriously than Spain. The remembrance of such events may be recorded as plagues and famines, but pharaohs don't like to brag about disasters and would not record them on temple walls. Such events may help us to give estimated time lengths to periods of disorder.

A more recent fixed date that can help us be specific about our calendar of events is 763 BC when there was an eclipse of the sun. Tablets from the Assyrian king Guzana mention that such an eclipse happened in his reign.

It must be emphasized again that dates given for kings and military expeditions are tentative. Dates later than 1000 BC are more easy to pin down, but we must keep in mind that historians cannot even be explicit about the date for such a relatively recent event as the birth of Christ.

2.3 Megaliths

Another method of dating early events and human wanderings is to investigate the early human's housing and entombment sites. One of the basic needs for any human is housing. Animals make nests to protect themselves in their environment. Some seek shelter in trees or caves. The human being is still able to enjoy a camp-out at night sleeping under the stars. Where did the early pair or community find housing? There are caves all over the world, some fed by underground rivers. Some caves have paintings left by early artists that prove they were inhabited. Other caves have remains deep under the cave floor such as those near Peking, China. Some caves used for early housing may be deep under water, due to rising sea levels. Some caves remain to be explored, like those in India. What marvels might be found 150 feet below ground level in the Ajanta caves of India's north Deccan? When caves became overcrowded, humans expanded out into their environment. They fashioned homes from trees, stones, and animal skins.

Stones as Memorials. The building of homes and communities across the earth went hand in hand with the erection of structures to worship the vastness and the unknown. This is because we human beings are subject to death. We humans respond to death in a variety of ways. What better way to remember our beloved dead than with something as permanent as rock! There is a theology concerned with tomb-stones. In the United States we view a field of tombstones, and we all know that under the dirt are many commemorated bones. We accept it as quite normal, and we even question someone's wish to be cremated, and we marvel when someone has their ashes dropped from an airplane to be scattered over a lake.

When a member of an early community died, sometimes they buried the body on the floor of the cave, or under the house. Sometimes these communities would exert themselves to put together more lasting monuments that reflected a desire towards the eternal, a recognition of something more durable than themselves. These desires are reflected in their grave burials with placement of the dead under a stone, or under heaps of stone (to keep off hungry predators). The more important people were awarded bigger stones, and became the subjects of godly legends. Piles of stones became holy places to commemorate people who were worthy of remembrance and to symbolize ideas of spiritual existence not clearly understood.

Commemorative *megalith* (meaning *great stone*) monuments have been found from Ireland to Madagascar, and even in Korea and Colombia. The one English speaking peoples hear the most about, Stonehenge, is of fairly recent date, having been built from 2400 BC to 1400 BC. Folk from the continent of Europe brought grain, cattle, and the idea of burial of the dead under mounds, to the British Isles. The Beaker people from Holland, in the process of trading for tin, inspired sky and sun worship. For this worship we find giant stones set up. A Mesopotamian dagger symbol etched on one of these stones proves there were travelers and knowledge from as far away as the Middle East. We are amazed today at the size of these Stonehenge structures and the knowledge of astronomy that they display. The transporting and setting up of these gigantic stones is possible by any pre-metalworking farming society. The labor may have been done by the religiously inspired.

Humans all over the globe seem to have a similar response to the infinite. They need a structure to connect them to what is greater than themselves. The builders of these structures in far distant countries were often not in communication with one another across time or distance. It must be that our common physical and emotional make-up, produced the same result although cultural groups may have been incommunicado. Of course, in some areas builders observed others' masterpieces, and were affected culturally. Other civilizations arrived at similar stages many years apart, as if a basic need or burial information carried across many generations.

Widespread Megaliths. Structures in the ancient city of Jericho show that the megalith technique was available in 8000 BC. The megaliths in Europe are dated about 5000-3000 BC. There are megaliths on coastal Spain, central and coastal France, Denmark, northern Germany, Sweden, Ireland, Scotland, and England. At Hagar Qim on Malta there is a megalith dated to 3000 BC. There is one at Giovinazzo on the heel of Italy and one at Castelluccio on Sicily. There are also megaliths on Corsica and Sardinia. At Shimish, Morocco there are ancient sun-oriented megaliths under the old Roman walls. Denmark's Lindholm Hoje necropolis contains 682 stone-bordered boat-shaped tombs, and dates from the Bronze Age. Megaliths on the west coast of France at Teviec and Hoedic date at 5800 BC. Loviet, near Paris, dates 5000 BC. A megalith in Portugal is dated at 4500 BC. There are megaliths at Tustrup and Bygholm Norremark in Denmark, and at Gaj, Sarnavo, and Wietrzychowice in Poland. Bulgaria has monuments in South East Thrace on the shores of the Black Sea. The Bahrein Islands in the Persian Gulf about 13 miles off the coast of Saudi Arabia have megaliths dating back to the third millennium. Megalithic constructions are found in Algeria, Sudan, Ethiopia, Palestine, Caucasus, Persia, Baluchistan, Kashmir, India, South Africa, and Madagascar. Those megaliths in the Magdalene Valley in Colombia are dated as having been erected as late as the 6th century BC. Did humans from Asia bring to this hemisphere a megalith knowledge programmed into their genes? Can peoples separated by vast distances have thought transmittal? Perhaps we can credit the early human with the ability to travel over vast distances, and to remember over lengths of generations, and to reminisce the ways of the ancestors. Story tellers can keep much culture alive for their audiences from one generation to the next. **Signs of Travel.** By tracing megalithic dates in the Deccan, Pakistan, Caucasus, Anatolia, Europe, Spain, and Ireland one could track the travels and religious beliefs of tribes from India and Persia northward. All megalithic structures may not be visible. Smaller, less noticeable megaliths may be buried in drifting sands or sunk under alluvial silt.

Besides having sun-oriented megaliths, Shimish, Heliopolis, and Lake Titicaca, all had in common the papyrus raft. They also had the same name for a similar animal. The South American *kinkajou*, resembling a raccoon with a powerful grabbing tail, has a range from Mexico to Brazil. The name *kinkajou* was given to it by the Tupi Indians of South America. The name *poto* given to it by Central American Indians is similar to the name, *potto,* used in Africa for a lemur of similar size and shape. This is one fragile link between the animal words of Africa and those of Central America. Can travelers from Africa have established themselves in Central America? Or did those established in Central America boat to Africa?

How many times have unrecorded Europeans visited the Americas before the advent of Columbus? There is a megalithic construction in southern New Hampshire dated to before the time of Christ. There is also the question of whether or not Hebrews fleeing Palestine in 70 AD reached the coast of Florida and eventually died in the hills of Tennessee.

In tracking down the tribal travels of our ancestors we might start in Japan and travel westward. Yamato tribes in Japan of 300 BC had large burial mounds. They put bronze mirrors with the shape of the Egyptian ankh symbol in their tombs. We do not know what their customs were 3000 years earlier, but they were doubtless following ancient practices. The people on the Japanese islands have been there a very long time. They were the earliest known makers of pottery about 11,000 BC. They also may have been early with burial sites or they may have copied burial customs reported by their traders in foreign lands.

An agricultural civilization developed in the Indus region of northwest India between 6000 and 2000 BC. These Indus and Harappan peoples may have burned their dead, not buried them. Megaliths builders south of the

Indus in the South Indian Peninsula of the Deccan, north in the Turkish Hittite area, and in Troy were also cremated. Southeast Turkey had cremation burials dated to the latter part of the third millennium. At the same time interval, right nearby, would be graves with skeletons buried in contracted positions with their heads towards the south east, as if two differing religious customs existed side by side. Both cremation burials and body burials may have been commemorated with large stones. Later enhancements may have been statuary. With cremation burials there would be no visible remains. Commemorative statues would usually remain in place as landmarks. At Mohenjo-daro in the Indus area, there has been found a soapstone statue of a priest king. Statues of similar looking individuals are evident at Nimrud-Dagh in Turkey.

Conquerors of a country might cart away burial building blocks to build homes or city walls, not having in mind their meaning or purpose for the dispossessed people. They also might give superstitious honor to the spot, or they might appropriate it and enlarge upon it. Plagues could demolish whole towns, and leave them without inhabitants for centuries. Those coming in might set fire to such a place to cleanse it, and thus destroy cultural information.

Astronomical Knowledge. Megaliths have been shown not to be haphazard structures. Humans 10,000 years ago could observe their surroundings as well as we can today. They may not have kept records long enough to know about variations in true north due to gyrations of the earth on its axis, but their monuments tell us that they knew much about positions of the sun and moon over time.

At Stonehenge there is a great circle with 56 chalk colored holes equally spaced to help early humans calculate the phases and eclipses of the moon. Not many of us today know that in a span of 56 years there are 223 lunations, or three cycles of moon rise (one moon cycle every 18.6 years). Eclipses occur at the same point in this lunation cycle. The early power group, who knew this, could predict eclipses, and thus confound important people who were not equally knowledgeable. With such wisdom they were able to control both rulers and a rowdy populace.

We see amazingly accurate astronomical knowledge being shown by the pyramid builders about 2700 BC. Egypt has a fairly late date for megalithic cultural attainment. The Great Pyramid built by Cheops has a shaft that opens out to the night sky, so that the star Sirius at its spring equinox midnight culmination was visible from the dead pharaoh's tomb chambers. This star was sacred to the Goddess Isis. In 3000 BC the heliacal rising or first morning appearance of Sirius occurred about June 25th, their

New Year's Day. Sirius or the Dog Star (Orion's Dog) is in the constellation Canis Major (Big Dog). Another astronomical architectural feature is that the sides of the great pyramids point to the sunrise on the vernal equinox. How amazing that the early Egyptians could manage such precision when we have trouble making our houses come out square!

Another star important to the Egyptians was the former pole star Vega. It served as pole star 13,000 years ago and will serve in like manner 13,000 years in the future. Today Polaris is the star that is closest to true north. We have these changes in pole star due to the earth's gyroscopic rotating pattern that it completes every 26,000 years. The Egyptians didn't know about this shift in the northern sky as it happened over such a long period of time. For early astronomers objects in the heavens became symbolic for religious beliefs on earth. The heavens were an assumed location of the gods.

Egyptian statuary frequently represents a god giving the ankh symbol to the pharaoh as a symbol of life. The ankh looks like a cross with a circular loop at the top. The circular loop may contain a polished piece of metal usable as a mirror. There is an ancient ankh box in Egypt containing a mirror very similar to boxes customary to Japanese entombments. The ankh symbol has also been found at Stonehenge.

Spiritual Aspects. Together with the materialistic structural knowledge of tomb building, went a spiritual body of knowledge and religious beliefs. Some of our predecessors seemed to believe that the spirit of the ancestor would come alive in the stone. The pharaoh's spirit was supposedly present in his statue. Today, we cherish a photograph; and when we view a talking image on video of someone who is no longer with us, isn't there some association with his spirit? Early peoples didn't have video, so they made do with something substantial like big rocks.

The Khassia people north of Syria placed their dead in stone chests with flat slabs on top so that the living could sit on them. They used these amphitheaters of stone chests for public gatherings to discuss community problems, and thus the guiding spirits of the ancestors were right there with the living to help them make wise decisions. Burial sites were community property. In some cultures burial sites were under the control of the religious specialists. We have the example of the Egyptian priest class guarding the pyramids. We have the catacombs incorporated into church edifices.

Some megalithic builders may have acquired their stone-building wisdom from previous knowledge of such structures, but other groups may have commemorated their dead from out of spiritual inner knowledge or from some urge built into our gene structure. We have assumed that we can learn about the travels of our ancestors through viewing age and pattern of megalithic structures. Some clay or brick structures may have begun as watch towers or for storage purposes. Perhaps pyramid building began as granaries. When they migrated from an old home because of starvation or oppression or just looking for new worlds to conquer, those who remembered would build as their ancestors had done.

This tracking of Megalithic constructions helps us to visualize some of the wanderings of the early human. These megaliths also show that the human was reflecting about his relationship to the unknown in the environment. The megaliths are evidence that the evolving bodily structure of the human was accompanied by similarly evolving reflective thought, or an evolvement of soul. It is difficult to trace the materialistic wanderings of tribes, but it is even more difficult to speculate on the development of what we term *soul* or *spirit*. In instances where there are vast distances between sites, we can believe in thought transferal on a spiritual level, or we could assume physical travel with knowledge carried by individuals.

Seen from Above. The North American continent displays the work of the mound builders. The Cahokia Mound, a truncated pyramid in East St. Louis, Illinois measures 1000 feet by 725 feet, and is 100 feet high. The Etowah Mound on the Etowah River in north Georgia has three truncated pyramid mounds. There are archaeological puzzles to which we do not have satisfactory answers. The Serpent Mound 500 meters long in the hills of Ohio, was built 2000 years ago of white chalk. It is best seen (as a large serpent) from a great height above the ground and was built over the crater of a meteorite. The Serpent Mound is similar to the White Chalk Horse of Uffington in England, which horse has proportions like the horses on Celtic coins. The horse in England was associated with the Celtic goddess Epona. It is 360 feet long, and was carved 2000 years ago. Serpent worship was practiced in India, and has surfaced in many cultures as a worship of power and wisdom. Were there more possibilities of a spirit-to-spirit communication on a religious level in ancient times? Even today we hear about bi-location. Saints and other meditative individuals are said to have their body or a visible spirit in two widely separated places at the same time.

There is still room for materialistic transport of ideas. We should credit the early human with a bit of inventiveness. Her brain was the size of ours, and she was challenged by her environment. She may have had spiritual flights, but she may also have flown physically. She observed the birds in air, and like many others, even before the Wright brothers, she probably figured out ways to be airborne. The Japanese and Chinese had giant dragon kites, and flew small passengers for short distances. The Greeks have the legend of Icarus who flew too near the sun, and melted the wax that held on his wings. Egypt has religious memories of mirrors and the sun god in its ankh symbol. The Japanese also had great faith in the sun god and in shiny mirrors, and could have heated up an air balloon with radiant heat from a gleaming piece of light weight metal. From Japan, sun and wind worshipers may have made their way to North America, where there are cross emblems of the sun god (and four wind directions) on structures in the Arizona desert which are visible from the air. They might also have gone to the Serpent Mound location on the Ohio. If they had the ability to rise from the ground, even briefly, in some type of balloon or glider, they would have been received like one of the gods. Balloons are run by the simple principle of hot air. This would be a possible concept for the early human who might have made a balloon out of very thin hide, silk, or rice paper parchment, attached a mirror, and been borne aloft in a reed basket on a breeze. Persons who had faith in that which created the sun and wind, and that which gave them the materials of nature to use, are much like us today. Such a person would have had enormous trust in the powers of creation.

2.4 Writing

Writing is a marvelous form of communication. When we write down our innermost thoughts, we can inspire and inform people across the boundaries of time. We can build structures of love between generations. A great deal of effort is required when languages are changed from century to century. One has to be a specialist in languages, and try to understand the place name changes, the meanings behind the god-words, the anthropomorphic and symbolic thought of living souls from different cultures. Yet with all our differences, we are similar. We live in communities that try to be under-standing and loving. We try to get along with the vagaries of the earth and others. We worship divinity. All this started with some early humans who put down marks on sticks and stones and communicated their thought to the future.

Because the early human did not have full blown writing skills, that doesn't mean she was not intelligent. Her brain was the same size as ours. Writing was not necessary for a successful life. Language and communica-tion were important, but there was not much need for written records. The necessity for counting came first, before writing and sounding out words. If you owned sheep, you had to have a way to keep track of how many sheep you had. Trading required that certain items be notated. Number systems began to use symbols to represent ideas. First they used a bag of stones or a knotted string to count sheep. Later they could make marks on stone. Legal documents were an important item. Early community members could use symbols such as a sandal to express ownership (Ruth 4:7). They could use clay figurines. The particular community would be able to interpret the symbolism.

Clay tokens were used from about 8000 BC to record amounts of grain or animals. They could be impressed with a sharp stone or stylus. People became interested in putting their name or their brand mark on the tokens. Names or places could be represented by pictures. Eventually, some pictures began to represent certain sounds. An alphabet was put together, so that any sound you could make would have a proper alphabetic representation.

Intermixing of Multiple Systems. Mesopotamia, Egypt, and the Indus Valley are known to have produced three different systems of writing at about the same time. Examples of Sumerian notation exist from 7000 BC, and by 5000 BC it was more versatile. Very early the Harappans had a special script that has been difficult to translate. The Sumerians in Mesopotamia and the Hittites from Turkey used cuneiform signs which started off being pictographs, but which turned into wedge shaped markings as writers became more expert. These markings could represent either words or syllables. Cuneiform was used by the Sumerians who had 600 characters, the Hittites (350), the Babylonians, the Elamites (200 characters), and the Persians (only 39 characters) from about 3000 BC and onward. Written words were basic and simple. Some Sumerian words with their meanings are: LU=people, URU=city, KUR=country, and KI=place.

It is thought that the Sumerians and their language came from the Caspian area using a Turkish dialect. They arrived about 7000 BC in the Jordan and Euphrates valleys. We can coordinate a calamity in the Caspian area of 7000 BC that would necessitate the exodus of a farming community. From studying lake sediments it has been learned that the Caspian area underwent desertification. As climatic conditions changed, tribes were forced to migrate to find new lands in which to dwell peaceably.

Such migrations can be traced through use of archaeology and linguistics. Hunters and fishers formed very mobile groups. Agriculture made folks a bit more stable, but the soil would wear out, and farmers would have to move on to a new land. This helped to spread the human community across the globe. Needing new soil, the earliest stone-using agricultural communities of Central Europe moved across the country from the middle Danube to the lower Rhine. Warrior bands and herding groups were mobile.

Wheeled vehicles helped to make migration easier for people about 3500 BC. Oxen could haul carts and were useful in farming. The horse was not as desirable as the ox for farming, but about 1600 BC, it was tamed for riding, for speed, and for war chariots. With the aid of the horse, mankind became more competitive. The horse made it easier for the hill people to raid the people on the open plain. Tribal groups formed alliances. City states made treaties. Nomadic groups found it harder to graze and hunt.

The Sumerians were not left alone in Mesopotamia for very long. They were joined by a Semitic group who perhaps were fleeing the rising of the Indian ocean or the desertification of the Indus area and Arabia. These two cultures mingled fairly peaceably and came up with an improved culture. When the Semites moved into Mesopotamia and adopted Sumerian cuneiform writing, they also borrowed stories of gods and shaped them to fit their own needs and beliefs.

In northern Mesopotamia there were invaders of a different type. There was an early legendary hero called Nimrod. On a hill called Nimrud-Dagh, lie toppled statuary that resemble the statue of the priest king of Mohenjodaro in the Indus Valley. The tribal group who built this sanctuary spoke East Semitic, or Akkadian. They came from east of Arabia. Other related Semitic languages in the ancient Near East were Canaanite, Ugaritic, Phoenician-Punic, Moabitic, and Hebrew.

A third language group from north of Turkey came on the scene speaking Aryan. This spread, so that by 1000 BC Aryan dialects were spoken from India to Central Europe. Between the Carpathians (mountains between Poland and Czechoslovakia) and the Caucasus seems to be the origin for these Indo-European languages.

Each secluded tribe developed differences in language and culture in their isolation. Aramaic was the prime language spoken after the time of Cyrus the Conqueror about 500 BC. Writing, written records, and stela proclamations were a means of unifying diverse elements in a conquered population. The word *stela* (or standing stone) comes from the Latin word which means to set up or to stand. Having written records has contributed greatly to our knowledge of the course of history, and to our ability to deal with present events.

Egyptian Writing. Because they kept records of the Nile floods, Egyptians produced a calendar of flood levels beginning in 4241 BC. Writing was also used for notations in foreign trade. A legendary individual is credited with inventing writing. The Egyptians honor a god of knowledge and research called Thoth, who is represented by the ibis. He supposedly created writing and was the scribe of the gods. Later on in history this Egyptian god was incorporated in the Greek pantheon as Hermes Trismegistus, the god who was three times great (Hermes=messenger, Tri=three, and megistus=majestic). The god Thoth may be patterned after the vizier Imhotep who was architect, astronomer, priest, writer, sage, physician, and built the Step pyramid at Sakkara for his king Zoser. Later, the Greeks worshiped Imhotep under the name of Asclepius, god of healing.

Early pictographs in Egypt conveyed words and concepts by means of hieroglyphics. Ancient Egyptian writing had three forms, hieroglyphics, hieratics, and demotics. Hieroglyphs or holy writings were reserved for the temple and were used only by priests from 3000 to 2000 BC. The earliest extant list of kings is the Third Dynasty. During the Middle Kingdom, hieratics, a cursive form of glyphs, were used by the scribes and the business community (about 2000-1700 BC).[5] A more common form of writing called demotics was developed in the New Kingdom (1600-1000 BC), which was used by the common people and may have been used by the early Hebrews.

Hieroglyphics were used with little variation from 2000 BC to 300 AD. A hieroglyphic sign could be used in three ways– as an object or idea, as a syllable or part of a word, or as a limit or subtraction from a previous pictograph. In early times there were 24 hieroglyphs that each represented a single letter and about 50 that stood for two letters together. There were many other idea and noun pictures with combinations of all of the above. These hieroglyphics could be read from either direction, and were usually read in the direction in which the pictured birds faced.

Often in the cartouches or name plates of the pharaoh or his dignitaries, the signs could be read up or down. These name plates were like the emblems on shields or family coats of arms, or insignia such as we have today in company advertising, and they could be read in differing directions.

There is much variation in the translation of the names of important people in early Egypt. As hieroglyphics can mean a separate letter or can stand for a whole word, and can be read from left to right, right to left, or upwards or downwards, we can have different opinions as to the proper spelling of early names. Our English word *pharaoh* itself, as the Hebraic name given to the kings of Egypt, comes from the P-RA or PH-RA of the hieroglyphics, which contains a sun and actually means *great house.*

Early scribes had not settled on a proper way to do their writing. Even today different languages are written in different directions. Arabic is read from right to left, English from left to right. Japanese starts from what Americans would think of as the back of a book. Some ancient Greek went back and forth on the page as a farmer would plow a field.

Writing was transmitted by traders. Cycladic obsidian was traded in the Aegean to make stela and statuary. The Cycladic Island culture of 7000-2000 BC preceded the Minoan culture in the Aegean. These cultures were destroyed by the volcanic eruption of Thera. The Minoans were on Crete, a large island south of Greece, from about 3400 BC to 2000 BC. King Minos had a large navy, and this helped to make the seas safe for trade. Early writing developed on Crete about 2700 BC. Those on Crete traded as far away as Marseilles, and this trading helped their writing skills, and those of other cities.

Even though they were composed in Egypt, the Amarna Letters of about 1400 BC were written in cuneiform, the language of diplomacy of that time. From 1200 BC alphabetic writing was used in Syria and Palestine. It was used in the Davidic Monarchy, the Lachish letters, and on seals. After the times of the conquering Alexander the Great, Aramaic, Greek, and Hebrew were used.

Statuettes. Writing enabled early peoples to use the written word instead of symbols in their legal dealings. The Gravettian culture in southern Russia and other cultures in the Near East had small figurines of fat women. One can only make suppositions about these household trophies. They may represent a fertility goddess. They may have been toys for children. Little boys may have been given bows and arrows; little girls, statuettes. A more grown-up possibility is that the figurines represented a marriage contract. When boys came of age, they joined the hunt. When girls came of age, they were betrothed. If these figurines are legal documents, they may show the woman had been legally delivered into the keeping of her husband. A loin cloth promised a virgin. Looks and skills were not guaranteed, but fertility was guaranteed, or a woman could be returned in disgrace to her parents. The important thing was not the head (or beauty), not the hands (or willingness to work), but the important thing was to produce offspring. If it became necessary to ''break'' a contract, you simply smashed it in the presence of witnesses (like Moses reportedly smashed the Ten Commandments when he came down the mountain and saw the idolatrous calf of gold).

Some statuettes were molded whole and then broken. Could they represent women whose marriages failed? There must have been as many marital upsets then as now. Think of our ancient phrases, *broken marriages*, *broken contracts*. We sometimes refer to women who have been abused as *broken* women. Back then, when contracts had to do with stone, one spoke of *broken*. Now that they have to do with paper, and we have greater psychological understandings, we have better words to describe marital relationships that have gone wrong.

Another possibility for incompleted statuettes is that they point up a religious reality. Human beings never see God completely. Therefore the statue of the goddess is not made whole so as to conform with this belief.

With the figurines, some of the nipples are broken off. There is a connection between broken nipples and a womanly tradition of grasping nipples in a time of deep sorrow, as an expression of grief so deep that the living nourishment of love ceases to flow. We have an expression in these latter days about "the milk of human kindness." After writing developed, these figurines were less common.

Statues and sandals were symbols that could be used to replace the written word. Other pre-writing statements of position and title are still with us. Some of the ancients flaunted their importance on their clothes, with the wideness of fringes on their garments. We copy this symbolism by having bars and stripes on uniforms.

Today we have experienced many modes of communication, phone, radio, TV, FAX, to let the world know what is important to us. We blare forth much that would be better left unsaid. The ancients were able to use a stylus and clay tablets to communicate myths, epic tales, hymns, law code, and all that was best in their society. The dross was not considered worthy to be set in clay.

2.5 People Who Traveled

We have at least two ways of knowing about our past geological history. We have scientists who can read the story in the rocks or in glacial ice, who can tell about ice ages and tectonic movement of continents. We also have myths from our ancestors that speak of their world being destroyed by fire or water. The Bible retains threads of these myths. It tells of a time of great rain and flooding. The Bible is a communication that is a wonderful witness to evolution; it is a gift given to us by the Holy Spirit speaking through the human tongue and hand.

If we take these early tales as humanity's collective remembrance of what their grandmothers told them, we can believe that at some point there was a lot of rain. When this rain came, it eroded the hills that had been denuded of trees. Perhaps trees had been over-harvested, as they were a major energy source, both for cooking food, and for warming dwelling places. Erosion silt clogged the rivers and flooded into deltas, even as in Bangladesh today. With the topsoil washed downstream, gathering-type farming became difficult. Animals were over-harvested. As the ice caps melted, rain poured down and the Adriatic became a sea rather than a plain. Peoples underwent mass migration seeking friendlier climates.

We have the beginnings of our present civilization in this post glacial era (9000-3000 BC). Archaeologists have many artifacts from this era in Palestine, Egypt, Iraq, Iran, and Turkey, but much information has disappeared and decayed in the silt of the dried-up riverbeds. There are also wadis in the Sahara and in the Arabian deserts that were flourishing rivers, with active communities on their banks. The community groups that had lived successfully in these areas had to find new locations for their activities. Unfortunately, there usually were other groups ahead of them in the most habitable regions.

Ancient Jericho. Archaeologists often term civilizations by the name of a present day landmark. The Natufians who founded Jericho are named after the Wady en-Natuf in southern Palestine. Jericho, one of the world's oldest known cities, was in existence in 8000 BC. The founders of this neolithic settlement came from the north, and were peaceful and pastoral people, harvesters of grain, and skilled flint workers. They hunted gazelle, formed early urban communities, and had ceremonial burial of their dead. The remains of the Natufians show that they were about 5 feet tall, with delicate features, such as specimens of other people from the north at that time, but they also had some Neanderthal resemblances. They may have come to the area near the Dead Sea, from the Lake Van region in eastern Turkey or from the Caspian Sea and Volga Delta which were experiencing a drying out. Early peoples may have continually been in exodus mode. The fact that some of them made walls around their encampments shows that rights to an area were often contested. There were probably many stories about the successive walls that were built at Jericho, and about the different heroes that succeeded in getting through the walls.

Clues to Migrations. As people and tribes traveled in search of quality living conditions, they intermixed with groups already established in the land, and absorbed the oral traditions of those groups. Often the men would kill each other, but frequently women would be spared and forced into labor as secondary wives or slaves. These women would tell their grandmotherly stories of previous times and of ancient gods, their "old wives tales." From these traditions and the eventual setting down in writing that followed, we are able to trace the possible movement of tribes in the ancient Near East area. Information can be gained from researching into the names of places and people, and also from disregarding these names as red herrings thrown across the track (because some story teller just didn't remember the correct name after 2000 years and had to come up with a realistic or appropriate substitute that was meaningful to her audience). What we get out of stories from the past is conditioned by our experience of the present. We of the sliced bread generation find it hard to imagine a world where there was no sliced bread or a world without bread.

In the Paleolithic or Old Stone Age, the human used stone weapons cut by chipping. In the Neolithic or New Stone Age, humans smoothed their stone implements. In the Old Stone Age groups of hunters forced large

Early Developments in The Near East

500,000 BP	Ice Age hunters used chopping stones.
400,000 BP	Spears made of wood hardened by plunging into fire.
250,000 BP	Hand axes.
150,000 BP	Stone blades with sharp edges.
45,000 BP	Triangular points on javelins.
25,000-10,000	Cave art in India and Mesopotamia.
9000 BC	Beginning of post glacial era, hunting, fishing as usual. Bows, battle axes, and sling shots.
9000-8000 BC	Last occupation of cave sites by food gatherers with late Paleolithic tools; the move from caves to open air.
8000-7000 BC	Huts; domestication of dog, goat, & pig; early villages; pre-pottery, neolithic Jericho.
7000-6500 BC	Beginning of agriculture; reaping and storing of grain; mud brick constructions, fortifications.
6500 BC	Statuary and stone vessels; containers needed to store grain against mice; granaries.
6500-5500 BC	Invention of pottery(earlier in Joman culture of Japan). Kiln fired brick in architecture; domesticated cattle.
5500-5000 BC	Metallurgy in Turkey & Iran to store grain; for swords; irrigation in south Mesopotamia (between the rivers).
5000 BC	Ubaid temple to Ninhursag, Sumerian mother goddess. Religious architecture - Eridu near Ur on the Euphrates.
5000-4000 BC	Farming in Egypt, irrigation on Nile. Irrigation systems, drainage systems in Indus Valley.
4000-3000 BC	Writing on tablets and standing stones, cylinder seals, art; urbanization by the rulers of Mesopotamia.
3500 BC	Wheeled carts.
3500-3000 BC	Dense population and prosperity; city of Uruk covered 5 square kilometers, international trade flourished.
3000 BC	Dynasties in Sumer; travel of pastoral tribes between Havilah and Shur (India and the wall of Egypt).
1600 BC	Horse and chariot used in warfare.
1500 BC	First true alphabet of 32 letters.
1279-1212 BC	Rameses the Great reigned in Egypt.

And where was
The One God of All The Nations
when all this was going on?

animals over cliffs, and clubbed them to death with axes. In the New Stone Age mammoths became scarce, so humans began domestication of animals. They also began to cultivate grasses.

Let us imagine a world where fruit is on the trees and bushes, where animals are plentiful and easily taken. Some animals are more trusting than others and can be tamed. Humans believe that it is their duty to reproduce, and they enjoy performing this duty. They enjoy life. They proliferate. They eat more game. They grow out of their caves, and as they spread farther north, they find it convenient to put on hides to protect themselves from the elements. They learn to drape these hides over poles and stones, and soon you have thriving communities of primitive housing. They have fire, so they have the opportunity for roasted meat. Sometimes, as there are quarrels over land and hunting rights, they even roast each other.

Communities come and go; leaders rise to power and fall. Little bugs that are the carriers of disease, and microbes that are invisible to the naked eye destroy populations. Crops perish in droughts, and earthquakes disturb settlements. Early people had many reasons for mistrusting each other and for changing locations.

Disease and Plague. Those who lived in southern Russia and Tibet about 8000 BC may have fled famine or plague. They were hunters and gatherers who used simple tools to cultivate grain. There were two job categories, the hunter-fishers and the farmer-herders. One group felt that there wasn't room enough for both. Perhaps that is where we get the stories of a wrathful God approving the destruction of people (Deuteronomy 2:35 and Joshua 8:2,27). We get rid of rats today out of fear that they are diseased and that their diseases will destroy us. We feel that God goes along with this destruction of the other life form because it preserves our safety and our health. We are not quite ready to make pets out of rats. The early Hebrews felt they had a right to destroy, as they had heard how ancestors perished from plagues after being kindly to the conquered. They were not ready to risk plague and ruin. One explanation for the apparent destruction of Neanderthal man is that he was slaughtered by the more aggressive *Homo sapiens*, whenever they met up. Perhaps the Neanderthal demise was due to transmission of disease, similar to the European giving small pox to the indigenous peoples of America about 1700 AD.

Disease may be one weapon the environment uses against overpopulation. Susceptibility to illness is built into our genes. Faith healers believe we can change this susceptibility by positive thought patterns. When there are negative thought patterns from population pressures, overcrowding, and violence, a disease like AIDS has the opportunity to become more effective.

Effects of The Flood. In 30,000 BC hunters were in the Lena and Angara River Valleys in Siberia north of Lake Baykal. In 8000 BC there were Stone Age hunters along the Danube in Germany for its 1700 miles length to the Black Sea. In 7000 BC these hunters and fishers had built community huts at Lepenski Vir on the Danube. The hunters found that domesticating animals insured a food supply. The early hunting economy shifted. Land became something to fight over. It also became over farmed, and farmers had to migrate to find better soil.

More and more trees were cut down for housing, cooking, boat making, and firing bricks as the population got denser. Humankind became an unruly lot. The Bible says God was upset with all their shenanigans. Things went wrong with the eco-system, as when the dinosaurs ate too much. A melting of the ice caps took place, it rained, and the oceans rose. Some of this was kept in the collective memory of the people and retold by story tellers all over the world.

After the flood there were still many people left in various areas, but the low plains such as the Adriatic, were now sea. Those who fled to the hills and had a few animals, managed to continue the human race. The Basques with their language that is unrelated to the rest of the Indo-European group of languages, are doubtless a community that lived through the flood, and their ancestors predate the second tidal wave of humanity that swept across from India to England. The Tibetans and the Chinese remained aloof in their own areas.

Back in the hills of southern Russia and Iran, the survivors of the flood had fire, had caves to live in plus the knowledge of housing, were gathering fruit and grain and domesticating animals, and still multiplying. There were earthquakes due to shifting continental plates. They moved south down the river valleys and through the mountain passes. Trading remnants from trade routes show where tribal wanderings could have taken place, especially if you had boats. Travels were not limited to boats, donkeys, and foot power; they tamed the ox and constructed a very usable wooden wheel. From India across the mountains to the Caspian, up the Volga, east to the Baltic, they traveled; from India southwest, to ports on the Persian Gulf and Red Sea. In good weather travelers could even go north around the top of the Scandinavian Peninsula. There were trade routes from Mesopotamia to the Mediterranean, to the Black Sea, north on the Don River (which lies near the Volga at one point) and north on the Dnieper; also, west on the Danube and north on the Rhine. In the third to first centuries BC, Strabo, Pliny, and Pomponius Mela record that a merchant, Pytheas, sailed in 400 BC to a land called Thule. Much earlier than then, the Sumerians knew that there was a land to the north where it was dark all day long in winter. Other old long forgotten trade routes can be observed today from satellites which show the remains of packed sand below the desert surface.

The travel routes from India through the Himalayas are not as impassable as one might think. Through the Karakoram Pass, one can reach the central Asian republics of Tadjikistan, Ujbekistan, and Turkmenia. Through Sikkim and through the Kumaon Himalayas, one can cross into Tibet. Using the northwest passes of Kej and Dasht, one can cross through Iran and attain western Asia and Africa.

Tools. The very early tool making human used these passes. It is thought that the African hand ax spread through these corridors. It may have passed in either direction between Africa and India, but hand axes most likely originated in Africa. The early human groups had two distinct tool types, heavy hand axes and the smaller pebble tools for scraping and cutting. The more delicately crafted pebble tools are found in China, Central Asia, India, and Africa. This tool distribution tells us something about human migration. In India there are found both hand axes and pebble tools. (There are chopper tools all over India dating from 400,000-200,000 BP. In the Mesolithic era, they progress to flake tools.) The hand ax is found in both Africa and Europe. Pebble tools and cleavers are absent in Europe, but present in both Africa and India. In Central Asia and China, there were no hand axes, only pebble tools. India and Africa seem to be the intersection point of different methods of early tool making. Pebble tools radiated out of the Indian area, and hand axes, out of the African area. Does this make India and Africa the point of origin of the various strains of humanity? Can we trace the development of the human being through her choice of tools? Hand axes could have existed in India with Australopithecus, and moved across the warm belt to Arabia and Africa when the ice was covering Europe. Then when there was a glacial warming, people and axes moved northward to Europe. Back in India, a response to this same glacial warming might have been invention of more precise tools and a movement of people northwards to Tibet, Russia, and China. Another theory is that Paranthropus types used hand axes, and her kind never made it north of India, while Australopithecus spread further and used more precise tools. Later in Europe, tool innovations came in with the Acheulian tool industry where they were in use at water holes 500,000 BP.

2.6 Boats

There is no reason to think that the early human made all her journeys by foot. If you spent a lot of time fishing, crabbing, or gathering oysters, you undoubtedly figured out how to swim with logs to assist, and the use of boats followed naturally. Log boats could have been in vogue with early tool makers. The indigenous people living on New Guinea in the present day have long canoes made out of logs. They stand astride this boat and with a shaped paddle move swiftly through the water. This may have been a mode of transportation for a very long time. They tied their logs together with vines and made rafts that could hold more people, and even transport animals. They put huts on top of their rafts, for housing.

There were boats being used off the coast of Japan in 18,000 BC. Cyprus had boats in 12,000 BC. We know this because the pygmy hippopotami disappeared from Cyprus around that date, as humans came in their boats and hunted them and ate them. They left datable bones behind. Boats spread to Denmark by 6,000 BC. With practice, sea faring became safer. The compass was invented about 2,000 BC, making it easier to reach one's destination.

In 1947 Thor Heyerdahl plus five companions sailed the raft Kon-Tiki 4,300 miles in 101 days. They traveled from Callao, Peru to the South Sea Islands showing the plausibility and endurance of that type of craft for trading and migration purposes. Likewise Eugene Savoy sailed a reed and bamboo boat 2,000 miles along the shore from Peru to Panama. In 1970 Thor with seven companions took off from Safi, Morocco in a sail boat made out of 200,000 papyrus reeds, and arrived 57 days (and 3270 miles) later at Bridgetown, Barbados, 300 miles off the coast of South America. He found that the ocean currents carried him precisely in the direction of the Columbus landfall. Using a fairly primitive raft, early men could have gone vast distances. If you were out of favor with the people in your tribal group, you might take to the seas to escape their wrath. Those ancient sailors landing on South America did not carry with them the knowledge of the wheel. Perhaps the wheel wasn't needed in the South American jungle. They didn't need wheels to make the ocean journey; they needed only boats.

What kind of boat you used depended on what materials were available. Where logs were plentiful, they would help to support a person in the water. They worked better if they were hollowed out, and paddles helped steer better than hands. One early boat employed in the Tigris-Euphrates area was shaped like the body of a horse, so that the rider could use both his hands and feet to propel himself through the water. A papyrus canoe called a *tankwa* was used by Abyssinians on Lake Tana. It was about 30 feet long and could carry 20 men. Reed canoes were and are still used in South America off the coast of Peru. When such a boat becomes water logged, it is dragged to shore and dried.

Other sea craft were stitched together with twine and skins. A *kayak* could be waterproofed with animal grease. A bas-relief from Nineveh showing the customs of 2500 years ago, portrays a large round basket covered with ox hides. They may have waterproofed it with ox grease. The modern *guffas* used on the Tigris today are similar, but use bitumen for caulking. The use of bitumen back in ancient times was also possible as pools of tar were available.

Off Polynesia the war canoes of the Maoris could carry 100 men. The *feluccas*, or sailboats, of the Egyptians on the southern Nile would float down stream with the tide and work their way back with the wind. They are still in use for trade and transportation.

House boats are used as homes by many off the coast of southeast Asia. The *khele nao* is a covered traveling boat used on the rivers of north Burma. The *dhoni*, a model used off Ceylon, has two pontoons with a little house resting on them. The Chinese *sampan* has a mat covered roof. These or something similar may have been the model for the biblical Noah's ark.

Many early families depended on the bounty of the sea for their food even though travel was undoubtedly dangerous. We hear about early sailors in Homer's description of the Greek warrior Ulysses. Their ideas of what the world was like, were hampered by their lack of knowledge and their map making abilities (see pages 194, 195). Thus all kinds of boat travel undoubtedly contributed not only to trade in goods but also to the wide-spread interchange of religious and cultural beliefs.

Footnotes
1 Harappan seal.
2 The *King of Battle* story in Amarna collection tells of merchants from Akkad.
3 *Encyclopedia Americana, Volume 2*, USA Americana Corporation, 1949, p. 372.
4 Christos Doumas, ''Thera and The Exodus,'' *Biblical Archeology Review, Volume XVII No. 1*, Jan./Feb 1991, p. 48.
5 Normandie Ellis, *Awakening Osiris*, Phanes Press, Grand Rapids, MI, 1988.

III

Civilization

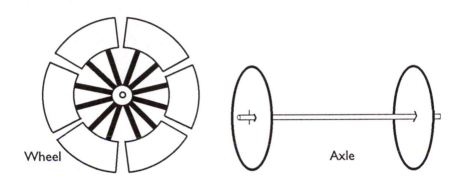

Wheel   Axle

3.1 In The Indus Valley

About 65 million BP the continent of India detached itself from Africa and slid across the in-between waters to hook firmly onto the bottom of Asia 15 million years later. At the same time Australia and Antarctica moved downwards. At the point of attachment of India onto Asia, the Himalayas pushed up and are still rising (but very slowly). Where the plate of Asia crunched against other tectonic plates, there were massive disturbances. There are still earthquakes in the Europe-Asia area today due to this grinding of continental plates.

The life forms on Asia, Australia, Antarctica, and India had similarities. These continents had come through the age of the dinosaurs and entered the age of mammal formation. Pre-monkeys may have been riding through the sea on the back of India, like passengers on a tremendous evolutionary Noah's Ark. The same animal types may have been riding Antarctica down to glacial extinction.

Early Turmoil. When this traveling boat of various species docked onto Asia, the creatures had to evolve drastically in order to survive. This subcontinent of Asia was a very dramatic place. About 900,000 years ago the upper Siwalik range in India was experiencing heavy tectonic movements. This was a warm interglacial period. An ancient Kashmir lake was cut up and the River Jhelum emerged. Other rivers forming at this time were the Indus and the Sohan. The rivers of India were in a continual state of flux from pluvial sediments (during interglacial periods), from tectonic movements, and from evaporating away in dry wind blown phases (when there were polar glaciations in northern Asia). There is evidence that people were living through these developments. A pebble tool industry and hand axes were found in the Sohan River area in Kashmir, dated to 300,000 years ago.

The area that is the Ganges Basin has a 500 meter thick alluvial deposit.[1] We can tell from scientific readings taken in oyster beds that at 130,000 BP and 35,000 BP, there were extraordinary high sea levels. High sea levels mean low ice at the poles, and a warm period for earth. The animal or people forms that may have been around, were kept busy scurrying up to high ground. If she fled to the hills for safety, the early human was met with the terror of earthquake. The fittest, the smartest, and the most agile were the ones who came through such upheaval. We must marvel at the ability of the human to survive, and at the wisdom of God to make such possibility of survival. When we look at India today and see what damage can be wrought by severe monsoons, and how villages are washed into the sea, we can relate to what the early human had to endure.

The river valleys were colonized by peoples with knowledge of copper, brass (alloy of copper and zinc), and bronze (alloy of copper and tin). Lake bed areas were used by groups who dug pits to dwell in and harvested vegetation. Hills and terraces were occupied by hunting groups. Originally, some of these cultures may have come from further east and south (such as Malay, Sumatra, or Java). Some names we have given to these cultures are the Ochre Color Pottery people, the Copper Hoard peoples, the Banas, the Malwa, the Kayatha, the Jorwe, and the Harappan in the Indus valley. The Harappan people are named after the present day site of Harappa but this name is also recorded in the Indian scriptures, the *Rig Veda,* as the *Hari-Yupiyawe.* The Hebrew scriptures, the Bible, have the patriarch Abraham associated with a relative or place name of *Haran* which is similar to *Hari.* They also have the name for God as *Yahweh* which is similar to the second half of *Yupiyawe.*

Climatic Changes. These various population centers in India were heavily dependent on climatic conditions. The Indus area which was the center for the ancient Harappan civilization (about 3000-2300 BC), has had its wet and dry periods. When its was too wet, civilization was flooded out. When it was too dry, populations had to move elsewhere to find food. For instance, Sambhar Lake near Harappa is 10,800 years old. Between 8000 BC and 1600 BC rainfall was good. In 1600 BC the lake became salt and dried up. It was dry for 700 years. Then in 900 BC it returned again. Such undulations as these caused population shifts. About 1700 BC Aryans came from the Caspian area and settled on the Indus, enslaving the remnants of population which they found there. These Aryans may have been the descendants of the earlier Harappans coming back to their ancestral home, when the area they had retreated to, became unlivable.

Remote Migrations. In times of glacial meltdown, with flooding of lowlands and land-bridges, the early human may have fled northward through mountain passes to Tibet for security. Other passes led from the Indus northwest.[2] From Tibet it took the human tens of thousands of years to infiltrate China, and develop northern Mongoloid characteristics. There is unbroken cultural development in China and India. Indian farmers still chant the sayings of the ancients, and if we could understand their words, we might hear clues to the background of biblical stories. Humankind migrated onwards to Japan where the archipelago had risen from the sea about 30 million BP. Early Japanese show some Neanderthal features. From Tibet westward wanderers may have taken another few thousand years to interbreed with other groups and produce the Neanderthal population in northern Europe. Those leaving the Indian subcontinent by the coast line could have become the Capoid race in Cush or East Africa. The Capoids, traveling to North Africa and meeting up with Neanderthal cousins across the Italian or Spanish land bridges, could have generated the Congoid peoples. We are all children of the same productive earth. Color of skin is a minor surface variation.

Dating early human occurrences in India is more difficult than dating in Africa at Olduvai Gorge. At Olduvai there are layers of volcanic material that can be dated, while in India there has been no volcanic activity, only earthquakes. Radio carbon can date back only to 40,000 BP, so Stone Age events are beyond its range. Dating approximations must come from dating gravel sediments and shell beds. There are Paleolithic sites all over India except where recent flood silting has buried and covered over evidence. Other mounds or evidences of early civilization may be sunk into the sands of India or drowned in the sea. The archeologist DuBois found early man on Java, reasoning that a warm climate would be the place to search. Explorers may find evidence of early civilizations near the sea coasts of Java, Ceylon, and Malaysia.

It is possible that early migrants from the drying Caspian area left tent-like houses of stone and wood, traveled south through mountain passes and along river valleys, and took up residence in an area extending from Palestine across Persia to India. Jungle had made this area too lush to be livable, but as the earth dried, it became more attractive to herders and cultivators of the soil. Still later invaders pushed up into Persia from India, as India suffered periods of too much rain. Persia, too, had its periods of earthquake and desertification. Still other groups who we call *Aryans*, retraced the steps of their ancestors, pushed earlier herders and farmers up into the hills and down into the southern tip of India and Ceylon.

At Bhimbetka near Bhopal, India, there is an area of 10 square kilometers where there are 800 caves and rock shelters, with deposits dating back to early tool-making periods. Unfortunately, there is no charcoal for radio carbon dating, and no volcanic deposits for potassium-argon dating. The remains of various animal species can help fill in dates. Certain horse, cattle, and elephant species existed at specific times and then became extinct. Their bones can date sites of human habitation. In the River Belan area a mother goddess figure was found in gravel dated to 18,000 years before the present. Rock paintings at Bhimbetka demonstrate the early human's belief in magic, or in God's care.

Town Sites. Early sites at different locations may be buried in silt, but others have been discovered and excavated. In the Indus Valley there is a series of village cultures scientifically designated as pre-Harappan and Harappan. Such civilizations are attested to, by large mounds at Mohenjo-daro in the Sind area, at Harappa in West Punjab, and at Chanhu-daro near the mouth of the Indus. They are situated on old river courses, and had wells, drains, brick-lined public baths, and toilets. These ruins confirm the existence of a pre-Aryan civilization spread over the northwest subcontinent. At the mound of Dabar-kot in the Zhob valley of north Baluchistan, this Indus culture is archaeologically bracketed by two other distinct cultures. Likewise, under the Indus culture at Harappa is another pottery culture.

There is an early Indian civilization at great depth in the flood silt at Kalibangan, southeast of Harappa on the now dry Ghaggar River where bull figurines have been found. The Ghaggar is the modern name for the ancient River Saraswati (named after the goddess of knowledge) which legend says flowed directly to the sea, but now is an inland river. On most of these ancient mound excavation levels, there seemed to be no palaces or fortifications, but remains seemed to testify to small villages with a chieftain who lived in the same type of house as his peers. Other better planned cities were built on top of these destroyed towns, by invading cultures, perhaps from Sumer or the Caspian. Pre-Harappan levels date from 3500 BC. A late pre-

Harappan level at Kalibangan dated before 2490 BC contained a mud brick fortification as if they were worried about marauding neighbors or religious oppression. This may have come to pass, for in the Harappan period they had developed a caste system, and needed slaves or low caste people to dump the jars they used for bodily wastes. In this period, fortifications become commonplace. Having slaves is liable to make one fearful for one's safety. Oppressors need fortifications to protect what they have gained out of greed.

At Mohenjo-daro, (which means *Mound of the Dead*), there was a drainage and irrigation system. A brick bath house had a deep end, and may have been used for religious purification purposes. The temple ruins had an enclosure for a sacred tree and two seated male sculptures. These statues were made out of steatite (soft stone). The granary in Mohenjo-daro had a floor area of 9000 square feet. It seemed that all the members worked in the communal storage of grain.

Early Worship. India is bound by the mountains on the north and surrounded by ocean, and one would expect it to be relatively unaffected by outside influences and to have a uniform religious system. However, it contained different ways of worshiping divinity even in adjoining areas (as it does today). At Kalibangan on the river Ghaggar there were fire altars and worship for the Mother Goddess cult. Kali was the name of one of the forms of the consort of the Hindu god Siva in her aspect of destruction (or burning). Brahman was associated with the fire god Agni. At Lothel there were also fire altars. Evidence of frequent flooding in Harappan times (2500 BC-1700 BC) may have caused the fire worshipers to leave for other climes.

Besides the fire altar worship, there were other religious strains present in pre-Aryan India. There was Rudra, a yoga-type god, the Lord of Creatures. Mohenjo-daro seals show trees, with a horned goddess sitting in a peepul or sacred fig tree. There were ghats or steps at a landing place for religious bathing on the river, as there are in India today.

The hymns of the *Rig Veda* are the oldest literature in any Aryan language. They may have been set down in writing by the Aryans, but the stories may be pre-Aryan material. The Sanscrit-speaking invaders or Aryans from the north brought new ideas to refresh the Indian culture. Their transportation was a little easier than that of previous migrating groups. They had two-wheeled ox-carts with wooden wheels and axles. They settled in the towns which the Harappans had abandoned several centuries before, such as Mohenjo-daro on the Indus and Harappa on the Ravi. These archaeological mounds are not located on these same rivers today as the rivers have moved or filled in. A site at Kot-Diji near Mohenjo-daro shows sixteen layers of occupation, the top three being Aryan. There is a fortified town underneath an unfortified Aryan settlement. The Aryans came into an empty town, which may have been deserted due to climatic conditions.

The new cultures which came in brought superior writing skills, and set down the legends which had been handed down by word of mouth. The *Vedic Hymns* are dated 1400-1000 BC; the *Brahmanas*, 1200-800 BC; the *Upanishads* 900-500 BC.

Harappan Culture. The older Harappan civilization lasted at least 1000 years. Their clay tablet writings have never been satisfactorily deciphered. Some tablets are written from right to left and then back again from left to right, as a farmer ploughs a field. Early tablets were used to count and to sell animals. At the beginning of Chapter II is a sample of an inscribed stone seal.[3] This may be a bull or it may be a picture of a unicorn, an ox-like beast with one horn. Tigers, crocodiles, and rhinos were also on seals, and composite grotesque animals such as one combining the face of a man, the tusks of an elephant, the horns of a bull, and the hind quarters of a tiger.

This Harappan civilization took thousands of years to develop. Pre-Harappan roots were with the cave artists of 25,000 BP. These early peoples gradually learned the arts of domesticating animals, smelting bronze, trading in wood and ivory, carving sculpture, growing wheat, barley, sesame, cotton, melon, and dates, using mud bricks for building blocks, using irrigation, and planning their cities with drainage and water supply. These farmers kept cattle, buffalo, pigs, and sheep. Camels (not yet in use in Egypt), horses, asses, and perhaps even elephants were used for transport. Because the people of India had earlier tamed their animals, the Saharans of 5000 BC were herding domesticated cattle, and had herds of sheep and goats.[4] Their farming method was cross hatch planting where rows ran from east to west, and from north to south in the same field. Much civilized activity was going on in India, and this knowledge traveled to distant places. Pottery variations show tribal relationships. There is evidence for trade contact between the Harappan community and Sargon I of Mesopotamia.

Civilization has its problems. Having fire made it possible to fire bricks for building. The consumption of major vegetation caused by the firing of millions of bricks, bared the land, reduced transpiration of moisture, and impaired the climate. Treeless lands encouraged flooding. Flooding destroys irrigation setups, and gives the land a heavy salt content that sours it for farming. Thus, early civilizations had a very finite life, often less than a thousand years for rise, decline, and exodus.

In a considerate manner the later Aryan invaders of the Indus valley allowed whatever earlier inhabitants of the land they found there, to live on, under the conditions that they would do all the dirty work for them. Perhaps their idea of God was of a God who wanted you to treat the stranger with a certain amount of empathy. This early supposed kindness on the part of one group to another, in allowing them to live as servants, firmed in place the caste system of India, which has endured to this day. Many of those who have practiced slavery down through the years have felt themselves to be kind and noble in their support of a people they felt to be less capable.

Some of the Harappan population preferred exile to servitude and fled away. When these Tamil speaking people were driven beyond the Indus, their territory became known as Hindustan, the land beyond the river, the territory of those who were forced to move on. Some of the people of this early Indus civilization shifted to the Ganges because of the Aryan invaders and formed a fairly stable civilization from about 1000-500 BC. Other groups moved westward and northward. Rice had not been used in India before 1000 BC, and its appearance may have helped to feed the people in the Ganges area. The rice goddess became an important symbol.

When at its height, the Indus civilization had trade which included imports of gold from Southern India, from Afghanistan, and from the River Kim area. Other imports were lapis lazuli, silver and copper from Afghanistan, turquoise from Iran, and jade-like fuchsite from southern India. Names for the Indus Valley or their trading outposts, may have been *Meluhha* or *Makkan*. Their territory stretched from the shores of the Arabian Sea (300 miles west of Karachi) to the Simla hills and southeast to the Kim River on the Gulf of Cambay. Because of a lack of reliable dates for Indus artifacts, they are sometimes dated by their similarity to artifacts in other countries. Of course, if these other dates are wrong, so are the Indus.

Folk tales. One of the ancient myths is contained in an epic poem called the *Ramayana*. This is considered to be both an elaborate allegory and a fragment of prehistoric Hindu mythology. It first existed for a long time in an oral version and acquired many varying, but related forms. It supposedly was first chanted by the two sons of Rama. Parallels are found in the *Arabian Nights*.

Rama's wife Sita is carried away to Lanka Cave on the island of Ceylon by Ravana, the king of the demons. Rama rescues his beloved by bridging the waters between Ceylon and India with an army of monkeys led by the monkey king or god, Hanuman.

3.2 The Sumerian Civilization

As we have seen, the climate caused confusion in the world of the early human being and aided in the emergence of the hunter-fisher groups into the farming and herding groups. When the Adriatic was dry land, the peoples of the Gravettian Culture of the southern Russian plain spread from caves to artificial dwellings and also migrated south and west. Signs of similar culture are found in Germany which can be dated from 15,000-12,000 BC, lasting into 8000 BC. The European hunting-fishing culture was in its closing phases 5000-2000 BC. This culture is represented by objects such as a dugout canoe from the Netherlands dated at 6300 BC, and stone lined graves at Brittany of 4000 BC. The Halaf was an early culture on the river Khabur in northeast Syria near Turkey. Its typical shrine was a round house with a tent out front.

Artisans and Traders. Early developments in creativity included metallurgy, which started with copper and tin, and their alloy bronze. The Euphrates ancient name was *Urudu*, which means *copper river* as copper came from north of the river source area. (The ancient name of the Tigris was *Idiglat*, meaning *arrow*, as it was a faster flowing river.) Gold was traded from southeast Asia. Ophir, which may have been India, was known for its gold. Even further east than India was the Kim River in southeast Asia, and *Kim* means *gold*. Chryse was known as the Land of Gold.[5] India may have traded for gold with the east, and then exchanged this gold for other goods in the west. People traveled to Ophir by sea (I Kings 9:28 and 22:49). The route would be down the Red Sea and across the Indian Ocean. Sumerians and Akkadians traded with southern Anatolia, Syria, Dilmun and Makkan (down the Persian Gulf), Elam and Aratta (Persia), and Meluhha (the Indus).

Writing was invented in Mesopotamia about 3500 BC. In the Mesopotamia of 8000-6000 BC there were village settlements such as Ugarit (7000 BC), a Canaanite city near the Mediterranean coast of Syria. Later about 1500 BC it could boast of a library of cuneiform and hieroglyphics. Jarmo (6500 BC) was an early town in the Zagros Mountains of Iraq. In the Sumer of 3100-2350 BC, city states were Eridu and Ur near the sea coast, and Lagash, Uruk, and Umma, inland and up-river. As the rivers frequently changed their beds, the dominant position of certain cities would also change. In 2750 BC there was a major shift in the course of the Euphrates. Canals were dredged to keep open the former channels. Today the major route of the Euphrates is even further to the west.

Trade developed between groups, leading to peaceful exchange of ideas and early inter-communication, that somewhat offset the exclusivity of the city-state. The Sumerians brought copper and tin down trade routes leading from the Transcaucasian Mountains and across the Black Sea, overland and then down the Euphrates. Egypt got copper supplies from the Sinai. An archaeological site on the Sinai has been dated at 100,000 years ago. The ancient tin country was Anaku, location uncertain. This source of tin may have been in Turkey, or as far away as the Mediterranean. Cyprus means *copper* and was visited for this resource. The island of Akrotiri (or Thera) which essentially disappeared in 1628 may have been the tin island. In Phoenician times trading for tin ranged as far as the British Isles. There are offering stones at Stonehenge (circa 1600-1500 BC) that display carvings of Mycenaean daggers, also the ankh symbol for life (a cross with an oval for the top) such as was pictured in Egyptian art. Phoenicians built typical square wells, and some of these wells in Cornwall, British Isles, confirm that trade and population moved over vast distances. The Mid East developed more rapidly than other regions because it was a pass-through area and received cultural information from distant areas such as Spain, China, and Africa. Sun god and ankh mirror symbols may have passed from Japan to Egypt or vice versa by water routes or land routes near Sumer.

Sargon I. On the negative side some greedy leaders found it was easier on their purse strings to demand the raw materials as booty or taxation. Power plays and greed caused more strife. As these notions of power and control developed in the Tigris and Euphrates area, ruling dynasties were formed. Power passed from one city to another. There were powerful dynasties in Kish, Uruk, and Ur. Early notable strong rulers were Mesilim of the Third Dynasty of Kish and Ur-Nina and his grandson Eannatum, in Lagash. The city of Lagash was overcome by Lugal-zagesi, King of Uruk. Lugal boasted of conquering other cities from the Persian Gulf to the Mediterranean. Then Sargon I, the King of Akkad (or Agade or Hagade or even Hagar), came on the scene and wrested supremacy from the Sumerians. The date for Sargon I is in question. It may be as late as 2300 BC or as early as 3200 BC. Sargon I was part of Semitic movements invading from the Arabian wilderness.[6] With Sargon of Agade the language of the land changed from classical Sumerian to Semitic Akkadian. Some archaeological mementos connected with him are a circular steatite seal with an Harappan type scorpion and inscription, and another seal with a bull-motif. In Egypt dated at approximately 3100 BC there is the mace head of someone known by the formidable title of King Scorpion, who was the predecessor of King Narmur (about 3050 BC). A scorpion is a large spider which has a stinger in its tail. This Scorpion King is credited with the digging of a canal, while Narmur is said to have diverted the waters of the Nile.

Can the Scorpion King of Egypt be Sargon I of Mesopotamia? Sargon preceded his grandson Naram-Sin in Sumer but these reigns are given Mesopotamian dates as late as 2300 BC (which are unreliable).[7] Sargon and the Akkadians seized power in Sumer and went up by Turkey to places like Haran in north Mesopotamia, and Arrapkha or Kirkuk in Turkey. Arrapkha has a name similar to Harappa, and this may imply a common ancestor or family ties. Sargon's soldier-traders, overrunning Sumer, and leaving triumphal statuary in southwest Turkey, may have gone on to Egypt where they left memories of an ancient King Scorpion. Presumably, Sargon's ancestors were descendants of Noah's son Shem, and from the east, such as Persia or the Indus area. Semites living in Israel many years later would naturally include myths similar to the Sargon-hero stories in the semi-historical tales of their tribe.

Sargon of Akkad may be considered to be the first potentate. A potentate is a sovereign or monarch wielding great power, a King of Kings. There is a question as to the location of Akkad. It may have been a Semitic settlement. It may have been a barracks for the Semitic soldiers who served the Sumerian royalty. It may have been a palace establishment. Akkad may have acquired the latter meaning of king, or great house. The name *Sargon* means *true* or *legitimate king*. His Semitic throne name was *Sharrum-ken*. He may have been called by other names in other countries such as *Aga Mennon* or *Akka Menes* (meaning *great Akkadian*).

Sargon may have been great, and he may have been a true king, but the story of his beginnings emphasize that he was not legitimate. The legend says that his mother was a temple prostitute, one of those supposedly chosen women who served the god in the temple by being available for sex, if one of the god's adherents felt inspired by the god to have sex. After Sargon was born, it was difficult for his mother to perform her temple duties and see to the needs of her son, so she made a little water proof basket, and floated him on the river (as in the story of Moses). A water carrier, coming to draw water, discovered Sargon, and brought him up as his son. Sargon entered the palace service as a youth, and was so talented that he rose up rapidly in the ranks to vizier, from which position he led a revolt.

Nineveh and Other Restorations. Other interpretations of Sargon's name bring up images of a rebel leader in an army encampment. In the area of Nineveh, there has been a great wall unearthed that is called Sargon's wall. This wall may refer to Sargon II, a later day Assyrian king, or it may be a rebuilt wall of the original Sargon's encampment. Nimrod may be the name that other populations had for Sargon, and the vicinity of Nineveh may be where he chose to locate his establishment. It would be a place easy to defend, yet still a place from which he could float down the Euphrates and undertake trading or raiding expeditions.

Nineveh, as described in the *Book of Jonah* was such a great city that it took three days to walk across it. There is a large area of ancient mounds in northern Mesopotamia where the River Zab meets the River Euphrates.

Fairly recent Assyrian kings, Ashurnasirpal II and Sargon II, who were interested in antiquities, may have refurbished old ruins in this area about 800 BC, and put their name on more ancient palaces. Their sphinxes, tiger-men statuary, and inscriptions may have been archaeologically displaced from a previous era of history, that of Naram-Sin. We have our museums today for the 100 to 1000 year old works of art. These Assyrian kings also felt the need to preserve the history that had gone on 2000 or more years before their time. These Restorer kings may have caused chronological confusion by taking ancient artifacts and placing them in settings of a more recent date. Around 1400 BC Shalmaneser I acquired Naharayim (northern Mesopotamia). He built up the city of Calah and restored the temple at Nineveh. He was succeeded by his son Tukulti-Ninibi who restored the palace at Ashur. Still later Ashurnasirpal (884-858 BC) re-restored Calah. He was succeeded by Shalmaneser III, also a restorer. There were five historical cities in northern Mesopotamia, Nineveh (near Mosul), Calah (modern Nimrud), Ashur (near Kalat Sherkat), Sargina (Khorsabad), and Arbela (Arbil). Sargon II admired the achievements of Sargon I (who ruled 2000 years earlier), and he may have built his capital, Khorsabad, where he believed Sargon I had had his capital.

Another instance of restoration in central Mesopotamia is the shrine of Ishtar of Agade which is situated in the Merkes quarter of Babylon. It was refurbished by Shamshi-Adad, a much later king who was interested in antiquities. Nabonidus (555-538 BC) states on a cylinder inscription that the cornerstone of a temple from the time of Sargon I had been put in place 3,200 years before. This would date Sargon I at 3700 BC. The number used in this inscription may also be translated as 320 years, and may refer to Sargon II.

On a mountain north of the Euphrates, is a worship site dedicated to Nimrod called Nimrud-Dagh. On this hill are toppled heads from giant statues which lie scattered on the ground. Statues may have been erected there at various dates, some being as recent as Greco-Roman times. Others may be of greater antiquity and may go back to the days of Sargon and Naram-Sin. In the Indus Valley at Harappa, there is a soapstone statue of an Harappan elder whose beard and facial expression are similar to a fallen head on Nimrud-Dagh. Sargon's Semitic ancestors may have come from the Indus Valley, and brought their statue making skills with them, or Sargon may have gone in both directions and been the inspiration for both statues.

Kings ruling in Sumer had been of Sumerian stock, but as more Semitic peoples gathered in the area, some of them became rulers and carried Semitic names as well as Sumerian. There was intermarriage between the two peoples, and there was exchange of language. Mebaragesi, King of Kish and Mesilim, shortly before the time of Sargon, was probably Sumerian, but used a Semitic name.

Geography of Early Peoples. From time to time mountain people invaded Sumer from the north, the northeast, and the northwest. One possibility is that Sargon's Semitic forbears may have come via Persia from India. Sheep would have fared well if herder groups crossed through mountain passes with streams of running water. This north west route would have given them a chance to mingle with tribes from what are known today as West Pakistan and Southern Russia. Biblical Eden, a land to the east of Palestine, is described as having the River Pishon for one of its borders. The Pishon encircles the land of Havilah (Genesis 2:11) which is a part of the Indus valley system. Havilah is reported to be a country rich in gold and precious stones. Diamonds may have formed there from the previously mentioned meteor. Genesis 10:25-29 describes Havilah with Sheba, Ophir, and others as the sons of Joktan who is a son of Eber (or Heber or Hebrew). It is to be noted that there is an Indian Cush and an Egyptian Cush, and that these two areas are accessible to each other by sea or by crossing the bottom of the Arabian peninsula. The two Cushes claim descent from a common ancestor.

Gods of these early peoples include Khaldi whose name means *God of Heaven*. Other tribes called those who served Khaldi, *Khaldeans*. The area moon god was Sin. Thus we have rulers who use Sin as part of their name. The sun god was Shamas; the rain god was Adad. Ishtar was incorporated into the Babylonian religion under the name of Sharis.

Growth of An Empire. Government in Mesopotamia before the time of Sargon depended on a circle of judges chosen from among their peers, a circle of the wise and powerful. One of these men would be the convener of the meetings, and the decider of what should be discussed. He would be the governor of the city, and would usually listen to the will of his colleagues and the mood of the people. At first he was chosen from among his group, but after awhile, the office became an hereditary one, and the ruler would be known and addressed as *king* or *lord*.

Either through military might or through invitation, Sargon became the king of city after city. He began by ruling in Kish, the mid area of Mesopotamia, and in Ur, the dominant city in the south, and then went to the cities on the northwest Euphrates. He allowed the local rulers to govern themselves, but he was generous with his wisdom and advice. He was accompanied by his military force.

The land that Sargon ruled had for a long time been the land of the Sumerian people speaking the Sumerian language. More and more Semites entered the land from the east and west, to partake of its culture, and to make out economically. They would hire themselves out as farmers or as paid soldiers. They learned the Sumerian language of their conquerors, but so many of them came that Semitic became a dominant language. Sargon, as a Semite, found it easier to run the country using his native tongue, and after his time the common language spoken in Mesopotamia was called Akkadian.

Up north in Turkey (or Anatolia) a group of merchants heard of the wisdom of Sargon, and invited him up to their wooded country to settle their disputes. Sargon went up and was greeted as befitted a king, solved their problems, and added the merchant community to his empire. There are memorabilia of Sargon in Turkey. A seventeenth century BC Hittite text says that Sargon was in Asia Minor and campaigned up the Khabur River.

The possible Sargon title of *Nimrod* (*Nimravus* means *sabre-tooth tiger*) is given to an extinct volcano, Nimrud-Dagh (Nimrud's Mountain) north of Mesopotamia overlooking Lake Van. Lake Van has water whose consistency can be compared to washing soda (sodium carbonate). It doubtless didn't please the taste buds. The people in that area were great wine growers, and improved their water with wine. The legend of Noah's drunkenness may have been circulated here as alcoholism may have been a community problem (Genesis 9:20-21). Legends often acquire local names as they pass through a territory. The use of the names *Noah* and *Ararat* for the flood story (which may have been told of a flood elsewhere) shows that the carriers of Bible legends passed through this area north of Sumer.

A stela, or rock tablet, of Sargon has been found at Cyprus, an island off the coast near Ugarit. Sargon also went to the island of Crete and to the city of Byblos on the coast of Palestine. He boasted that he had trade with the people of the Indus, and Harappan beads, pottery, and ivory objects have been found in ancient Akkadian houses. Trade was very important to both kings and merchants, and also to the people. They liked the crafts from foreign countries. The Achaemenid Royal Road from Sardis in Asia Minor (the city of the legendary Croesus) to Susa in Persia, had been in use since 7000 BC. Sargon would go personally to communities that had something to trade. He would be treated royally, and local rulers would be honored to give him their daughters for his royal entertainment. Stelae or statues would be erected to commemorate such an event. If royal treatment were lacking, Sargon's soldiers would round up recalcitrant citizens and take them back to Mesopotamia as slaves.

Naram-Sin. Sargon ruled about fifty years, facing a lot of opposition near the end of his life. His twin sons took the throne upon his death. The youngest son, Rimush, ruled first for eight years, and was killed in a palace coup. The older twin Manishtushu, ruled for fourteen years. Then he, too, was executed. Stories told about Manishtushu relate that he crossed the Lower Sea in ships, and that he defeated thirty two kings and occupied their country up to the silver mines. He brought diorite from mountains beyond the Mediterranean Sea, which may be describing marble from Italy. He founded the Ishtar temple at Nineveh.

The next to rule was the grandson of Sargon, Naram-Sin. Naram-Sin claimed to be "king of the four quarters of the world." He called himself a god. Later day Assyrians (in northern Mesopotamia) worshiped a self made god called Ashur. Not too many of the people living in southern Mesopotamia were ready to worship such a god. In the time of Naram-Sin, the people of the south and the Hebrew population didn't like to bow down to emperors who called themselves god. They revolted. A statue of Naram-Sin was found near Dohuk in northern Iraq. With much travel to parts of his far-flung empire, it must have been difficult for Naram-Sin to hold the empire together.

Naram-Sin waged war against Elam (Persia) in the east and the Semites in the west (Syria, Jordan, and Canaan). There is a stela of Naram-Sin, King of Sumer and Akkad, which shows him celebrating his victory over the people of the Zagros Mountains. Behistin in the Zagros Mountains con-tained three language groups, ancient Persian, Susian-Elamite, and Babylonian-Assyrian. These people that he is fighting and oppressing may be his distant relatives. This picture may commemorate either the king's victory or defeat. When ancient kings returned from warring expeditions, they had to say they were the victor, (whether they were or not), and brag about their exploits. If the other party in the conflict did not have stelae and architects and scribes available, no one would ever hear his side of the story. In this stela the king is shown climbing the mountain, while an enemy with a broken spear begs for mercy. The two stars of the goddess of war Ishtar are in the sky. Some of these mountain people in Mesopotamia were fierce fighters called the Guti. These Guti warriors maintained a far flung commercial activity. In 2680 BC Gudea of Lagash is reported as importing Lebanese cedar.

There is a possibility that Naram-Sin was the warring leader who razed Ebla in Syria. Ebla was on the trade route from the northern Euphrates to the Palestine coast. Ebla's ruins have tablets referring to the five towns mentioned in Genesis 14:2, Sodom, Gomorrah, Admah, Zeboiim, and Zoar. Sodom and Gomorrah may have been leveled in an earthquake of 2350 BC. A change in the course of the Euphrates is also recorded about 2400 BC, leading us to suspect that the Near East was a turbulent place at that period.

The Sumer-Akkad kingdom founded by Sargon and Naram-Sin lasted

Mesopotamian Dynasties

Dates given for early dynasties are merely to establish which reign followed which and are approximate as it is difficult to estimate reigns which took place before periods of instability. Dates set down here give preference to short periods of disorder. There may have been many rulers whose reigns were not recorded. For this reason I would like to emphasize the possibility of the following dates: Sargon I - 3100 BC, Naram-Sin - 3050 BC, and Hammurapi - 1947 BC.

2750-2334 BC Early Dynastic II, III
2630-2600 BC En-mebaragesi of Kish
2600-2425 BC First Dynasty of Ur
  (including Pu-abi, Mes-ane-pada)
2570-2342BC Kings of Lagash
  (including Ur-Nanshe, Uru-inim-gina)
2340-2316 BC Lugal-zagesi,
  King of Umma, Uruk, and Sumer
(2334-2154 BC) Akkadian Dynasty
  2334-2279 BC   Sargon I
Above date may be about 3100 BC
  2278-2270 BC   Rimush
  2269-2255 BC   Manishtushu
  2254-2218 BC   Naram-Sin
Above date may be about 3050 BC
  2217-2193 BC   Shar-kali-sharri
(2141-2118 BC) Rulers of Lagash
  2141-2122 BC   Gudea
  2121-2118 BC   Ur-Ningirsu
(2153-2113 BC) Rulers of Uruk
  2123-2113 BC   Utu-hegal
(2112-2004 BC) Third Dynasty of Ur
  2112-2095 BC   Ur-Nammu
  2094-2047 BC   Shulgi
  2046-2038 BC   Amar-Sin
  2037-2029 BC   Shu-Sin
  2028-2004 BC   Ibbi-Sin
(2017-1794 BC) First Dynasty of Isin
  2017-1985 BC   Ishbi-Irra
  1934-1924 BC   Lipit-Ishtar
(2025-1763 BC) Larsa Dynasty
  2025-2005 BC   Naplanum
  1834-1823 BC   Warad-Sin

  1822-1763 BC   Rim-Sin
(1894-1595 BC) First Dynasty of Babylon
Above date may be 2049-1750 BC
  1894-1881 BC   Sumuabum
Above date may be 2049-2036 BC
  1880-1845 BC   Sumulael
  1844-1831 BC   Savium
  1830-1813 BC   Apil-Sin
  1812-1793 BC   Sin-muballit
  1792-1750 BC   Hammurapi
Above date may be 1947-1905 BC
  1749-1712 BC   Samsuiluna
Above date may be 1904-1867 BC
  1711-1684 BC   Abi-eshuh
  1683-1647 BC   Ammiditana
  1646-1626 BC   Ammisaduqa
  1625-1595 BC   Samsuditana
Above date may be 1780-1750 BC
(1813-1741 BC)   Kings of Assyria
  1813-1781 BC   Shamshi-Adad I
  1780-1741 BC   Ishme-Dagan I
Period of unrest, which may reflect
date of 1628 Thera eruption.
Unknown dynasty of about 11 kings
(1521-1171 BC)   Kassite Dyn.-16 kings
(1170 -730 BC)   Elamite Dynasty
  1170-1153 BC   Merodash or
                  Marduk-shapik-zer
  1152-1147 BC   Ninurta-nadin-shumi
  1146-1123 BC   Nebuchadnezzar
(1363-609 BC)   Kings of Assyria
  883-859 BC   Ashurnasirpal II
  721-705 BC   Sargon II

two centuries. Naram-Sin's practice was to conquer cities and collect loot, but he allowed each separate conquered city to keep its own *patesi* or priest-king. After Naram-Sin, the Guti descended from their mountains and destroyed Sargon's civilization for a period of instability. The Book of Judges speaks of a period when everyone did as he pleased. The Sumerians and the Semites eventually rallied under Utu-hegal, King of Uruk. In the mid third millennium BC, Sumer, Akkad, and Susa (Elam or Persia) came under the control of Ibbi-Sin, King of Ur, forming a great civilization. At Ur they used kiln fired bricks which were an improvement over mud bricks, so they could build a great city. The date of this kingdom may be as late as 1800 BC. Accepted dates may be off by hundreds of years, as they often depend on undated periods of instability. Also, dates may be calculated from one known eclipse date of the moon, which should have been calculated from a much earlier eclipse.

Babylon. The next grave historical action was that the Persians under Ibbi-sin's control revolted, invaded Mesopotamia, took Ibbi-sin captive, and destroyed Ur. Ur was on the southern Euphrates near the Persian Gulf from 3500 to 1850 BC. When the Euphrates shifted its course, there was a loss of power for the rulers of Ur. Ur had controlled the Mesopotamia area, but the Elamites (from western Persia) invaded this area, and made their capital city Babylon, on another part of the river. This changed the nation's name to Babylonia.

With the fall of Ur, the *Amorites* (or people from the areas west of Babylon, such as Syria, Jordan, and Palestine) were also flooding into Babylon. We know this because their names were on tablets, and from other linguistic evidence.[9] Babylon became a polyglot community as in the Tower of Babel tale. Because of these incursions into Babylon by these Semitic speaking people known as Amorites (or Martu) King Shu-Sin about 2000 BC built a wall to keep out foreigners, known as the Muriq-Tidnim (which means *keep away the tribes*). These migrant people stabilized, reproduced, got plentiful, and eventually became the new leaders.

Babylon was seized by Hittite groups from Asia Minor. Still later (about 1500 BC) the Kassites from northeast of Babylon became rulers in the Tigris-Euphrates area. The Khaldeans migrated to Babylon between 1100 and 875 BC from the west. The Assyrian Sargon II, in the mid 700's BC built his citadel in the city of Khorsabad. The Assyrians fell in 600 BC and the Babylonians rose to power. Between 626 and 539 BC Nebuchadnezzar II was ruler. Babylonia was part of the Persian Empire from 539 BC to the time of Alexander the Great (331 BC).

3.3 Legends Associated with Sargon

<u>Greek Legends.</u> In the *Iliad* Homer (who lived about 900 BC) tells about a mythical character Agamemnon (meaning *Great King*). This may have been an actual historical person, the over-lord of Greece and Corinth, with his royal seat at Mycenae in the Peloponnesus. Just like Sargon, Agamemnon presides over feudal chiefs who do their own thing, but obey him because he is consecrated to his position by Zeus. Agamemnon, in this Trojan War legend, is the son of Atreus and brother of Menelaus, the King of Sparta, whose wife Helen has been abducted by Paris, son of Priam, King of Troy.

When Homer talks about Troy, he describes it as a city with a population of at least 50,000. When Schleiman excavated Troy it turned out to be a small place about 600 feet across. Did the legend originate in some other city and get attached to a city that would hold interest for a Greek audience? Homer is describing events that supposedly took place over five hundred years before. He is weaving together threads of different stories that he has heard from story tellers who have heard them from other story tellers. He is still trying to keep his facts straight. He has heard of a *great king* who ruled some place at some time, and he puts this king into his story. Perhaps Sargon of Agade (or Akkad) becomes Aga Memnon, or Minos, or associated with the Minotaur, a man with a body of a bull, who ate human flesh. Mesopotamian statues were frequently animals with human heads, or animal heads with human bodies. The bull and the lion were favorites. The name *Nimrod* has lion-tiger associations. There were winged sphinxes. If Sargon had paid a visit to Athens or even to a city in near-by Turkey, and had not been treated royally, he might have carried off some of their citizens as booty, and left a royal statue of himself to remind them of their obligations to him. The Minotaur legend says that Athens sent a yearly tribute of edible people to this people-eating Minotaur, until a Greek hero, Theseus killed him and freed them from their bondage.

Other tales have a more kindly Minos, as the ruler of Crete, and son of Zeus and Europa. Minos is a wise law giver and a lover of justice. He has a grandson who is also named Minos.

<u>Egyptian Ties.</u> When we turn to Egypt, we have the historian Herodotus declaring that Menes was the founder of Memphis, which he built on a piece of ground that he recovered from the Nile by altering the river's course. Menes introduced the worship of the gods into Egypt, as well as a more elegant style of living. This early dynasty, called the Thinite Dynasty, ruled from a place called Thini (similar to Sinai). The second king of this rule, Narmur, wore both the red crown of Northern Egypt and the white crown of

Southern Egypt. He was drawn in over-large proportions to designate his godly status. Pharaoh Menes may be Sargon, or a relative of Sargon left behind to encourage trade with Egypt. The Sphinx, which is of unexplained origins and Mesopotamian appearance, may be a rock carving commemorating Sargon or Naram-Sin. The Egyptian name for the Sphinx is the *Father of Terrors*. Menes and Narmur are two names that are mentioned by the Egyptians in connection with the unification of Egypt. Egyptian dates being arguable and names being spelled differently, it is possible that a leader Menes and a godly ruler Narmur were the force that caused Egypt to join together. These rulers may have had ties to Sargon the Great, or Aga Menes, and to his grandson Naram-Sin.

There were some people who didn't like Sargon, Naram-Sin and their ways. According to an early stela, the kings of Akkad were dreaded in Sinai and on Cyprus. The later Achaemenid rulers of Iran, Cyrus and his descendants (558-330 BC), take their name from an ancient claimed ancestor of Cyrus, *Achaemenes*, or *Akkad Menes*. Did Sargon in his pursuit of trade and prosperity for his empire leave his name, his gods, his writing, his culture, and his descendants in Egypt, Persia, and Greece?

Legends Associated With Sargon's Daughter. Another interesting Greek story is told of Iphigenia, daughter of Aga Memnon, who was to have been sacrificed to Artemis (the goddess Diana). This sacrifice would ensure that the Greek ships would have a favorable breeze, so they could sail off to war. At the moment of sacrifice, Artemis snatched Iphigenia away to Taurus, which are mountains in Asia at the head of the Euphrates. There Iphigenia served in the temple to Artemis (Diana), where she was obliged to sacrifice every Greek who came that way. When her Greek brother Orestes came, she could not bear to sacrifice him. The two of them took the image of Artemis and fled safely away.

This sacrifice of Aga Memnon's daughter recalls the story of Jephthah's daughter in Judges 11 and 12. Jephthah was, like Sargon, the son of a prostitute. The elders of Gilead invited him to go to war for them against their enemies, and promised they would make him their leader and judge. This was a very important battle for the son of a prostitute, and Jephthah vowed that if he won the battle, he would sacrifice whatever came to meet him on his return home. As it happened it was his only daughter who came out to greet him, and so he had to sacrifice her. She requested that he allow her a little time to mourn this sad event, so she went in the wilderness to mourn. For this reason young Jewish women of early times would make a retreat to commemorate the sacrifice of this maiden.

An interesting archaeological accompaniment to these myths is the unearthing of the royal tombs at Ur, which have artifacts displayed in the British Museum. The museum plaque describing them reads as follows:

These tombs are unparalleled in Mesopotamia. Their original significance remains debatable.

Woolley's original theory that they were indeed 'Royal Tombs' was natural, given the wealth of finds. There are many analogies from other cultures for human sacrifice in connection with royal burials. There is only one apparent reference to the practice, however, in all Mesopotamian literature.

An alternative, stressing the close connections that existed in Sumerian civilization between royalty and priesthood, is that the tombs belonged to officials, especially priestesses, of the Moon God of Ur. The practice of human sacrifice might then have been restricted to this particular cult, which would explain its absence elsewhere.

One might have hoped that personal titles written on cylinder seals found in the graves could resolve the issue, but they tend to be equivocal, possibly but not necessarily royal.

Other suggestions have been that the principal occupants of the tombs were priests and priestesses put to death after Sacred Marriage ceremonies, or that they were substitute kings and queens, killed to avert bad luck.

Sargon's daughter, Enheduanna, was set up as high priestess in the Ur temple to the moon god, and she is credited with writing hymns some of which are extant. She is depicted on a limestone plaque offering sacrifice to the god. As chief servant of the moon god of Mesopotamia, she may be associated with the moon goddess Diana of other nations. This may be recorded in the second part of her name, *duanna*.

If Sargon had a vow to sacrifice his daughter, he surely would have given her the most stylish funeral available. Early tablets refer to the bad luck that pursued Sargon and Naram-Sin towards the ends of their reigns, much as we referred to the 'bad luck' of the Kennedys in their notoriety. It isn't surprising that someone who had so much charisma and good fortune as a Sargon, should also have had his share of dramatic difficulties.

Looking back at these three similar stories which must have been told and retold in the early Near East, we can see a progression in ethical beliefs. Early Near East practice was to offer child sacrifice to God. Sargon offered his daughter to a god's service. Jephthah offered his daughter as a direct sacrifice to God. The goddess intervened to save Iphigenia from those humans who misunderstood the wishes of a goddess, even as God intervened to stay the hand of Abraham.

Arthur Legends. These stories traveled tremendous distances and bridged different times and cultures. In their retelling they would emphasize different aspects of truth as seen by the various cultures. We have said that government in early Sumer depended on a local king surrounded by his peers. The Greeks opposing Troy followed this same system. In English legends we have the example of King Arthur and his knights of the Round Table. The name *Arthur* comes from the Persian *Arthura* which comes from *Athura* which has a connection with *Ashura* which comes from *Ashur*.[8]

These *Arthur* words are also connected with the Hindu word for moral law. The Sargon-Arthur type of rule was not forgotten by kings that followed in history. Government by constitutional monarchy with a supreme king, a council of ministers, and a council of lesser kings was described in a text on government written by a statesman in the Indian Maurya Empire (322-200 BC). This document was called the *Arthashastra*.

The King Arthur legend may have traveled over the centuries with the Celts to Britain. Arthur, the son of Uthyr was supposedly the king of the Silures in the Sixth Century AD who married the Lady Guinevere and hosted the Knights of the Round Table. He reigned twelve years in peace, then conquered Denmark, Norway, and France; slew giants in Spain; visited Rome; and then hurried home because of the faithlessness of his wife and his nephew Modred. He was buried on the isle of Avalon. Perhaps Arthur was a Celtic chief, a leader of the Cymry of Cumbria, a group in England who migrated there from the orient. Their religion, associated with the Druids, is said to have Hindu, Persian, and Egyptian origins. Elements of Arthur's story may be from the Sargon legends.

Other Legends. The *Gilgamesh Epic* from the Sumerian city of Uruk was composed before 2000 BC. Gilgamesh, the powerful king who built Uruk, was arrogant, oppressive, and philandering. The people complained to the gods, and the gods chose a champion <u>hairy</u> hunter named Enkidu, a Sumerian wild man, to give Gilgamesh a come-uppance. The gods' plan failed as the two heroes became friends. The hairy hunter, Enkidu, reminds us of the biblical hairy hunter, Esau.

The goddess Ishtar fell in love with Gilgamesh, but he spurned her. She got the high god Anu to send a bull to trample the city. Enkidu killed it, but unfortunately got killed in the process. Gilgamesh feared for his life and left for safer parts, in a search for *Utnapishtim*, the Sumerian version of Noah. Gilgamesh is pictured in Sumerian art between two lions. There is a seal from the Indus civilization that shows a god or hero grappling with two tigers. The Indus legend may have come first in an oral version and then been written down later by the Sumerians.

Flood legends were plentiful. The *Gilgamesh Epic* character called Utnapishtim (meaning *he-found-life*) survived the flood like the biblical Noah. There is an Akkadian flood story featuring the name *Atrahasis* (meaning *extra wise*) dated 1900 BC. Atrahasis is given seven days warning of the flood. Another Sumerian flood story comes from Nippur 1700 BC and the hero is *Ziusudra* (*long life*). The Han Dynasty scholar Wang Chin is a Chinese Noah. His family fled to a mountain for safety.

A Sumerian legend on a different topic is that of Etana, a king who is desirous for an heir, as Abraham also longed for an heir. This may be another shared myth and is one of the earliest fables to be written down. Its main characters are an eagle and a snake. In order to procure the plant of birth, Etana takes a ride on the eagle's back as he tries to reach heaven.

3.4 Other Cultural Contributions

Gifts from early Babylon are division of day and night into twelve hours each, division of the year into twelve months, and division of the week into seven days. The days were named after the planets, and astrologers collected data on heavenly occurrences. There was an effective system of weights and measures, as is necessary for trading purposes. Sargon established workable governmental administration, encouraged trade, and built irrigation systems. Sumer may be the earth's first known nation, and perhaps have set down the first writing and compiled the first laws.

Sumer furnished the earliest documents referring to international law and treaties and made the earliest attempts to settle disputes by arbitration. Laws were needed when Amorite and Elamite populations descended into Mesopotamia. Early law codes were one in Lagash by Uruka-gina (2351-2342 BC), one in the Akkadian city of Eshnunna by Ur-Nammu (2112-2095 BC), and one in Sumerian by Lipit-Ishtar of Isin (1934-1924 BC). (Dates given here may be several centuries off.) These codes bear resemblances to the Covenant Code of Exodus 21-23.

When writing abilities were better perfected, the laws were further worked on by the Amorite leader Hammurapi. (Debatable date is 1792-1750 BC.) The Hammurapi Code revised the earlier Akkadian and Sumerian regulations. It contained divorce regulations. The main principle of the code was that "the strong shall not injure the weak." There is a stela of Hammurapi which shows this king adoring Marduk, the Babylonian sun god, who is giving him a copy of the laws.

3.5 The Egyptian Civilization

The word *Egypt* comes from an ancient name for Memphis, which meant the *House of Ptah's Spirit* or *Hikuptah*, which was translated by the Greeks as *Aigyptos* which we have Anglicized to *Egypt*.[10] Our language changes, and our earth also undergoes changes. The Nile region had gradually changed from an impenetrable jungle to a green area along a fairly accessible river. **City Gods.** Tentative beginnings of the Egyptian civilization were about 10,000 BC due to good climate and plentiful vegetation. At the dawn of civilization Egypt was slow to awake. The people along the river had their own settlements. They had fairly friendly relationships with other towns along the stretch of river and boats to travel back and forth. From the southern reaches of the Nile where there was still vegetation and hunting grounds, came tales of animal faced gods and goddesses that would help them in their hunting. Reverence for God's power was represented by the crocodile. The most important city in southern Egypt was Edfu. The nobles of Edfu were believed to be descendants of the falcon god Horus. The villages in northern Egypt had other gods. They worshiped God's power in the sun and the wind. They told stories of the creation of the earth. When those who ranged the area between India and Egypt rested from their travels in the Nile delta area, they told their tales of suffering sons, and murderous brothers, and these stories became interwoven with Egyptian tales, giving rise to legends of gentle Isis and the beloved Osiris.

As one Egyptian city gained in importance over the others, the particular god of that city would become the head god of the country. The priests who served that god would become a powerful political group. Thus, as centuries passed, gods went in and out of favor. Names of gods changed. Gods exchanged characteristics. The common people worshiped the local gods and lived their everyday lives with their beliefs in something that guided the whole process. Priests and rulers kept control of each other and the population by professing to knowledge about the official god.

Among the official gods were Ra (Re), the sun god, the supreme god of the Old Kingdom, and Amun (Amen, Amon) of Thebes, the hidden god, the supreme god of the later dated New Kingdom. The sun god-aspects were given different names according to the time of day– Kheper when rising, Ra at midday, and Atum (Atem, Temu) when setting in the west. Ra was more often associated with the sun, and Amun, although incorporating the power of the sun, was more of a creator and compassionate father.

At Memphis on the west bank of the Nile between the pyramids of Giza and Sakkara, the local god Ptah was early named supreme. His consort was Sekhmet, the Great Lady, and their son was Nefertem. Across the Nile and a few miles to the north at Heliopolis (or On) was the territory of the sun god Ra. The creation of the world supposedly took place at Hermopolis in north central Egypt near the present city of Minia. Here, the primeval hill rose out of the waste of water, Nun. At Thebes in mid-Egypt Amun was lord and Mut was his lady. Amun had begun as an ithyphallic fertility god of the nearby village of Koptos. Gods change, as the ideas of those worshiping change.

In the times of the Middle Kingdom, Senwosret I of the Twelfth Dynasty combined Amun and Ra together as Amun-Ra. This worship was interrupted in New Kingdom times by Akhenaten I of the Eighteenth Dynasty who named the all-powerful god of solar energy as *Aten*. Horemheb of the Nineteenth Dynasty returned his country to Amun-Ra and multi-god recognition. The local priests of the temples had to shift back and forth in their god-allegiances to conform with the beliefs of the ruling pharaohs. The chief priests were open to political appointments and to political downfall.

The Nile usually flooded its banks at the proper time, and the farmer planted his crops. Day followed day, and year followed year, and there was no need to attempt control of one's neighbor. Mother Nile was good to all, and if the flood didn't come, they all knew they would all starve together. This fairly comfortable life style along the Nile, placed Egypt a bit late on the cultural ladder. Nomad raiders had an easy take over which changed this slow pace. 5000 BC was the pre-dynastic period in Egypt. Around 4000 BC society became more stable and there was pictorial communication.

Date Keeping. Before writing, record keeping was sketchy, and date keeping was necessarily haphazard. Take, for instance, date-keeping in Egypt. It is difficult to date intermediate periods of turmoil. Some chronologists take 1850 BC for the beginning of the New Kingdom in Egypt, but some would place the New Kingdom at 1570 BC. Disputed dates for the beginning of the Hittite Empire are 1740 BC or 1590 BC. It is better to state dates approximately to keep the sequence of reigns in proper order. We have some Egyptian kingly reign sequences thanks to the Egyptian historian Manetho of the third century BC, who did research on the subject and left us his information. Other inexactitudes of time enter in, as when early people express a long period of time using the number of 40 years, as it covered a normal life time.

Dates between Egypt and Mesopotamia do not jibe precisely. At some point in Egypt's idyllic history, a foreign element saw an opportunity for gain. An early dynasty in Egypt is headed up by a man named Narmur or Menes or Aha. Kings had several different names, because if someone knew your real name, he could acquire magical control over you. Your public name that you put on monuments was not your secret real name. For instance, Moses found out the name of God, by asking, so people knew that Moses had a measure of control or influence over God. There is the legend that the goddess Isis tricked the sun god Ra into telling his name. Thus Isis was an honored goddess in Egypt for a long time. But the gentle Isis and Osiris were replaced with Ra, or power, when the need arose to do battle.

Foreign Influences. Who was this Narmur? Was he an Egyptian or a foreigner? Where did he come from? The names of the first Egyptian rulers are like the names of those in Mesopotamia. *Menes* is similar to *Mennon*. *Narmur* is similar to *Naram*. *Aha* is similar to *Akka*. We have a celebrated ruler in Mesopotamia called Naram of Sin (the moon god), and we also find that pre-dynastic Egypt honors a ruler called Narm. Keep in mind that their spelling was not like our spelling, they didn't use vowels, and their writing was in haphazard directions. There also may be a connection with the biblical Nimrod. The Bible mentions Nimrod as the first great leader who led his people off to conquer. Early heroes had special battle names, and they also had titles related to their favorite god, such as *favorite son of Baal*. Writing was almost non-existent and usually without vowel sounds, written from left to right or vice versa, or upwards or downwards. From what written remains we have, we can only pick a few consonants, and say that the biblical Nimrod had a name that contained N, M, R, and D.

Perhaps a foreign leader marched a group of men around, and pressured all the towns along the Nile to agree that he was the chief with whom they would trade. When he was absent due to problems in his home kingdom, they went back to doing their own thing and worshiping their own local gods, yet continuing to have one special king of Upper and Lower Egypt. If they saw that Narmur's god was good to him and made him powerful, they doubtless would say a few prayers in that direction, and include that god in their worship. Also, the Sumerian ruler Naram-Sin had made a god of himself! His representations are twice the size of a normal human. This idea is continued in Egypt. We have Egyptian palette pictures of an oversize King Narmur of Egypt. He conquered Northern Egypt and wore that crown. He is also depicted wearing the Southern Egyptian crown, and surveying dead Northerners. These portrayals are very similar to Sumerian monuments. They belong to the period of foreign conquest. Narmur of Egypt could easily be Naram-Sin of Sumer!

The Sphinx. The assarion coin worth a penny or a farthing was not too valuable in the time of Christ as Assyria was no longer an important country. Assarion coinage was issued when Assyria was dominant and was valuable then, but when Assyria lost power, this coinage became worth little. When it was valuable, it was distinguished by its tiger or sphinx representation. The sphinx hearkens back to the worship of Ishtar and the tiger associated with the name of Nimrod. This all brings to mind a possible origin for the sphinx of Egypt. The Sumerians may have conquered Egypt for trade purposes. A prince of Sumer may have united the villages along the Nile, under his banner, and bound them to Sumer through trade. He possibly brought along his culture, writing, stelae, house and pottery designs, religious beliefs, and coercive weaponry. Before this, each group of Egyptians had been content to dwell in their own town, to quietly do their own thing, and to worship their own special god. But the Sumerian prince "opened up" Egypt, and after awhile, the enlightened Egyptians decided to outdo their subduers. Those with a drive to freedom and power, threw off the yoke of the foreigner, and took over the title *Uniter of Egypt*. The expelled had to leave behind the great sphinx carved out of rock, as a symbol of Sumerian benevolence. If there were any degrading Sumerian inscriptions on the Sphinx, they were chiseled away, and replaced with proper Egyptian titles. There was an Assyrian type beard, a symbol of authority, which was hacked off. The sphinx's beard is located today in the British museum. It was found buried in the sand under the Sphinx's chin.

A foreign element had entered Egypt, as much later, Commodore Perry of the United States opened up Japan. A warlike power monger from Sumer could easily have intimidated those who lived near the Nile Delta. A symbol that was important in Mesopotamia was that of the winged tiger with a human head. Mesopotamian rulers sat on thrones decorated with such figures. If a Mesopotamian despot wanted to emphasize that he had control in Egypt, he could have had a giant animal with a human face carved in the rock near the subject city. The sphinx statue near present day Cairo is 187 feet long and 66 feet high. Winged sphinxes (kerubim or seraphim) can be representations of the goddess Astar or guardian angels. From this subjugated and impressed trading center the invading soldiers could have floated down the Nile rattling their swords threateningly, and thereby changed the religious perspective of many in that river valley. The Egyptians were not slow. They quickly learned the raiders techniques and formed their own dynasties. They improved their writing abilities. They worshiped the powerful gods. It was easy for a united Egypt to oust threatening invaders.

Pyramid Building. The head of the giant Sphinx at Giza was claimed by some later nationalistic Egyptians to have been built by King Khafre of the Fourth Dynasty. However, it is thought that the pyramids were built after the Sphinx. During the Third dynasty, about 2700 BC, the construction of the pyramids began. Imhotep constructed the Step Pyramid at Sakkara for Pharaoh Zoser. Sekhemkhet is remembered by a Step Pyramid. Khaba has the Layer Pyramid at Zawiyet el Aryan (between Giza and Abu Sin). Nebka has the Unfinished Pyramid. Huni, a pharaoh of the Third Dynasty, was builder of the first true pyramid at Meidum. Senefru has the Bent Pyramid and the Northern Pyramid at Dashur. This Third Dynasty pharaoh, Senefru, secured the throne by his marriage to a woman described as Daughter of

God, Hetep-Heres, the daughter of Huni.

The Fourth dynasty (about 2600-2400 BC) was a prosperous era with great control, and the large pyramids were built. Khufu (Cheops) built the Great Pyramid at Giza about 2580 BC. The third largest pyramid was built by Mycerinus about 2540 BC. Two thousand years later the historian Herodotus calls Pharaoh Mycerinus "pious and just, not like his predecessors," leaving us to wonder about the previous builders who may have oppressed their workers or their slaves. This pyramid of Mycerinus had an underground connection to a valley temple. Food offerings to the dead at the false door of Egyptian tombs were collected by priests. This priestly subterfuge furthered the cult of the dead (and helped to feed the priests). These actions helped to maintain the belief in the pharaoh's spirit. If the mummy were disturbed, the spirit could supposedly retreat to a statue of that person, so statue likenesses of nobility were placed near tombs. It was believed that the pharaoh was the form or body in which the god chose to dwell. When the pharaoh died, the god would take up residence in the pharaoh's first born son.

When we look at the dynasties in Egypt, we see a long list of strange, hard-to-pronounce names. These rulers' reigns covered thousands of years. Some of them were strong rulers and subjugated surrounding countries. Others were beset with internal problems. Some were non-Egyptians. At times conquering foreigners ruled Egypt from cities in the Nile Delta area. The amazing thing is that there were so many centuries of orderly rule with little military oppression. The Egyptians are calm and easy-going like the flowing of their river. Even in today's often violent world, they are trusting and friendly. The ancient priesthood and the natural abundance of the Nile Valley helped to keep the people domesticated like sheep with their shepherd pharaoh. The word *pharaoh* did not mean *king*, but meant *great house* (per-o) or *protected place*. Egypt was the pharaoh's sheep fold.

The Old Kingdom Dynasties Four, Five, and Six honored Sun God Ra. Smaller pyramids came with the Fifth dynasty (about 2400-2300 BC), and we assume there was less authoritative control, or times were harder, or the pharaohs were dying off at a younger age with less time to have grand tombs built. Our presidents often rule longer than did the Egyptian pharaohs. With the Seventh to Tenth Dynasties there was considerable instability. The rulers feared that robbers would defile the tombs. Thus they built their tombs further south.

With the Eleventh Dynasty, there is the mortuary temple of Montuhotpe I (about 2050 BC) at Thebes. As hundreds of years pass, there are changes in tombsites, capitals, customs, gods, and language. For instance, the endings of dignitaries' names such as Im<u>hotep</u>, Montu<u>hotpe</u>, and Amen<u>ophis</u> change from *hotep* to *hotpe* to *ophis*.

The Twelfth Dynasty was Nubian, and its first ruler was Amenemhet I (about 1990 BC). His successor, Senwosret I (about 1971-1925 BC), built a temple to Amun, the hidden one, and also a shrine to Montu, the hawk-headed war god. He made Thebes the capital city.[11] There was a period of weakness between the Twelfth and Eighteenth dynasties.

Sobekhotpe II of the Thirteenth Dynasty temporarily restored order about 1740 BC. After the so-called Shepherd Kings of Sobekhotpe III, Neferhotpe I, Si-Hathor, and Sobekhotpe IV, disorder ruled again.[12]

The Hyksos. About 1670 BC Egypt was invaded by the Hyksos (which means *foreign rulers*), a west-Semitic speaking people. These Amorite tribes entered Egypt and ruled from Avaris in the Delta as the Fifteenth Dynasty.[13] The Amoritic kingdoms and the Hyksos had been disturbed by two new groups out of Turkey. One group was the Hittites under a leader called Mursilis. He entered Babylon and overcame the Hammurapi Dynasty. Hurrians, with a capital called Mitanni, were a second agitating group.

Humankind kept reproducing and being inventive, and in the Near East area, someone processed iron. The Hittites from Turkey shared this knowledge with the Hyksos who went to Egypt and left this invention with the Egyptians. Iron made more effective weapons, and those who were out to conquer and gain land for themselves, could use iron-tipped weapons to quickly subdue others. Exodus relates one problem with iron chariots and heavy armor– they don't float.

About 1570 BC Seqenenre and his sons Kamose and Ahmose expelled the Hyksos and Canaanite overlords who had been there more than one hundred years. The new rulers were the Thutmosids, Ahmose the Liberator and his son Amenophis I. They ruled at Thebes.[14] The tomb of one of Ahmose's soldiers contains an account of this victory which changed the Near East power set-up. North Syria was dominated by Aleppo (the state of Yamkhad), the Orontes Basin was under Qatanum, and the upper Jordan Valley, of Galilee and Palestine, was under Hazor. All these states had a common origin and spoke dialect Amoritic. Under the Eighteenth Dynasty (about 1570-1350 BC) Egypt became the dominant power of the Near East.

Temple Builders. Thutmose I (about 1500 BC) was the first pharaoh buried in the Valley of Kings across the Nile from Thebes. He built the 3rd, 4th, and 5th pylons (or entrance gateways to inner temples) at the Thebes shrines of Karnak and Luxor. Thutmose III built the 6th and 7th pylons. Queen Hatshepsut built two obelisks and the eighth pylon besides having a giant burial temple constructed across the Nile. Thutmose IV (about 1400 BC) fulfilled prophecies about being a messianic ruler when he cleared the sand off the half-buried Sphinx (about the time Adoni-zedek was King of Jerusalem as in the story of Joshua 10). Thutmose's son, Amenophis III, the husband of Queen Tiy (about 1375 BC), was a great builder one hundred years earlier than Rameses the Great. Was he the builder for whom the Hebrews slaved? The famous statue of "Memnon" (the Greeks gave this statue a Greek name) is really Amenophis III. Amenophis III built a temple to the god Thoth at Hermopolis and to Khnum at Elephantine. He lined an avenue at Thebes with sphinxes and constructed the main entrance pylon. He was a prolific stela writer.[15] In 1385 BC Amenophis IV was born, the *second* son of Queen Tiy. Did the death of the first born son of Amenophis III, lead to the story of the pre-exodus plague which killed the first born?

Akhenaten (Amenophis IV) was the creator of the sun temple and also proposed the monotheistic sun god religion. Horemheb returned his people to the multi-god representations and destroyed the sun temple, hiding its stones in the 9th and 10th pylons. Pylons built in 1340-1330 BC by Horemheb and in 1295 BC by Rameses II were filled with the refuse of the monotheistic constructions of Amenophis IV.[16] If rulers didn't like the politics or religion of their predecessors, they destroyed the pertaining masonry and stelae. These gigantic temples to the gods of Egypt are among the wonders of the world. Thebes remains a dramatic proclamation of our faith origins, in spite of its being sacked by the Assyrian Ashurbanipal in 663 BC and by the Persians under Artaxerxes III in 343 BC.

In times of strong pharaohs, it was necessary to have a good foreign policy. Native rulers in Palestine took a personal oath to serve Pharaoh. Some of their relatives were sent to the Egyptian capital at Thebes and received an education in partial confinement. When the native ruler died, the Egyptianized relative was sent home to rule. Prisoners of war were sent as servants to the temples. So many foreigners came to Egypt for one reason or another, that alien deities had shrines in the temples, such as the Canaanite goddesses of fertility, Anat and Kadesha. At Memphis there was a temple to Baal and Astarte. Some Egyptians took to these representations in their needs, and some of these foreign god myths were incorporated into tomb and temple hieroglyphics.

3.6 Egyptian Stories - Tale of Sinuhe

With the ability to write, Egyptian scribes composed works about the same time as the pyramids were constructed. Ipuwer in *Admonitions* foresaw a bright future with the advent of a Messiah. Nefer-rohu told of a gloomy future in his writing to King Senefru. He also wrote *Dialogue With His Soul*

Dynasties in Egypt

	12,000-6,000 BC	Late Paleolithic rule
	6000-3100 BC	Pre-dynastic, city states
Old Kingdom	3100-2980 BC	1st Dynasty (Thinite) Menes, Narmur
	2980-2890 BC	2nd Dynasty (Thinite in north), unknown in south
	2890-2670 BC	3rd Dynasty (Memphite) Zoser, Sekhemkhet, Serus, Khaba, Nebka, Huni, Senefru, step pyramid at Sakkara
	2670-2490 BC	4th Dynasty (Memphite) Cheops or Khufu, Dedefre or Radjedea, Chephren or Khafre, Menkure, Mycerinus, Shefsefka, 3 great pyramids at Giza
	2490-2365 BC	5th Dynasty (Memphite) Userkaf, Sahure, Nefererkare, Sheperskare, Neferefre, Niuserre, Menkanher, Djedkare, Unis
	2365-2200 BC	6th Dynasty (Memphite) Teti, Pepi I, Userkare, Merenre I, Pepi II, Merenre II, Nitocris
Middle Kingdom	2200-2175 BC	7th, 8th Dynasties (Memphite) **Instability**
	2175-2140 BC	9th,10th Dynasties (Heracleopolite) Kheti-Achthoes
	2140-2000 BC	11th Dynasty (Theban) Sehertowy Antef I, Wahankh Antef II, Nakht-neb-tep-nefer Antef III, Nebhepetre Montuhotpe I, Se'ankhibtowy Montuhotpe II, Nebtowyre Montuhotpe III
	2000-1788 BC	12th Dynasty (Theban) (Nubian from Aswan) Amenemhet I, Senwosret I, Amenemhet II, Senwosret II, III, Amenemhet III, IV, Princess Sobekkare Sobekneferu
	1788-1567 BC	13th-17th Dynasties(Hyksos=*foreign rulers*)**Instability** Sobekhotpe I, Sekhemkare, Sobekhotpe II,III, Neferhotpe I, Sihathor, Sobekhotpe IV, V, Ya'ib, Aya, Meribre Sheshy, Bnon, Merwoserre Ya'qob-el, Seuserenre Khayan, Aqnenre Apopi, Asehre Khamudi
New Kingdom	1567-1348 BC	18th Dynasty (Diospolite) Senakhtenre Tao I, II, Kamose, Ahmose, Amenophis I, Thutmose I, II, Hatshepsut, Thutmose III, Amenophis II, Thutmose IV, Amenophis III, Akhenaten, Smenkhkare, Tutankhamen, Ay
	1348-1198 BC	19th Dynasty(Diospolite) Horemheb, Rameses I, Seti I, Rameses II, Merneptah, Seti II, Siptak
	1198-1085 BC	20th Dynasty (Diospolite) Setnacht, Rameses III, Rameses IV-XII
	1085-945 BC	21st Dynasty (Tanite)
	945-730 BC	22nd (Libyan-Bubastite) Shishak I, Osorkon I, II
	730-525 BC	23rd-26th Dynasties (Saite, Ethiopian)
	525-332 BC	27th-30th Dynasties (Persian rulers)
	332-31 BC	Alexander, Cleopatra, Ptolemaic Period
	31BC-395 AD	Roman Period (late 2nd century-641 AD, Coptic)

Dates given for early dynasties may be off by two hundred years, but they give an idea of the time sequence involved. Periods of instability also have questionable dates.

by *The Man Weary of Life* in which he found no consolation except in death. Other popular works were *An Instruction of Amenemhet I* and *Satire on The Trades*. The book that every knowledgeable Egyptian had to read was *The Tale of Sinuhe.*

An approximate date for Sinuhe is 2300 BC, after the pyramids were built. The date for Sinuhe could be earlier than 2300 BC as Egyptians were writing fairly skillfully in 3400 BC, and keeping a type of calendar in 4241 BC. On the other hand, the date could be later. The pharaoh's names in the earliest copies of the story are pharaohs of about 2000 BC, but a later scribe may have updated the names to reflect his contemporary political reality.

The content of *Sinuhe* is as follows. Sinuhe overheard a secret, was filled with dismay, and fled from the capital city of the land of Egypt. Amenemhet, the old king, dies, perhaps by conspiracy, and Sinuhe might know who killed him. The younger partner on the throne was Senwosret who was momentarily returning from a military campaign in Libya. Amenemhet must have been an unpredictable old codger, for he was ''feared like Sekhmet in the year of the plague.'' Sekhmet was the goddess of battle and the consort of Ptah. She was shown as a woman with a lion's head.

In fleeing, Sinuhe met a man who was afraid of him. This is similar to Moses, who was questioned by a fellow tribesman, ''Will you kill me as you killed the Egyptian?''

Sinuhe's flight takes him across the water of a small lake, where he wades or swims across the southern end. He spends the day in the open fields, and then is ferried across the Nile in a barge, without a rudder, with the help of the western breeze. He passes by the quarries of Gebel Ahmar near Heliopolis or On, and sneaks past The Wall of The Prince, built as a protection against Asiatics and Sand-farers. On one of the delta islands, Kem-wer, he falls in with friendly Bedouins, who give him refreshment.

He set forth for Byblos, and went even further east to Qedem (or Kedme which means *east*). There the Prince of Upper Retenu, Enshi, son of Amu, took him in, married him to his daughter, and gave him a tract of land, rich in fruits, wheat, and barley. *Enshi* or *ensi* may be a title for the local governor. These people lived in encampments, and had herds of cattle, and flocks of sheep and goats. This, too, has similarities to Moses who married the daughter of a chieftain. The Prince made Sinuhe a captain in his tribe, but in spite of all this kindness, Sinuhe was homesick for Egypt.

He returned to Egypt by way of the land of the Philistines. (Of course, in 2000 BC, there were no Philistines on the coast of Palestine.) He reached the frontier of Egypt at the garrison of Wawet-Hor on the Nile. (*Wawet-Hor* means *The Ways of Horus*, Horus being a major god of Egypt. *Mount Hor* means the *Mountain of the God Horus* or simply the *Mountain of God.*) The pharaoh sent ships to escort Sinuhe to the court at Ethet-Toui (a place name associated with the pyramids of Amenemhet I and Senwosret I. The pharaoh welcomed Sinuhe back, and gave him magnificent living quarters.

3.7 Early God Stories

The early god legends developed from stories about ancestors who had behaved in a noble or godly manner. In the upper Jordan valley at a site called Eynan, a Natufian chieftain is buried with his head facing Mount Hermon. In this tomb lies a skeleton with severed legs placed near the body. This can lead to gruesome thoughts about early Natufians. Either it was a common thing to dismember someone when you buried them, or it was such an uncommon thing, that it was remembered in folk lore. The Natufians were a Caucasian group that came from the north. They both harvested crops, and did hunting. It was natural for them to cut animals apart, and they had effective weapons to do this. The tombsite dates about 8000 BC.

The Natufians also had phallus shaped pendants made of obsidian obtained from Lake Van. They may have traded with people from the Lake Van region, or there may have been a direct religious or tribal connection with phallus paintings on cave walls in India. The religious group in India may have had traders, herders, or relatives who traveled to Lake Van. From Lake Van they may have migrated to the Natufian site in the Jordan Valley. From the Jordan, some of their members may have boated to the Cyprus town of Khirokitia and left pendants dated to 6500 BC. There was also phallic-connected worship in Egypt.

There are other ancient stories that tell of dismemberment and similar catastrophes. When his woman is raped, a member of the tribe of Benjamin cuts her dead body up and sends the pieces to his fellow tribesmen (Judges 20). One early story that tells of a fight between brothers which specifies their differing trades, is the story of Cain, the farmer, and Abel, the herder.

Another story that speaks of dismemberment is the Egyptian tale of the goddess Isis. This legend tells us that two gods produce four offspring– Isis, Osiris, Set, and Nephys. Isis and Osiris become a married pair and likewise Set and Nephys. Unfortunately, Set kills Osiris, hacks his body into many parts, and hides them in various places. Isis still loves Set and forgives him because he is her brother. She goes out hunting all over for the body parts of her husband, and her sister Nephys helps. One of the places which she searched was the area of Byblos, which is in the area of the tombsite mentioned above. In some myths, Osiris is said to have died in Byblos. Isis was known for her gentleness and ability to heal. She gathered the parts together, Osiris was resurrected, and Isis became pregnant from this pieced-together husband. She produced a child, Horus, represented in Egyptian art with the head of a falcon. This child born after his father's death, was the one who had the duty of avenging his father by pursuing his wicked uncle Set. Both Isis and Osiris became early god figures. Horus, in his turn, is taken under many different names into the religious beliefs of other nations.

3.8 The Soul and The Community

In order for us to find remains of early pre-humans and early humans, they must have been pretty numerous. Small pre-humans mammals may have been here 75 million years ago competing with the vanishing dinosaurs. Soon early human types populated the globe. They walked upright and spread all over. They had brains that were intelligent enough to use tools to acquire their food. They had many wonderful physical capabilities. They had to use their strength and wits to survive on earth with large, extraordinary mammals. The Chinese have legends of great dragons that destroyed many people. Grandmothers kept little children in line by telling them to be good or the world spirits would let the monsters come and eat them.

The spiritual side of humanity is correlated with civilization. The ability for reflective thought, the awareness of the needs of others, and the willingness to cooperate despite diversity, are all aspects of spirituality that have existed to some degree from the beginning of humankind. These aspects of spirituality have contributed to the civility of peoples and the growth of civiilization.

Little mother and father birds have enough where-with-all to take care of the needs of little birds. Gorillas are tender with their babies. Certainly the early bi-peds could take care of their young. When dogs can enjoy scenery and give companionship, should we think less of our early ancestors than of dogs? The first humans may not have understood the future or the past too well, but they could make choices, and must have been inwardly appreciative of their immediate and chosen blessings. Can we visualize people with physiques, drives, feelings, and reasoning abilities like ours in environments that presented quite different challenges than those to which we are accustomed?

From archaeological remains at cave sites and from graves, we can see that the early human believed in the spiritual, and leaned on the spiritual. We find evidence for evolution of the spiritual in our own living genes. In the genetically programmed growth of the child of today, it is possible to observe similarities to the development and needs of the early human. The infant crawls, then rises to her feet and stands and walks. She learns to talk.

She learns about herself. She learns to share with others. There is an element of choice and a directing will. We lay out possibilities of behavior before the child, and we tell her that she can choose her path. We point out that she is responsible for her actions, that screaming is a waste of time and energy, and that there is a world waiting for her footsteps. With this physical process in both the individual and human evolution, hopefully there are corresponding spiritual possibilities. Today the spirit that made the earth, is still with the earth, guiding it, and still with the individual human, guiding her, but giving her the freedom to enhance her own formation.

It seems that in the development of our souls, we have not changed very much from our ancestors who lived 10,000 or even 20,000 years back. We still *compete* with others for our livelihood. We fight as if fighting were the accepted mode of behavior. "...history has followed a number of natural laws. One is the biological law that once a species has evolved, it will not change into another species for a long time. That is why the biological capacities of man are geared to the life of a hunter, and hence why the most satisfactory civilizations are those that permit the full expression of those capacities."[17] We will have to keep playing football games and cops and robbers to please the warrior palette within.

What will happen in our world of today, if we cannot contain our biological instincts? When our sexual urges prompt us to over populate the earth and when warlike leaders can aim weapons that destroy total populations, we must fear for the destiny of the human race. We may go the way of the dinosaur and the mastodon. Our physical capabilities have outpaced our spiritual controls. Our weapons and war machines are used thoughtlessly in slaughter. "When man's culture outgrows the fixed dimensions of the earth, a moment of human as well as physical climax faces man."[18] Perhaps we need to clearly see the disruption before we can change direction and grow spiritually. If we achieve spiritual control, our destiny may be beyond the earth.

When people are nourished with care and understanding, they are more capable of controlling physical fears of bodily harm and are freed to help in the positive evolvement of the earth. The human can choose to be kind. Is it safe to be kind? Those who stood quietly while others threw stones at them, rapidly died out. It seems that evolution of the human being encouraged the growth of competitiveness and egocentric fighting for survival. However, this competitive tendency was countered by the community urge– in order to survive one needed the help of others. To reproduce, one needed another. Those who survived were not just competitive; they also had the quality of being able to cooperate. The early human seems to have had the same ability to love and to harm as humans do today. She had the same opportunities to see God's presence in nature and in her fellow humans. It is in the ability to cooperate that humankind now needs to excel.

We are spiritual beings under God's care. If we believe a vast purpose created and cares for this creation, we must believe in our spiritual component, our God-instilled, God-directed energy. Human kind (and animals, too), are not just physical quantities. They can possess characteristics, such as empathy and loyalty. They can be afraid. They have spiritual components. These components may be attached to their bodies, as a result of chemical and physical reactions which are difficult to understand. As the human has walked across the earth, how her spiritual part behaved, had a direct influence on how her body evolved, and vice versa. Our spiritual imaging still influences our bodily activities.

We have this unique quality called a soul. It arose from somewhere and is with each of us today. Compassion and understanding the joys or sorrows of others, are marks of this soul-entity. We speak of *great souls* as if some souls were larger and some, smaller. Some physical surroundings may produce greater souls with encouragement of selection of the fittest. There is the possibility that as in selection of species, one dominant soul type may produce a genetically viable line, while another varying line may fade away like the Neanderthals. Those with peaceful souls may be the remnant that will inherit the earth, while those who are most contentious may gradually die off. We all have this ability to use our spiritual component or soul to choose our path. We can choose to empathize with the diversity of others. We can help guide each other towards fulfillment.

One's soul, one's reflective self, can also descend to the depths of despair, but God will not leave us there. She will not let that holy part of us suffer corruption. The Psalmist (16:10) affirms that "God will not leave my soul in hell!" We can assist each others' souls out of the pit.

The development of love and responsibility happens best in civilization with groups of people. The lone individual can meditate on the God he finds in nature. The small family member in the wilderness does not have to figure out how to get along with the masses. He doesn't really have to be polite to anyone. He can boss his wife around (or vice versa) and no one will object. Certain capabilities were necessary for pre-civilization souls as the bodies they inhabited roamed through pleasant woods. When people gathered in towns and cities so that the bodies these souls inhabited were packed closely together, were their souls affected? A soul in the fairly solitary wilderness could satisfy her needs and her greeds without too much trouble. A soul in a packed city may have had trouble satisfying her needs, and also had to consider whether the satisfaction of her needs or greeds was depriving others. What does a soul look like when it has been searching the town for days with no food in its stomach? What does a soul look like when it shares its bread with a starving person?

When we live close to others, they become concerned with our behavior, even against their will. Drunkards and drug takers become a public problem. We may not want to associate with them, but they must be helped. We are offended by seeing their prone bodies lying in the gutter. We call them *lost souls*, and we worry about the collective *soul* of America as so many degenerate into debauchery.

When humankind gathered in groups and built cities, all these souls were brought into closer proximity. It was more commonplace to communicate beliefs, commonalities, and differences to each other. When there is communication with another, the mind can develop. Likewise souls can be stimulated to unite and to produce loving communities. Competitiveness and community building both require effort. We learn to live with others, and our souls adjust to this. Human correspondence can be both uplifting and degrading. One can communicate high ideals, or one can authoritatively command obedience to imperfect regulations. An individual soul can meditate and come close to God. People in groups can worship and God will inspire their community. Many religious groups today seek ''union with God'' through a combination of practices. There is the practice of solitary meditation; there is the practice of responsible action; there is the practice of compassion.

The cultivation of humankind's inner attitudes, that relate to soul, was variously furthered by religious systems. The human worried about the rightness or wrongness of others' religious beliefs. There were problems that the communities of souls had to solve. If my idea of God is different from your idea of God, whose God should we worship? Along the Nile there were many instances of cities worshiping their favorite aspect of god. If three cities are unified by a strong military leader, which god will they choose to worship? How does a group reconcile their beliefs in three different gods with a belief in one God who loves them specially? Egypt and Sumer both had this problem. They proposed trinities of gods to please the priests and theologians. The common people continued to worship whatever god they found speaking in their soul. If this god were a gentle god, they lived peaceful lives. If this god was a god of war, they went to war under that God's banner and died gladly and proudly.

As the human being enlarged her horizons, there was growth of competition, division into oppressed and oppressors, self-righteousness, exclusivity, and intolerance. Ethnic groups formed. Nations rose and fell. Religious group leaders convinced adherents and themselves that the gods had given them absolute truth. Conquerors felt they showed virtue in the enslavement of others. Instead of killing a captive outright, you allowed him to live and to become your slave. If you were the master, it was to your advantage to continue the social systems that were in place. Varying ethical concepts grew through the exchange of ideas and the improvement in communication through trade and language ability. As groups interacted with one another, new methods of living and new ideas were born.

Today, we humans, like our predecessors, are still subject to emotions of fear, anger, hatred, and lust. These may be buried deep in our subconscious. Once there, they can rise to the surface repeatedly, even becoming an addiction. But we have also developed the ability to recognize these thoughts, set them aside, and replace them. Repeated replacements with thoughts of empathy, understanding, compassion, and forgiveness– all aspects of kindness, have contributed to the further *creation of kindness*. With this increase of kindness, we grow the total soul of the earth.

Footnotes

1 D.P. Agrawal, *The Archaeology of India*, Curzon Press, London, 1985, p. 7.

2 There are many ways to arrive in India. When Alexander the Great marched east in 327 BC, he did not take the main road through the Khyber Pass, but circled north among the Hindu Cush and came down a tributary of the Indus.

3 Ruth Whitehouse, *Dictionary of Archaeology,* Facts on File, 460 Park Ave. S, NY NY 10016, 1983, p. 207.

4 George E. Stuart, Editor, *Peoples and Places of The Past*, National Geographic Society, 1983, p. 141.

5 Stuart Piggott, *Editor, The Dawn of Civilization,* McGraw Hill, New York, 1961.

6 Siegfried Herrmann, *A History of Israel in OT Times*, SCM Press LTD, London, 1975, p. 18.

7 Some dates in Babylon depend on eclipses of the moon. The moon has lunation cycles, and historians may be dating from later lunation cycles.

8 Celtic priestesses carried these word-of-mouth tales of Arthur across Europe.

9 John Bright, *A History of Israel*, Westminster Press, Philadelphia PA, 1972, p. 50.

10 P.H. Newby, *The Egypt Story*, Abbeville Press, New York, 1975, p. 106.

11 Donald B. Redford, *Akhenaten The Heretic King,* Princeton University Press, Princeton, NJ, 1984, p. 13, 97.

12 *ibid.*, p. 99.

13 *ibid.*, p. 15, 100.

14 *ibid.*, p. 9, 11, 14.

15 *ibid.*, p. 43.

16 *ibid.*, p. 66.

17 Carleton S. Coon, *The Story of Man*, Alfred A. Knopf, New York, 1954, p. 8.

18 *ibid.*

IV

Heroes and Heroines
Abraham to Joseph

Next let us praise illustrious men,
our ancestors in their successive generations.
The Lord has created an abundance of glory,
and displayed his greatness from earliest times.
Some wielded authority as kings
and were renowned for their strength;
others were intelligent advisors
and uttered prophetic oracles.
Others directed the people by their advice
by their understanding of the popular mind,
and by the wise words of their teaching;
others composed musical melodies, and set down ballads;
others were rich and powerful,
living peacefully in their homes.
All these were honored by their contemporaries,
and were the glory of their day.
Some of them left a name behind them,
so that their praises are still sung.
While others have left no memory,
and disappeared as though they had not existed,
they are now as though they had never been,
and so too, their children after them.

Ecclesiasticus 44:1-13

4.1 Myth and The Hebrew Historians

In the previous chapters I have set down history, archaeology, and evolutionary science, plus some personal and debatable opinions of what went on during the formation of the world and in the makings of early civilizations. My conclusions may be unusual, and though I have prayed for God to inspire me, some of my hypotheses may be rising out of an overactive creativity.

The authors of the Pentateuch, or first five books of the Bible, were faced with the same dilemma. How did they view the time slot which has been presented in the preceding three chapters? There were several different main authors contributing to the Pentateuch. The Jahwist author used the name of God as *Yahweh*. Another author named God as *Elohim*. Later authors were the Priestly and the Deuteronomist editors. All these writers came up with a story of human evolution gleaned from ancestral information that reflected their political events and included ethical observations. Many colorful threads and swatches combined together give an informative, imaginative, and interesting finished product.

Prototypal People. Like the Harappan, Sumerian, and Egyptian civilizations, those of Bible times have comparable words that define collections of ancestral humanity. They would not know the meaning of the words *Indus* or *Egypt*. They used names of tribes and *prototypal* people to build their message. These prototypal people may not be actual people but represent unnamed tribes or groups of people and their actions. Where we would speak of musical instruments being invented by some indefinite early person, they would say that a prototypal person with a specific name invented musical instruments. This name might describe a location or a time period or it might be translated as *singer of song* or *player of harp*. People in later ages might not be able to recognize these prototypal names for what they are, especially with the differences of our present day languages. If there were a people bound together by certain ethnic and ethical ties for many years, the biblical writers might condense this long lived group into the name of one man. Then they would tell myths about this prototype to show the religious and cultural beliefs of the group.

Beauty in The Message. The forming of a myth may be compared to what goes on in a kaleidoscope, a monocular device filled with tidbits of paper or glass. You put it up to your eye and twist the far end of the mechanism and your multi-mirrored pattern switches its design. To a small child there seems to be an infinite number of patterns available, some more beautiful than others. When I was a child, I was glad to have such a marvelous toy. Then one day it broke, and I felt somehow cheated to learn that all the beauty I had been seeing came from such flimsy chips of material.

When I have finished discussing the origins of myth, I hope you won't feel cheated or disappointed. I hope you will remember all the beautiful combinations that were put in place, and the thrill you had at viewing each portrayal. Above all, you should keep close to heart the ethical teachings that are "to be treasured more than the finest gold" (Psalm 19:10).

When we spread out the colorful collection of stories from our kaleido-scope before us, we find that as we keep searching deeper and deeper, we continue to make new finds. The Bible was written centuries or even millennia after some of the events it records. We cannot determine firm historical dates for Abraham, Isaac, Jacob, Joseph, or Moses. Only when we come to Joshua and 1400 BC Canaan, do archeologists and biblical authors find common ground. However, the biblical books of Joshua and Judges do not entirely agree about the date for the conquest of Canaan.

The biblical authors of 1000 BC wrote these pieces of history and pre-history as God permitted them to see it. They did not have the broader view we have today. However, they did have the inspired knowledge of many holy people who were their predecessors who had thought deeply on God's ways with the world and its people. They also had folk tales of their ancestors that told of memorable happenings. We can learn much from the Bible that can fill in gaps in the story of humankind that we have pieced together from our archaeological discoveries. The writers often speak in parables and use prototypes. They preface their Genesis history with the fairy tale beginning line of *in-early-times* (Genesis 2:5). They do not expect to be taken literally when they use anthropomorphisms (such as God having hands), or to be understood scientifically when they talk about physical happenings (such as people turning into pillars of salt). Their scientific knowledge was vastly different from our body of scientific knowledge.

Biblical Dates. We cannot expect to find correct dates in the biblical stories. Even the sequential timing of events may be altered if necessary to make a theological point. Their time was not calculated as we calculate time. The ages of the patriarchs given in Genesis 5 are not their accumulation of years. Their number systems were not in modern Arabic. They could not handle millions and billions any better than our minds today contemplating the U.S. national debt. To add up the generational years between Abraham and Moses as recorded in the Bible will not give us a correct answer as to how many summers came and went between the birth dates of these men. Because the story of Abraham is derived from mythical origins, its time slot is an indefinite number of years before that of Moses. We have no way of knowing precise dates for myths or their country of origin. We do not know if parts of the Abraham story have been pulled from some Egyptian folk tale or from Egyptian happenings more contemporaneous with David, or from other parts of the ancient world. If we place the story of Abraham back only 1000 years from the latest accepted date for Moses, we lose sight of possibly earlier origins. We confine it, and we misinterpret the theological insights that are carried along from religious beliefs that pre-date the Hebrew. If we believe the legend to be totally Hebrew, we may be blinded by our present day conceptions of Hebrew culture, and we don't allow ourselves to see the full beauty and potential of the myth.

The Authors. The Bible has a wonderful way of telling us about our earliest beginnings. The Jahwist author-editor of the Bible writing in David's time, who relates many of these folk tales, may have been either male or female. The Deuteronomist author several hundred years later may have been Huldah the Prophetess (II Kings 22). In order to emphasize this possibility of feminine authorship, I will refer to these authors as *she* rather than *he,* so that the reader can envision a scholarly scribe *or* an industrious intelligent woman working under God's inspiration. The Jahwist author who set down these wonderful words inspired by God, tells us in the best way she could, the stories she has heard from her ancestors. She uses the names that would make the most sense to those of her day who would read her words. In our day we interpret her words according to our present civilization. We know much more about geography, migrations of peoples, place names, languages, and ice ages than the author could have been expected to know, yet we often interpret her words in a very literal manner, as if she were a member of our own generation. However, our ancestors were as shrewd, intelligent, and investigative as we are today. They could remember long lists of ancestor names. They knew certain geographical facts and could travel vast distances by foot. There is an ancient map that indicates that someone in the times of Naram-Sin (about 3000 BC) had heard about the long winter nights in Siberia north of Lake Van in Russia.

Our author knew that God created the heavens and the earth. We do not know if she viewed God as a patriarchal old man in the heavens, as a power behind the movement of the sun, as a marvelous unifying spirit, or as a combination of all these. From her writings it seems that God inspired her to believe in a First Cause. This First Cause made all the marvels that she beheld in her everyday life. God created the stars in the heavens and the animals upon the earth. She wrote that this was a good earth God created, even though she knew of the improper actions and the sorrows that humans foisted upon one another.

Early myths capture for us a bit of humankind's prehistory. They let us in on what went on before there was writing, perhaps even before there was much verbal communication. We make a grievous error in trying to date stories that tell us reasons for human social behavior, such as Abraham's sacrifice of his son, or the circumcision of Moses by his wife. At some point in pre-history, human sacrifice, especially of first born sons, became more than mothers could bear, and a theological explanation was needed to end this abuse. Similarly, circumcision became an accepted practice for religious and health reasons, and was made into religious law. The biblical authors explain these social changes by inventing ancestor stories that make the point clear.

The author knew that some early human beings had formerly lived off the plenty of the land. She did not write of the pre-human being on earth one million years ago, because in her time, there was no concept of time as long as a million years. She could speak of tribes and heroes and notable acts-of-God. She realized that some areas had problems because of changes in climate and geography, so that people had to migrate. There is the myth of Abraham's migration and Isaac's subsequent return for a wife. It is told in the context of *Ur of the Khaldeans*, a city in Mesopotamia. *Ur* may be simply a handy name to use. *Ur* means *city* and the Khaldeans worshiped Khaldi, *The Lord of Heaven*. The myth may tell about a migration and return between places whose names had been long since forgotten.

4.2 Creation, Garden, and Flood

Thus heaven and earth were completed with all their array ... there was as yet no wild bush on the earth nor had any wild plant yet sprung up ... However, a flood was rising from the earth and watering all the surface of the soil ... Yahweh God fashioned the human being and breathed into her nostrils a breath of life (Genesis 2:1-7). The Bible gives an orderly account of God making this whole marvelous creation, and readers three thousand years later have no reason to doubt its description. Heaven's and earth's *array* may be stars and sun and moon, or it may refer to God's helping spirits, or it may mean the arrangement of seas, rocks, and continents. There was a time on earth when there were no plants, and a time when God sent rain to water the soil with interglacial ice melt. After the soil was ready, God created the human and breathed life into her.

Yahweh planted a garden in Eden which is in the east ... A river flowed from Eden to water the garden, and from there it divided to make four streams. The first is named the Pishon, and this encircles the whole land of Havilah where there is gold ... The second is named the Gihon, and this encircles the whole land of Cush. The third is named the Tigris ... The fourth river is the Euphrates (Genesis 2:8-14). The beginnings of the Hebrew tribe were eastward of the land of Palestine where the biblical authors were writing their world history. The beginnings may even have been east of Mesopotamia, for many of the traditions seemed to have a start in the Tigris-Euphrates area but may have been brought to that area from still further east. Joshua 24:2 claims that the ancestors came from "beyond the river" which river may be the Indus or the Oxus. If Joshua 24 were referring to the Tigris and Euphrates, it would have to make the word *river* into the plural *rivers*.

We often think of the Bible as being a book about Israel and its history in the land of Palestine. However, Palestine is where David ruled and the author who wrote about David was acquainted with its place names and its language, but the history she is relating comes from other lands and languages. The times that her hard working contemporaries looked back upon, were times that had faded in memory and took place pre-Israel, and even pre-Mesopotamia. Men and women lived off the fruits and animals produced by Mother Nature. There were no cities of Babylon and Ur. They did not till the ground, and there was food for all. When the population thickened, each group had to work harder for sustenance. Ethnologists believe that tilling the ground and the beginnings of agriculture did not start in Mesopotamia, but north in the Caucasus or west in India or Afghanistan.

The places where they roamed free, and also where they began to diligently labor, were probably not in Palestine, but eastward towards Persia, Arabia, India, or even Japan. One of the earliest cultures was located on the islands of the Japanese archipelago where the first known pottery was crafted in 11,000 BC. Many Bible stories come out of Mesopotamia, but these stories may have originally come from some locale further east which had developed earlier. We are able to recognize the later stories and cultural statements that came from Egypt to the west of Palestine. But the Eden tradition is much earlier than Egypt. The Eden story does not mention the famed Nile as one of the rivers that watered the garden, so we must look for these rivers in the opposite direction. When a geographical location is given as Cush, we should remember that there are two lands of Cush, one is west of Palestine near Egypt, and the other is east of Palestine near India. The spread of this Cushite group across Arabia may have been furthered by an ancient river, which dried up circa 3000 BC, running from present day Kuwait to Medina. Could this river be a candidate for the Gihon? The territory that was occupied by the Cushite group bridged two bodies of water, the Red Sea and the Persian Gulf, and extended from the Indus Valley westward across the tip of the Arabian Peninsula, into African Ethiopia. Before these gulfs of water formed, this may have been the land area of descendants of Australopithecus and of the Capoid Homo sapiens.

When Genesis speaks of the Pishon and the Gihon as two of the four rivers watering paradise (the other two are the Tigris and Euphrates), they might possibly be referring to the *Pishin* (which is still a name for part of the Indus system). The Pishin or Indus did water the territory of Havilah or western India. The Gihon is more difficult to locate, but the Bible says it has to do with Cush. In the northern part of the Indian Cush is an area called Margiana which is drained by rivers in the Oxus system. One of these rivers may have been named the Gi-on. What today is known as the Oxus may have had the earlier name of Gihon. These four rivers, the Tigris, the Euphrates, the Indus, and the Oxus, encircle the Iranian plateau which was lush with fruit and melons and may have been the land remembered as Eden.

In dimly remembered time the people dwelt in a beautiful garden. They were expelled from this place where all their needs were met, and were kept out by an angel with a flashing sword. What better way to describe the disappearance of a beautiful land by volcanic fire, earthquake, or other natural disaster, than to say an angel kept them out?

Settlements. [*Cain*] *became the builder of a town, and he gave the town the name of his son Enoch* (Genesis 4:17b). Cain is the prototype of farmer, builder of a town, and trader. Farmers, forming groups utilizing the land, were more in need of regulations to help their members get along, than were the hunting groups. Cain, the farmer, was punished for his wrong doing, by having to wander over the earth. This wandering would make it fairly difficult to farm. He may have taken to the seas, becoming a trader-merchant. Merchants need exploitable areas that can produce items for trade.

The biblical author knew that there had been people before the period of great rain. Between 10,000-8000 BC, the end of the Pleistocene, the climate modified rapidly and severely. With the retreat of the ice, the rain belt left North Africa. Before this the Baltic had been an inland lake, and the North Sea and the Adriatic had been dry ground. Fertile areas crept northward, after the receding ice.

According to the time line of the Jahwist author, this town which Cain built was a pre-flood town, as Cain came before Noah. Archaeologists date the influx of water at about 10,000 BC. The Bible states that there were towns on earth before Noah, so the people who built Jericho about 8000 BC knew what they were doing, for there had been previous towns upon which they could model their structures. The biblical time line is confirmed by the archaeological record, as pottery remains from pre-flood civilizations in Mesopotamia have been found below the flood silt.

We can speculate that Cain's town may represent one of the very early towns that were flooded out in Mesopotamia, in India, in Malaysia, or even between China and Japan due to melting of the polar ice caps. After the time of Cain and after the flood, known Neolithic settlements were at Jarmo in northern Iraq, Jericho, Ras Shamra on the Mediterranean coast, and the largest at Catal Huyuk in Turkey about 7000 BC. There were village settlements on the Danube (6000 BC), and farming and herding settlements at Mehrgarh west of the Indus (6000 BC). There may have been localized floods after these dates.

Biblical Prototypes. *Jabal was the ancestor of the tent dwellers and owners of livestock* (Genesis 4:20). The Bible tells us that there were early people who dwelt in tents and tamed herds. The first domesticators of animals seemed to have lived in the Indus-Afghanistan area. If we consider the plateau of Iran to be associated with the Garden of Eden where food was free for the grabbing, then the Indus area may have been where the human being learned how to shift for herself.

Jubal was the ancestor of all who play the lyre and the flute (Genesis 4:21). In our history there were people who were musicians. At some point there were the first people on earth who sang and laughed and called to one another. Before that time, voices could not sing. Imagine a world without laughter and without song. Imagine a world where there was no sense of humor. Imagine a world where there were no dancers. Back in the mists of pre-history, somebody told the first joke.

Tubal-cain was the ancestor of all metalworkers, in bronze or iron (Genesis 4:22). We know that there was a Bronze Age and an Iron Age when humans became familiar with metals, and could create metal objects to serve their needs. The biblical author in giving us the prototypal ancestor of Tubal-cain, confirms that the people of David's age knew about these early metal workers. Women were mentioned as connected with these trades. Tubal-cain is described as having a sister Naamah, a mother Zillah, and a relative Adah. Women as cooks may have been the first to notice the melting of metals in cooking fires. Men are often credited with inventions, but women are equally inventive. Women as having less strength to move heavy objects may have invented wheels and rollers. Muscular men would be more inclined to use strength rather than to invent tools to move an object.

Enosh was the first to invoke the name of Yahweh (Genesis 4:26). As Moses was the first to call God *Yahweh* as described in Exodus 3:14 and 6:3, the meaning of insert 4:26 may be that Enosh was the first to call on God under any name. It seems certain that God was addressed by many people by many different names, but somewhere there was a first human to call on God. When we look back at our evolutionary history, we can see that at some point people did not call on God, and then later on, they did. Our biblical author, recognizing this, calls this prototype by the ancestral name of Enosh, as there were legends which associated this name with a good and holy man. Enosh may have been the first formal visionary, for Genesis 5:24 says that he vanished when God took him. There is confusion with the names *Enosh* and *Enoch*. These men are variously described as the son of Seth, the son of Cain, and the son of Jared in Genesis 4 and 5. The biblical author is combining different threads of tradition.

The author of Genesis employs prototypal devices to tell us about the progress of the human race. We are given Adam and Eve as types of the first humans. The author relates that there were other human beings around when Adam and Eve were thrown out of the garden, because she has their son Cain marrying some of them. The names *Adam* and *Eve* are prototypal names. Adam means *man*, and Eve means *mother of the living*. Cain kills his brother Abel. Ab-el means *God is his father*, implying that Abel is the favorite of God and follows after goodness. Adam and Eve have a third son Seth. There was a pre-flood division of people into those descended from Seth and those descended from Cain. This may be interpreted as the die-off of the godly such as Abel due to non-resistance, the aggression of unpredictable individuals such as Cain, and the everyday trials of your average person Seth.

The sons of God, looking at the daughters of men, saw they were pleasing ... The Nephilim were on the earth at that time (Genesis 6:2-4). The first section of this quote could be misinterpreted. Taken literally, it could mean that all men were born of God, and women were merely human. These ideas came from the same early myths that Homer had heard. Our author relates her passage to the heroes or godly people of the days gone by. She has heard of those ancient nobles who were thought to be favored by the gods, or who proclaimed themselves gods (such as Naram-Sin). Similar stories are told in the Phoenician tradition by an ancient author named Sanchunyathon. Hittite texts also speak of Hurrian myths that contain similar material. This man-as-god and woman-as-human scenario may have kept women believing in their secondary status.

Verse 6:4 speaks of the Nephilim who are also referred to in Numbers 13:33 as ancient giants. There doubtless were some larger humans and many variations in the shapes and sizes of humanity, as there are today. Homer tells of the giant Cyclops, and stories often tend to exaggerate and to make large people more massive than they really were. The author wanted to set down her generation's knowledge about the sizes of people of former times. **The Flood and Noah.** *The flood lasted forty days on the earth* (Genesis 7:17). Forty days in biblical language is synonymous with a long time. Forty years simply means many, many years. Four hundred years may mean millennia. Generational count may be very haphazard, and may omit ancestors of lesser importance. When we read that it rained for forty days, we are being told that it rained an extraordinarily long time. When we read that multitudes of people wandered for 40 years in the wilderness, it may mean 100 years. We don't know, and neither did the biblical author.

Noah, a tiller of the soil, was the first to plant the vine (Genesis 9:20). Again, we have prototypal examples. Noah is described as the first farmer. We know that there were many people turning to farming around the same period in history. We do not know who was the actual person who made the first mental decision to farm. Even Adam is described as believing that he would have to till the soil and earn his food through the sweat of his brow. Noah is also described as the first wine maker, and the first person to become drunk. How do you explain to people where wine came from? It may have been discovered many times by many different farmers or fruit harvesters.

These people farmed somewhere east of Palestine, and their ancestor stories originated in places to the east, associated with ancestor names. The Bible author tells us that after the flood, the ark came to rest on Mount Ararat. She places the ark on Ararat because that is at high mountain with which she is familiar. Her listeners or readers will get the proper message. However, if Noah is a citizen of a land to the east of Palestine, his ark may have come to rest further away, perhaps in the Himalayas. The description of the boat that Noah made is also very interesting. It is a type of house boat used off the coasts of China and India. There are many flood legends in India, and today there are still floods there. The flood story may be an oral account of an event that occurred about 9000 BC before the invention of writing and may relate events far away from Palestine. Similarly, the Moses and Sargon baby-in-the-basket stories may have been told about a third person being rescued from a river other than the Nile or the Euphrates.

Genealogy. Genealogies in the Bible are difficult to interpret. They give us information on ancestor names, but they also can help us understand disconnections and in-family rifts. Imagine yourself making up your family tree today. Do you want to include the uncle who was the "black sheep" who disgraced the family name and was sent to prison, or would you rather omit him altogether? Some other public recorder of events might include him, and confuse future genealogists. Do you put in that your relative married a foreign woman and consequently came to your house and tried to convert you all to his wife's religion, or do you take him out of your family tree, and let him be remembered by the wife's family?

The two genealogies of Jesus (Luke 3:23-38 and Matthew 1) are substantially different. One list is trying to show that non-Jews were involved as Jesus' ancestors. The other is trying to prove his Jewishness. The Gospel of Luke is written for a Gentile audience, and Matthew, for Jews.

Those who put in genealogical listings in the Bible have agendas that involve more than 'who begot whom.' Genealogies help to broaden our understandings of early people. We can relate ancient problems and disturbances to similar upheavals today. The genealogies also serve the fundamental purposes of reminding us of our togetherness with and responsibilities to those who went before and to those who come after. They reinforce the concept of the ''communion of saints.''

Blessed be Yahweh, God of Shem, let Canaan be his slave (Genesis 9:26). The historical underpinnings of this short blessing and condemnation are very interesting. This statement sums up the later day relationship between the Semites, descendants of Shem, and the Canaanites, descendants of Noah's son Ham. Biblical curses were saved for your enemies' ancestors. The Semites didn't have much good to say about the people who lived in the land of Canaan (Genesis 10:15-19), particularly in the time frame before 1200 BC (the date of much of the oral biblical material).

Where did the people who lived in the land of Canaan come from, and why did the Semites or children of Shem dislike them so intensely? When the tribal Semites came from the east to the land of Mesopotamia, they were fleeing climatic problems and having a population explosion. The land of Mesopotamia was known by various names. In the Akkadian language it was called *Sumer* or *Shinar* (Genesis 10:10, 11:2, 14:1) or *Sinar*. The Sumerians called themselves *Kiengir*. As more and more Semites pressed into the land of Sumer, some of the Sumerians who didn't like these foreigners, moved out of Sumer westward into the land of Canaan. Another way of spelling Canaan is *Ki-en-a-nim*, which means people from Kiengir or Sumer. The name of *Cain*, as trader, may also be reflected in the *Ki-en* name. The bad blood between Semites and Canaanites probably began in Mesopotamia where disparate ethnic groups had trouble getting along.

The name *Canaan* came to be understood as a land designation rather than a people and contained other groups beside those Sumerians forced over from Sumer. The Amarna texts of Egypt (about 1400 BC) name this land as *Kinahhi* or *Kinah-na*. The *Alalakh* texts of the Mitanni kingdom (northwestern Mesopotamia) from about the same time, speak of the *Ki-in-a-nim*. The other nations were aware of the land of Canaan and its varying population. The dislike of the Hebrew Semites for the Canaanite people is reflected in the names used in their myths.

These are the descendants of Noah's sons (Genesis 10:1). The Bible gives us the names and genealogy of peoples of pre-David times. These listings may not reflect actual genetic lines, but may represent tribal groups and relationships which were political, geographical, or linguistic. We find David forming his twelve tribes through political and geographical ties as well as through the incorporation of what may have been actual sons of Israel. The whole idea of the designation, *Sons of Israel,* may be a way of telling us that these tribes were people who had established themselves in the land of Israel, and who had sworn political allegiance to each other and to the God of the land of Israel. Tribal leaders could perform the ritual of blood brotherhood by splitting open their veins and mixing their blood. Perhaps there were marital ties. Sometimes we are told why tribes did not get along. It is frequently blamed on unworthy actions of ancestors.

Likes and dislikes of tribal groups continued to change even after the Genesis genealogy. The Jahwist document of David's time, claimed Sheba as a son of Joktan from Eber (Genesis 10:25-27). I Chronicles 1:9 which is a later listing near the time of the Babylonian exile, presented Sheba as descending from Cush. There may have been political reasons for David's inclusion and for the later disfavor.

From the long list of Noah's descendants, language and history experts have worked out some possible correlations of ancient names with present locations. Genealogy names may represent tribes rather than individuals. The name Japheth is similar to Iapetos, a Greek mythical hero, and his descendants include people in the Aegean and Turkish area. The Gomer are the Assyrian Gimir-ray, which become Cimmerians, which tribe crossed Europe as the Cymry or Cythians or Celts. Gomer's sons are the Ashkenaz (Cythians), the Riphath (on the Philistine coast or perhaps descended from a branch of Joseph), and the Togarmah (from near Carchemish). The name Gog may refer to Gyges in Lydia, the west part of Asia Minor. Tubal and Meshech were landholders in what is modern Turkey. Javan's sons were the Sea Peoples, Elishah (Cyprus), Tarshish (Turkey), Kittim (also Cyprus), and Dananites (from northern Palestine to the Danube). Ham, as the tribe of the disgraced son of Noah (Genesis 9:24), includes the enemies of the Hebrews, Cush (Ethiopia and Havilah), Mizraim (Egypt), Put (questionable location), and Canaan. Ham's other tribal partners are Raamah, Sabteca, Sabtah, and Dedan (on the Asiatic side of the Red Sea).

When the Bible tells us of Noah's descendants, it may be telling us that the forming of the races was a peaceful process, that Shem went in one direction and fathered the Semites, Japheth in another direction and fathered other races whose names were known in Solomon's time, and Ham stayed right where he was and began the Canaanite race. These seemingly confusing insertions of geographical and tribal lore may eventually help biblical students to unravel relationships between peoples and migrations.

Cush became the father of Nimrod who was the first potentate on earth (Genesis 10:8). Cush, a descendant of Noah's son Ham, is the prototypal ancestor of the peoples from the Indian Havilah Cush and the Ethiopian Cush. The Cush territory or tribe may have to do with the original spread of peoples when India, Arabia, and Africa separated, after they had been jammed together in tectonic collision. The Cushites related most closely to Nimrod are those east of Mesopotamia in the direction of Havilah. The description of Nimrod fits neatly with the achievements of a prototype which combined Sargon I and his grandson Naram-Sin. In order to confuse matters, these kings had Semitic origins which would classify them as being descended from Noah's son Shem. Genesis 10:10-12 says that Nimrod first was king of Babel, Erech, and Akkad in the land of Shinar or Sumer. Then the Assyrians or Ashur built Nineveh, Rehoboth-Ir, Calah, and Resen. In this list of cities the name Rehoboth-Ir (which means *gigantic city*) may be an adjective for Nineveh. Archeological layers at Nineveh have been dated back to 6000 BC. Calah may have contained original construction from Sargon I, but its antiquities were rebuilt by a later day monarch, Ashurnasirpal II (883-859 BC) after the time of the Davidic biblical author. Resen may have been a military construction or a place to house trader-soldiers. Historically, some of these cities may have been taken over and enlarged by Semite kings (descended from Shem, son of Noah), while the Bible states that the kings who built these cities were descendants of Cush, the son of Ham, the son of Noah.

Shem's sons, according to Genesis 10:22, are Elam, Ashur, Arpachshad, Lud, and Aram. The Elamites were hill tribes in southern Mesopotamia and Persia from shortly before the time of Sargon I up to and including the time of David. Ashur may describe the Semites who had ties to the Assyrians. Arpachshad may be the Harappan peoples on the Indus. Lud, or Lot, was a group in eastern Iran, and Aram spread across Iran from the Aral Sea and the Caspian down through Arabia. In Genesis 10:23 Aram's sons are Uz, Hul, Gether, and Mash. These were all Semites, or people who had allied themselves with the Semites. Arpachshad eventually fathered Eber who is in the list of patriarchs after the flood (Genesis 11:14). From Eber comes the word [*H*]*ebru* or the present tribal term, *Hebrew*.

What is known as Arabia today may not have been the land of Arabia of pre-biblical times. The term *Arabia* may have been used to designate all of southeast Asia. They didn't have precise maps to set locations. They only knew that somewhere in the distant past there were tribes claiming descent from Eber, the brother of Peleg, with the names of Havilah, Ophir, and Sheba. Peleg (or Phalek) was a descendant of Shem. The Bible states that his name means that in his time the land was divided. This could be speaking of either a political or geographical division. Geographically, India and Arabia had been pressing on Asia and causing earthquakes in many areas. This tectonic plate movement is still in process. It may have caused deformations in the Dead Sea area, or more massive eruptions that made a desolation of vast areas. This division in Peleg's time may have referred to a relatively simple shift of earth that changed the bed of the Euphrates.

Babel and Language. [*The town*] *was named Babel therefore, because there Yahweh confused the language of the whole earth* (Genesis 11:9). When we investigate languages, searching for blood bonds among tribesmen, we find that the Elamite language has little in common with Semitic. The Guti (or Gudea) language of the Mesopotamian mountain dwellers was associated with the language of Elam. These mountain tribes may have been remnants of pre-flood people who spoke a pre-flood language. If the biblical author claims Elam as a Semitic group, it may be because the Elamites took the Semitic side in some battle waged against the Semites.

Another pre-flood language may be that of the original Hittites. The Hittites or Hatti spoke *Hattic* (or *Boghazkoy*). Heth, the ancestor of the Hittites, is described as the brother of Sidon and son of Cain in Genesis 10:15. This Hattic language was neither Semitic nor Indo-European. When the country was overrun by a conqueror, it kept the old place names but used the conqueror's language which was *Luwian*.

In opposition to the pre-flood language of Gudea, Elam, and Hatti, the Semitic and Hamitic languages had a common ancestry.[1] Shem and Ham may have had their differences but were linguistically linked together. Aram was a descendant of Shem, and Aramaic was a dominant language. Arabic was another Semitic language division. The North Arabic languages were spoken by the Arabs of Arabia. The Southern Arabic or Southeast Semitic languages were ancient Sabaean, Minaean, Ethiopic, and more recent tongues with links to Akkadian.

The story of the Tower of Babel in Genesis 11:1-9 is an explanation for the development of languages. The author makes note of language differences, and her theological explanation for this is that people did not seem to be understanding of each other. From her perspective in history the confusion of tongues ensuing from the building of cities in Sumer would be worthy of the name of Babel. This biblical mention is in the correct time sequence, as it takes place after the flood. The list of patriarchs after the flood brings us up to the introduction of Abraham (Genesis 11:26).

4.3 Abraham and Sarah

One myth that is written firmly into our hearts is the story of Abraham and Sarah. In telling us this legend, the biblical author is relating to us the origins and beliefs of the various religious faiths. She acquired the background for her account of Abraham's beliefs from ancient oral traditions. Abraham believed in a God concerned with people. The writer gives us hints on the growth of faith in the prototypal human being. Abraham acquired his beliefs from earlier groups. Perhaps we can tell something about the origins of this legend by investigating the meanings of the names used by the writer.

Names and what they mean are a very important part of a myth. The storyteller will often tell us something about the hero or heroine's name to make the story more clear. Both the hero and the heroine in this legend undergo name changes, so we have many derivations to discuss. In Genesis 17:5 Abram becomes Abraham, which the writer says means *the father of many nations*. Likewise, in Genesis 17:15 Sarai becomes Sarah, *the mother of nations*.

Names and pieces of the Abraham story can have come out of any country or tribe, any time before its composition date by the Davidic author about 1000 BC. There were many pieces that made up the totality, and there must have been theological reasons why the ancient story teller put the pieces together in the manner she did.

Indian Possibilities. Let's examine different sections of the Abraham myth. Could a thread of this story have come from India? The names *Abraham* and *Sarah* can be interpreted as names with Indian roots. In the religious tradition of India there is a god-like pair who represent truth, justice, and the nobility of one's ancestors. The god/hero *Brahma* has as his main consort, *Saraswati*. Brahma is the most important god in the Hindu trinity. *Ab* in the Near East means *father*. If we called our ancestral hero *Father Brahma* (or *Ab-Brahma*), we would get a name very similar to the name Abraham. The name of the Hindu god Rama can also be tied into the name of Abraham before his name was changed from Abram. The name *Ab-Ram* means *my father is Ram*, or *my god is Ram*. Both of the biblical names, *Abram* and *Abraham* are associated with Hindu beliefs. If the Hebrews' legendary ancestor was the hero Rama, and if Rama worship went out of style, while the more universalist hero Brahma became popular, there would be good reason to have a change of ancestral names. The biblical author could be telling us about her tribe's religious beginnings. The first ancestors believed in the Hindu god Rama; then there was a broadening of beliefs. Rama was more of a feared model to be worshiped; whereas Brahma represented the god-like capabilities of every man. If there were a tribe called the Sons of Rama, and if they expanded their religious outlook, they could have changed their ancestral or tribal name, to suit their changing religious beliefs.

Sara. Checking out the name of *Sara*, we find that *Saraswati* is one of the names of the Hindu divine mother goddess, who was the union of power and intelligence from which organized creation arose. She is sometimes referred to as the daughter of Kali. (Kali was also named Durga.) Saraswati revealed writing to man and was the mother of poetry. She was goddess of speech, and queen of learning, wisdom, creative arts, and song. She was usually represented as riding on a swan or a peacock and held a lute and a manuscript. She was considered to be the personification of the River Sarasvati (Sarsuti), which presently flows in the northern part of Uttar Pradesh, and dries up in the desert of Rajputana. This river is mentioned in the *RigVeda* as ''She who goes pure from the mountains as far as the sea.'' According to a Hindu writing, *The Mahabharata*, the flow of the river to the sea was ruined by the curse of the sage Utathya. Saraswati was recognized as the universal mother and protector of all children, and in Persian folklore, as the mother of the divine child Skanda-Kumaris, the first human. Saraswati as mother of Kumaris, may be comparable mythologically to the heroine Sara who produced Isaac (or Ishmael by proxy). *Kumaris* in Persian and Hindu theology, was the first man or founder of the human race.

The heroine or goddess, Saraswati, is recognized by many Hindus as the feminine half of God. The masculine half could not create the human race without the help of wisdom and motherhood to soften his macho characteristics. God, as totality, is both male and female. For this reason in this book I sometimes use the feminine pronoun for the One God. It is not that I believe God to be feminine, but that I believe God contains both male and female aspects. If I use feminine pronouns, then readers will have the opportunity to look more closely at their beliefs about God.

If we used a shortened version of Saraswati, we would find ourselves saying Sara. The name *Sara* in Hindu, appears related to *sati*, which means real or true woman (*suttee*), from which comes the act of suttee, where a woman is killed by being burned with her husband's corpse on his funeral pyre. There is also the goddess Sita who is the model for a virtuous wife. A Persian variant on her name is *Sitarah*, meaning *star*. This name has similarities to the name *Sarah*. Sita is the consort of Rama whom we have also associated with Abraham. There is a myth among the Hindus of how the god Rama rescues his beloved Sita from the clutches of a demon king. This may be some of the background myth material for the problems that

Abraham has with Abimelech of Gerar in the Negev (Genesis 20:1-18). Abraham tells Sarah to state she is his sister, rather than his wife, and the unsuspecting ruler takes Sarah into his harem. When the king learns of this deception, he gives Abraham gifts and sends him on his way. There is a corresponding story concerned with a legendary pharaoh of Egypt in Genesis 12:10-20.

Early peoples traveling from India might mythologize their distant ancestors Abraham and Sara in their contemporaneous religious beliefs. If their prototypal ancestor or theology were associated with the name Ab-brahma, they would be called the children of Ab-brahma. The Bible refers to the Hebrews as *sons of Abraham*. There is a river in India called the River Brahmaputra which means *sons of Brahma*, which implies that some sons of Brahma lived along this river. The source of the Brahmaputra is in Tibet, where it is called the Dihang. Its next section is called the Brahmaputra, and when the Ganges joins it, then it is called by the Ganges name. Where it flows into the Bay of Bengal it is four or five miles wide. Perhaps some of the Hebrew tribes originated from this river valley.

Abram's Migration. *Yahweh said to Abram, "Leave your country, your family and your father's house, for the land I will show you"* (Genesis 12:1). A notable ancestor and pillar of the community or a whole group would leave the home town for other parts, if farming land went sour, or if trade made it necessary to travel. Both these reasons may have applied to the Abraham group in India. The Harappan civilization made good use of irrigation, but archaeologists have noted that its land wore out from overuse. If the group's trade were sheep herding, one would necessarily have to walk the herding trails from one end to the other, fattening the sheep on the way, and selling one's produce at either end of the long trek. If the tribal group started out from India, they may have gone to Egypt, but it is more likely that they would travel to a nearer city such as Tehran or Susa. With an ancestor named Terah (Genesis 11:27), there may have been a possibility that Tehran was a major end point of the herding enterprise. The patriarch Abraham is described in the Bible as having vast herds and making a journey to Egypt, but we must remember that the biblical author was using locations that would be familiar to her audience of 1000 BC Palestine.

Early shepherd-class Brahmans formed tightly knit tribal groups that would travel large distances to find grazing lands for their animals. The expression "from Havilah to Shur" (Genesis 25:18), may be similar to a present day expression, "the ends of the earth." Havilah was India and Shur was the wall built in Egypt to keep the Semites out. That was the known world and the range of the sheep herders as they plied their trade. They needed both winter and summer pastures. They needed a market at each end of their journey to sell their produce. This need for a market could cause both cultural exchange and aggression. Around 2000 BC, King Ibbi-Sin of Mesopotamia also built a great wall to keep out foreigners. This wall might also have been the Shur of the "Havilah to Shur" expression.

After several centuries such a group might find a better living traveling a different route with more fertile pasturage, rather than returning to its homeland. They would remember their priestly forebears and their tribal ties in tales and song, but they would grow new heroes based on their everyday experiences and their conflicts with other people who contested their grazing rights.

This group would also keep health and purity regulations that preserved their religious upbringing, and protected them from contamination by the peoples of the land through which they walked. They might be convinced of the necessity for circumcision. They might not eat roast pig, as shepherds would not have time to dig roasting pits every time they had a pig to roast. Cooking pig on a spit would not make the meat hot enough to kill disease-bearing worms. They might follow patriarchal systems which contained strict master-servant relationships.

Both the Indus and Tehran areas had caste systems. That of India was put in place very early. The master-slave relationship had been established even before the Aryan invasion into the Harappan region. This is indicated by the fact that the Harappan social system required dedicated laborers to build structures and remove sewage. Religious beliefs contributed to the system, requiring each person to have a certain station in life, and to perform to the best of his ability in that station. In times of famine or when battling foes, generosity could be shown on the part of the "haves" in the sharing of their produce with the less able or in allowing a captured enemy to live. The enemy thus reprieved was required to become a servant to his captors. In spite of recent legislation designed to eradicate this serfdom, caste is still present in India where it has been an institution for thousands of years.

Brahmanism. The origin of Brahmanism is shrouded in myth. Early followers of Brahma supposedly denied themselves and left all wealth and temporal advantage to others. They were not allowed to own property, and could not engage in any pursuit the object of which was to gain wealth. They believed in personal sacrifice and prayer as ways to serve divine being. These thinkers and meditators who were the elite in their society were supported by a caste system where others "less pure" fed them and carried their waste products.

The four great caste divisions are Brahmans (priestly), Kshatriyas (military), Vaisyas (shopkeepers), and Sudras (the servile class). Each great caste is not a group of equal individuals, but is further divided according to marriage regulations, trades, location, or labor. For instance, the Brahmans can be divided into several hundred sub-castes, who frequently cannot intermarry with or eat food prepared by another Brahman the next rung down the social ladder. In different geographical areas there are Brahmans who may be fishermen, farmers, porters, potters, or shepherds as well as resident priests. These subcastes doubtless arose out of necessity, as you cannot have a community that is all priests with no one to provide the vegetables or meat for offerings. In our present century 1886 separate Brahmanic groups have been officially listed.

Leaving "Ur." *Terah took his son Abram, his grandson Lot the son of Haran, and his daughter-in-law the wife of Abram, and made them leave Ur of the Khaldeans* (Genesis 11:31). The Abraham and Sara story could be describing a prototypal couple of the Brahman shepherd caste. Semitic groups with possibilities of such Brahmanic origins ranged with their flocks in the area between India and Egypt from 8000 BC to the present. These prototypal God-fearing ancestors would have had certain religious beliefs that they would pass on to their children. They would be described as having noble characteristics. Both Abraham and Sarah are people who laugh, who are amused at and in control of situations. In Genesis 17:17 Abraham laughs; Sarah, in 18:12. Those who laugh show they are in power and are not afraid. Those who laugh show that they have souls that can appreciate the creation made by God. Our religious ancestors were people who could laugh. They were godly, powerful people.

The Bible describes one of the places of their origin as Ur of the Khaldeans. The name Ur means *fire mound* according to one language translation, and *city* in another. As the Khaldeans were fire worshippers, this might be a logical progression, as the center of cult worship would very likely be the center of the civilization or the city of importance. The Bible in describing Ur of the Khaldeans, is describing still another aspect of the origins of Abraham's religious faith. We are given a description of the rites of the Khaldean faith in the sacrifice description of Genesis 15. Sacrificial animals are laid out in a precise pattern and then burned. This was one of the formal rites which the prototypal ancestor Abraham used to properly worship his God. It was a rite that was long established in the city of Ur. This rite of animal sacrifice was incorporated into the worship of the Hebrews and was used when they built their temple. It was set down by the biblical author to give a stamp of approval to those priests who performed such rites. What better way for a group of wandering shepherds to show their devotion than the sacrifice of animals!

Lot. *Looking around, Lot saw all the Jordan plain, irrigated everywhere– this was before Yahweh destroyed Sodom and Gomorrah– like the garden of Yahweh or the land of Egypt, as far as Zoar* (Genesis 13:10). Genesis 13 describes Abraham returning from Egypt with Sara and his relative Lot. Those who research the Bible give various dates for Abraham's visit to Egypt: 1920 BC according to years specified in the Hebrew text of the Bible, 2551 BC according to some interpretations of the Hebrew *Septuagint*, and 2876 BC according to more liberal interpretations. Because the Abraham legend evolved back in the mists of prehistory, another possibility might be that Abraham never went to Egypt but the stories of ancestral tribal movements were put in more local places to aid understanding. Abraham's "father" is said to be Terah, so a possibility would be movements to a city nearer to India such as Tehran. Haran is another ancestor name associated with Abraham (Genesis 11:31). As climatic changes occurred, another ancestral group many generations later connected with the name Isaac, might have traveled from Tehran to Haran in northern Mesopotamia. A third route in a later time slot might have been Haran to Palestine. When the sheep herding groups were based in Palestine, their particular ancestor was called Jacob, and their tribal name became the name of the land, *Israel.* The ancestor Jacob was considered the head of this tribe, along with Abraham and Isaac as distant tribal progenitors.

Yahweh rained on Sodom and Gomorrah brimstone and fire from Yahweh (Genesis 19:23). We can give a practical date to that part of the Abraham story which concludes with the destruction of Sodom and Gomorrah at the southern end of the Dead Sea, *if* the Dead Sea is the true locale. Archaeologists believe that these communities met a violent end about 2350 BC. We might be tempted to use this date to give reality to the story of Abraham. But this is principally a legend about someone called Lot, rather than about Abraham. The addition of the name of Abraham in this story may be a tenuous connection of one proverbial ancestor with another. Another Mideast earthquake date is about 2750 BC.

All these dates may be too late for the real beginnings of the Lot story. The association of the story of Lot with the Dead Sea area may be due to the time and location of the biblical writer in the Palestine of King David. She knew that the Dead Sea was a devastated salt marsh area where nothing would grow and that there were salt formations there. Her audience also would be able to understand the Dead Sea setting for the Lot story. We have always assumed that Sodom and Gomorrah were the original locale for the natural disaster described in Genesis. However, with myths being a collection of several pieces of history, the original story may have earlier origins and may relate to another disaster elsewhere. Another area associated with the name of Lot is in a country far to the east of Palestine. There is a tremendous desert area in Iran called the Dasht-i-Lut, or Desert of Lot. It contains saline swamps and a salt area. This may well be the original location for the story of Lot's wife. This also may be the land where Lot settled, as in early times this section of Iran was a beautiful garden where the world's first peaches and melons were cultivated. This may be the location of the nation of Lud mentioned in Genesis 10:22.

Genesis 14 tells the story of Lot's abduction by a roving band and of his rescue by Abraham. The kings described in Abraham's foray to rescue his relative have names of legendary famous kings who were not necessarily contemporaneous with Abraham or each other. They are useful names for getting across the moral of the story. These kings may not have lived in Palestine, but in locations east of Palestine. They may symbolize battles between the cities in Mesopotamia. The Valley of Siddim or the Salt Sea spoken of, may be geographical elements in the Lot area in Iran.

All these separate tales of ancestral doings are woven together to give ethical instructions to the people of David's time. They also serve to inspire and teach all people who have come afterward. From a theological viewpoint, it doesn't matter where the legend of Lot's wife arose. We of a later day can still get the message– In times of stress, don't look back with longing, or you will become unable to move forward to greater accomplishments. If you discover a new idea or new ways, do not look back to the supposed security of a former system, or you may lose your stride and are liable to become encrusted with inaction.

The Promised Land. One hypothesis is that Abraham represents the typical wandering shepherd from the Indus region which was deteriorating from climatic changes and from improper irrigation techniques. Such a wanderer would naturally long for a secure homeland with fertile soil. The land in Iran would look very good to a wanderer from a dried out India. If we are to accept that the myth of the Promised Land was originally linked with the story of Abraham, and not an improvisation thrown in to help stabilize the Kingdom of David, then Iran may have been the original Promised Land. The myth about land would fit reasonably with the dreams of the prototype Abraham.

Longing for An Heir. Another yearning of people might concern the need for an heir. Pieces for this part of the myth set down in David's time, may have come from other stories existing in Egypt and Mesopotamia. Abraham is frequently heard lamenting about his lack of progeny. There was a similar lament in Egypt, where a pharaoh had a problem getting his wife pregnant.

The Hebrew tribes had spent a lot of time in Egypt and it is likely they heard gossip about Egyptian leaders. What was interesting about an Egyptian monarch could serve to illustrate the facts of life to listening Hebrews, but would be more meaningful for Hebrews if told about their own ancestor.

One pharaoh, Akhenaten or Amenhotep IV, had a disease in which his hips grew wide. He had a beautiful wife, Queen Nefertiti. Most people who have Akhenaten's disease are sterile and produce no children, but Nefertiti had several daughters. We do not know who was the father of these daughters, but Akhenaten may have had good reason to lament that he had no sons. If these stories about wishing for a son were told around the campfires of the Hebrews migrating back to Palestine with Moses, storytellers may have exchanged the name of Akhenaten (who lived about 1370 BC) with the name of Abraham.

There are other stories that have as their theme the need for an heir. One of the earliest written stories in the world is the Mesopotamian myth of King Etana who searched for a magical plant that would give him a son. This story also may have influenced the biblical author in her writing about Abraham.

Those who serve God should be concerned with how their actions will affect people in the future. Abraham is accordingly depicted as being greatly concerned about his descendants. The theology of the Davidic writer of the Bible includes this emphasis on the generations to come, in her tales of the noble ancestor. Her message is that those who consider the well being of descendants and those who learn lessons from the past, are worthy of the present.

4.4 Relatives of Abraham

Terah. Other clues that supply knowledge about the mythical beginnings of Abraham, may be found in the names of his relatives. Genesis 11:22-32 tells of *Nahor*, his brother (also named as his grandfather), and of *Terah*, his father. The name *Terah* has the meaning of *breath*, such as the breath that was breathed into Adam. *Narayana* was the divine Hindu sage that taught humankind.

Then there are comparable place names. The ancient name of Terah is still present in the name of the principal city of Iran, *Tehran*. Abraham's relatives are referred to as *Arameans*. Northern Mesopotamia is the land of *Aram Naharayim*, or *Aram of The Two Rivers*, the country around the source of the Tigris and Euphrates. Assyrian inscriptions limit Aram to areas east of the Euphrates, giving west of the Euphrates to the Hittites and Amorites.
Hagar. Besides Sarah, another heroine from the Abraham legend was Ishmael's mother *Hagar*, the slave wife of Abraham. Semitic groups who

didn't approve of each other's actions, yet who believed they descended from a common root, could blame their differences on the mother. It would be handy to explain this mother as a lesser wife. Slavery and slave wives were common in Near East culture. The Indus Valley culture similarly used its caste system to separate people into better and lesser lineage. The Israelites admit that the Ishmaelites are also Semites, tribally related to them and coming from the same geographical and religious background as Abraham. We also notice that the name of *Hagar* or *Agar*, the slave mother of the Ishmaelites, has similarities to *Agade* or *Akkad*, a name associated with Sargon I and Naram-Sin. The Sargon dynasty was Semite and may have had Hagar for an ancestor.

There were political reasons for the Israelites to dislike other tribes such as the descendants of Hagar, even though they were related. Naram-Sin was a Semite and claimed a common ancestor with the Hebrews. On one of Naram-Sin's trading journeys across the north of Palestine to the coast of the Mediterranean Sea, the people of Ebla were discourteous to him and his troops. Naram-Sin retaliated by razing their city to the ground. Those other tribes dwelling in the Palestinian area were horrified by this action, and cut themselves off from any tribal relationship they might have had with the Semitic kings of Sumer. Although the incident happened about 3000 BC, memories of it were kept alive through oral traditions that connected the disliked person's name with other oppressive individuals.

In later Jewish history a person with a name similar to Hagar, *Agag*, a king of the Amalekites, is saved by Saul, yet hewn in pieces by Samuel before Yahweh's altar (I Samuel 15:1-23). The Amalekites harassed the Hebrews while the latter were on their exodus journey, so it was ordered that their memory should be blotted out (Deuteronomy 25:17-19). It was said that "Amalek, first of the nations, his latter end will be destruction."

The Amalekites may have been descended from Isaac through Esau rather than from Ishmael and Hagar. They were a branch of the Edomites or sons of Esau (Genesis 36:12). Esau fathered Eliphaz, who fathered Amalek, and thus the Amalekite tribe. Amalek's mother was Timina, a Horite woman. Hor has to do with Egypt, as Horus was a prominent Egyptian god. This woman's descendants were doubly disgraced as they were connected to both Akkad and the foreign gods of Egypt. The connection may go back to the time of Sargon I and Naram-Sin, who may have ruled Egypt from an encampment called Thina at the northern end of the Red Sea. Thina or Timina was a feminine name worthy of Hebrew scorn.

In the Book of Esther, Haman, the arch-enemy of Israel, is termed *the Agagite*, emphasizing his descent from Agag, king of the hated race. The tellers of folk tales found it necessary to have appropriate hateful names for the villains in their stories. Violence and hatred is difficult to forgive, but history proves that this is what we are called to do if we want a peaceful world. As the Jew named Jesus said, "Love your enemies; forgive the one who wrongs you seventy times seven times."

Keturah. Genesis 25:1 tells us that the prototype Abraham had other sons by a wife called Keturah. These sons settled eastward of Palestine, according to the reckoning of David's day. If the Abraham legend draws on stories from further east, Keturah's sons' possible settlement in Arabia, may place Isaac's land in the Dashti-Kavir of northern Iran or in an area at one time called Sacae (Isacae), north of the Indus Valley and south of Cythia. Sons of Keturah named in I Chronicles 1:32-33 are Zimran, Jokshan, Medan, Midian, Ishbak, and Shuah. Also mentioned is a tribe called the Kedar (from [Ketur]ah). Isaiah 42:11 requests that the Kedar also praise Yahweh. Isaiah hoped to see a time when Hebrews and the various Arab tribes such as the descendants of Keturah, would unite in worship of the Creator.

Ishmael and Isaac. The Bible emphasizes two main splinter tribal groups of the descendants of Abraham. One claims that *Ish*mael is their ancestor. They are called Arabs. The other includes an ancestor *Ish*aac or *Isaac* and a tribe of Jacob, also called *Ishrael* or *Israel*. These names beginning with *Ish* have mythical meanings. In early Hebrew, man=*ish* and woman=*ishshah*. *Ish* words are used in the formation-of-the-human story in Genesis 2:23.

Because there are matriarchal societies among primitive peoples, the Semites may also have had matriarchs among their primitive nobility. An early first woman was Iscah (Genesis 11:29), which name linguistically corresponds to Ishshah, which also is like Esther (Hebrew), Ishtar (Babylonian), or Isis (Egyptian). Patriarchal tendencies won out, and by the time of David, early heroines were pretty much ignored by biblical writers. Abraham's sons, Isaac and Ishmael, are explained as dual tribes with similar stories. If Abraham and Sara are the prototypes for an earlier part of the ethical myth of the ancestors, then Isaac as a second part was explained by being given the role of Abraham's son. The Bible doesn't tell us a lot about Isaac. He stayed pretty much in the same place. The living must have been good with no earthquakes or droughts to cause a dramatic migration.

Isaac was almost killed as a sacrificial offering by his father. The Arabs believe this near sacrifice was not Isaac, but their ancestor Ishmael. This story about child sacrifice informs the readers that the prototypal ancestor Abraham did not believe in such a practice, and therefore, to worship God correctly, they should avoid such actions. More of Abrahamic religious beliefs are displayed in Genesis 24:2-3 where his servant is required to make a phallic pledge to find a wife for Isaac. This servant used ten camels to go in search of this wife. This may have been an Arabic incident, for camels were used in Arabia more than in Israel or Egypt. Another thread connecting Isaac to earlier religious traditions is the Rama-Sita abduction myth alluded to in Genesis 26:7-11.

Like Abraham, the idea of an ancient father figure is found in the Hindu holy writing, *The Bhagavad-Gita*, Book 4, Text 1. "The Supreme Personality of Godhead said: I instructed this imperishable science of yoga to the sun-god Vivasvan, and Vivasvan instructed it to Manu, the father of mankind, and Manu in turn instructed it to Iksvaku." It is believed that God passes transcendental knowledge to those in authority, such as tribal leaders. The idea of Manu may be related to the idea of Abraham as the father of nations, and *Iksvaku* may refer to *Isaac*. Abraham, Isaac, and Jacob may represent a religious heritage rather than blood relatives!

Iranian myths say that the goddess Saraswati became the mother of the first prince-man, Kumaris. As we look at the names *Ishmael* and *Israel* (for Isaac's son, Jacob), we see that for the Arabs the name of the first son Ishmael, son of Hagar, means *the man who hears God*, while the descendants of Sara have the name *Israel* meaning man or prince of God. A prince is born of a legal wife, while a person who hears and serves is born of a servant wife. The idea of a prototypal first man, Kumaris, Isaac, Ishmael, or Israel, may come from the same mythical beginnings.

Esau and Jacob. *When the time came for her confinement, there were indeed twins in her womb. The first to be born was red, and as though he were completely wrapped in a hairy cloak; so they named him Esau. Then his brother was born, with his hand grasping Esau's heel; so they named him Jacob* (Genesis 25:24-26). Jacob is associated with the word *heel*, and right from the beginning of their relationship, Jacob had a hold on Esau. Can the story of the tricking of Isaac by his son Jacob in Genesis 27, be a mythical allusion to two tribes in the same area, one of which was notable for red hair and success at hunting?

The religious traditions of the prototype Isaac were handed down to two related tribes, the sons of Esau and the sons of Jacob. Edom, or the descendants of Esau, was a tribal division which sought the security of the mountains, like the mountain men of Zagros (the Gudeans and Elamites) who ruled for a time in Mesopotamia. The tribal name of Jacob might refer to the Semitic plains people or farmers who settled in both north and south Mesopotamia from 3100-2200 BC. Some of them went further west to Palestine and became known as Israelites. They remembered the religious teachings of a forebear who wrestled with God, and who handed down significant thoughts about God's justice.

Jacob tricked his father into giving him the blessing that was due his first born brother Esau. What can be the deeper historical significance of this tale? Is this an admission that the mountain people were the earlier tribal group possessing land rights? When Jacob fled his father's wrath, he traveled to the home of his uncle Laban. He worked for this uncle in the land of Qedem (which means people of the east and is the same land where the Egyptian hero Sinuhe was treated so well). This land was somewhere east of Canaan. When Jacob left the Laban place of employment to meet his brother Esau, the river he crossed is called variously, the Jordan (Genesis 32:10) and the Jabbok, a tributary of the Jordan (32:23). When Jacob left Laban and entered the land of Canaan, Jacob's name changed to Israel. In the biblical story, Jacob and Esau made peace by living in different areas (Genesis 33). Genesis 26:34-35 remarks sorrowfully of Esau's marital alliance with Hittites, a tribal group from what is now present day Turkey. This reflects a dissatisfaction of the Israelite group with the hill tribes' military alliance with Hittites.

Another insight into the religious views of the time of Jacob (which may have been influenced by Hittite customs) is given by the story of Jacob's wives. Jacob served his father-in-law Laban to acquire his two wives. Jacob was easily convinced by Laban that the elder daughter should be given in marriage first. He married both of Laban's daughters, Rachel and Leah, who were much concerned about their ability to produce children. When Jacob took his wives and left Laban's homeland, Rachel hid the statuettes of the household gods which she had stolen from her father. These household idols do not sound like worship of the One True God. The religious traditions of Jacob's family contained threads of Hittite religion and of the worship of Mother Goddess figurines. When Jacob's son Joseph was hijacked to Egypt, he probably carried in his heart his mother's worship of the Mother Goddess.

4.5 Joseph

Pharaoh named Joseph Zaphenath-paneah, and gave him Asenath the daughter of Potiphera, priest of On, for his wife. Joseph traveled through the land of Egypt (Genesis 41:45). There is much in the Hebrew scriptures about Joseph, son of Jacob, who rose to power in Egypt. With all this Hebrew publicity, surely there must be *The Story of Joseph* from the Egyptian point of view carved on some tomb wall. If we are to believe the Bible, there was a remarkable young foreigner who arrived in Egypt and was able to impress the ruling pharaoh with his wisdom. If such were the case, surely this man's story would be inscribed on the tomb wall of his pharaoh.

Generations coming after would remember his wisdom and quote it to one another. Perhaps they would forget his humble beginnings and that he was a foreigner. They would recall him only as a great example of Egyptian manhood, or perhaps even liken him to a god. If Rameses II was considered godly because he helped his people, shouldn't Joseph, a man who built great storage warehouses and saved the known world from starvation, have some memorial in the country he served?

Joseph is a Hebrew name, and the ancient Egyptian word for *Joseph* will not be familiar to us. It is not the present day Arabic *Yusuf*. Arabic was not the language of Egypt until long after the time of Christ. Joseph might have had an Egyptian title not easily recognized as belonging to Joseph, the Hebrew. The name Joseph itself may be a title. In English the name means *he shall increase*. What better name for a pharaoh's vizier than *one who increases his master's possessions*, or *one who possesses fullness*? The Bible says that Joseph traveled through Egypt on the pharaoh's business, presumably dealing out justice in the pharaoh's name. The pharaoh demanded of his ministers, "Can we find any other man like this, possessing the *spirit* of God!" He made Joseph governor over the *whole* land of Egypt (Genesis 41:37-43).

The Religious Milieu. To what kind of spirit of God was pharaoh referring? Did he realize that Joseph as a foreigner was brought up by a mother (Rachel) who reverenced household idols? Looking back today from our One-God monotheistic viewpoint, we feel that the early peoples of Egypt worshiped many gods. This may be a wrong impression. John West points out in *Serpent in The Sky* that the various religious centers in Heliopolis, Hermopolis, and Thebes were not advocating different gods but different aspects of god.[2] From one supreme Godhead came the nine natures of this One. The names of these nine God-aspects are usually given as Temu, Shu, Tefnut, Geb, Nut, Osiris, Isis, Set, and Nephthys. Others sometimes included are Ptah, Hathor, and Thoth, with Ra, the representative of sun and light, often the most powerful. In this super abundance of God-natures or God-aspects, Temu and Ptah, are often bound up together, with Temu being the transcendent, beyond us, creator God, and Ptah being the God who is immanent, within us, and recognizable by the human. If the pharaoh of Egypt wanted to say something impressive about Joseph, he could not have chosen better words than to say that this man possessed the spirit of God. The name of this immanent God-aspect, Ptah, might be placed before or after the name of Joseph to emphasize that Joseph was imbued with the spirit of this god. The Egyptian hieroglyphic for Joseph has certain linguistic similarities to the Spanish word for Joseph, *Jose* (pronounced Ho-zay). Joseph's Egyptian name may be *Hotep* or *Ptah-Hotep*. Many Hoteps and Ptah-Hoteps are recorded in Egyptian history.

Kagemni may also be a descriptive job-title for Joseph. The name *Kagemni* or *Khaemhat* (names would change slightly as hundreds of years passed) was an official title that at one time meant *the overseer of the granaries*. In another puzzling inscription Khaemhat's *father* or *predecessor* is named *Imhotpe* (or *Imhotep*). This may be saying that Khaemhat is a vizier in a long line of viziers going back to the famous vizier Imhotep.

Gifted Viziers. In searching for the name and personality of Joseph in the list of noblemen commemorated on tomb walls, we find that there are many possibilities for gifted viziers. Unfortunately, some inscriptions on tomb walls are repeated over and over. Scribes who prepared funerary tales had to do the writing on the wall while the pharaoh and his noblemen were still alive, so they often copied some information from the father's or grandfather's or predecessor's tomb site onto their current pharaoh's tomb walls. There are many examples of this type of repetition with the pharaohs. To determine which pharaoh performed the noteworthy act, one has to go through all the ancestral tomb inscriptions to find which is the earliest and therefore the original.[3]

One possible identity for Joseph as *Hotep* is as a nobleman in the reign of pharaoh Zoser of the **Third Dynasty** (about 2670 BC). This person named *Imhotep* was the physician of his pharaoh and also the architect of the funeral complex at Sakkara of which the Step Pyramid is the main feature. The other pyramids exceeded Imhotep's construction in size, but they copied his style. One of his architectural achievements was the use of limestone rather than brick for permanent buildings. Imhotep was made the patron of scribes and his wisdom was copied and recited. The later day Greeks deified Imhotep as the god of medicine, Asclepius. A later inscription from Ptolemaic times on a rock face near the First Cataract of the Nile, recorded an oral tradition that told of a famine in the reign of Zoser.[4]

Another possibility is that Joseph may be located among the **Fifth Dynasty** noblemen who ruled from Heliopolis (about 2490-2365 BC). As the Bible mentions the priests at On (Genesis 41:45), and as in this time period Ra was being worshipped at Heliopolis (another name for On), it is possible that Joseph may be this Fifth Dynasty vizier commemorated at Heliopolis not far from modern Cairo. We find in the Fifth Dynasty time period that pyramid texts at Heliopolis show funerary customs, prayers, and hymns oriented towards Ra.

We can search for Joseph among the Fifth Dynasty viziers– Ti, Kagemni, and <u>five</u> Ptah-Hoteps.[5] Ptah-Hotep, vizier of Pharaoh Djedkare of the Fifth Dynasty, wrote 43 instructions to his son. Some of the advice given is, "Be not proud because of thy learning," "Never utter words in heat," and "Report on a thing observed, not heard."

If these early writings are by the Hotep who was the Bible's God-filled, wisdom-filled Joseph, they may have been both Egyptian proverbs and have been carried over into the Proverbs of the Bible. The Egyptian *Book of Wisdom* directed to a son, introduces many of its lessons by "Listen, my son, to your father's instruction." Joseph had two notable sons, Ephraim and Manasseh. When Jacob blessed the sons of Joseph, he managed to bless Ephraim, the younger with a better blessing than that given to Manasseh, the elder. This may reflect that the people of Manasseh did not fully incorporate into the Israeli group, but became associated with the Ishmaelites in Arabia. Some proverbs have been handed down from this group in Arabia, which also may be the wise sayings of an Egyptian. The Bible's Proverbs 30 contains the sayings of Augur (a person who can interpret dreams or foretell the future), the son of Jakeh (Jacob?), of Massa (the tribe of Manasseh?).

Leading us to suspect this particular Ptah-Hotep is Joseph, is another report of a famine under the Fifth Dynasty. A double tomb at Sakkara memorializing Pharaoh Djedkare and his son (meaning *favorite*) or servant Ptah-Hotep of the Memphite Fifth Dynasty has tomb artistry with views of plentiful food, implying they came through the famine successfully.

Also, sometime during this Fifth Dynasty the Egyptians recorded on limestone rock the defeat of the Badawi (Bedouin) in the Sinai. Seshat, the inventor of writing and the goddess of history, claims that the Egyptians received 100,000 oxen and cattle, plus 200,000 each of asses, goats, and sheep as a result of this maneuver. This defeat does not correspond with the popularity Joseph had with his pharaoh, but it may be recording an earlier or later event. It also may be recording the friendly takeover of cattle that occurred when Joseph invited his relatives to live in Egypt.

Another possible date for Joseph is about 1600 BC when Egypt came under the control of foreign rulers called the Hyksos. Some of these **Fifteenth Dynasty** rulers may have been connected with people from Palestine, because many groups entered Egypt at this time. Their date is very near 1628 BC, the date for the volcanic explosion of Thera 70 miles north of Crete. This explosion caused many peoples to relocate.

Expansion and disruption in other nations led up to this period of turmoil for Egypt. The Hyksos in Egypt were both Western Semites (or Amorites) and Hurrians from further north in a kingdom called Mitanni. The Hittite kingdom in Turkey at 2000 BC extended into northern Syria. The Hittites (Hatti, Khatti, Kassites) about 1800 BC moved southward, put an end to the First Dynasty rulers of Babylon, and reached their zenith in the 14th and 13th centuries BC. In 1365 BC the Hurrian country of Mitanni was overthrown by the Hittites. In 1200 BC the Hittite Empire was itself overwhelmed by the Sea Peoples and was incorporated into the Syro-Hittite amalgam.[6]

Groups from Western Asia, the Mediterranean, Turkey, and the Near East had been entering Egypt for many centuries. The Egyptians called them *Apiru*. This name may refer to foreign sheep herding groups, or results of intermarriage of foreign elements in Egypt, and some people believe it may have a relationship to the word *Hebrew*. These foreign elements consolidated under Hyksos leadership and controlled much of Egypt from their capital at Avaris in the eastern Nile delta. The Hyksos could rule in Egypt as they had beaten the pharaoh's armies. However, they, as foreigners, did not have the support of the Egyptian people, and they did not have control of all Egyptian cities. The Hyksos may have introduced the horse and chariot to Egypt; also some more peaceful items, the olive and the pomegranate.

These stranger kings banished Amun from the pantheon because Amun represented the Egyptian elite. The expulsion of Set as evil, was also due to this foreign influence. Before this innovative Hyksos theology, both good and evil were deemed necessary for normal life.[7] Set, as evil, was the necessary antagonistic companion of good. Set, as sin, and as the idea of a devil, became the enemy to be driven out.

Egyptians from Thebes further down the Nile disliked these foreign kings. The Theban ruler Seqenenre and his sons Kamose and Ahmose engaged them in battle about 1500 BC. The tomb of one of Ahmose's soldiers contains an account of the expulsion of the Hyksos.

These regimes under the control of the foreign Hyksos and the Shepherd Kings may have had some connections with the sojourn of the Hebrews in Egypt prior to their exodus.[8] Of those rulers living in the Nile Delta town of Avaris, the pharaoh Merwoserre Ya'qob-el or Apachman (about 1640 BC) has in his name *Ya'qob-el* a phrase that could be interpreted as *God of Jacob*. (*Ya'qob* equals *Jacob*, and *el* equals *god*.) This ruler is probably not Joseph, for Joseph was not a Pharaoh but a vizier, and Ya'qob-el's reign was not long enough to include Joseph's more than 14 years of activities (seven years of plenty and seven of famine). Another Hyksos pharaoh after Ya'qob-el (about 1600 BC) is named Aqnenre Apopi or Apophis, a name which has evil connotations for the Hebrews. Sin and evil were associated with Apophis, the great serpent, the enemy of gods and of humankind.

It is possible that there was a famine throughout the Mid East in the years following 1628, because of atmospheric dust from the Thera explosion which hindered plant growth. It may be that Joseph's relatives or some group of Hebrews went to Egypt after that date. If they spent 400 years in Egypt, that would make the possible exodus date during the reign of Rameses II (circa 1250) about right.

On the other hand, the earlier Fifth Dynasty around 2450 may have been the time when foreign elements (including Joseph) first entered, and rose to power. Centuries later when the Hyksos got in control, they may have been the ones who "knew not Joseph" (Exodus 1:8) and persecuted the Hebrews. The biblical story tellers may be remembering a late exodus scene in the time of the Hyksos, when the Hebrews left and took a lot of other people with them. The biblical plagues described in Exodus 7-12 may be related to incidents that occurred in Hyksos times due to the explosion of Thera; or the exodus scene and the plagues may refer to another time and confrontation. With myths there is always the possibility that many different legends may be used and woven into one myth containing the many threads.

Still another possibility for the identity of Joseph can be found in the reign of a later pharaoh, Amenophis III of the **Eighteenth Dynasty** about 1415 BC. Pharaohs would use the name of a god as part of their name. For instance, *Amenophis* is broken up into *Amen* and *ophis*. This combination can be translated as *Amen is satisfied*, or as *the pharaoh is filled with the spirit of the god Amen* (or *Amun*).

Amenophis III took the throne as a teenager. He lived a long life and saw many viziers come and go. One of his favorite advisors was a native of Avaris in the Delta, who used his pharaoh's name of *Amenophis*, and also the name of *Khaemhat*, as special servant of Amenophis. Foreigners in high office in Egypt were sometimes given Egyptian names, more often than not compounded with the name of the reigning king. This vizier Amenophis was the son of Hapu (or Hapiru? or Apiru? or Hebrew?). This person was deified like the earliest vizier Imhotep. We know this because the Egyptians represented him by a larger-than-life statue.

Again, there is some wisdom written down. Some of our biblical proverbs (such as 22:20) are attributed to *The Wisdom of Amenemophis*. This *Book of Wisdom* may refer back to previous books of wisdom written by previous viziers. The name *Amenemophis* may be a later day version of Pharaoh Zoser's vizier *Imhotep* prefaced with the name of the god *Amun* (or *Amen*), and where the ending of *emophis* equals *Imhotep*. The name *Amen-emophis* may be a variant on *Ptah-Hotep* with the in-dwelling God being recognized as Amun instead of Ptah. In the religious beliefs of 1415 BC, Amun was back in style and was described as the "hidden god" who made mankind and created the animals. After a thousand years, a few changes, such as having the *hotep* ending shift to *ophis*, and having a different name for god, should be expected. Another fact leading to name changes is that there were no vowels written down in early hieroglyphics. The glyphs for Amenophis would contain only M, N, P, H, and S.

Amenophis III moved his capital from Memphis to Thebes, an action that implies he had a trusted overseer who could substitute for his lord in either section of Egypt. Amenophis of Hapu, the vizier, was known for his architectural work at Thebes for his pharaoh. He built the Colossi at Memnon as part of the mortuary temple of Amenophis III.

Amun was the god-aspect of the upper class, priests and warriors. Shortly after the reign of Amenophis III, his son Akhenaten, who disliked the power of the priests, announced his belief in One God whose energy was the sun. Can this religious renewal have been instigated by belief or opposition to a foreign theology? Akhenaten discharged the priests and nobility who had served his father and put parvenus in high administrative posts.[9] If Joseph were vizier under Amenophis III, then he would have rapidly been defrocked of his powerful position by Akhenaten. It may be that Amenophis III outlived Joseph, for the Bible implies that Joseph and the Hebrews were favored by Joseph's pharaoh during that pharaoh's reign.

In this Eighteenth Dynasty time period we also have viziers and assistant viziers of the pharaoh who have the name *Mose*. The vizier *Ramose* was the younger brother of the vizier Amenophis, son of Hapu. *Ptahmose* was another vizier in the south at this time and high priest of Amun. The name of Moses may come from this era, but some of the myths told of Moses may be from much earlier traditions.

Joseph's Land. *"Never mind about your property for the best that the land of Egypt offers is yours"* (Genesis 45:20). Joseph's acceptance of pharaoh's offer to stay in Egypt may indicate that he had not concluded anything about the precise location of a land promised to the descendants of Abraham. He is eager and willing to settle in Egypt. The territory where the Hebrews lived in Egypt was called Goshen. It was the fertile northern pasturage area. Other areas in the early civilized world had this name. There is also a territory of Goishon in Iran. This is similar to the name of the River Gihon which watered the Garden of Eden. When the pharaoh gave this territory to Joseph, he gave the best land in the region to the Hebrews, a true Land of Promise, land that was later known as the land of Rameses (Genesis 45:20; 46:28-34; 47:11, 27; 50:8; and Exodus 9:26).

Taxes. *Thus Joseph acquired all the land in Egypt for Pharaoh, since one by one the Egyptians sold their estates, so hard pressed were they by the famine* (Genesis 47:20). A harvest tax had evidently been collected for quite awhile, but tomb statements report that officials collected a great harvest tax in the year thirty of the reign of Amenophis III. These may be two different types of tax. A harvest tax is also described in Genesis 47:13-26. The biblical author may be gently complaining about Joseph's strict measures towards the common people. The Egyptians and any foreigners in Egypt were happy to be alive after the famine, but Joseph's economic policies may have set in motion procedures that later caused resentments that made his descendants uncomfortable. From that time forward a fifth of the produce of the land went to Pharaoh. Only the priests were exempt from this double tithe.

As Joseph in the Bible was supposedly the *first* one to set a 20% tax on the commoner, the proceeds of which went to the pharaoh, the son of Hapu of 1415 BC may not be the biblical Joseph, but a vizier from a later time period. The harvest tax had been collected for quite awhile, and was calculated proportionately to the height of the Nile flood. When there was a good flood, there was a good harvest. On the other hand, a 10% tax may have been collected from early times, and Joseph may have been the one who doubled it.

Prototypal Joseph. The story of Joseph may be a combination of some or all of the identities listed above. He may have been Zoser's vizier *Imhotep.* He may have been one of the *Ptah-Hoteps* and been present in Egypt in 2450 BC. He may have ruled with the Hyksos or been *Amenophis, Son of Hapu.* The Joseph story may be built up from parts of a series of great viziers, as was commonly done for heroes in Egypt. The Bible story of Joseph is not giving us history, geography, and architecture, as much as it is giving us the story of the human's relationship to divinity and to her fellow human. It is telling us what has gone on in the development of the world, but relating it all to God's care for God's creation.

When Genesis 45:8 says that Joseph was appointed to a high position, it describes his title as *Father to The Pharaoh,* or as one of the respected elders in the pharaoh's household. This honorary title came into vogue in a certain period of time, and does not mean that Joseph was called by this title. The only dating that can be understood from this title is to say that the writer in David's time was writing after this title was in use. If Rameses II used this title, it does not mean that Joseph was vizier under Rameses. If Zoser or Djedkare or Amenophis III did not use it, that does not exclude Joseph from being one of their viziers. The title is stated as seen from a 1000 BC viewpoint.

Joseph stayed in Egypt with his father's family; and Joseph lived a hundred and ten years (Genesis 50:22). Biblical age may have more to do with the quality of a person's life than with chronological age. Perhaps all the people with the job description of *Hotep* were recorded as having the same age. Amenophis, son of Hapu, vizier to Amenophis III about 1415 BC, was able to say in his funerary inscriptions, "I am a righteous man. I have attained eighty years in the favor of the king. I shall complete 110 years."[10] This may have been the approved formula for the scribes to place on the tomb walls of a Hotep or Joseph.

All these tomb inscriptions of Hoteps may spring from the fame of the early Imhotep who was so great that the Greeks and Romans turned him into their God of Healing, Asclepius. (When the Greeks and Romans conquered Egypt, they absorbed some of the Egyptian religious ideas.) The other Hoteps following in his footsteps acquired pieces of his fame. One of them wrote words of wisdom to his sons. One of them was a son of Jacob.

As the biblical Joseph may be a combination of these Hotep myths, his ancestors, the Patriarchs, who are described in the Bible before him, are likely to also be composites of myths. This enhances rather than diminishes the value of the biblical writings. It deepens our understandings of the historical views of the writers and enlarges the scope of the lessons learned from history.

Footnotes

1 E.A. Speiser, *Interpreters Dictionary of the Bible, Volume III*, Abingdon Press, New York, 1962, p. 238.

2 Normandi Ellis, *Awakening Osiris*, Phanes Press, Grand Rapids, MI, 1988, p. 21.

3 Hieroglyphic scenes on tomb walls may not apply to the particular pharaoh being commemorated, especially if there is a dynasty connection. To keep dynastic control hieroglyphics imply that a previous leader's strength and foresight is extended into the present reign. If we run across a tomb design of a kneeling Asiatic captive paying respect to a pharaoh, we must check out the tombs of his predecessors to see if this is merely a rerun. Thus we have the theme of Libyan captives repeated by Sahure (2458-2446 BC), Neuserre (2416-2392 BC), Pepi I (2289-2255 BC), Pepi II (2246-2152 BC), and Taharqa (690-664 BC). The real Libyan campaign may have been even earlier than 2458 BC. This information is from *Atlas of Ancient Egypt*, John Baines & Jaromir Malik, Facts on File, New York, 1980, p. 34. Another example of repetition is found in *The Ancient Egyptians*, Jill Kamil, American University in Cairo Press, 1988, p. 67.

4 Jill Kamil, *The Ancient Egyptians,* American U. in Cairo Press, 1988, p. 44.

5 *ibid.,* p. 89.

6 R.F. Tapsell, compiler, *Monarchs, Rulers, Dynasties and Kingdoms of the World*, Facts on File, Park Avenue, NY, 1983, p. 66.

7 J. Gardner Wilkinson, *The Ancient Egyptians*, Bonanza Books, New York, 1989, p. 331.

8 R.F. Tapsell, *loc. cit.,* p. 69.

9 Donald Redford, *Akhenaten*, American University in Cairo Press, 1989, p. 165.

10 *ibid.,* p. 47.

V

The Way Out of Egypt

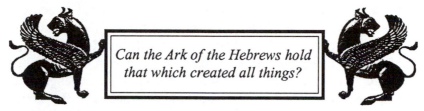

> *Can the Ark of the Hebrews hold that which created all things?*

5.1 The Person, Moses

The myth of how the Israelites came into Egypt is only part of the story of God's care for all people over the millions of years we have been reviewing. Nevertheless, it is a cornerstone of many current belief systems. The time arrived, spoken of in Exodus 1:8, when there was a pharaoh who knew nothing about Joseph. The Israelites became the oppressed. The myth of Moses and the *exodus*, or *going-out*, emphasizes God's love for the oppressed, and reminds us of the presence of God through time.

The Bible As History. When asked about the first five books of the Bible called the Pentateuch, people usually agree that they were written by Moses or by scribes of the Moses tradition. They tend to believe that these early scribes knew all the factual information about the patriarchs, and that they speak to our day with an authoritative historical voice. Some of us assert that the Holy Spirit is speaking through their writings. For that reason we designate the scriptures as *Holy* Scriptures. I, too, believe that whoever wrote the Bible, did so at the urging of the Holy Spirit within.

We often do not think about whether the persons influenced to write by this Spirit were black or white, male or female, Hebrew or Egyptian. They may not have been Hebrew <u>male</u> scribes of the Moses tradition. In fact, the *Moses tradition* evolved and rose to importance in the time of David and Solomon and the even later time of the building of the second temple. It may include much more than what went on in the actual lifetime of Moses, who never entered Palestine or worshiped in a Jerusalem temple.

To test whether the Bible is being historical, mythological, or theological, we must use other tests such as biblical-contemporary stelae, archaeological data such as pottery, ancient literature, or even other sections of the Bible itself. Some stelae and tomb hieroglyphics by pharaohs may be kingly boasting for purposes of propaganda, but there is usually some historical truth in them. Archaeological finds can verify dates. Other biblical sections can reinforce the theological message, using varying symbols and stories. **The Exodus Setting.** In the millions of years that humans inhabited the earth, there must have been thousands of mass migrations to escape natural disasters or human-made oppressions. Because of the Thera volcanic explosion, for example, people pressed eastward from the disturbed Mediterranean, displacing other populations. Droughts and earthquakes added to some of the migrations. This left some groups with the urge to return to the lands from which they had been evicted. One such migration is described in the Book of Exodus. The Hebrew exodus may not have been a single datable incident, but may have taken place under different leaders at different times. The biblical author combined these different events and described them as happening to one group under two leaders, Moses and Joshua. The personages of Moses and Joshua may also be combinations of myths. There were events that happened to other tribes which eventually ended up in Palestine. In 1177 BC there were Sea Peoples who were pursued by pharaoh's armies. These tales had to be included, too. There were religious customs and laws to be obeyed. These were important to record. All this information was put together by the biblical authors in story form, so that it would be easy to follow and to remember, similar to the treatment of the stories of Abraham and Joseph.

The Bible relates all these cultural and political maneuverings from an ethical viewpoint, that helps us in the present day to look beyond battles and politics. We are advised not to trust in princes or even in the ordinary human being. We are to put our trust in God, and to promote justice in our personal lives. The ancestor tales of Abraham and Sara and their offspring give us many examples of good and bad behavior, and help us to decide proper courses of action. Are we to treat our wives like Abraham, and docilely allow them to be put in the local king's harem (Genesis 20)? Because we are clever about genetics, are we to appropriate the father-in-law's flocks and herds as Jacob did (Genesis 30:32-43)? We understand that we are to love our spouses, and to deal honestly with our in-laws and with all others. We are told about the exodus event in order that we might meditate on God's loving care for all people, especially the oppressed.

Baby Moses. The biblical exodus story tells us that Moses was set adrift in the reeds by the Nile. This may never have happened, but may be a tale with theological implications. The Bible is not telling us facts and figures; it is giving us theology, the story of how God takes care of the people of the world. Moses is the mythical figure who is the carrier of the message of a God concerned with the welfare of earth's people. The stories told about him are similar to those told about other heroes. A baby-in-a-basket tale is told about Sargon I, King of Akkad about 3000 BC, the charismatic Semite who rose from small beginnings to rule over all of Mesopotamia. As a baby, he was found floating in a basket. It would appear that elements of the basket story came by way of Mesopotamia, as the biblical papyrus basket (Exodus 2:3) is smeared with tar which is found in Mesopotamia. Nile boats were made of buoyant matting and didn't depend on tar. There also were wise persons in India who were floated in baskets on holy rivers, at the mercy of the gods who controlled the rivers. These males who were to serve their people were drawn from the power of the water by people of faith and given proper education for their future greatness.

The Name, Moses. *(Pharaoh's daughter) treated him like a son; she named him Moses because, she said, "I drew him out of the water"* (Exodus 2:10). The name *Moses* may have watery connotations, but it may also have other meanings. It may be a title rather than a personal name, and may come from the same type of word construction as the name of Rameses the Great. Rameses can be divided into two words– the god's name *Ra,* and *Moses* meaning *son of,* or *servant of.* Moses in the Bible has an Egyptian name similar to Ra-moses and Thut-moses. Hebrews reverently omitted God's name as too holy to speak, or perhaps dangerous. This may be why there was no name of a god associated with this particular *servant of* name. In every day life, Moses may have used a common name. Followers used his official name *Moses* as it was more respectful and it honored him as God's servant.

Other languages have their own way of spelling *Moses,* and there were other legends from north and east of Palestine using variations of this name. The Hittite name *Mukshush* is related to the name Moses. It is found in a document called the *Maduwattas Indictment* which names Mukshush as a supporter of King Attarissiyas. There is an area in North Syria called the state of Mukishe. This may be where Moses spent some of his time. The name Moses is also related to the name Mopsus, a sage of Greek legend, who wandering after the fall of Troy, supposedly founded Greek colonies in Pamphylia and Cilicia in Asia Minor. An inscription in Cilicia has Moses claimed as an ancestor by an 8th century BC chieftain of the Danoi, the tribe of Dan which moved northwest and had ties with the Homeric Greeks.

The Palace Household. When myth-weaving storytellers introduced the tale of Moses, they wanted to impress the audience with the fact that the hero was truly a great man. If Moses had a good education, seemingly one of the requirements of greatness, his reading and writing skills had to come from somewhere. The storyteller couldn't say that Moses had a Bachelor of Arts degree, because such things hadn't been invented in Moses' day, so she stated that the hero came from the pharaoh's household. Someone from the pharaoh's household would have a good education in writing, astrology, priestly duties, and handling war chariots, horses, and people. He might be an authority on Egyptian gods and belief in afterlife. He might even have been a specialist in writing hieroglyphics on tomb walls for the future entombment of his pharaoh.

However, if the pharaoh died, he might lose his job. The new pharaoh might have other favorites that he would want inscribing wise and spiritual thoughts in his tomb. Pharaohs didn't last very long in office, and scribes did go in and out of favor in Egypt. We have heard about an ancient scribe Sinuhe who got out of favor with his pharaoh about 2300 BC.

Mixed Marriages. *Moses fled from Pharaoh and made for the land of Midian* (Exodus 2:15). There he married the daughter of the priest of Midian. Joseph, his predecessor, married the daughter of the priest of On, or Heliopolis, where the sun god Ra was worshiped. Are these priestly daughters put into the Bible story to let the reader know about the incorporation of other ethics into the Hebrew amalgam? What sort of a God did the priest of Midian serve? When Moses describes his God to Pharaoh, he tells Pharaoh that he must take the people into the wilderness to worship this God (Exodus 5:1). Moses' God is the God of the Wilderness. Moses had experienced this God in a wilderness setting in his confrontation with the Burning Bush (Exodus 3:1-6), and he knew that he had to go to the wilderness to properly worship this God.

5.2 Comings and Goings of Peoples

After this, Moses and Aaron went to Pharaoh and said to him, "This is what Yahweh, the God of Israel, has said, 'Let my people go, so that they may keep a feast in the wilderness in honor of me'" (Exodus 5:1). Moses and Aaron had to give reasons to Pharaoh for their need to leave the country. There weren't official passports, and a large group of people did constitute a threat to the safety and order of the Egyptian nation. The religious explanation for their exodus retreat is further elaborated upon in Exodus 8:22– *"We sacrifice to Yahweh our God animals which Egyptians count it sacrilege to slaughter. If we offer in front of the Egyptians sacrifices that outrage them, will they not stone us?"*

Yahweh said to Moses and Aaron, "Pharaoh is adamant. He refuses to let the people go" (Exodus 7:14). Early civilizations had many challenges and calamities. We don't know which might have related to the migrations to and from Egypt. For example, when the explosion of Thera occurred, there may have been very difficult times for Egypt. The air was poisonous from volcanic ash, causing lung malfunctions and making boils on animals and humans. Such disasters sound similar to the period of the Ten Plagues set down in Exodus. Plagues described were (1) the river's waters are turned into blood (Ex. 7:17-24), (2) frogs (Ex. 8:2-14), (3) lice (8:16), (4) flies (8:21-31), murrain on cattle, horses, asses, camels, oxen, and sheep (9:3), (5) boils on man and beast (9:9), (6) pestilence (9:15), (7) hail and fire, with flax and barley smitten (9:18), (8) locusts (10:4) which came on the east wind and were cast out by the west wind, (9) darkness for three days (10:21), at which point the Israelites traded their heavier possessions for jewels that would be easy to carry, and (10) the plague of the first born (11:5). Then there was a strong east wind (14:21) that parted the Red Sea and enabled them to go through dry shod.

From approximately 2400 to 2000 BC, there was a culture decline and widespread destruction in Palestine. The number of communities diminished sharply. Many cities suffered destruction. A second major period of disorder occurred from 1600 to 1200 BC. Should we explain this as due to Moses and Joshua, or pinpoint earthquakes, plagues, famines, and volcanic disturbances for the consequent cultural unrest? For the same period of time, 2400 to 1200 BC, the Hapiru were referred to in texts as troublesome people in the land of Canaan. These roving bands agitated through the countryside.

5.3 The Exodus Under Moses

Joseph went up to bury his father, all Pharaoh's servants and the palace dignitaries going up with him, joined by all the dignitaries of the land of Egypt, as well as all Joseph's family and his brothers, along with his father's family. They left no one in the land of Goshen but their dependents, with their flocks and their cattle. ... Then Joseph returned to Egypt, he and his brothers, along with all those who had come up with him for his father's burial (Genesis 50:7-8,14). The first Hebrew body in the Goshen community to exit Egypt was probably the dead body of Jacob who had made his son Joseph promise to take his corpse back for burial in his home country of Palestine. This must have been a marvelous pageantry which displayed the solidarity felt by Egyptians and Hebrews. The Hebrews all returned to Goshen with apparently little thought of staying in the land of Palestine for any reason. Then, Goshen in Egypt was their 'land of milk and honey.'

The first group to exit Egypt *en masse* may have been people fleeing plagues and persecution. They may have had a leader such as Moses. Historical archaeology confirms only small pieces of the exciting story that the Bible relates– that back in history there was a person who worshiped God and was out of favor with the pharaoh, who led a group of dissidents into the wilderness. This group stayed as nomads in the wilderness for many years. Their leader died, but other leaders rose up and eventually they left their nomadic way of life and settled in the hill country of Palestine. There are several possible time slots for such an exodus. One possibility is the first period of disorder in Egypt, around 2400 to 2100 BC, corresponding to Dynasties Six through Ten, when many foreigners settled in the delta area.

Archaeologist Emmanuel Anati believes that during the **Sixth Dynasty** reign of Pepi I (about 2350 BC), the Egyptians conducted a number of forays against Asiatic populations. One commander named Uni describes his oppressive actions against ''sand dwellers'' similar to the Exodus account. The Admonitions of Ipu-wer, a writing of the 6th Dynasty (about 2300 BC) shows some similarities with the description of the Ten Plagues. A date range different than 2300 BC is given for the Hebrew exodus by statements made in the Book of Exodus 15:4– *The chariots and the army of Pharaoh he has hurled into the sea.* The Egyptians didn't have horses and iron chariots until after the Hyksos rule about 1600 BC.

A prophecy proclaimed during the Nubian **Twelfth Dynasty** (about 1900 BC) says, ''The Asians will not be permitted to come down into Egypt that they might beg for water in the customary manner, in order to let beasts drink.'' One way the Egyptians had of managing foreign populations was a long *shur* or wall. If Hebrews passed near this check point, they would be turned away. They had to know how to avoid border control points and find other ways to enter Egypt. The *Story of Sinuhe* (about 2300 BC) which has much in common with both the Moses story and the Joseph story, speaks of an ancient wall that assisted the pharaoh's soldiers in their control duties. Hagar headed for this wall when Abraham deserted her and Ishmael (Genesis 16:7). The wall eventually disappeared due to natural causes, so that by 1300 BC, it was no longer an obstacle. When the Hebrews left Egypt, they didn't take the main highway to Palestine (Exodus 13:17), but the back roads, so this border outpost may have been in place. This would give a date earlier than 1300 BC for an exodus departure.

Another date for plagues and possible mass exodus is after the Thera volcanic explosion which may have been responsible for famine and discontent. Excavation on Thera shows that the island was occupied from 4000 BC to the explosion, about 1628 BC. There were artists, ship building, crafts, a pleasant civilization. The eruption which took place was greater than that of Krakatoa in the Indian Ocean in 1883, when it became dark more than 250 miles from the explosion. The darkness in 1883 lasted more than a day, and there were 100 feet high waves more than 30 miles away. The explosion on Thera was larger. This massive volcanic blast may be one of the strongest in history. It wiped out the Minoan culture on the island of Crete, and made living unbearable on the shores of the Aegean because of tidal waves and ash fall-out. This explosion initiated a movement of peoples, which continued to trigger wars for hundreds of years. In the second Egyptian period of disorder occurring after the explosion of Thera, foreign rulers took leadership in Egypt, as the Thirteenth to Seventeenth Dynasties ruling out of Avaris in the delta. These *hyksos* or foreign rulers were expelled by the **Eighteenth Dynasty** from Thebes, which could have been another radical changing of power that precipitated an exodus.

5.4 An Exodus Related to Sea People

The sons of Israel left Rameses for Succoth, about six hundred thousand on the march– all men– not counting their families. People of various sorts joined them in great numbers; there were flocks, too, and herds in immense droves (Exodus 12:37,38). The Israelites left a location in northern Egypt to begin their exodus journey. Apparently the ruling pharaoh was present in that same city for he seemed to be readily available for conversations with Moses and Aaron. There was a city in the northern Nile Delta area, where much building went on during the **Nineteenth Dynasty** rule of Rameses II (1279-1212 BC). The biblical author calls this spot the city of Rameses. This does not necessarily mean that it was called by that name when the Hebrews left on their journey, or that the Hebrews did their slave labor there for Rameses, or that Rameses II was the ruling pharaoh at the time they left. Or it may mean all of the above. The only thing we can be reasonably sure of is that the city of Rameses was a handy geographical designation that would be understood by the readers of Exodus about 1000-800 BC. We also know that a previous name for the city of Rameses was Avaris. This city was inhabited under a different name by foreigners and Hebrews around 2500 BC. This is where the Hyksos shepherd kings held court about 1600 BC. Rameses II restructured it about 1250 BC and thus dedicated it to himself as the city of Rameses.

Let me give an example of how a myth teller might pick a place name. If I were to tell you about an Indian group that lived on Manhattan island one thousand years ago I would say, ''These Indians lived in what is now New York City,'' or ''these Indians lived on Manhattan.'' If my audience came from Los Angeles, they might not know what was meant by *Manhattan*, so I would say, "These Indians came from the area of New York City." My myth location is basically correct. However, I don't know the name the Indians gave their home one thousand years ago, and the Indians wouldn't know that I was referring to their territory.

The Bible tells us that the Hebrews left on their exodus journey from the city of Rameses, and many have interpreted this to mean that the great pharaoh Rameses II pre-dated the Hebrew exodus. The writer, male or female, Egyptian or Hebrew, slave or free, set down the facts of the ancient exodus journey, during the reign of David about 1000 BC. There may have been other oral tellers of the Moses tale anytime before that (possibly 2400-1000 BC). As grandmother passed the story on to granddaughter, as priest passed it on to priest, many changes in nomenclature could have occurred.

If the city built by foreign labor (perhaps including Israelites), was the city of Rameses,[1] then the pharaoh in the biblical story may have been Rameses II. The eldest son of Rameses II died about 1260 BC which reminds us of the plague of the first born. These clues (of builder-ruler, of city name, and of first born death) seem to point to Rameses II as being a possibility for the pharaoh of the Hebrew exodus.

The whole Nineteenth Dynasty of Egypt (1292-1184 BC) had problems with foreigners, similar to the problems that exist between refugees and their host countries today. It is difficult to say for sure which particular pharaoh led which battle, as names would be replaced on stelae and temple wall scenes as soon as a new pharaoh took office. Pharaohs of the Nineteenth and Twentieth Dynasties are dated *approximately* as follows:

Rameses I (1292-1290 BC).
Seti I (1290-1279 BC).
Rameses II, The Great (1279-1212 BC) Battle of Kadesh 1275 BC.
Merneptah (1212-1202 BC) Canaanite Campaign (1211-1209 BC),
    victory over Sea Peoples announced on 1207 BC (Merneptah stela).
Amenmesse (1201-1199 BC).
Seti II (1199-1193 BC) also bragged of battle in Canaan.
Siptak (1193-1184 BC) ends Nineteenth Dynasty.
Setnacht (1184-1182 BC) starts Twentieth Dynasty.
Rameses III (1182-1151 BC) tax collection was instituted. His land and sea
    battle with Sea Peoples of 1177 BC is described in his mortuary temple at
    Thebes.

There is a scene of conquest on the North Wall of the Rock Temple of Rameses II in Nubia. The king in his chariot under the protection of the falcon god Horus, charges a horde of fleeing Bedouin tribesmen. Two prisoners are bound to the chariot pole. Another scene shows Rameses II and his son capturing a Syrian fort and slaughtering its defenders. Tribal groups are known by their distinctive clothing. At the Battle of Kadesh on the Orontes River in Syria (1275 BC) between Pharaoh Rameses II and the Hittite army leader, Muwatallis, both claimed victory! Later rulers Rameses III and the Hittite king, Hattusilis III, made a peace treaty, in which a balance of power was achieved. Some of those fighting on the side of the Hittites may have been Hebrews.

The second son of Rameses II, Merneptah, also of the **Nineteenth Dynasty**, who ruled from 1212 to 1202 BC, was in Israel putting down rebellions. He, too, could have been the biblical pharaoh whose chariots drowned in the waves. He conducted a Canaanite campaign in 1211-1209 BC. Merneptah, who ruled from 1212 to 1202 BC, fought the Sea Peoples and the Libyans and is also noted for a stela describing his campaign against those in Israel.[2] The stela describes the expedition thus:

Canaan has been plundered into every sort of woe.
Ashkelon has been overcome.
Gezer has been captured.
Yano'am was made non-existent.
Israel is laid waste (and) his seed is not.
Hurru has become a widow because of Egypt.

This gives us the information that some people named *Israel* were living in Palestine and were calling themselves *Israel* in 1211-1209 BC. According to the picture, the Israelites were possessed of war chariots. However, the Egyptian activity may have hampered them from settling in more desirable locations. Joshua 15-19, in recording the allotments to various tribes, mentions the spring of Nephtoah, which may be named after Pharaoh (Mer)neptah, and was a boundary point.

Our Bible seems to ignore events described by the above mentioned stela. This is 200 years before the time of David's author, and should have been in the tribal memory of the Ephramites. Was David playing it down, because he wanted his people to ignore Egyptian politicking? Was the pharaoh Merneptah guilty of exaggerating to influence his populace? The stela demonstrates that Israel was a settled people in Palestine around 1209 BC.[3] This stela is confirmed by a scene on the wall in Karnak Temple, but there the carnage wrought is credited to Merneptah's successors, Amenmesse and Seti II, due to replastering and re-engraving of name plates. Both Canaanites and the non-Canaanite Shasu are depicted in these Merneptah reliefs on the Karnak Temple wall. The Canaanites wear ankle-length clothes. The Shasu wear short kilts and turban-style headdresses. Whether the Israelites were considered by the Egyptians to be Canaanites or Shasu, *Israel* was a name given to a people well established in Palestine in 1209 BC.

Another period for an exodus may have been still later under the **Twentieth Dynasty** when a group of Sea Peoples, with their families traveling in carts on the sea coast, and their boats at sea, were attacked by the navy of Rameses III who ruled 1182-1151 BC, in a foray that was described as a great victory. This information is on a 133 foot long scroll written after the death of Rameses III. This battle may have been a draw, as the Sea Peoples were left to live peaceably on the coast and became known as the Philistines. Such boasting of a battle by a Pharaoh does not mean that the particular pharaoh was in the battle. He may simply be reminding his audience of someone else in his dynastic line who performed such a deed, implying that he, too, is capable of such ferocity. This practice is observed in Egyptian tomb and temple drawings. There may have been an attack on emigrants moving their families along the coast toward Canaan in ox-carts, while those traveling in ships participated in a naval battle documented at 1177 BC. The group mentioned as the "people of various sorts" in Exodus 12:38 may have included the persecuted Sea Peoples, the Danoi, who were depicted on Egyptian victory markers as being harassed by the pharaoh's soldiers.

The Sea Peoples associated with the Hebrews were the Danoi or tribe of Dan (also known as Danuna, Danubians, or Northerners). Other Sea Peoples were Tjeker (Turkish), Shardana (southwest, Sardinians), Weshesh (Westerners), and Philistines.[4] The Shardana or Sherden were mercenaries who fought on the Egyptian side, against other Sea Peoples. They are portrayed in the reliefs of Rameses III as having horned helmets like the Vikings 2000 years later. The Sherden and other foreign elements, were often forced labor used by the Egyptians to man their garrisons in Canaan.

The sons of Israel went out from Egypt fully armed (Exodus 13:18). This resorting to arms sounds like they left Egypt as free men who were defiant of the pharaoh. It seems that they may have had more devious plans than simply worshiping their God in the wilderness. It is not surprising that the Pharaoh felt he had to have his soldiers keep an eye on them. If foreign people go about a country fully armed, the established rulers of that country naturally get a little edgy.

Dating. As the ruling pharaoh seemed to be available to Moses for easy consultation, we might date the exodus by asking when pharaohs had their capital city in northern Egypt. The rulers of the Third through Tenth Dynasties were in Memphis in the northern Nile Delta (2900-2140 BC). Memphis was a city well known to the Hebrews. It is mentioned in Isaiah

19:13, Jeremiah 2:16, 44:1, 46:14,19, Ezekiel 30:13, and Hosea 9:6. The Twelfth Dynasty were Nubians who ruled from Aswan in the south, and made Thebes (about half way down river) the capital about 1900 BC. The Hyksos rolled in with their iron chariots and horses and ruled from Avaris in the delta region about 1600 BC. Thus the exodus pharaoh could have been one of these Hyksos (meaning *foreign rulers*). The Nubians and Thebeans learned how to use horses and war chariots and combined forces to chase the Hyksos out. They had control of northern Egypt, but continued their rule from Thebes in central Egypt. If pharaoh had horses and chariots that sank into the sea, such offensive weaponry arrived in Egypt during or after the Hyksos time period.

Another possibility is that one part of the Hebrew exodus was at an earlier time that did not have iron chariots, but when the Sea Peoples were chased by Pharaoh's troops about 1177 BC, their tale also became incorporated into the exodus story. The Bible describes and combines different incidents. The tales of oppressed peoples, when told by a sympathetic story teller, might tend to run together. The latter day author probably wasn't sure of the facts, but wanted to be faithful to all her sources.

There are possibilities of exodus from Egypt from 2300 BC to 1177 BC with the Sixth, Twelfth, Nineteenth, and Twentieth Dynasties. Early legends may tell of Moses, in the wilderness about 2300 BC, and the material for the more recent events described in exodus stories may have spanned a hundred year period from near 1279 BC to near 1177 BC.

5.5 The Parting of The Waters

God did not let them take the road to the land of the Philistines ... Instead, God led the people by the roundabout way of the wilderness to the Sea of Reeds (Exodus 13:17-18). The Israelites did not leave Egypt by the main highway, but took a more circuitous (and possibly secretive) route. Moses and the tribes, or some group of refuge people fleeing Egypt, supposedly crossed either the Red Sea or the Sea of Reeds between two walls of water which God held back. Their route is much debated, and may actually be a legend about a combination of routes, and a combination of water events.

One tradition holds there was an escape along the shore of the Mediterranean Sea; another tradition says that a group went by a Red Sea route. An exodus group of people may have taken the northern route by the Mediterranean Sea where there were reed marshes. One route (Exodus 14:9, 15:4, 15:19, and 15:22) speaks of Pi-ha-hiroth by the sea, and Baal-zephon. Here the sea mentioned is specified as the Red Sea. When just the word *Sea* is used in Joshua 24:6, it is understood to mean the Mediterranean, as the most important sea to the early world.

Yahweh drove back the sea with a strong easterly wind all night, and he made dry land of the sea (Exodus 14:21). This phenomenon has been shown to be possible in a certain section of the Red Sea when the wind blows strongly from the east. It could have easily been like a Cecil B. DeMille production though the walls of water may not have been as high as in the movie.

The Egyptians gave chase (Exodus 14:23). They entered onto the sea bed, but God clogged their chariot wheels. There are different versions in the Bible. One (beginning in Exodus 13:17) is quite dramatic ending with the army of pharaoh drowning (Exodus 14:28). In the account given in Psalm 136:15, the pharaoh himself drowns. This drowning of the pharaoh is also in the Islamic tradition, but the original Book of Exodus account is silent on this matter. In Joshua 24:7, the Lord protects the people from the charioteers by spreading a thick fog. Exodus 14:19-20 also speaks of fog.

These accounts may be describing the reedy lake north of the Gulf of Suez, called the Bitter Lakes, or another lake bordering the Mediterranean, Lake Sirbonis. Either of these might be a logical route for refugees who did not choose to take the king's highway out of the country. Papyrus reeds used to grow in the Bitter Lakes. The papyrus root was an edible item, and if you were moving hungry people across the sands of northern Egypt, you might pick up a square meal at this spot. There was a narrow neck of land between the Mediterranean and Lake Sirbonis. This might have been a place where horses and chariots got bogged down in the sand.

Picture a mixture of Hebrews and others, the "people of various sorts," dissatisfied with a regime or living conditions they could no longer endure. They sold their homes to Egyptians for transportable gold and silver and kept their flocks to support them on their journey. What held this motley crew together during their long association? The Sea Peoples came from the west; the Aramean tribes came from the east, the wilderness of Arabia.[5] Perhaps some were descended from Hapiru, tribes from northeast of Egypt in the direction of Palestine, who intermixed with other foreign elements. Perhaps their religious beliefs held them together. In a long stay in the wilderness, myths from Egypt and other more distant places could have been woven together and adopted, thus reaffirming the group's solidarity.

When the women, children, and slow moving cattle, approached the narrow neck of land stretching along the shore of the Mediterranean, between the Mediterranean and Lake Sirbonis, they could look back and see soldiers and chariots in the far distance, presumably up to no good. The refugees marched steadily across. It could have been about an eight mile trek. If tidal conditions were such that the isthmus narrowed down to a strip ten feet wide, just one lead chariot bogging down could debilitate the whole pursuing army. If the charioteers were handicapped in such a manner, they were probably glad to call off the chase. The protecting God of the community had shown love and concern for the community, and the group was able to march on towards the Holy Mountain to thank their God for their deliverance.

5.6 Holy Mountains

Yahweh will descend on the mountain of Sinai in the sight of all the people. You will mark out the limits of the mountain and say, "Take care not to go up the mountain or to touch the foot of it" (Exodus 19:11-12). For the people of Moses' time, the Holy Mountain was off limits, perhaps because of seismic disturbances. The people were allowed to approach in the direction of the *holy*, but they needed mediators like Moses to speak to God for them. Today we do not think of the *holy* as inaccessible. Active participation in the faith of one's choice is encouraged. Muslims are invited to make pilgrimages to Mecca. We visit shrines to the saintly and pray for miracles.

Visiting "Mount Sinai." When my daughter invited me to climb the mountain where God appeared to Moses, I gladly made the trip to the southern Sinai. As my husband, my daughter, my granddaughter, and I struggled up the mountain with flashlights in the dark of night with a guide named Moses, my daughter informed me that the mountain we were tackling might not really be the true Mountain of Moses; the true one might be another mountain nearby named St. Catherine, or it might be elsewhere on the Sinai Peninsula. The mountain we were climbing had been chosen by people who wanted to believe it was the Holy Mount described in the Bible.

We arrived at the top of the mountain in time to view the sunrise, and were joined by a group of tourists who delighted us by praising God and singing English-language hymns in Korean. We could feel a oneness with one another and with the *Ten Commandments* and God's peace and justice. It did not seem to matter then that this might not be the same mountain that Moses climbed to receive the commandments.

This experience started me thinking about why certain places become rated as holy. I wondered if God's justice and concern could be felt on other mountains, with or without the edifying worship of Christian Koreans. I thought of other mountain-top appearances, such as that of Mary at Medjugorje. A loving community gathers, and in the course of their worship, they are given instructions through a visionary on how to live a good life. Some members of the community are transformed in response to these insights, and rules and regulations are set down to assist further transformations. One person becomes the leader, and the rest follow his instructions believing him to be more knowledgeable than themselves. Supposedly he has mountain-top vision, and having climbed the Mountain of Moses in lower Sinai, I can believe in the clarity of mountain-top vision. On mountain tops, one can see for almost forever, and one can feel that one knows what is important and what is unimportant. What is important is God's care for us and the earth; what is unimportant is the exact location of the mountain.

But we humans are curious, and we like to track things down. We like to know the particular time and place of biblical events. We like to speculate on the personalities and trials of Moses and Miriam and Zipporah. Where was Moses when he saw the Burning Bush? *Moses was looking after the flock of Jethro, his father-in-law, priest of Midian. He led his flock to the far side of the wilderness and came to Horeb, the mountain of God* (Exodus 3:1).

When the youthful Moses fled from Egypt, he escaped to Midian which is located east of Sinai, north of the Red Sea, south of the Dead Sea, and south of the land claimed by the Moabites. The Moabites were descended from the incestuously created offspring of Abraham's relative Lot (Genesis 19:37). Abraham had a son Midian by the woman Keturah (Genesis 25:1-2). This son, or tribe of Midianites, took up residence away from the territory Abraham gave to his son Isaac (Genesis 25:6), so Moses was fleeing in the direction of a distantly related tribe. It is possible that the land of Midian extended west into the Sinai Peninsula, and that Moses didn't have too far to go.

Mount of The Burning Bush. One possibility is that there are two mountains associated with Moses, one for the Burning Bush theophany, and the other for the presentation of the commandments. In southern Sinai there is the Moses peak where my family climbed to commune with God at sunrise. At the base of an adjacent mountain is St. Catherine's Greek Orthodox monastery which has hosted traveler's since 500 AD. At that time the local population had no idea where Moses had tarried 2000 to 3000 years earlier, but when the Orthodox monks at the monastery told them there might be a connection with Moses, they were happy to go along with the story. They even came to believe that a certain strange and ancient tree growing in the monastery garden, was the Burning Bush. This tree had its tap root under what was the main altar of the monastery a thousand years ago, but grew outwards when the building was constructed on top of it. Those telling the original story about this plant being the Burning Bush may have had purely theological interests. They may have felt that the Moses' tale was one of the spiritual reasons for the existence of their monastery, so important that it had to do with the main altar of their edifice. On the other hand, when Moses fled to Midian, he may have seen the Burning Bush on this solitary mountain side. In their enthusiasm, later-day worshipers may have connected the Hebrew exodus site to the Burning Bush site.

Some pilgrims coming to visit this proposed place of Moses' vision may feel thrilled that they are in contact with a holy relic such as the Burning Bush (whether substantially correct or not), and through belief in these relics, may come closer to the spirit of God. The material object, such as a bush, has done well in carrying the spiritual message. The important thing is that the spiritual message has been carried. People have received the message, and through their prayers, the place truly does become holy.

We can say the same thing for the Catholic Church. It is imperfect. It is of distinctly human, as well as spiritual construction. It is full of errors, but it has carried the message. For that reason we can call it a *Holy Church*, and we can call its leader, *Holy Father*. Some may feel that *Holy Father* is a title that should belong to God alone, but it is imperfect people like us, living in an imperfect world, who through our strivings toward perfection, make people and places holy. We have canonized a mountain in the southern Sinai, and for that reason pilgrims have had a true religious experience there.

We have canonized certain books of the Bible, while other true words of Jesus may be waiting to be found in the apocryphal gospels or in other as yet undiscovered or unacknowledged texts. Other true words of God may have been written by Muhammad on misplaced plant leaves or leather scraps, and other words of God may still be unspoken or unwritten. Our knowledge of theological matters is highly imperfect and speculative. We take myth for fact, and spiritual symbolism for physical location.

Mount of The Ten Commandments. Another possible location for the Holy Mountain is in northern Sinai. Sinai is a land twisted and divided by many mountains, any one of which would remind a traveler of the majesty and greatness of God. Scholars have long speculated on the routes that Moses and exodus groups used when leaving Egypt. The Bible gives us a log of an exodus journey in Numbers 33:3-49. Events and names are also set down in Numbers 9:1, 10:33, 11:4, 16:1, 20:1, and 21:1;10-35. Many place names are given, and some are unrecognizable. Archaeologist Emmanuel Anati[6] referring to the exodus journey described in Numbers 33, proposes locations that satisfy him as to possible number of days needed to travel the distance between water holes. This trail leads him directly to Har Karkom or Mount Hor in the Negev desert of northern Sinai.

One name that reappears in the Bible as having to do with the Hebrew's exodus journey, is that of *Paran*. The later prophet, Habakkuk, affirms that *Eloah is coming from Teman, the Holy One from Mt. Paran* (Habakkuk 3:3). *In the second year, in the second month, on the twentieth day of the month, the Cloud lifted over the tabernacle of the Testimony. The sons of Israel set out, in marching order, from the wilderness of Sinai. In the wilderness of Paran the Cloud came to rest* (Numbers 10:11-13). *Then the people left Hazeroth, and camp was pitched in the wilderness of Paran* (Numbers 12:16). *At Yahweh's bidding, Moses sent them from the wilderness of Paran* (Numbers 13:3). As Moses sent explorers from Paran to Canaan, Paran must be north in the Negev and not a hundred miles down in south Sinai. The desert of Paran must be near the Holy Mount and near Canaan.

The archaeologists have been able to help us out. They have dug around the supposed "Mountain of Moses" in southern Sinai and have found nothing that would indicate a tribal encampment or worshiping groups at this mountain area at any BC date. However, at Har Karkom (or Hakbar, or Hor, or Mount of the Egyptian god Horus, or Mountain of God) in the Paran area of northern Sinai directly south of the Dead Sea, there are archaeological remains that testify to great use of the site by worshiping nomads about 2300 BC.

What time did Moses live? General scholarship places him at about 1300 BC, but the Italian archaeologist Emmanuel Anati speculates that some exodus groups may have left Egypt as early as 2300 BC. Anati goes back to the Pentateuch to see if there is verification for this archaeological data, and proposes the biblical material of Exodus is not New Kingdom Egypt of the 13th century BC, but dates from ten centuries earlier.[7] If the date for Moses is 1000 years earlier than previously believed (similar to the date for the story about Sinuhe of 2300 BC), then the dates for Abraham, Isaac, and Jacob also get pushed back 1000 years or more.

If the Moses and Joseph myths are combinations of stories about different Egyptian viziers and several exoduses from Egypt, then it is easy to believe that the Abraham, Isaac, and Jacob stories cover numerous, and not just three, generations. For the sake of simplicity, the Davidic author has compressed these myths in order to give us the message of a caring God.

The Holy Spirit uses the tool of myth to teach. Some parts of the myth are merely props or a vehicle to carry the more important parts of the story. The location of the "Mountain of Moses" or the "Mountain of God" is an illustration of this. For those of us who live in the United States, there is no need to know the exact location of this mountain. We can get all the theological benefits of the Moses story by reading the Bible. The myth carries the message of the Holy Spirit very well. We know that God spoke to Moses and that Moses obeyed God, and these acts of God and Moses are received by the Holy Spirit in us, incorporated into our inmost beings, and hopefully result in a manifestation of the fruits of the Spirit for us and for others around us. To have someone tell us that Moses lived 1000 years sooner or later than we formerly believed should not bother us much, as long as they did not insist that the theological message associated with his story was incorrect.

We look back and think that people in those days were either righteous believers in the one true God (that we like to think we worship today) or misinformed idol-worshipers. In reality, there were thinking people of many opinions. There were those who admired the qualities of truth, justice, compassion, nobleness, and infinite being, and worshiped the one God who possessed those qualities. There were also meditative people who divided up these qualities and represented them separately as they needed them. These latter believers would worship a goddess of justice represented with a feather for her head, if they were oppressed; or a powerful god depicted as a crocodile, if they needed a warrior-protector. Then there might be worshipers who combined the one-God spirituality with practical variations depicting other god-aspects. As we are varied people with different person-alities, we worship the one God in many ways.

We must not assume we are superior intellectually, culturally, or legalistically to either Bedouins, Egyptians, or others of the early Near East. Look at what we admire—the power and speed of a polluting automobile, the wealth of a cheating stock-market tycoon, the physique of a football player, the youthful beauty of a virgin or non-virgin. What is the one true God we all worship? The one true God is beautiful, generous, powerful, and loving. We can represent this God by comparing God to the person Jesus, beautiful in soul, rich with the qualities and gifts that matter most, with power to transform lives with his teachings on loving concern. What was the God of Moses like? We really don't know, but there at the Mountain of God, this God laid out some rather strict community regulations. This God seems to have been a God who sought to further loving concern in the community.

5.7 The Ten Commandments

Then God spoke all these words. He said, "I am Yahweh your God who brought you out of the land of Egypt, out of the house of slavery. You shall have no gods except me" (Exodus 20:1-3). The people believed that there were other gods, some of which did not adequately represent the true God, even as we today give our allegiance to things (such as excessive materialism) that lead us away from justice and loving concern. The God they followed through the wilderness proclaimed that they should pay no heed to these "other" gods.

Egyptian Sources. Moses was brought up in Egyptian cultural traditions. It is easy to see that Egyptian regulations predate the *Ten Commandments* of Moses. The Bible accuses him of killing an Egyptian. Moses wouldn't have had to flee from the Pharaoh's wrath for this killing if the Egyptians had no recognized sanction against murder.

Inscriptions from Egyptian tombs beginning about 2600 BC have cautions similar to the *Ten Commandments* which determine who will be admitted to the afterlife. The Egyptian afterlife rituals on tomb walls show the deceased's heart being put in a balance against a feather. You get no afterlife unless you can truthfully say, "I worshiped God. I was kind to my neighbor. I did not kill anyone in cold blood." These affirmations are from the *Egyptian Book of The Dead*.

The *Ten Commandments* also have parallels with the *Instructions to Meri-Ka-Re* from an Egyptian text dating to about 2300 BC.[8] The young prince is commanded, "Revere the God, copy (honor) your fathers and ancestors; do justice; do not distinguish the son of an important person (of wealth or position) from a poor man."

Mesopotamian Sources. Another source of law was Mesopotamia which was not a very law abiding place. The rulers of the small city states must have tried every trick in the book to keep their populaces under control. In the Mesopotamian city of Lagash about 2350 BC, King Uruka-gina established *The Righteous Laws of Ningirsu* whose purpose was to stop exploitation of the poor. After him, there were the law givers Ur-Nammu of Ur (300 years before Hammurapi) and Lipit-Ishtar of the city of Isin (150 years before Hammurapi). Hammurapi's Code revised the older Ur and Isin regulations. The date for these law codes may be 300 years off. Dates for Hammurapi have been argued various ways. If we take the earliest tentative dates for the time of Hammurapi as 2123-2081 BC, and the latest dates as 1792-1750 BC, the early date of 2350 BC for the Moses' code as an influence on some of the Mesopotamian codes is a possibility.

The *Ten Commandments* may be an effort on the part of the inspired biblical writer to explain the origins of their accepted tribal law by giving a prototypal ancestor. Both Moses and Hammurapi were Semites, and played important roles in the body of Semitic folklore. Our dates for each of them are indefinite. They may have been contemporaneous.

About this date of 2350 BC, the Near East and the Dead Sea area had volcanic and seismic disturbances. Smoking mountains and earthquakes are described in Numbers 16:31 and Exodus 19:18. The Moses myth contains interweavings of earthquakes, law codes, and rebellions against Moses' authority, implying these events came in the same time frame. When confronted with an unruly people in the wilderness, the neophyte Moses put into practice the rules and regulations he knew about, and with God's help, came up with a workable legal system. This innovation in community governance turned out to be reasonably successful. If we consider the date for Moses' community at the base of Mount Hor to be the pre-Hammurapi date of 2300 BC and allow time for the news of this experiment in community rule to travel, then one of the sources of Hammurapi's use of law may derive from the Moses experiment. On the other hand, Moses may have borrowed from Hammurapi.

There is a famous engraving showing Hammurapi receiving the laws from the hand of his god Marduk. However, this is kingly propaganda. It would never do to say that a leader acquired the law from historical predecessors. Hammurapi was able to control his population and to consolidate his kingdom because he adopted and used pre-existing laws such as those that his predecessors had formed. Governors in Mesopotamia wrote on clay tablets and set up carved monuments, so that people would know the laws. The Bible reports that Moses' laws were inscribed on stone (Exodus 32:15-16). The breaking of these tablets may have been a symbolic action related to the breaking of their covenant pledge by the children of Israel. Hammurapi, as royal ruler, had his laws carved on stelae, on mountain sides, and in other public places where his subjects could see them, and where they could be read to the populace.

If we use this early date of 2300 BC, we find that the law did not easily follow the early tribes into Palestine. In Palestine or Canaan, there were periods of disorder followed by the temporary rule of judges. Each little city state was governed by a ruler, and these rulers sat uneasily on their thrones. The major activity for those times seemed to be kings going out to war against kings, as if it were a form of entertainment or an activity to keep young men occupied. Today we have the less violent sports of football and soccer. There were also the occupations of farmer and herder in the Canaanite lowlands. The people were bound together not by laws, but by opposition to common enemies who wished to usurp their territories.

From 2600 BC Egypt to the present, rulers have used legal systems to help keep order. The 1000 BC biblical author of David's time was reporting that as history progressed, people formulated and were guided by codes of law. The author may be trying to emphasize the need for a legal system to deal with the social and political complexities of her times. She may have derived parts of her story from priestly traditions and other parts from the Hammurapi legend.

The *Ten Commandments* have continued to spread and to keep people in order. They have been incorporated in church laws, and they still strongly influence our behavior today. Their origin may have been on the Mountain of God, from out of the dedicated heart of Moses, or drawn from the wise pronouncements of the *Righteous Laws of Ningirsu* or the tomb writings of Egypt. In any case, we can accept the hand of God guiding our insights.

Thou Shalt Not Kill. According to the Bible, Moses not only killed a man in Egypt, but was also responsible for quelling an insurrection which took place in the wilderness community as a result of his leadership style. This incident, the destruction of Korah, Dathan, Abiram, and On when the earth ''swallowed them up,'' is related in Numbers 16 and can be associated with an earthquake. This story may portray theological concerns, as it is about representatives of other religious groups. The names of the dissenting individuals may tell us something about the nature of the dispute. The name *On* is a name given to the establishment that followed the sun god Ra at Heliopolis. *Dathon* may have to do with regulations of the god Dagon. *Korah*, as son of the female clan ancestor Aholibamah, related to Esau, may have to do with the feminine aspect of the Edomite religion. Numbers 16 may be bringing to our attention stirrings of religious intolerance.

The violent actions of Moses and the wilderness community are reconcilable with their community-oriented legal system. Moses and his followers did not apply the *Ten Commandments* in their dealings with people considered to be outside their community. Those who believe their God is the omnipotent God, or that their religious practices are the only allowable ones, are often ready to kill the challenging or opposing groups. Basically, we can never know absolutely about God, but if we kill off all the dissenting voices, then they do not trouble us with their views, or make us worry about whether we are right or wrong.

We like to believe that God is on our side when we march off to war. We often refuse to see anything positive about the enemy, so much so, that we kill innocent children in our self-righteousness. In our present day communities, we allow anyone who wishes to possess guns, and to use them if they feel threatened. We vote in our representative governmental assemblies to support massive armies whose use may become abhorrent, as in the Vietnam War. We still do not seem to have a grasp on *thou-shalt-not-kill* regulations or *just-war* theory. We are blinded by our intolerance, which rises out of fear and uncertainty.

As we are imperfect, we must accept the fact that our knowledge is imperfect, and our laws are imperfect. We have been attempting perfect law and order for centuries, and are still way off the mark.

5.8 Joshua and Jericho

"Yahweh the God of Israel says this, 'In ancient days your ancestors lived beyond the River—such was Terah the father of Abraham and of Nahor—and they served other gods. Then I brought your father Abraham from beyond the River and led him through all the land of Canaan. I increased his descendants and gave him Isaac. To Isaac I gave Jacob and Esau. To Esau I gave the mountain country of Seir as his possession. Jacob and his sons went down into Egypt. Then I sent Moses and Aaron and plagued Egypt with the wonders that I worked there. So I brought you out of it. I brought your ancestors out of Egypt, and you came to the Sea; the Egyptians pursued your ancestors with chariots and horsemen as far as the Sea of Reeds (Joshua 24:2-6). This reading gives us the compressed history of the tribe of Joseph which was divided into the two half-tribes of Ephraim and Manasseh. As the Genesis author has told us (2:8), the beginnings of this people were far to the east. From beyond some River, the ancestors traveled through Canaan and down to Egypt. It is important that the related tribe of Esau is given the mountain territory. If the Hebrews respect their ancestors, they are to respect the rights given to Esau's descendants. On their way out of Egypt they come to the Sea. When the Sea is spelled with a capital letter, it is usually interpreted to mean the Great Sea, the Mediterranean. The Sea of Reeds is also mentioned.

Conquests. This story from the Book of Joshua has a slightly different interpretation of the exodus event and seems to confirm the pursuit by horses and iron chariots. If we are to visualize different sets of people leaving Egypt at different points of time, the Joshua story seems to reflect a group in the period shortly after Hyksos rule in Egypt. This later group may have come from Paran, circled the land of the Edomites, and then proceeded up the east side of the Dead Sea where it subdued the people of Transjordan under Sihon, king of the Amorites. They crossed the Jordan and came to Jericho.

Go up into the Negev; then go up into the highlands (Numbers 13:17). *Israel took all these towns, and occupied all the Amorite towns, Heshbon and all the towns under its jurisdiction* (Numbers 21:25). *Then Yahweh said to Joshua, "Now I am delivering Jericho and its king into your hands"* (Joshua 6:2). *I will put into your power the king of Ai, his people, his town and his territory* (Joshua 8:1c). *From Mount Halak, which rises toward Seir, to Baal-gad in the Vale of Lebanon below Mount Hermon, he captured all their kings, struck them down and slaughtered them* (Joshua 11:17). We read about the taking of Jericho in Joshua 6, and the taking of Ai in Joshua 8. Archaeologists who worked at these sights believe that these two conflicts took place, but not in the lifetime of the same heroic leader. Perhaps all conquering generals of that vintage were given the name of Joshua. In retelling tales, it may have been difficult to remember the correct name, and the name *Joshua*, meaning *savior*, was a very appropriate name to employ. We learn from Numbers 13:8 that another name for Joshua is *Osee*. This sounds like the Spanish *Jose*, and reminds us of the Egyptian *Hotep*. The names *Joshua* and *Joseph* appear to come from similar roots.

Archaeologists believe that Jericho was not heavily occupied from 1600 to 1200 BC. It suffered an earthquake and burning about 1400 BC. Ai had been an important town in 2400 BC, may have suffered seismic disturbances shortly thereafter, and remained sparsely settled until just before the Hebrews moved in about 1200 BC. Its constructions may have been further weakened from the earthquake that affected Jericho, and people who dwelt there were certainly psychologically shaken. Being weak and few in numbers, they would have succumbed easily to invading foreigners.

Other Peoples in Palestine. Joshua 10:1-5 tells us that the Amorite Adoni-zedek whose reign is thought to be about 1405 BC, was King of Jerusalem when Joshua was in the Jericho area. Five Amorite kings formed an alliance against the Joshua group. Besides Adoni-zedek, they are named as Hoham of Hebron, Piram of Jarmuth, Japhia of Lachish, and Debir of Eglon. The date for the members of this alliance substantiates the Jericho destruction date of about 1400 BC.

We have a later date of 1177 BC for the Egyptian battle with the Sea Peoples. Joshua and his followers may represent the tribal group of Ephraim, son of Joseph, fighting its battles back in the hills. The exodus of the Sea Peoples may be the story of the tribe of Dan (which eventually headed north of Ephraim) and other more southerly Hebrew tribes which entered Palestine from the southeast, such as Judah. Perhaps Judah never went to Egypt but was a tribe which dwelt precariously in southern Palestine. The Hebrew tribes (sometimes known as Shasu pastoralists) settled into the land of Palestine, particularly in the hill country of Mt. Seir which was populated by the tribe of Edom (with whom they were politically or ethnically connected).

Joshua, Son of Nun. Joshua 3:16 reports that the refugees crossed the Jordan dry shod. This may sound like a repeat of the Exodus-Red Sea crossing, but it was probably a separate incident, and there is a natural explanation. Every so often due to earthquake activity in the valley, mud slides block the river. When a slide temporarily stops the flow of the river, then people can walk across dry shod. There is even time to gather stones from the middle of the river to make an altar. Flow cut-offs in the Jordan due to quakes and mud slides were recorded in 1160 AD, 1267, 1546, 1834, and 1906 AD. If such a miracle happened during 1400-1100 BC, it could be tied into the Exodus material.

In Egypt the pharaohs had the custom of naming themselves after an aspect of God that they favored, or one from whom they claimed protection. For instance, the pharaoh would be described as the *son* or *servant* of Ra. Such a pharaoh would have for one of his names *Ra-meses*. Those fleeing Egypt after being exposed to this custom, may have used it to express their belief in God's providence.

They carried this custom in their cultural repertoire, and their names, such as Joshua, Son of Nun, may not reflect a genetic father, but may be a way of telling people that Joshua was favored by a certain aspect of God. Joshua is identified with miracles of water, and as such might be described as a favored son or servant of the God who ruled the waters. It is interesting that one Egyptian name for the waters out of which the world was created, is *Nun*. The Egyptian priests at Memphis promoted the idea that the God Ptah was himself the eternal ocean Nun that existed for all time and out of which both the earth and Atum-Ra, the sun god, were created.[9] Thus the name *Joshua, Son of Nun,* may be referring to a religious idea. In Egypt at Heliopolis (or On) which was the original settlement of the Joseph-Ephraim-Joshua tribal line, it was taught that the creation of the world occurred at Heliopolis when the land rose up out of the primordial water Nun. In this context, it would be natural for a savior (Joshua) coming out of Egypt to claim the protection of God under the name of Nun, and it would be natural that a promise of land would be part of this primordial water story. Some ideas of the legend of God giving the land may have come to Palestine with Joshua. Through miracles of water, God gave the land to the Ephramites.

Another spot in the Hebrew Bible where the God Nun is known by his absence, is in Psalm 145, verse 13b. This Psalm uses the letters of the alphabet to indicate the verses. In Hebrew, *nun* is the name for a letter of the alphabet, and when it is the turn for the letter *nun*, the verse and the letter are omitted. The Hebrews believed that it was appropriate to omit the name of God out of respect. In this case, the name of God was considered to be Nun, the God who rescued them from the pharaoh by means of water. This missing verse can be found in Christian Bibles.

5.9 The Ark of The Covenant

Palestine between 2300 BC and 1100 BC was a turbulent place. There were at least five major approach points by what were later known as the Twelve Tribes. The Moses group (perhaps 2300 BC) approached from Egypt via Paran and may have gone northeast of Israel. Ashur, or the Assyrians, may have come from the north. Joshua of the Ephramites, or half-clan of Joseph, entered from the east by crossing the Jordan (1400 BC). Sea Peoples entered from the west after 1177 BC. Members of the tribe of Judah may have originally come from the Zagros Mountains and could have entered Israel any time before 1100 BC.

Articles of Worship. In 2300 BC, the first people coming from Egypt may have worshipped gods in the Egyptian manner, or coming into the land where Baal was worshipped, may have felt that they should worship the god who was prominent in that land. Because they may have spent a long time at the foot of Mount Hor, or the Holy Mount, they may have had a more permanent altar there enshrined in a tent (Numbers 3:25). Was this god they were worshipping still related to the in-dwelling Egyptian god, Ptah? Was it similar to the god Baal often represented as a bull? Was it a god of healing and wisdom portrayed by a serpent on a staff? In the Moses exodus story we are told of the *Ten Commandments*, the Golden Calf, and the Bronze Serpent. Exodus 25-31 defines "a system of worship which goes back to Moses and contains elements of great antiquity, but with these are mixed others which reflect the development of worship in the course of the history of Israel."[10] Early groups emigrating from Egypt may have continued to follow some Egyptian religious practices.

We do not know what sort of God the average exodus person believed in, but the commandment, "Have no other gods before me," leaves open the possibility for other gods. People believed in those days that if your god won a battle for you, then he was more powerful than the god of the side which lost. The Israelites are advised not to worship these other gods, which evidently existed in the minds of the people. In the time of Joshua, some people still admitted the reality of other gods, but believed that these other gods were secondary to their Hebrew God.

Ancient peoples made altars to their various god representations. In the cities there would be magnificent temples. In the smaller towns and farming villages there would be sacred groves, or altars set up under holy trees. The prototypal ancestor Abraham worshipped under an oak at Mamre. (*Mamre* means an elevated plain, which name does not specify any particular country.) If you were a wandering tribal group, it was necessary to carry the symbols of your God with you, because you could not raise stone altars at every stopping place.

Hillside altars would consist of heaps of stones or offering tables and

Possible Dates for Exodus Happenings

About 2670 BC	Step pyramid built for Zoser by Imhotep of Third Memphite Dynasty.
2600-2300 BC	Ethical statements on tomb walls in Egypt similar to those of Ten Commandments.
2490-2365 BC	Fifth Dynasty noblemen include 5 Ptah-Hoteps, one of whom wrote instructions to his son.
About 2500-2300 BC	Ra and Ptah important gods at Heliopolis.
About 2400 BC	Ai becomes a ruin & is unoccupied until 1200 BC.
2350 BC	Seismic destruction in Dead Sea area.
About 2350 BC	Egyptians record a defeat of Bedouin in the Sinai.
About 2300 BC	A great famine.
About 2300 BC	Archeological remnants of a nomadic community at the foot of Mount Hor in northern Sinai.
About 2200 BC	Semitic tribal movements, Mesopotamia & Syria.
About 2200 BC	Political instability under 7th and 8th Memphite Dynasties.
2000-1800 BC	Nubian 12th Dynasty forbids Asians to bring their flocks into Egypt.
1628 BC	Thera erupts causing plagues, tribal movements.
About 1600 BC	Hyksos rule 15th Dynasty at Avaris in Nile Delta.
1415-1377 BC	Pharaoh Amenophis III of 18th dynasty has vizier Amenophis, son of Apiru, who wrote *Wisdom*.
About 1400 BC	Adoni-zedek is local king of Jerusalem.
About 1400 BC	Jericho is destroyed. Joshua may have led attack. Southern entry point by Israeli tribes from east.
1279-1212 BC	Rameses II, the Great, the builder.
1275 BC	Battle of Kadesh on the Orontes River, Syria. Horses and chariots were used by both sides.
1250-1220 BC	Northern entry near Mount Ebal by Israelites approaching from the east.
1207 BC	Merneptah stela records the name of Israel. Battle scene from Israel on Karnak temple wall.
1182-1151 BC	Reign of Rameses III, tax collection was instituted. Certain foreigners in Egypt feel oppressed.
1177 BC	Egyptian fight with Sea Peoples described in tomb of Rameses III and on Harris papyrus scroll.
1151 BC	After death of the strong pharaoh, Rameses III, Israel has the opportunity to emerge as a nation.

had poles that held up god symbols. The common people could worship at these sacred spots. Activities in the city temples were more controlled, and priests at these city sites were enlisted to carry out services that often were secret in nature. Architecture in city temples could be very elaborate. Wilderness worship was less formal. Exodus 25 describes a wooden chest which would keep the holy objects secure, and could be carried wherever the tribe went. This chest or Ark of the Covenant may have been decorated with representations of cherubs (Exodus 37:7-9). It contained the two *Tablets of the Law*, Aaron's rod, and a pot of manna (described in Hebrews 9:4). It had support rings so that it could be easily transported. Later biblical authors believed that there must have been an Ark of some sort included in the wilderness journeys.

It is likely that migrating peoples had some religious symbols that they treasured, such as stone inscriptions of their community regulations, and a box to contain them. The Book of Exodus does not describe a cart for this ark, perhaps because carts had not yet come into common use, or because it was difficult to take a cart through the wilderness. At some point in their wanderings, leadership was transferred from Moses to Joshua. The Ark and its symbols were also transferred, for the Ark is spoken of in the story of Joshua, chapters 3 and 4, as being carried over the Jordan River to hold back that river's waters. In Joshua's day the *Ten Commandments* were carried in the Ark, as the Israelites are described as surrounding the Ark in the valley between Mount Gerizim and Mount Ebal, and pledging their allegiance to the laws of God (Joshua 8:33). Also, the Ark of God was prominent at Bethel when angered Israelis wiped out their brother tribe of Benjamin (Judges 20:27).

If Joshua can be dated at 1400 BC, a lot of time went by in Palestine before the anointing of Saul as king and the founding of the kingdom of David. Rulers of city-states and judges came and went. Soldiers won and lost battles, but the memory of Joshua lingered on. Joshua's group had carried the Ark of the Lord across the Jordan, and marched it around the city of Jericho until the walls fell down (Joshua 6). The Ark was carried up Mount Ebal where Joshua wrote on stones a copy of the *Law of Moses*. Surely, some of the Hebrews carried the law in their hearts, and believed in a God of justice and truth.

In another story (I Samuel 3:3), the Ark of God was at Shiloh. The Israeli troops carried it into battle against the Philistines, and they lost the battle and their Ark. The Philistines set the Ark up in their temple to Dagon at Ashdod, and the statue of Dagon was found fallen on its face before the Ark. This didn't seem like a positive sign to the Philistines, and they sent the Ark back harnessed to two milk cows, accompanied by gold tokens. It arrived at Beth-shemesh, and was taken from there to Kiriath-jearim to the house of Abinadab (I Samuel 7:1).

The Ark just before the time of David may have been a powerful symbol among the Israelites as a result of the reaction of the Philistines. It also was an important part of the story of the Ephramite exodus group under Joshua. If David wanted to consolidate his kingdom and acquire the support of the Ephramites, he needed to adopt this symbol as his own, to increase his popularity. David had the Ark transported to a new location. It was on a cart, and Uzzah put out his hand to steady it, and was zapped with a disease and sudden death (II Samuel 6). It was finally brought to Jerusalem. Further legends about the Ark have it presently located in Ethiopia. The Book of Maccabees 2:5 suggests that Jeremiah hid the Ark before the Jews were taken prisoner to Babylon.

For those who trusted in God, the way out of Egypt led into new religious and community experiences.

Footnotes
1 *BAR* May/June 1992, p. 76.
2 Frank Yurco, "Picture of Israelites Found In Egypt," *BAR* Sept./Oct. 1990, pp. 21-37.
3 Frank Yurco, *loc. cit.*
4 Other directional names of tribes are Benjaminites (meaning people of the south), Qedem (meaning people of the east), and Amorites (those who lived in the west).
5 Siegfried Herrmann, *History of Israel in OT Times*, SCM Press, London, 1975, p. 21.
6 Emmanuel Anati, *Mountain of God,* Rizzoli, New York, 1986.
7 *ibid.*, p. 287.
8 *ibid.*
9 Jill Kamil, *Ancient Egyptians*, American University Press, Cairo, 1976, p. 38.
10 Alexander Jones, Editor, *Jerusalem Bible*, Doubleday & Company, Garden City, NY, 1968, Footnote after Exodus 25.

Possible Dates for Old Testament Events

First cities	Early cities in Near East..............................8000 BC Cain built a pre-flood city.......................... ? BC
The Flood	Ocean levels rose post Ice Age...........16,000-9000 BC 5 foot flood silt level recorded in India..........3000 BC Calculated by adding biblical ancestor ages....2285 BC Story of Sumerian flood hero Utnapishtim....2000 BC Story of Nippur flood hero Ziusudra.............1700 BC
Abraham and Sarah	Brahman, Rama worshiped in India before....4000 BC Seismatic disturbances in Land of Lot, Iran..........? BC Seismatic disturbances in Dead Sea area........2350 BC Ur is powerful city in Mesopotamia.....3000- 2000 BC Dates when adding ages of ancestors.............1920 BC
Joseph in Egypt	Imhotep of Third Dynasty.................................2670 BC Ptah-Hotep of Fifth Dynasty.................2490-2365 BC Dating Joseph by biblical calculations.............1720 BC Hyksos rulers, Fifteenth Dynasty......................1600 BC Amenophis of Hapu,Vizier of 18th Dynasty..1415 BC
Floating Basket Myth	Sargon I...3100 BC Moses, accepted biblical dating.........................1355 BC Hindu poet Kabir..500 BC
Exodus	Remains of community at base of Mt. Hor....2300 BC Egyptians have horses and chariots..................1600 BC According to biblical years.................................1276 BC Sea Peoples leave Egypt (Rameses III)............1177 BC
Zoroaster	Religious instructor of Persian kings........? or 600 BC The Jews Esther and Mordecai in Persia..............? BC
Ten Commandments	Hindu law giver Manu......................................4000 BC Shepherd of the Ningursu.................................2350 BC Egyptian tomb injunctions................................2300 BC Hammurapi Code...1900 BC According to biblical calculations.....................1275 BC
Joshua	The taking of Jericho...1400 BC According to biblical calculations.....................1234 BC
Tribe of Judah	Gudeans of Zagros Mts. are traders..............3000 BC Gudeans are rulers in Lagash...........................2300 BC Judah in Palestine, David is king......................1000 BC
Ark of Covenant	Taken to Ethiopia..900 BC Hidden before Babylonian Captivity................587 BC

VI

The Other Gods

The Hindu Trinity of Brahma, Vishnu, and Siva[1]

6.1 Religion in The Indus Valley

When we listen to myths, we are impressed with both the truths they tell, and the wild imaginings they contain. Myths help humans to learn social ethics and to come to grips with their inner fears. Myths give us a quick glance at our doubtings and allow us to release our tensions with laughter.

When we look at the representations of God that people have dreamed up, we wonder where these ideas of God can have come from. As we are unique individuals with our own unique experiences, we each have our own perceptions of deity. Nirguna Brahman (a neuter noun) is the Hindu deity, the universal divine spirit and ground of all existence, the God <u>without</u> attributes. His agent is known as Saguna Brahman who has personal attributes and can be imagined by his devotees. This personal divinity is known by the further names of *Pitamaha* (The Great Father), *Prajapati* (The

Lord of Creatures), *Swayambhu* (The Self-existing), *Parameshti* (The Abider), and *Lokesa* (Ruler of The World), all good names for describing deity. He is often represented with four heads and four arms, holding in one of his hands a portion of scripture. The Hindu sees God as being without human limitations. To express the greater than human power of a god or goddess, he or she is shown with many hands. Hindus use multiple appearances to describe the various characteristics of the supreme eternal One.

Aspects of God. The impersonal Brahman is the ultimate principle of which the Saguna Brahman, Vishnu, and Siva are personal aspects. The Hindus believed in *being*; this being was called Brahman, the unique self or *atman*, which was considered to be the infinite center of every life, the spark of world soul within each individual. God could appear in different forms, and there were heroes or avatars who possessed the *being* of God. Thus the name of God could easily change, and also the dominant characteristics of God.

This dominant God at one time was identified as Vishnu. Vishnu came to earth as the avatars of a fish (when no <u>man</u> was available), a tortoise, a boar, a man-lion, a dwarf, the hero prince Rama, and the cowherd Krishna. Vishnu was also associated with Indra, the war god of the Aryans, who helped these outsiders to gain a foothold in India. Vishnu as Vamana the Dwarf, changed to a giant, took three paces to measure the universe, and thus claimed the earth for humankind. Narayana was the divine sage that taught humankind. Shesha was the cosmic serpent. Ganesh was the god with the elephant face. The monkey god was Hanuman. While there were different interpretations for some, each was seen as an aspect of the one true God, Brahman.

These god-aspects are served by priestly individuals who use approved rituals. The god is mediated to the people through the priest or shaman. The people are taught that the carnal and spiritual selves of humankind are at war. The practice of *dharma* or natural virtue is the necessary basis for human law and ethics. Truth (*satya*) and order (*rta*) are desirable as opposed to disorder (*anrta*). *Karma* is the path of activity. Each act a person does affects us all. This is the ethic of personal responsibility. The individual will have the future that she creates. *Karma* has to do with the belief that one's actions determine the fate of one's soul. *Karma* can only be performed with the help of the body.

God In All Creation. The spirits of God were seen everywhere, in all of life. In some of Brahman's name changes, he was worshiped as the Fire God Agni. There also were fire altars for the Mother Goddess cult of Kali. There was a holy drink, *soma*, made of a drug derived from hemp. The lesser gods were called *devas*, or shining ones, with another name for the father God being Dyaus. The assemblage of lesser gods around Dyaus contained Indra, the god of war, weather, and the thunder bolt; Surya, the sun god, like Helios or Apollo, worshiped also in Egypt and Japan; Varuna, the heavenly king in his celestial palace; and Rudra, the grim archer, also known as Siva, whose consort was Parvati. This hierarchy of gods encouraged belief in a hierarchy of people, and Indian culture easily incorporated a class system. **Earliest Writings.** A common Indian saying is, "There is only one God, but he is called by many names." Rama appears as three different incarnations of Vishnu, the Trinity of Bala Rama, Parasu Rama, and Dasrat Rama. The model wife, Sita, of Dasrat Rama was carried away to Ceylon by the king of the demons Ravanna. Rama rescued Sita with the aid of a band of monkeys who helped him across the water. There are Iranian legends of flying carpet abductions. There are similarities to Abraham's wife Sara being housed in the harem of the king as in Genesis 12:10-20.

The personal Brahman was considered to be the author of the *Vedas* (*veda*=knowledge). Sections of the *Vedas* called the *Brahmanas* contain no philosophy, but describe how the Brahman priest should conduct ceremonies. The writing down of these scriptures may have taken place 2000 BC, though orally, they are much older. The *Vedas* contain expressions of earlier cultures and also the beliefs of the Aryans who invaded India from the northwest about 1500 BC. These invaders spoke a tongue related to Greek and Latin, which evolved into Sanskrit. Southern India spoke and retained the earlier Dravidian language. The Brahman culture unified all these conflicting beliefs through tolerant Hinduism. Ancient India did not have many temples or images. Shepherds from this area would not burden themselves with representations of the God whom they sensed all about them. Why make an image for God when you could see his power in the elephant? Images in the Indus Valley proliferated only after the 5th century BC when people became more stationary.

The Hindu philosophy, based on the universal divine spirit Brahman, was carried by traders to many lands. The paths of traders and hence propagation included routes to Persia, Turkey, and the coastal sea routes west to the mouth of the Tigris-Euphrates, and east towards Japan. Tribal migrations penetrated these beliefs into Mesopotamia, Palestine, and Egypt.

6.2 Power and Love in Mesopotamia

Philosophers and traders talked over these important ideas of what God was like, and why God made human beings. As God made the human, and as the Spirit of the One God permeates all the earth, God knew what the human was thinking, and God helped the human in positive directions.

There were many God ideas that the Israelites gathered in the wilderness. As the Hebrews grazed their flocks through the countryside, talked with local people, and married local women, they learned about the gods that came out of Mesopotamia. The early gods of the southern section of the Tigris Euphrates Valley were joined by other variations of godly qualities in the northern area of Assyria near Hittite territory.

Earliest Ideas. The early farming communities trusted in the God of Nature to give them produce. Life was not all a Garden of Eden. Tribal disputes over land or irrigation rights easily led to wars that took on religious overtones when each side in the argument felt they had a special God who they believed was on their side. As the human being evolved from farming into civilization, she began to experience the sort of creature she was and the possibilities before her. One of the humans' prime responsibilities was the creation of the future generation, and some of religious ethics was devoted to items such as phallic energy, circumcision, and the place of temple prostitutes. The Bible encourages humankind to "be fruitful, multiply, fill the earth and conquer it" (Genesis 1:28).

From very ancient times, before civilization, the Mother Goddess cult was carried over into the worship of Ishtar in Mesopotamia. Tales were told of how the goddess Ishtar descended to hell and rose again, and of her brother/lover Tammuz.[2] In early stories Tammuz was the son, and Ishtar was the daughter of the water god Enki-Ea. There is an ancient belief that a king's son (*Tammuz* in Assyrian or *Damuzi* in Sumerian) died for all living creatures. He returns to earth one day each year to pay for the release of Ishtar from the underworld. Immortality was conferred upon him for his sacrifice, and there is the celebration of his annual triumph over death.[3] This festival is symbolic of the revival of nature in spring. *Damuzi* is translated as *son of life*.

The myth of the god-man who suffers has its roots in earlier religions. Osiris, a god-aspect in Egypt, was dismembered but somehow rose again through the healing powers of his wife/sister Isis. Tammuz in Mesopotamia died and was brought back to the land of the living by his sister. These myths describe the love of the human sister for her brother. Ezekiel 12 complains of the weeping for the god Tammuz by the women of Jerusalem. Coincidentally, the New Testament describes the weeping of the women of Jerusalem for Jesus carrying his cross, as he gave his life for others. This story emphasizes that a human can love with a god-like love, as it tells how one human died for all humans

The early Sumerian legends tell us more about the fashioning of the human than the personality of God. The gods gathered together and spit into a common vat out of which came the first man, Kumaris. All these aspects of God had a hand in forming the man, and bequeathed him possibilities of acquiring their godly characteristics. Those in Mesopotamia may have seen one creator God behind this cooperative godly fashioning of the human, but they apparently do not make authoritative pronouncements about this God. **Local Views of God.** The god *Ashur* is worshiped in Assyria, but this name is not used in Babylonia. Naram-Sin, as ruler in northern Mesopotamia, had proclaimed himself one of the gods (perhaps as one imbued with the spirit of God), but not everyone believed this. Other deities or aspects of God in Mesopotamia were *Anu* (God of Heaven and Angels), *Bel* (Father of The Gods), *Sin* (Moon God), *Shamash* (Sun God), *Ninib* (God of The Hunt), *Nergal* (God of War), *Nuski* (Bestower of Scepters), *Beltis* (Mother of The Gods), *Ishtar* (Leader of Heaven and Earth), *Bel* or *Merodach* or *Marduk* (Lord of Babylon), and *Ea* (God of The Sea).

As the centuries passed, gods exchanged names and characteristics, according as to what was needed in the culture of the times. The Babylonian god Marduk killed Tiamat, the goddess of the sea, and fashioned the universe from her body. This is described in the myth *Enuma elish*. In this period, people may have been changing from ideas of a God as a provident Mother Nature to that of a warrior protector.

The Supreme God Concept. As in India, the concept of a Brahman type of primary God, with supporting aspects of God, struggled for acceptance. Finally, a type of One-Supreme-God worship was consolidated in Marduk. He is described as being the cover God for other god aspects. "Sin is Marduk, the illuminator of the night, Shamash is Marduk of justice, Adad is Marduk of rains, ..."[4] Marduk became a name for the one supreme God.

Exports and Derivations. Bel or Marduk or Asari were alternate names for the primary God. Early in civilized time, Asari had his name changed to Osiris when traders brought his worship to Egypt. Vowels are interchangeable as they were not designated by early scribes. The name *Asari* was easily changed to *Osiris*. Ishtar of Assyria was Inanna of Sumer and had cult centers at Agade, Kish, Uruk and eventually all over the Mediterranean and in Britain. Her sacred beast was the lion. She had attributes similar to Isis of Egypt who portrayed mother-son, mother-husband, mother-brother love, but Ishtar of Assyria matured into a rather violent goddess who led her people off to war. As time passed men felt more comfortable with male gods leading them in battle. From the mother love that was displayed in the early Ishtar characteristics, humanity's beliefs evolved to a notion of gods who protect us in battle, and mow down the adversary in an unmotherly fashion.

There are many variations on the name of Ishtar, the chief female goddess in the Near East. She has a name very similar to the heroine Iscah, the daughter of Haran and sister of Lot in Genesis 11:29. Other names are Innini, Anat, Astar (Abyssinia), Athtar (Arabia), Ashtoreth (Jewish), Anaits (Persian), Sharis (Khaldean), Cybele (Phrygian), Astarte (Latin), Demeter (Greek), Aphrodite (Greek), Venus (Roman), and others. Ishtar was also known as *My Lady* or Belti. Belti is the feminine aspect of the god Baal or Ba-el or Bel worshiped by Jezebel. The consort of Marduk, Zarbanit, was known as *Our Lady* or Belit-ni. The title of Tammuz was *My Lord*. When these myths traveled to Greece, Bel became named the Greek word for Lord, or *Kyrios*. In following ages there is the transferal of the *Our Lady* title to the Virgin Mary, and the *Kyrios* title being applied to Jesus.

When we look back, the kind of past we see is conditioned by our experience in the present. We draw inferences from the material of the past, but we are not seeing reality as the ancients saw it. When ancient Assyrians said *Lord*, they meant Baal, and we do not know how they visualized Baal. Did they see Baal as the statue of an idol, or did they see the One Supreme God of Heaven caring for all the earth? It's also hard to say how the early human treated her neighbor, or how her environment caused her to behave. We look back at the city of Ur, and we see that both priests and priestesses performed fabulous rituals. There was a mass funeral of these priests and priestesses. We wonder if they believed in an afterlife and in a just God who would reward them for their voluntary sacrifice. What more can a human being sacrifice to her God than her whole life?

6.3 Beliefs of Ancient Hebrews

The Bible is about the majesty of God, so we would expect to read a lot in the Bible about how the human being worshiped God. There has always been much variety in this worship. Each of us is different and sees God from her own particular viewpoint. Then, as now, people were confronted by those who thought God had spoken clearly to them. Human beings would gather in groups, and some would follow a charismatic leader to death, even as in recent events at Jonestown, Guiana and Waco, Texas.

Abraham. The Pentateuch authors relate that Shem fathered Eber (the progenitor of the Hebrews) and speaks of the God of Abraham, the God of Isaac, and the God of Jacob. She mentions the household gods of Laban, stolen by his daughter, Jacob's wife (Genesis 31:32). We hear of the altars to foreign gods set up in the temple for Solomon's wives (I Kings 11:1-13).

We are told that Abraham came from Ur of the Khaldees and had an ancestor Haran, or was connected with the city of Haran. The city of Ur was in the southern portion of the Tigris-Euphrates valley, and Haran was far to the northwest where the Euphrates is fairly close to the Mediterranean and to present day Turkey. To the north of this is the hilltop site of Nimrud-Dagh where there are fallen memorials to legendary kings. More directly north of Ur, in the Tigris region, and near Turkey, are the towns of Arrapkha, Nineveh, and Ashur. These are closer to areas where even today fire altars and Zoroaster hold sway with some of the indigenous population. A description of a fire sacrifice by Abraham (Genesis 15) is similar to Khaldean fire offerings. Abraham is called the son of Terah of Khaldea. The Khaldeans worshiped the One Supreme Lord of Heaven, Khaldi. It was easy for this mythical figure, Abraham, to abandon polytheistic paganism for he was evidently not a committed polytheistic worshiper but a worshiper of the One Lord of Heaven.

The biblical author may be giving us the prototype Abraham as the early worshiper of one supreme Lord. Belief in one supreme deity by an individual can be seen as a relationship between God and that individual. This relationship is holy, as Abraham is known as the *Friend of God*. Such a relationship is brought about through meditation and through seeking to understand God's will.

There is also a very fine line to be drawn between those who worship one God and those who worship one God who has many portrayals, or who can be described by many different terms. Even in our day there are groups who worship one God under three aspects. This Unity is called by some Christians, the Trinity. Trinities of the one in-dwelling God were worshiped in ancient Egypt and are worshiped in present day India. In the Hindu Trinity, Brahma is God The Creator, Vishnu is God The Preserver, and Siva is God The Destroyer (and Renewer). They represent One God in his past, present, and future actions.

The biblical author depicts Abraham as having some notions of the Trinity of God as in Genesis 18:1-2, God appeared to Abraham as three persons. On the Egyptian temple walls, the pharaoh is usually pictured standing with three aspects of God. The visages of Abraham's three visitors are not described, but Egyptian tomb drawings often showed the deceased nobleman in the company of three gods. The noble or pharaoh was shown with a human form and visage, but the god representations had animal heads and bodies which were either male or female.

There may have been an individual named Abraham with a wife Sara, but it is not necessary to have had such a pair. Abraham can be at least in part a mythical prototype constructed out of tid-bits given about Father Brahman of the Hindus as the good father of a believing people, about Akhenaten of

Egypt, and about other notable men. The thread weaver of David's reign could use any material about any great man that preceded her 1000 BC date. Akhenaten lived about 1350 BC, previous to her time. The Mitanni, Tushratta, is dated about the same time. Rameses II (1290-1224 BC) is before her time. She could have used mythical material about any one of these famous leaders or stories about anyone much further back in history. **Isaac and Jacob.** The God beliefs of Abraham, Isaac, and Jacob tend to be quite distinct. God is "the God of Abraham, the God of Isaac, and the God of Jacob," rather than simply "the God of Abraham, Isaac, and Jacob." This is because the ancestors were separated by many generations and reflect different land areas and cultural views. Gods were overseers of different sections or types of land such as mountains or deserts or towns. The god of the desert must be able to control the sand storm. The god of the town has more to do with morality. The God of the *Twenty Third Psalm* is more gentle than the God who aided the sacking of Jericho.

There seem to be differences in the way Abraham worshiped and the way Isaac worshiped, as well as differences in the way Moses worshiped and the way David worshiped. If we are to believe that the early Hebrew myths associated with an ancestor named Abraham came out of India, where Brahman was the good spirit internalized in and concerned with humanity, then we are being told one aspect of the Hebrew religion. If the Bible tells us of fire offerings, we see another aspect. If we see that Abraham believed in child sacrifice, and was led to drop that belief, then we learn something more about early Hebrew beliefs.

This belief in child sacrifice persisted. Jephthah (section 3.3) in the time of the Judges was willing, albeit reluctant, to kill his daughter for an oath he had made (Judges 10, 11). A Hebrew chieftain in the reign of King Ahab (874-853 BC) offered up his own sons as a sacrifice to ensure the safety of Jericho when he rebuilt it (I Kings 16:34). Other children were left on the hillside to die and found by compassionate people, such as the prophet Ezekiel (Ezekiel 16:4-6). It is no wonder today that we have those who see no harm in, and those who oppose abortion. We have spent a long time trying to settle our priorities in regard to who shall live.

When Abraham made his covenant with God, Genesis describes how he laid out his offering (15:7-11). This may not be a description of what Abraham did, but a description of what his many-times great-grandchildren did to validate priestly offerings. These sacrificial customs of Canaanites and Israelites were copied after the priestly rites that had evolved in the temples of Egypt or on hill tops eastwards from Palestine. Thank goodness they decided not to have human sacrifice! A similar sacrificial strain developed in the Aztec culture, but they used human beings. Carthaginians used human beings for sacrificial offerings. Chinese left babies on hillsides for dragons to devour. South American Indians in Peru allowed themselves only two children, and destroyed the surplus. Abraham was tempted to use human beings for sacrifice. Today we have evolved to unbloody sacrifice on our religious altars. Some people may still see a necessity for bloody sacrifice of human beings in war, as pleasing to God.

When the biblical author reports on the relationship of God and Isaac, the individual has progressed to family status. There are relationships among family members that are to be straightened out. The God of Isaac is a strict God concerned with the rights of primogeniture. This God shows concern for Isaac and finds him a wife from the tribe of Abraham's brother Nahor. As Abraham left this brother in the country of his birth, worshiping the local gods, Isaac's wife Rebecca comes to her husband still believing in those local gods. For a third time the Bible repeats the legend of how the king found the patriarch's wife beautiful (Genesis 12:10-20; 20; 26:1-11). Abimelech is blamed for two of these incidents. It seems that the biblical author is being very careful to write down all threads of tradition. She is telling us how men should cherish their wives, and also telling us that God protects those who serve him although they are in a foreign territory.

Time passes, and the relationship between God and Jacob has advanced from family to tribal proportions. The God of Jacob is the powerful God of the land who wants brother tribes to dwell in peace. Jacob acts rather independently, wrestles with God, and ends up accepting God's care for himself and his family.

Jacob's son, Joseph, went through trying circumstances, and experienced God in his Egyptian prison conditions as a most immanent God. The biblical author expresses how she thought each of the ancestors felt God's care.

Jacob's descendants had word of mouth tales about various happenings in the land of Egypt. These tales illustrated God's love for all humanity. The Bible is theology. It tells us about a loving God using representative examples. David's scribes emphasized David, Judah, and Jacob as God's special people. These biblical heroes should serve merely as illustrations, for all people are God's special people. The biblical author's emphasis on David was necessary to legitimize his usurpation of kingship and his control of the other power structure, the priesthood.

Jeremiah. The 600 BC prophet Jeremiah is also a product of his time. In Jeremiah 31:31-35 he emphasizes that the race of Israel is to endure. He perhaps did not realize any more than racially concerned people of today that his ancestors came from many locations, and that when we carefully consider our origins, we find we are all related to one another and to the earth. We are united in our humanity, but diverse in our genetic structure. The <u>human race</u> is capable of great endurance. God will surely save a remnant. It may be necessary for the remnant to evolve to greater gentleness and humility.

We should not be fascinated with one particular history or one particular people. All people are important to the God who created them. The world is full of agony and misunderstandings in all its quarters, and God has concern for all. When you consider the suffering of those in Jericho, those in Ai, those in Egypt, those in Mesopotamia, in India, the suffering of the Cro-Magnons, the Neanderthals, all the wonderful people that God has made, how can we say that God commanded one privileged group to kill the others off? Groups make mass killings of other groups out of jealousy or fear. The message of the Bible is that we should love one another, not fear one another. We should treat the other people dwelling in the land with respect, or the land will be taken from us. We must respect all ethnic and religious groups all over the earth, or the earth will be taken from us.

The tribes of Israel were in Palestine 1400 BC or earlier. This group of blood-bonded tribes remembered stories of a sojourn in Egypt, a wandering in the desert, disputes among early ancestors, and the name of a father-type or tribe founder back in a time when there were no written documents, and one memorized lists of progenitors' names. David's author collates previous unwritten material and gives us Moses, Exodus, and the Tribes as reasons for a united relationship among diverse peoples. What is more important for all people everywhere today is that these people felt themselves to be the beloved of a monotheistic God. The true message of the Bible is not separatism and elitism, but the love of God for all peoples everywhere. If diverse tribes could unite under David and the Mosaic God, surely our modern divisive races, creeds, and sexes can give respect to each other as we acknowledge One Creator God.

Pulling It All Together. This picture of the one true God, possibly drawn by a woman in the reign of David about 1000 BC, is for the purpose of keeping religious and temporal order in the Kingdom of David. For her masterful tapestry, she uses threads of myth from many different cultures, Egypt, Assyria, Babylonia, and India, and also reinterpretations of such myths from the tales of wandering tribespeople in the desert lands in between. She may not realize that she is using such colorful and various information. She may only be repeating what she has heard. What she has assimilated has given her tremendous faith in the God Yahweh. David may have been content with any god that would unify the tribespeople, but this writer insists on the pre-eminence of the One God, and her instructive words have transmitted this God to generation after generation. She used fable and allegory to carry her message, and she supplied names that were convenient to her purposes.

The Abraham ancestor myth and service of his God may have encompassed over two thousand years. Isaac was an ancestor figure from another era and area. Jacob or Israel is the ancestor connected with the land of Israel, and thus more tied in with the God of that land. However, when one of Jacob's sons went to Egypt and became famous, much religious input was absorbed from Egypt. This Egyptian lore was added into the amalgam of beliefs that had come from the Indus Valley, Tehran, northern Mesopotamia, and the land of Canaan to make a comprehensive ecumenical God for the people of David's Palestine.

6.4 The Theology of Egypt

Early Diversity. Before the rule of dynasties, Egyptian towns had their own view of God. They expressed different characteristics of God in terms of God's creatures. Each town had its own idea of what was powerful. The crocodile was feared and worshipped for its power. The cow was honored as a holy resource. The cat goddess Bast was the solar goddess with the gentle heart. The lion-headed goddess of Memphis, Sekhmet, consort of Ptah and goddess of war, was a more roaring type of cat. She was the goddess of scorching heat. These gods were often represented with animal heads and human bodies.

Many god stories and god names of Egypt have their beginnings in Mesopotamia, which in turn heard tales from the Tehran area and further east. The Syrian war goddess Astarte was adopted by the Egyptians and associated with the moon and Hathor. Hathor was the goddess who took care of women. She wore a solar disk between the cow's horns on her head, or sometimes she was seen simply as a cow. Khnum was the god of fertility and creation who made humans on his potter's wheel (as in Isaiah 64:8). One of Khnum's consorts was Satis (like the Hindu Sati) whose name meant *she who runs like an arrow*, and who was associated with the rapid currents of the Nile. An important deity was Thoth. He began as a moon god. He and his consort Seshat invented letters, time, and record keeping. Thoth was shown as a baboon or ibis, or a man with the head of a baboon or ibis.

As we have seen in Chapter III, all the lesser gods of Egypt eventually consolidated depending on which city had the most power. Trinities of gods developed. At one point, the sun god Ra was most powerful. At another time the combination of Atum-Ra was worshiped.

The One God of Egypt. The Davidic author of 1000 BC tells us about the One God of Moses. She surely had heard about the different aspects of God that were worshiped in Egypt. She didn't want her fellow Hebrews to worship those representations. In her portrayal of the God Yahweh, she was using information that was common to her time and culture. She could be using information about the One God of Pharaoh Amenhotep IV. This *Amen*hotep changed his name from referring to the god *Amen*, to Akhen*aten* because he came to believe in *Aten*, the one God of energy, all powerful. If Moses were in the wilderness about 1250 BC, he would have savored the same philosophy that had led Akhenaten to proclaim one God around 1300 BC. If Moses existed earlier around 2300 BC, he would not have had the insight into this 13th century Egyptian pharaoh's belief. However, the Davidic author would still have been able to use the Akhenaten material, and could have given the God of Moses the later day characteristics of the God of Akhenaten.

Akhenaten was disgusted with the Egyptian priesthood that had amassed power and wealth and corroded the people. In 1370 BC he moved his capital north from Thebes to his chosen temple site, Akhetaten, in Middle Egypt on the east bank of the Nile across from Hermopolis, and undertook a religious renewal. Akhenaten believed himself to be the *Beloved of The Sun-disk*, that this monotheistic type of god had a personal love for the pharaoh. Akhenaten's attitude understandably annoyed the powerful priesthood at Thebes, and upon his death, the other Egyptian cities went back to worshiping their local gods, and the capital was returned to Thebes. Those who worshipped the new idea of one absolute God in one form may have had to go underground or think about leaving the country. Some of these religious ideas may have been internalized by the Sea Peoples who traveled along the coast into Palestine circa 1200 BC.

A hymn to the sun god on a stela by Akhenaten's architects Suty and Hor singles out the sun-disc and describes him as "one who created everyone and made their life."[5] Fragments of Akhenaten's announcement of the new god state his belief that the old gods had failed to operate properly. This new god is absolutely unique and located in the heavens, and described as universal, transcendent, creative, and all-powerful. Some of the epithets used for this god are: "the august god of the primordial moment," "Harakhty the great sun-disc, the fashioner of brightness," "the living sun-disc who brightens the land with his beauty."[6] Ra-harakhty, or the rising sun depiction of Horus, is shown as rays of energy from the sun disc, often with feet on the end of the sun rays.

One of Akhenaten's objectives was to cleanse the temples of their strange animal-headed representations of God. These gods were seen by some as the many characteristics of the one true God. Others believed they were idols and worried that the less knowledgeable were giving improper reverence to good luck tokens. The reduction of the sun god to a nonhuman disc was an attempt to rid religion of the human form and to reduce priestly control. In the hieroglyphic script of Akhenaten's time, figures of animals and humans were avoided. A few symbols such as falcon, sphinx, and bull connected with the sun-cult were left on stela inscriptions. The pharaoh recognized the Disc as "the one who built himself by himself, with his [own] hands– no craftsman, knows him!"[7] This thought expresses belief in a God who is far beyond human comprehension.

Infusion of Egyptian Ideas. The Egyptians passed on to the foreigners dwelling in their land many of their ethical values. They had a concept of justice which was called *maat*.[8] Maat was the quality of goodness and truth which was considered as an inheritance from the elders. It was to be prized more highly than the material gift of wealth, which misfortune could easily take away.

Other Egyptian theological thought that carried through to David's time was that "the *ab* is the heart, the seat of knowledge, wisdom and understanding;" and *khu* is "the inspiration, the message of the gods." The *ab* is what the human may learn in silent meditation.[9]

The beliefs of the wandering tribespeople who settled temporarily in Egypt were heavily influenced by the religious discussions and the priesthood of Egypt. Coming from an arid nomad life-style, they found much comfort and stability in the well watered towns along the Nile River. If they stayed for the biblical tally of 400 years, they certainly acquired many of the positive Egyptian cultural habits. The Josephites incorporated customs of the cult at Heliopolis (or On). Later migrating groups had their choice of Egyptian multi-god representations, or One Unseen God. With intermarriage their beliefs undoubtedly reflected some of the beliefs of their spouses. Joseph, for example, married the daughter of the priest of On, and was therefore very knowledgeable of that theology. Aaron, as chief priest in the wilderness, may have served his apprenticeship in an Egyptian temple. Women in Egyptian temple services acted in the capacity of cantors. Miriam, therefore, may have been exercising her duty as the proclaiming cantor in the timbrel and dance episode of *Exodus 15:20-21*.

The tribal groups probably "went to church" in the local Egyptian temple with the rest of the townspeople. We can't say that as good Hebrews, they went to the synagogue. The synagogue wasn't present as an institution until after the Babylonian captivity. As tribes dwelling in the northeast of Egypt, fellow travelers and inhabitants of their ghettoes probably included those from Persia, Babylon, Libya, and Ethiopia. These groups needed a place to sort through their thoughts about God and their personal problems, as we do in our churches today. To some extent, all these foreign or traveling people of ancient Egypt worshiped in the local temple and supported the local temple priests.

When people live in the foreign quarter together and worship their special god in a corner of the community temple (dedicated to the primary city god with free room for other gods and goddesses), they are bound to develop a certain amount of community rapport and religious toleration. We should encourage more of such community mingling today. Our church leaders should not restrict us to closed communities. When worship is in special separate locations, there is a tendency towards elitism.

The Exodus. Regarding the Hebrew exodus myth, we can say that a group of people of foreign ancestry left their area in Egypt, probably for a mixture of political and religious reasons. They claimed belief in a God who was interested in their community group and in their travels. They believed their God was urging them to leave Egypt and the domination of the pharaoh, and that this God's loving concern for them was demonstrated by certain miraculous occurrences, one of which was their safe passage through the waters. This God that guided them had Egyptian symbols and ethics attached, and the Israelites carried with them into the wilderness a certain respect of the priesthood. They developed a priestly cast modeled after the political elite of Egypt and the hill-top shamans of Canaan.

6.5 Gods In The Wilderness

Moses fashioned a bronze serpent which he put on a standard, and if anyone was bitten by a serpent, he looked at the bronze serpent and lived (Numbers 21:9). Serpents are respected by some and feared by others. Amaunet, the consort of Amun, was represented with a serpent's head. Serpents intertwine on the Asclepian medical symbol. Satan is represented as a snake. Moses proposed the serpent as a positive symbol. One time period's symbol for healing is another time period's symbol for idolatry. The later day King Hezekiah felt that some of his countrymen were offering sacrifice to this symbol. *It was (Hezekiah) who abolished the high places, broke the pillars, cut down the sacred poles and smashed the bronze serpent that Moses had made* (II Kings 18:4).

When a group of politically oppressed people gather in the wilderness together, they are liable to come from many different backgrounds. There is opportunity for interfaith dialogue and for greater understanding among individuals. We think of the Moses group as homogeneous, worshipping the Hebrew God *Yahweh*, but perhaps they had never heard of such a name for God. If they worshipped one God, that God may have had many different names. The names we call God are varied, and give a hint as to the kind of God we feel we need. Some of us call on a Lord of Battle. Some of us believe in a God of Love. Most have decided that there is one God who is more powerful than the others. Some in the wilderness may have been meditative yoga type worshipers inspired by Brahmanic ideals. Others may have believed in a God concerned with family well-being or with a particular tribe. Moses may have emphasized a God who demanded legalistic obedience. A source of dissension in the wilderness must have been when one group insisted their special God was the most powerful.

Then Yahweh spoke to Moses, "Go down now, because your people whom you brought out of Egypt have apostatized. They have been quick to leave the way I marked out for them; they have made themselves a calf of molten metal and have worshiped it and offered it sacrifice (Genesis 32:7,8). Worship of a serpent may have come out of Egypt with the tribal group. The serpent was at times a representation of wisdom and of healing. In the Genesis 3 description of the creation the serpent is described as the cleverest of the animals. What virtue or characteristic of God could the wilderness people be worshiping in a golden calf? Egyptians worshiped the quality of sustenance displayed by the cow goddess Hathor. If you were hungry in the desert, you would pray to a god or goddess that would feed you. Those from Mesopotamia believed in the strength of the bull, and worshiped a representation that was half-bull, half-man. A bull represents power.

But why a golden *calf*? Two generations after David, Jeroboam of the Northern Kingdom of Israel made two idols whose description is translated as golden calves, and set them up for worship in the shrine-cities of Bethel and Dan (I Kings 12:29). These may have been *small* statues of cows, rather than small *cows*, as Jeroboam had spent some exile time in Egypt where Hathor, the cow goddess, was a protectress of the people. The Golden Calf in the wilderness may also have been a *small* image of a cow. This may reflect a type of worship that was common among the Israelites and their fellow-travelers when they were dwelling in the desert. It also may have to do with worshipping the female aspect of God. There are inscriptions from the 8th century BC in the vicinity of Hebron and the Negeb that show some Israelis worshipped a Lady God along with their Lord God. These inscriptions refer to the Lord's wife *Asherah* which is a name for the chief

Canaanite goddess. Other Hebrews who were soldiers at Elephantine in southern Egypt worshipped *Anat Jahu*, a goddess they regarded as the wife of the Lord God of Israel, in the 5th century BC, Anat being another name for Asherah.

Before the advent of Zoroastrianism, other gods reigned in Persia and surrounding territories. Asherah was wife of the Canaanite supreme god El and by him, the mother of seventy deities. We have heard of El, the God of the mountain, from the *Elohist* biblical author. We find other uses of the number seventy in the Septuagint where seventy wise books are written by God's messengers, and in the Sanhedrin where seventy wise persons rule the people. The goddess Asherah is called the "Bride of Heaven" in an 18th century BC inscription credited to the Amorite population of Canaan. Nearby, on the Mediterranean coast of Syria (modern Ras Shamra, ancient Ugarit) Ugaritic texts from about 1400 BC call Asherah the mother of the great god Baal, and the goddess Anat is considered to be his sister. These goddesses were imported into Egypt in the 13th century BC, as Pharaoh Rameses II called himself "the companion of Anat." A Persian or Canaanite princess may have been given in marriage to an Egyptian ruler, and imported elements of her faith with her. A more warlike means of transport may have been conquering armies. Asherah's Egyptian name became Qodshu or Qedeshat (Star of the East). Egypt already had associated the goddess Isis and the Dog Star.

When the Hebrews reached the Holy Land, Gideon pulled down the Asherah pole by night (Judges 2 and 6). He didn't want to risk the wrath of all her female adherents. As time passed and more princesses were traded in order to cement treaties, Solomon married other royalty and built an Ashtoreth (Asherah) sanctuary (II Kings 23). Manasseh, king of Judah (696-641 BC) set up a graven image of Asherah (2 Kings 21:7).

The Amorites, also known as Amurru which means *Westerners*, were a class of people in northwest Mesopotamia who spoke northern Semitic. Since about 2800 BC these nomads had been pressing onto the Fertile Crescent and overrunning Palestine, and their numbers may have included Hebrews, Gudeans, Assyrs, Arameans, and others similar to the description of the prototype Abraham. They claimed Baal as their god (3000-2500 BC). He was known as Adad in Mesopotamia, and as Hadad in northern Syria. Stories told about Baal 'way back when,' are found in religious apocalyptic literature such as descriptions of battles won over sea monsters, serpents, and seven-headed dragons.

Baal and bull worship frequently go together. Baal was worshipped in Egypt as a result of conquered peoples being transplanted. The Israelites in the desert were easily persuaded to pay their respects to a golden calf. The Greeks encouraged the worship of *Serapis* (*Osiris* dropping the first letter 'O' plus the name of the sacred bull *Apis*). Some in India hold the cow sacred. Bull worship is connected with the astrological signs. For many years the dominant sign has been the goat, Capricorn. Before that was the Age of the Bull, accounting for bull worship, and before that, there was the Ram. Recently, we have entered the Age of Aquarius, the Water Carrier.

When the commandment says that they are not to bow down to other gods (Exodus 34:14), it admits the existence of other gods or other possibilities of objects to worship. It wants the Israelites to acknowledge that Yahweh is the first and foremost God, and superior to these other gods. In the Bible these lesser gods are later de-emphasized and transformed into the cherubim and seraphim that sing around God's throne. In the 50 BC Dead Sea Scroll material these lesser ones are described as the gods of knowledge and spirits of God who proclaim the majesty of God.[10]

For the Israelites in the desert Yahweh was the God of the Covenant, but that troublesome god Baal, supported by Jezebel and fought against by Elijah, was also called by his adherents, Baal Berith, meaning the God of the Covenant. Who was copying whom? The name Baal implies ownership. It is the name of the god who possesses the land and the people.

6.6 Mythical Heroes and Heroines

Each country had its heroes and heroines. Some are interchanged between cultures and countries. It is hard to say if some heroes originated in India and flowed north, or if they were first admired in Persia or in the Caucasus. We are most interested in those heroes that are associated with our own cultural background. Christians and Jews come from the tradition of Abraham and Moses, and we use those familiar names for our role models. According to our religious beliefs, we call these heroes *demi-gods*, *avatars*, *angels*, or *saints*. If we don't have role models, we manufacture them. People of today admire Martin Luther King, Jr. and Sai Baba. Sometimes lesser heroes will take people's fancy and be catapulted into fame. The economic community has dramatized Santa Claus. Mrs. Santa Claus has been proposed.

Early heroes were men and women who were great enough to be remembered for their acts and their beliefs. Stories of heroic characters are also sometimes created to illustrate a principle. For example, Genesis 11:28 speaks of Ur of the *Khaldees*. The name of Ur is given as a name that will be understood by people of 1000 BC. Abraham's Ur may have been another city holy to the Khaldeans, such as Kalibangan in India where there were early fire altars. Lot's wife may have met her end in a desolate eruption many miles to the east of the Dead Sea. Isaac or Ishmael may have been prototypes of the idealized first born, as was the Iranian, Kumaris. Jacob and Esau may have been prototypes for the typical tribal disputes among brothers. Other biblical stories may have sprung from Mesopotamia, such as the tale of Jephthah's daughter.

The locale of a myth also can be changed. Genesis and Exodus contain myths from India and Mesopotamia, with Palestinian place names, in order to justify and support the monarchy of David. More importantly they are used to make a theological statement that proclaims God made the earth, and that God will give us a peaceful existence on earth, if we are kind to the earth and to each other. We are all God's beloved.

Footnotes

1 J. Newton Brown, Ed., *Encyclopedia of Religious Knowledge*, Brattleboro Typographic Company, Brattleboro, VT, 1840, picture from p. 622.

2 Rostovtsev, *History of Ancient World, Volume I*, Oxford Press, London, 1930, p. 19.

3 *Mythology of All Races, Vol. V*, "Semitic," Cooper Square Publishers, NY, 1964.

4 Joan Oates, *Babylon*, Thames & Hudson, London, 1986, p. 172.

5 D.B. Redford, *Akhenaten*, Princeton U. Press, Princeton, NJ, 1984, p. 172.

6 *ibid.*, p. 173.

7 *ibid.*, p. 175.

8 Jill Kamil, *Egyptians*, American University Press, Cairo, 1988, pp. 91, 92.

9 Normandi Ellis, *Awakening Osiris*, Phanes Press, Grand Rapids, MI, 1988, p. 24.

10 *Songs for the Holocaust of the Sabbath*, 4Q400.

VII

David

The Ecumenist

As the fat is set apart from the communion sacrifice,
so David was chosen out of all the sons of Israel.
He played with lions as though with kids,
and with bears as though with lambs of the flock.
While still a boy, did he not slay the giant,
and relieve the people of their shame,
by putting out a hand to sling a stone
which brought down the arrogance of Goliath?
For he called on the Lord Most High,
who gave strength to his right arm
to put a mighty warrior to death,
and lift up the horn of his people.

Ecclesiasticus 47:2-6

7.1 The Rising Star

Anointed by God. *The oracle of Balaam son of Beor, the oracle of the man with far-seeing eyes ... I see him--but not in the present. I behold him--but not close at hand: a star from Jacob takes leadership, a scepter arises from Israel* (Numbers 24:15). *Samuel took the horn of oil and anointed (David) where he stood with his brothers; and the spirit of Yahweh seized on David and stayed with him from that day on* (I Samuel 16:13). Back in the early cultures of Egypt and Mesopotamia, it became important for a ruler to have a good relationship with his god. If you weren't in the hereditary line, it was advisable to have a respected prophet anoint you. There must have been many prophets of the various gods still known in Israel, but David proclaimed that the sacrament of his anointing was performed by Samuel, a prophet of Yahweh.

The Giants. There are giant killing exploits that have been recorded in Hebrew history. We are assured in I Samuel 17 that David was the killer of a giant whose name was Goliath. David is described as the son of Jesse of the tribe of Judah. David's official name *David* meant *leader* or *chieftain*, and the Bible uses these formal titles when talking about him, but he had another more personal name. Bathsheba probably didn't call David, *Chief* or *Leader* or even *My Lord*, anymore than I would call my husband by those terms. It would have sounded sarcastic. What was David's personal name before he became the great leader? Might his victory over the giant also be reported in I Chronicles 20:5 under his real name where Elhanan (meaning *mercy of God*) of Jair (meaning *light* or *enlightenment*) from Bethlehem killed Lamhi, a brother of Goliath from the town of Gath? In II Samuel 21:19 Elhanan reportedly kills Goliath. Could David's true name be Elhanan? Could the name of his God be the God of Light such as Ahura Mazda? In II Samuel 21:17, David is described by his followers as the Light of Israel. Other official giant killings are given in II Samuel 21 where it is reported that Abishai, David's nephew, killed the giant Dodo of the tribe of Rapha, and thus saved David's life. Also Sibbecai of Hushah killed Saph of the tribe of Rapha. Jonathan, the son of David's brother Shimeah, killed a six-toed giant of the tribe of Rapha.

David and company were obviously out to get these giants of the tribe of Rapha and the town of Gath. I Chronicles 7:24 says the men of Gath killed Ephraim's sons. David would certainly make allies of the Ephramites if he avenged them. But another strange thing is that one of the sons of Ephraim is named Rephah (or Rapha) which is the name of the tribe of the giant Dodo. This sounds like it could be a case of brother fighting brother, or the descendants of Joseph fighting each other. David, in siding with the dominant group, made allies of the Ephraimites.

Early Developments. David's early years led him to be empathic with the under dog and to be an able manipulator and administrator. He could see clearly the mistakes of his predecessor, Saul. Saul's son Ishbaal ruled for two years after Saul's death. He was king over Ashur, Gilead, Jezreel, Benjamin, and the important tribe of Ephraim. This name *Ishbaal*, or *man of the god Baal*, may have been given him by the biblical author to emphasize his unworthiness as compared to David. Through intrigue and perfidy, Ishbaal lost his life and his supporters. David claimed nonparticipation in the killing of Ishbaal, and sorrow for the deed. This helped to heal the wounds of Ishbaal's followers. David knew that in order to unite the unwieldy group of tribesmen behind him, he would not only have to be a unifying symbol himself, but he would have to incorporate their varying cultures and religions.

David cemented his position by his marriages. While on the ladder up, he was happy to marry a daughter of Saul. Later, she became a drag around his neck, as a symbol of an oppressive former king, and he had to put her in the back of his harem. His marriage to Abigail, the wife of Nabal the Calebite, also had political overtones (I Samuel 25) as did his marriage to a woman from the city of Jezreel (I Samuel 25:43). Could his affair with Bathsheba (presumed to be black in accord with her name, Sheba) and the consequent kingship of her son Solomon have been an attempt to acquire the support of the black community at home and abroad?

7.2 Contemporary Politics

Saul was killed in 1011 BC. David reigned from 1011-971 BC, and Solomon, from 971-931 BC. Pharaohs contemporary with the Kingdom of Israel were of the 21-25 dynasties (1070-685 BC). This was a period of instability for Egypt after the strong Twentieth Dynasty reign of Rameses II. One of the reasons that an upstart like David could rule in Palestine was that there was a power vacuum in 1000 BC. Egypt and Babylonia were temporarily set back. The Minoan-Crete sea-island culture had ended about 1628 BC due to the eruption of Thera. The Philistines, one of these displaced Sea Peoples had become entrenched in southern Palestine. Dor and Akko, more Sea Peoples, settled in northern Palestine, and in between were Ashur, Zebulon, and Dan. Midas, king of the Phrygians, moved into Turkey about 1200 BC. The Sea Peoples are recorded in a battle with Rameses III of Egypt in 1177 BC. Sidonians are mentioned in II Kings 16:31. The ruler of Tyre is the King of the Sidonians. They are described in Genesis 10:15-19 where Sidon is called the first-born of Canaan. The land of Canaan had just been freed from Egyptian and Hittite overlords. The Assyrian army of Tukulti-Ninurta I destroyed the Hittites in 1200 BC. Phoenicia was freed up to trade and expand. Back in the hills, King David overcame the military power of the Aramaeans.

Roving peoples would fight to overcome the people of a city, if they needed that land for themselves, but at some point we begin to get kings and leaders who gathered soldiers around them and fought for land out of glory as well as need. Perhaps they felt they were doing their god or goddess a favor by increasing her territory. Perhaps they feared the unknown inhabitants of nearby territories, and felt they would be safer if they ruled over them. Why do grown men have to buckle on swords and march out to battle? Is it a hang-over from going out to hunt, and finding meat for food? What instincts in our genes, or fears in our psyches make us band together to kill or even to bad-talk an opposing group? When the solution to most problems is talking it out and trying to understand the other, why do men plot for germ warfare and build tanks and fighter planes for aggressive purposes?

In our world of today we can look around and see the same set of alternatives. Human beings have the choice of fighting for territorial rights like animals, or of using their spiritual components and sharing the earth creatively with each other.

Man's competitive urges became more pronounced when the horse was tamed and man started riding along at greater speed. At some point, due to numerous battles among rival nations, there was a power vacuum in the Near East. God, it seems, took this opportunity to demonstrate the positive features of an inclusive community.

7.3 Justifying A Kingship

The Need for Mythology. David the King had to explain to the people why an insignificant upstart such as himself, could exert supreme authority from the wadi of Egypt to the Euphrates. Usually, suzerainity was applied from the outer reaches of these boundaries, with the land in between being a disorganized place to conquer. To mold a united nation from among the many wandering tribes in the area would be a difficult task. People would not be willing to give military support to a commoner with no royal forbears. The need arose, in order to hold the financial and military backing of the people, to give supporting mythology to this claimant of kingship. It was also necessary to justify David's wresting of authority from Saul, the previous king.

The Promised Land. It was entirely natural for each tribe to hope that its God would lead them to a better condition of life as time went on. Their myths supported that hope. Tribes of wanderers were promised land. There are many myths about people being blessed by God with land.

In India there is the dwarf Vamana, an avatar or enfleshment of the Indian sun god Vishnu. Avatar means *one who has descended*, as the god Vishnu descended from heaven to earth. The dwarf, Vamana, secured land for the people, by changing into a giant and taking three strides. His first step covered earth; his second, heaven; and his third came to rest on the head of Bali, king of the genii, and pushed him into the nether-world. The god Bali is related to the Canaanite Baal or the Mesopotamian Bel. There is a Persian parallel to this Hindu myth in the three steps of the hero Amesa-Spenta. The Nordic tale of a plowman contains this same theme.

When this legend passed through the Holy Land, its unbelievable aspects were detached, and the words of the God who owned the land were spoken to the hero or prototype Abraham. Abraham replaced the dwarf Vamana as the one who walks across the land and learns of God's providence. *Yahweh said to Abraham after Lot had parted company with him, "Look all around from where you are toward the north and the south, toward the east and the west. All the land in your sight I will give to you and your descendants forever ... Come, travel through the length and breadth of the land, for I mean to give it to you"* (Genesis 13:14-17).

We all want a safe and fruitful land. Therefore, this was a good theme for an innovative king to use. The origin of the *Land of Promise* idea may have come to David from many sources as well as from the myths of the legendary ancestor Abraham. It might easily have also been a myth sung by an Egyptian, Persian, or Hindu about some other hero with some other land boundaries. Perhaps it was a marching song for shepherds, to speed weary feet. What better way to march than in step to music and a promise?

After David, the promise of the land is enlarged upon. The material in Deuteronomy and Numbers may have been set down many years after David's reign. *Yahweh your God is bringing you into a prosperous land, a land of streams and springs, of waters that well up from the deep in valleys and hills, a land of wheat and barley, of vines, of figs, of pomegranates, a land of olives, of oil, of honey* (Deuteronomy 8:7-8). More specific boundaries are in Numbers 34:3-12.

God's Promise to All. Perhaps the Spirit had these particular boundaries of the Hebrew myth written down, to describe the natural yearning of every people for peace, security, and prosperity, as well as to proclaim the glories of David's kingdom and to lay out and justify David's boundaries. When reading that promise of boundaries today, we receive from that same Spirit, a flood tide of God's loving concern for all those who serve God. We do not have to limit our belief to certain land boundaries only for a specific genetic line.

We must believe in the spiritual message for all peoples of God's earth. All peoples are God's concern and in God's loving care. Genetics and the tracing of one's inheritance shows that one group is never pure and perfect. Genetics leads us to believe that we are all related to one another, and that we are all imperfect.

The boundary lines described in the Bible included a diverse assortment of tribes and former enemies, in an attempt to share crucial resources like land and water. They confirm the tribal locations of the people of David's time, so that the squabbling over land and water rights could be minimized. Learning from that, if we could better share the land, water, and other resources of our earth today, as given to all peoples by a loving God, we would minimize the need for guns and warfare.

7.4 Many Tribes

When David came to power, there were many semi-nomad tribal groups living in Israel. Genesis 29, 30, and 49 and Numbers 1:5-15 name twelve tribal names, Reuben, Simeon, Levi, Judah, Issachar, Zebulun, Benjamin, Dan, Ashur, Gad, Naphtali, and the Joseph tribes of Ephraim and Manasseh. I Chronicles 2:1-2 reports the same names. The Levites are a caste rather than a tribe.

Ancestral Roots. *Jacob sent messengers ahead of him to his brother Esau in the land of Seir* (Genesis 32:4). *Here are the descendants of Esau, the father of Edom, in the mountainous region of Seir ... These are the chiefs of the Horites in the land of Seir ... Here are the kings who ruled in the land of Edom before an Israelite king ruled* (Genesis 36:9, 30, 31). The tribe of Edom which traced its descent from Esau, is not embraced as a member of the big happy family, even though it has recognized family ties. Perhaps Edom was too connected with the Hittites. Genesis 26:34 states that *when Esau was 40 years old he married ... local women, Hittites*. Other members of the tribal family may have had bad relationships with Hittites. The Bible maintains that the tribal relationship between Jacob and Esau was stormy but ended peacefully.

The Song of Deborah (Judges 5) gives some very ancient tribal information. Only ten tribes are mentioned. Tribes who came to the aid of Barak are Naphtali, Zebulun, Ephraim, Benjamin, Manasseh (Machir), and Issachar. Those who refused to help were Reuben, Gilead (Gad), Dan and Ashur. Here, Benjamin is the kin of Ephraim. The enemy of Barak is Jabin of Hazor. His general is Sisera of Harosheth-ha-goiim. The tribe of Judah is not mentioned. Jabin and Sisera may be related to the tribe of Judah. The Judahites may have been on the wrong side in this battle, so their tribal name is omitted.

In the Book of Joshua a man from the tribe of Judah disobeys orders and is stoned to death (Joshua 7:16-26). Achan, the son of Zerah, was the name of this disgraced individual. David's general and relative, Joab, is the son of Zeruiah, a name similar to Zerah. Were Joab and David related to Achan?

Recognizing the confusion in the various traditions, the biblical author organizes the story of ancestry by using the number twelve, denoting fullness, and being as inclusive as possible. This number twelve may describe all tribes dwelling in all the land available. This may be as inclusive as all peoples living on the face of the earth.

The biblical author uses the names of friendly tribes in her known world that are willing to support David. The tribe of Ashur, seemingly named after Leah's son Ashur, may be a group of friendly Assyrians entrenched in a nearby area. It may also represent an invitation to other Assyrians who would like to be in alliance with David.

There were many Levites, priests, and hilltop shamans in the land at the time of David. The inclusion of the Levites as a tribe was an invitation to all religious specialists to support David and receive official support from the citizens. This Levitical group was not in place at the time of the Exodus, although Moses is described in Exodus 2:1 as being of the tribe of Levi. The actual historical fact may have been that Moses and Aaron were hilltop shamans. David, in his intuitive community building, gathered the varying religious specialists of his time under one banner. The historical Aaron was noted as the prototype of this group by the biblical author. The brother-sister relationship of Moses, Aaron and Miriam (Exodus 6:20 and Numbers 26:59), may be describing a religious continuity rather than common parents.

The Tribe of Judah. Our storyteller found it necessary to state David's tribal background. The ancestor Judah is given one of the more noble parts in the story of Joseph (Genesis 44:14-34). In Genesis 37:21 a pre-David tradition names Reuben as the hero in the first part of the Joseph story. It was also probably a well known fact that David did not belong to the Joseph-Ephraim-Manessah group, and may have been in opposition to them. It was necessary to incorporate the northern Israel tradition into the David amalgam. David could probably claim some Semitic ancestor, such as Eber, but he needed a closer tie than that, with the tribe of Jacob. These ties of sonship to Jacob may be nothing more than a claim to being an accepted tribe in the land of Israel at that particular moment of history. The biblical author had a lot of knitting to do in order to work Judah and David into the Jacob and Israel story. For this reason the Book of Ruth may have been written. It spoke well of the foreigner and sought to justify foreign marriages and alliances.

What constructive references do we have to David's ancestor, Judah? In Genesis 38, Judah did not treat his daughter-in-law Tamar justly according to her Leverite right to become pregnant by a male relative of her dead husband. She had to trick him into getting her pregnant by playing the prostitute. From this incident, according to the genealogy at the end of the Book of Ruth, she produced twin sons about the year 1200 BC, assuming David was born about 1000 BC. This genealogy implies that Judah was in Palestine in the time of the Judges. Judah's affiliation with Jacob may be fairly recent. The Judahites may never have made it to Egypt, and didn't have an exodus to look back upon. It would be wise for David to put his ancestor Judah into the exodus story of earlier times. Genesis 46:12 says that Judah's two oldest sons died in Canaan. The third son also seems to be located in Canaan. The Tamar incident takes place in Canaan. One of the sons by Tamar, Perez, may be the father of the Perezite tribe that the Hebrews are trying to displace in the land of Canaan. According to the Jesus genealogies in Matthew 1:3-6 and Luke 3:23-38, Perez is the direct ancestor of David. The Moabites were another tribe troublesome to the Hebrews. Ruth, a Moabite woman, is another direct ancestor of David. Abraham's nephew Lot fathered the Moabites and the Ammonites. One of David's strengths might have been that he was related to some of the pre-exodus dwellers in the land. Perhaps the Bible is trying to tell us that not only were many Israelis bonded because of ancestors who came out of Egypt, but also because there were inter-relationships among those already dwelling in Canaan.

A possibility for Judah and Judea may be the pre-flood Sumerian mountain people, the Guti or Gudea. The Judah tribe may be from the Zagros Mountains between Iran and Iraq. Around 2400 BC or earlier, the Guti descended from their hills and destroyed the power of the kings in the Tigris-Euphrates valleys. They weren't all uncultured mountain men. A Gudea *ensi,* or ruler, from Lagash called Uruka-gina or the *Shepherd of Ningirsu* encouraged late Sumerian art and formulated law. This law was written down and incorporated in the government of a later king Ur-nammu of the Third Dynasty of Ur (about 2200 BC) who had it inscribed on monuments. As an ancestor of David, the descendant of Judah or the Guti, this *Shepherd of Ningirsu* may be the inspiration for some of the Moses tradition. Power plays may have forced Gutis from Sumer over toward Palestine. Pressures in Palestine caused inhabitants to shift to Egypt. Egypt had chaotic periods when semi-nomads entered the delta area in 2200 BC and 1800 BC.

The name for another group from the Zagros Mountains was the *Su* or *Sua*. Some of the people who ravaged Ur may have been the ancestral line of Elam+Sua or E-sau. Sua is associated with the Persian city of Susa. An Elamite or Persian king named Shu-Sin ruled over the mountain tribes in Mesopotamia about 2200 BC. The Judea or Gudea or tribe of Judah may have been more closely related to Esau than to Jacob! For this reason the biblical author emphasizes the peace agreement between Jacob and Esau. David came to rule in a country named Israel, where many people traced their descent from Eber or Hebre, and these people deserved being named as belonging to the Hebrew tribe. Other tribes sprang from the pre-flood people who populated the hills. They were not Semites, Sumerians, Aryans, or Tamils. They had sought safety in the hills from fluctuating environmental conditions. Their language was pre-flood language which contained similarities to the language of other hill people who might have developed their language from Neanderthal influence. David, as a descendant of Judah, may have been from these hill tribes and of Gudean or Elamite ancestry. This very famous Hebrew may not have been a genetic Hebrew.

The Book of Judges opens with an account of how Judah took territory in the Holy Land. It says that the sons of Judah attacked Jerusalem and took it. However, this didn't happen until the time of David, so this section may be a later insert to gain prestige for the Judahites and Simeonites. Judah is not mentioned again in Judges until verse 10:9 which may be another insert. **Benjamin and Judah.** Benjamin was evidently a small group dependent on the larger tribe of Judah for its protection. Saul belonged to the tribe of Benjamin. Is that why Benjamin is given the part of the duped child in the Joseph story (Genesis 44:12)? Are we always to think of Benjamin as helpless and foolish? Eventually Benjamin is absorbed by Judah. In the myth tales of Genesis 44:18, Judah performs a good action for Benjamin. Such myths using character names were positive propaganda for David's politics. The tradition created by the biblical author can be seen as a propaganda campaign to rewrite Israelite history, or it can be seen as a monumental effort to set down the truth as seen from the Davidic viewpoint, in an impossibly complicated tribal situation.

The Tribe of Dan. At one point David took refuge with the king of the Philistines (I Samuel 27), a tribe which had settled along the coast and which gave Palestine its name. They had pottery like the Mycenaeans and thus were displaced Sea Peoples seeking a new homeland. Other Sea Peoples were also associated with the Israelite tribe of Dan. One thing the biblical author knew about the tribe of Dan was that it was the tribe of the famous Samson, whose treacherous girl-friend cut his hair to destroy his strength (Judges 16). Another fact was that according to legend, it was in the most northern section of the land. The word *Dan* is associated with the direction of *north*. At one point in time the tribe of Dan migrated from southwest Palestine to the northern location of Laish (Judges 18). How could an author in David's day describe the location or territory of the tribe of Dan when she probably didn't know herself, and even if she knew, she did not have the present day map-making ability or knowledge to enlighten her, or to assist her in enlightening others? A quick glance at early maps such as the one on the following pages, can give us an idea of the imprecisions with which our ancestors were faced. It is a marvel that they could travel so far and arrive at where they intended to go.

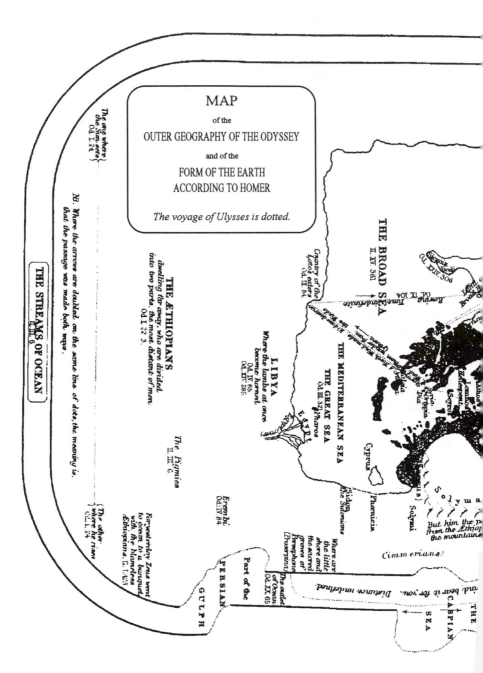

MAP

of the

OUTER GEOGRAPHY OF THE ODYSSEY

and of the

FORM OF THE EARTH
ACCORDING TO HOMER

The voyage of Ulysses is dotted.

THE STREAMS OF OCEAN
Il. XV. 6

THE ÆTHIOPIANS
dwelling far away, who are divided
into two parts, the most distant of men.
Od. I. 22. 3.

The Pigmies
Il. III. 6.

LIBYA
Where the lambs at once
become horned.
Od. IV. 85.
Od. XIV. 295.

THE MEDITERRANEAN SEA
THE GREAT SEA
Od. III. 37; Θάλασσα

THE BROAD SEA
Il. XV. 381

Country of the
Lotos eaters
Od. IX. 84.

LIBYA
Egypt

Cyprus

Phoenicia
Sidon
The Salamians

Solyma

Cimmerians

Part of the
PERSIAN
GULPH

From bi.
Od. IV. 84.

For yesterday Zeus went
to ocean to a banquet
with the blameless
Æthiopians. Il. I. 423.

CASPIAN SEA

How The World Looked to Pec

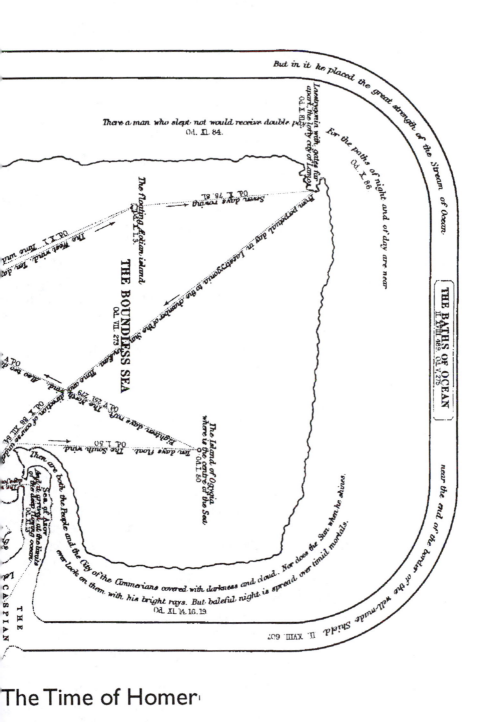

The Time of Homer

The maps in David's time did not show tribal locations the way we show states or counties on our maps today. Major objects like mountains and rivers could be approximately located, and north, south, east, and west were known directions. Even though some people in leadership positions felt that a certain town was under their control, they could never really ascertain how firm that control was, or what subversive elements were accepted by the population. This non-communication led to unreasonable fears, and to more warring factions. Also, the ethnic background and allegiances of the people might be in question. The best thing for David to do, was to assume that everyone wanted to join his team.

A story about the theft of idols by the tribe of Dan is in Judges 18. In this tale the biblical author gives her version of where the Danites acquired some of their religious beliefs. The tribe of Dan had connections with a group of Sea Peoples, the Danuna, mentioned in the 14th century BC Amarna Letters, displaced because of the explosion of Thera. Their name in Greek may have been the Danoi, or they may have been the Egyptian Denyen (in an inscription of Rameses III). They could also be the people in the Phoenician inscription from Karatepe called the DNNYM. Judges 5:17 tells us that Dan dwells in ships. Whatever tribe David needed to consolidate his support, was named in his litany. If he needed a peaceful northern frontier, it was well for him to have an ally there.

The Danites acquired traditions from Iran and India as they intermingled in Palestine. Other Danites brought traditions from the Mediterranean. They attempted to settle near Joppa according to Joshua 19:40-48, but were turned away, and conquered Laish or Leshem (Judges 18). Gathering on the coast of Palestine and continuing in the northward direction, they may have left their name on the Danube. In Roman times the lower Danube was named Ister which reflects the name of the Sumerian goddess Ishtar. The Upper Course of the Danube was called the Danubius. Rivers, as sacred, recall names of deities and also are called by tribal names. The travels of tribes can be traced by place names, some of which have existed until the present. The tribe of Dan may have made settlements in Denmark, Finland, and Estonia. They went on to Sweden, where they became known as Aesir (from Asia), Norsemen, and Vikings. David's connection with the tribe of Dan may have been a political necessity rather than a genetic affiliation.

The Complexity of Complexions. Some of the travels of the early human can be traced by skin color. It is speculated that David was fair skinned or *ruddy* (I Samuel 16:12 and 17:42), not brunette like your average Arab. Perhaps just his looks were against David. Why should a group of brown eyed, brown haired, olive complexioned people, accept the rule of a blonde or redhead? The Bible makes note of differences in skin color. People are whiter than milk, rosier than coral, and dark (Lamentations 4:7). These genetic differences can be caused by a wide variety of causes, possibly including volcanic disturbances with poisons being thrown into the air. During the last cycle of glaciations and warmings, groups of people were sequestered in closed areas and subject to inbreeding. Many lost pigmentation in their skin, so that today we have a skin tone range from albino to Nubian. Most of the people in the Mid East, then and now, have a bronze-tan skin tone. Some of this may have resulted from lighter folk from the Caspian mixing with Indians, Cushites, and those from southern Egypt. Some areas such as up in the hills may have been pre-flood people of lighter complexion. The Gudeans and people descended from Esau may have been some of these "pale faces." When Esau was born, he was described as having red hair (Genesis 25:25).

7.5 Interpreting The Biblical Author

The Underlying Messages. There are two main ways to read the Bible, literally and creatively. Like a kaleidoscope, you can peek in and see the beautiful picture, and you can hand it to someone else cautioning, "Don't jar it; it's so lovely. Keep it that way. Enjoy the beautiful scene." Or you can mix the bits in the kaleidoscope violently. You can shake apart characters, actions, historical snips and pieces, and get many enhancing and edifying insights. God's truth and inspiration are not static. God leads us as we grow in her knowledge and love. God is a way with ever varying scenery, not an end to be preserved stiffly.

You and I don't have to know the absolutely real route to the Holy Land or the exact chronological time of the journey. Those who related their beliefs in God and the ancestor tales to us, wanted to communicate the care that God had for people. Those of us today who search for God's presence, will find that message of caring concern on any mountain of God that they climb.

Whatever can be said as to which is the true Mountain of God, what were the origins of the *Ten Commandments*, who was Moses, and did he return to Egypt, we can definitely say that the Exodus stories added significant dimensions to the evolution of God as a God of loving concern. It is also important that these stories were written down so as to capture the sensitivities to those incidents of a later day person. Think how many people from that day to this have been influenced to more socially concerned behavior due to this 1000 BC setting down of tradition.

Tribal Routes. There were many wandering tribes in the area, as it was the cross roads between India, Northern Europe, Central Asia, and Egypt. If tribes couldn't get along, it was easy to take to the road or the waterways and set up a homestead some place else. If a foreign ruler conquered your country, he could order you to come to his country to do slave labor. If there were a famine in your area, you would walk and walk, until you reached the outer limits of the drought, and there abide, until the people who were originally there, got tired of you. Family groups often stuck together, but people also became assimilated with the people of the land of their refuge. It was very difficult to keep track of just who your ancestors were, but stories told around campfires established traditions that people could appropriate.

Genesis 10 contains some of the tribal history that we have been discussing, as seen from the view point of an author about 1000 BC. She is relating how the earth was peopled by the three sons of Noah. She knows that there was a time of great rain, and that some people with the help of a benevolent God, lived through this difficult period. Her ancestors were largely Semites and thus were descended from Noah's son Shem. Dan is to be considered one of the Twelve selected tribes of Israel, but the Danites are also considered to be the offspring of Noah's son Japheth (Genesis 10:4). In Genesis 9:26-27 we find the political statement that Japheth is welcome in the tents of Shem, and Canaan is not. For political purposes, the blood lines of the tribes have been extended backwards from Israel to Noah. It's too bad that our present day stereotyping of other races can't be eliminated by tracing our blood lines back to our common creator, God.

We think of Yahweh as firmly set in place from the time of Moses, but there were many people living in Palestine in 1000 BC who didn't know too much about this God that David had decided to serve. Judges 2:10 admits that there were in-between generations which neither knew Yahweh or had heard of the deeds that Yahweh had done for Israel. For a very long time the Israelites had lived among the people of the land of Canaan and had given them their daughters in marriage, and served their gods (Judges 3:6). The writer of the story of David combines all these threads of religion and history and gives them a necessary unity. "The narratives of Genesis are a composite of many layers of oral and written tradition, from many different time periods and social circumstances."[2]

Social Norms. The biblical tradition is very time conscious. Things are set down in the proper order. After the Genesis 1-11 telling of pre-history, 11:27 begins the patriarchal legends. These are set in the context of apparently well known historical events, although they are themselves, pre-writing and from a mythological background. These traditional tales established societal norms for the Davidic times, and have even lasted through to our day.

Behold the power of the written word!

Women were accorded a certain amount of respect in the time of David, as they often are when prosperity reigns. David's publicity agent brings up the problem of treatment of children of indentured servants or of slaves in her tale of Abraham's wives. It must have been evident that the women claiming descent from Sara and Isaac were treated with more respect than those claiming Hagar and Ishmael as ancestors. This may be a leftover from Hindu marriage customs when an upper class man married into a lesser class. The biblical author also discusses the rights of inheritance in the story of Jacob and Esau, and the problem of competition and jealousy between siblings or related tribes when telling of Isaac's and Jacob's sons.

If you are a story teller charged with justifying a kingship, your first step is to give your king a pedigree. It must be a pedigree that reflects his belonging as one of the people. David was very fortunate in having his loyal relative and general, Joab, as the second in command in his kingdom. He was also fortunate in having a chief scribe among his relatives and accomplices who could understand his needs, reinforce his chosenness by God, and write history from a unifying viewpoint. This scribe was also loyal to Joab, and distressed by Joab's death on the ascension of Solomon (I Kings 2:26-35). Solomon hired further scribes from Egypt to set down his particular mythology. His placement on the throne was due to one woman, Bath-Sheba (I Kings 1:11-40). His wisdom as ruler was proclaimed by another woman, Queen of Sheba. Unfortunately, due to Solomon's oppressive measures, the kingdom split in two, and rapidly disintegrated.

The pen, being mightier than the sword, the myth of David lived on, and is still being used in our day, to justify present day procuring of the land and domination of the people in the land. The Bible is not so much a history of Israel as it is a history of humanity. The names of the persons chosen to represent this humanity were names set down by a member of a changing and varied tribal population. These groups claimed to have something in common with an ancestor Jacob whose other name,Israel, was given to him by God (in the mythical story of Genesis 32:29-30). This similarity of name and locality give us room to form an opinion on their ancestry. Those people dwelling in the land of Israel are given the right to be called Israelites and to claim a common benevolent progenitor. We in the United States, proudly call ourselves *Americans*, using the name of a map maker, Amerigo Vespucci, to unite us. The ancient dwellers in the land of Israel were also bound together by a name that had historical meaning for them.

Stories in the Bible that are told to legitimize the kingship of David are the Moses law (which was the law code used by David), the twelve-tribal bond with the incorporation of Esau (to incorporate factions), the Joshua tie-in (to encourage cooperation by Ephraim and Manasseh), and especially the God of the Patriarchs as David's God (to establish an obedient priesthood). The Bible is the way that previous events were seen by David's public relations specialist. However, all this writing of history was also guided by the inspiration of God.

We are told much that is positive about David and Solomon, but we also hear about their problems. *The Court History of David* (2 Samuel 9-20 and 1 Kings 1-2) tells about the times of the author. There is a quantity of kingly propaganda included in this. When Solomon died in 922 BC, other authors, still inspired, but less tied to the power plays of royalty, give us hints of how things might really have been. I Kings 11:9-10 informs us of Solomon's imperfections. He is to be forgiven for his back-sliding, because he may not have been acquainted with the strict religious laws of Deuteronomy and Leviticus. The supposedly Mosaic laws in Deuteronomy are regulations compiled in the 8th and 7th centuries BC. The sacrificial system described in Leviticus is not the system used in the period of Judges, but what was done by Hebrews after the exile in Babylon. "Monotheistic Judaism was a product of the Exile, not earlier, as both the Bible itself and Jewish tradition strongly suggest."[3]

7.6 The Priestly Connection

There were priests of various sorts accepted by the populace in the land of Canaan, and they found ways to support themselves through the generosity of worshipers. Before the Davidic monarchy, there was household worship, with no main temple or shrine. Any Israelite male could officiate as an intermediary to God, build an altar, plant a tree, or set up stelae. There were food and drink offerings with festivals borrowed from Canaan. We read in Judges 17 how an Israeli named Micah hired a man who was classified as a Levite to oversee the worship to his silver idol. While some of the Hebrews may have transformed the *other gods* into the one Lord of Heaven, these gods from Persia and Canaan passed through Palestine to Phoenicia, and were transported around the Mediterranean. They were renamed by the Greeks and Romans. El became Cronos; Baal, Zeus; Asherah, Aphrodite; and Anat, Athena.[4] No wonder Saul's son (and David's opponent for the kingship) could be named *the man of the God Baal* or *Ishbaal*! *Baal* was another name for the High God.

Although David's predecessor Saul had attacked certain priestly clans, David gathered these miscellaneous priests together and made of them a coordinated group. He established a tithing and support system for the priestly community that kept them on his side, but under his control. Those who ruled in the city of Jerusalem before David were of the kingly and priestly Zadok line. It is not known what sort of God they worshiped, but they were pressed into the service for David's idea of the godly, as a way of incorporating them into David's supporters. Even David's sons were priests (II Samuel 8:18), but this nepotism was an acceptable proceeding throughout the Near East.

David had to employ priests who would support his kingship. He considered the religious antecedents of the priests who serviced the shrines of the land, and then appointed Zadok and Abiathar and some Levitical priests as his assistants (I Chronicles 15:11). Zadok supposedly had his pedigree established in I Chronicles 24:1, where he was tied in to Eleazar, a descendant of Aaron. (I Chronicles is written by an historian who was looking back about 500 years, and may not have had a correct perspective.) Saul was blamed for the slaughter of the Aaronic priests at Nob (1 Samuel 22:20). Abiathar was the sole survivor of the disaster at Nob, definitely anti-Saul and pro-David, and as such, was highly favored by David. Unfortunately, he did not believe Solomon should inherit the throne, and ended up disgraced by Solomon (I Kings 2:27).

The Paying of Tithes. The story of Melchizedek, the priest-ruler, is an updated insert from David's day that justifies the paying of tithes to priests (Genesis 14:17-20). King David's mentality-formers did not want to say that priests got their free portions because that was the way it was done in ancient Egypt. There is a moral question as to whether tithes go to support the needy or if they encourage a privileged aristocracy. Looking at the situation from David's viewpoint, he needed all the supporting bureaucracy that he could muster.

The combination of kings and supportive priests frequently makes for hardship on the common people. People are led to believe that in order to serve God properly, they must pay a temple tax or tithes to the priesthood. The kings encouraged this belief, so that the people are domesticated and the priests are placated. All those ruled are encouraged to believe God is on the king's side, and the king can do no wrong.

Acceptance of the tithes from Abraham, burdened Melchizedek with the guilt of Abraham who had slaughtered the opposing kings (Genesis 14:1-16). Tithes bind all those who don't want violence, into the power grabbing and guilt of authoritarian structures that commit violence. My taxes are used to purchase weapons of war, and my church contributions are used to deny equal rights for women. We meekly follow social custom. We hand out money for supposedly religious purposes, for lambs and doves for the altar.

We obey laws rigorously. We tell ourselves we are doing what God wants us to do.

Then suddenly a prophet arises and questions our social structures. Christ comes and chases greedy money changers from the temple. He loosens sacrificial sheep and goats and turns the temple into an uproar. We are asked to keep our temples holy.

The Ark. *Then David and all Israel went up to Baalah, to Kiriath-jearim in Judah, to bring up from there the ark of God which bears the name of Yahweh who is seated on the cherubs. At Abinadab's house they placed the ark of God on a new cart* (I Chronicles 13:6,7). David came on the scene when all the other rulers of the Near East were curling their tails between their legs, and licking their wounds. There had been ups and downs among the Egyptians, Sumerians, Akkadians, Hittites, Mitannis, Amorites, and other sundry tribes in the west Asian area. David realized that he would have to please a lot of diverse elements in the Palestinian population. One way to do this was to have the Ephramite God and this God's ark symbol on his side. He hoped that the Ark would help to unite the diverse tribes. For this reason he brought the Ark from its resting place on the holy hill of Kiriath-jearim. The other name of *Baalah* for this site helps us to see the openness and tolerance of early Palestinian worship for God under various names.

David established control over the Ark of Yahweh and made Jerusalem his religious and political capital when he imported the Ark there (2 Samuel 6:12-23) and pitched a tent for it near his palace. In David's first attempt to transport the Ark, Uzzah steadied the Ark of the Lord with his hand and was killed for being too familiar with divinity. This worried David, so he left the Ark with Obed-Edom who had good fortune for harboring the Ark. With this encouraging sign, David took the Ark on towards Jerusalem. The transporting of the Ark was celebrated with a festival of bread, dates, and raisin cakes. Raisin cake had been the celebration food for the Canaanite gods, but David managed to incorporate elements of different religions. This ecumenical aspect of David's reign added to his popularity.

The Ark had originally contained Aaron's rod, a pot of manna, and the two tablets of the law. When Solomon built the temple and deposited the Ark therein, it contained only the two stone tablets (I Kings 8:9). Some time between the authorship of I Kings and the time of the prophet Jeremiah, the Ark disappeared. The Ethiopians claim that it was given to an Ethiopian-Hebrew prince (the son of Solomon and the Queen of Sheba), when he went to study in Jerusalem. The Ethiopians have Ark replicas in their houses of worship. They believe that one particular site in Ethiopia holds the original Ark from the Jerusalem temple. On the other hand, II Macabees 2:1-8 states that Jeremiah hid the Ark when there was danger of the Babylonians desecrating it. The prophet Jeremiah himself assures us that in the Messianic Age, the Ark will no longer be needed (Jeremiah 3:16). The Ark is symbolic of God's presence with the people. We will not need symbols to reassure us when we are graced with love.

7.7 Our Debt to David

David's life and promulgation of the Bible immeasurably influenced those generations coming after him. He became the power structure which was to carry God's message. David was a politician who was interested in being a military leader or a king. He was a charismatic person who was able to understand the needs and fears of others. Having led a band of ruffians who were out of favor, and having been out of favor himself, he could sympathize with the down-trodden. He had faith in God's love and power. In his position of power, David sought to show that all men were brothers, and that all the tribes could get along peacefully. This may have necessitated his embracing Sea Peoples as brothers, and being polite to a weakened pharaoh. David was not only a politician; he was a diplomat. He needed some rules and regulations to keep order and to bind his diverse groups together. The Mosaic Code served well for this purpose. David became the head of the power group that carried Moses' message of the good neighbor. This required skillful handling of the priestly group.

As the land of Canaan was a hodge-podge of personalities and cultures, it had to make some accommodations. Canaanite art drew many elements together. The same can be said for Canaanite religion. The people living in Palestine 1200-1000 BC melded together Hindu, Khaldean, and Egyptian beliefs. They came up with a Brahmin-type God, associated with fire-sacrifice on high places, who was worshiped in an Egyptian-type temple.

In the sense that David gathered diverse elements together, David was an Ecumenist. We can also look at his part in history as that of the one who wove threads from many cultures and places into one vast whole. Only a charismatic person with the help of God could accomplish this marvel. For this we owe David (and God) heartfelt thanks. David absorbed all that was good, loving, and edifying for the community and built the Jewish nation from these roots. In his time there was a flowering of humanity.

As the human being is not perfect, neither was the Kingdom of David. There were problems of order, power, and control. However, these problems are developed and discussed in the Bible in a marvelous way using the tool of myth. We are given the freedom to make up our own minds about solutions for our time and culture. We are given insight into what religious and ethical thought came before David. We are given facts about Hebrew worship as performed in David's time. We are given temple worship and law as exercised 500 years after David. The Bible is an ecumenical volume that incorporates the religious thought of a world with an expanding consciousness. It catches this potpourri of beliefs, and we are graced with a gift fit for the soul of the earth.

The origins of a new religious worship were formulated in the time of David. They continued in the reign of Solomon with the construction of the temple. We are told that David gathered the material for the temple construction, and he also established commemorative celebrations in which all the people could participate. Solomon was not as alert to the needs and wants of the people. Perhaps building a temple that tended to be exclusive was a mistake. Perhaps allowing space in the temple for the gods of his many foreign wives and worshiping these gods (I Kings 11:5-6) was an affront to the established priesthood. Perhaps the phenomenon of David was a difficult act for anyone to follow.

7.8 Our Debt to The Biblical Author

<u>Insight and Interpretation.</u> The scientists have gathered information from the rocks on the mountain tops and from the sea beds, from meteorites, and from the skies. They have inspected the magnetic layers of the earth, and checked gene structures. They have come up with facts to support the beginnings of the human on the globe. At some point these humans start telling their own story, but the words they use come through mythological and theological backgrounds. Often, there are exaggerations to make a point, unbelievable anthropomorphisms, interchanging of gods and heroes, and all this is done by word of mouth. Next, writing comes on the scene, and someone faithfully sets down what has been passed from mouth to mouth for 25,000 or more years.

Have you ever played the game of "gossip?" The starter will whisper a phrase to the person next to her, and this phrase will be whispered from person to person until the last person in the chain announces what she has heard. It is invariably quite different from what started, as it has gone through many filters. The word *baboon* may be changed to *monkey*. *Pink* may turn up as *red*. *The pink baboon walked over the toad*, may emerge from the end person's lips as *the red monkey hurried along the road*. We make our interpretations and report according to our cultural understandings.

As we are all different, we must expect to have disagreements, and these disagreements can be used in a positive manner. We can all learn something if we listen respectfully to one another. My interpretations of what has gone before and of what is presently happening, come out of my cultural upbringing, and have to do with my desires for the future of the world. Others, who have had different experiences, will naturally have different interpretations. These interpretations should be discussed in consensus groups, so that everyone can profit from the maximum of knowledge and experience present in the group. Output is most often for the optimum good. It is possible that such groups can still come up with biased conclusions. For instance, they can decide to make war on another opposing group. However, if they invoke the Spirit of love asking for guidance, they will usually be led in positive directions.

The Jahwist Author. There is one main author who transmitted the greater part of the early pre-writing traditions. In order for her to accomplish this monumental work, she must have prayed often for guidance from her God. She looked at this material from a different perspective than we do. Several distinct race and language groups developed about 3000 BC. Archaeologists can tell us what stelae were written in what language. They can guess at whether a king's name is Sumerian or Semitic. They can relate the facts that are recorded in court records of different countries. All this will involve a lot of guesswork and assumptions. The biblical author had all these same problems when she attempted to relate events that went on before her time. The tool she had that we of the present day do not have, was a closer view of the oral tradition and the relationship of the customs of her times to the customs of earlier times.

Blood Relations. Many readers of the Bible assume that when the author uses names, she is giving us the names of real individual people. Her name usage may be culturally quite different. She may be giving us an historical progression of tribal movements. She is living in a culture where blood brotherhood could be formed by men slitting their veins and mixing their blood with that of another. They believed that they were all originally related, that the first man had been formed by the various gods spitting in a pot, mixing up the contents, and drawing out the original human. Thus when we accuse David of mistaking political ties for genetic ties, we are being culturally incorrect. We do not know how many of his ancestors mixed their blood with other clan leaders, thus forming ''blood brother'' ties. They did not know about genes and chromosomes. Today when we understand genetics, we are inclined to judge all ties genetically. We might be more peaceful if we could recognize that we are all spiritual brothers and sisters. We don't have to mix blood to prove a relationship; we are all from the same Spirit.

Prototypal Names. The biblical author was knowledgeable about vows of brotherhood and other cultural commitments. In her treatment of the patriarchs, she may not be giving us travels of individuals, but rather travels of whole tribes. She represents these tribes by prototypal names. The first land-associated ancestor she mentions is *Terah* which brings to mind a section of Persia in the vicinity of *Tehran*. She tells us that these people in Persia believed in many gods. It may be that she gives us a name that relates to what we know as the present country of India. A good name for this group of people that describes their type of religious worship is *Ab Brahman*. An offspring from this group is the tribe of *Isaac*, a people perhaps inhabiting a territory north of India named *Saac*. The tribe of Isaac lived away from the other sons of Abraham (Genesis 25:6). These other offshoots of the Brahman group or sons of Abraham established themselves in the Arabian peninsula, a country to the east of the writer's location of Palestine.

Isaac had two sons, Esau and Jacob. These may be names of tribes, rather than people. The tribe of Esau may have had the birth right to the land of Israel, as being there first. The name *Jacob* means *usurper* (Genesis 27:36). The tribe of Jacob, coming later, may have usurped Esau, and thus deserved the name of the land of *Israel*, or a name which meant *the prince favored by God*. We know that the culture and religious beliefs of Israel come from other tribal groups pictured under the names of Isaac and Abraham. Can the author be describing tribal trails involving Tehran, Indus Valley (West Pakistan), Saac or Sacae (northern Afghanistan), and Israel? Or is she only referring to a corresponding trail of religious beliefs?

Again, in her stories the author is probably not telling us individual incidents in the life of one person such as Abraham. She is giving us the ethical framework of her times. She is telling us, for example, that the ancestors felt that circumcision was very important. She is letting the people of her time know that fathers should not sacrifice their first born sons. It is true that we can read the Bible as if it were the history of distinct individuals such as Abraham and Isaac and absorb constructive ethical content. It is also good to realize that we can add bountifully to our historical, ethical, and scientific knowledge by attempting to read the Bible in the context of the times in which it was written.

Footnotes
1 James Cranstoun, Ed., *Classical Atlas*, Ginn & Company, NY, 1897, p. 3.
2 *BAR*, May/June 1990, ''Archaeology and The Bible,'' William G. Dever, p. 54.
3 *ibid.*, Dever, p. 57.
4 *loc. cit.*

VIII

Other Pieces

of

The Mosaic

The task of the messenger is to deliver messages.
Since this is the only possibility of intercourse between men,
he is accorded special divine protection.[1]

8.1 Developments After David

David had a great kingdom, but the world did not stop turning when he died. Kingdoms went out of style; other forms of government were tried. Prophets and charlatans roused peoples emotions, even as today.

After the reign of Solomon, son of David, the kingdom split apart. Hebrew kings descended from David ruled in the small section of Palestine around Jerusalem. The writers of the Bible picture some of these kings as good, and some, as evil. The word of the law of God was lost and Hebrew kings followed after "strange gods." The holy writings were found again in the reign of the young king Josiah (640-609 BC). Foreign nations made war on the northern break-away section of Israel and then descended on Jerusalem, carrying its king and important people off to Babylon (586 BC). This *Babylonian Captivity* lasted for approximately seventy years. Cyrus of Persia conquered Babylonia and proclaimed in 538 BC that any Jews who wished, would be allowed to return to Palestine to rebuild their temple.

The Jewish population in Babylon had been doing very well with their religious worship. They had scribes working on their religious books; they had support gatherings in their homes which developed into the present day synagogue service; they had festivals of remembrance. When the opportunity came to return and rebuild, many Jews stayed where they were. In seventy years, a person gets used to a foreign land, and it becomes home to her. The Jews who accepted Cyrus' offer were probably born in Babylon or Persia and may never have seen Jerusalem. A Hebrew group gathered together enough resources to return to Jerusalem in 522 BC, and had rebuilt the second temple by 516 BC.

The returning remnant found that after seventy years, they could not relate with the religious beliefs of the people in Palestine. Some of these people were the unimportant people who had been left behind in the Babylonian Captivity, and others were people who the Babylonians had relocated from other conquered territories. The Jewish settlers separated themselves from these Samaritans, reformulated their laws of purity, and forbade intermarriage with these people of the land. In 444 BC Ezra read the Jewish Law to those assembled in Jerusalem, and the little country became a theocracy. The Samaritans continued their own worship of God, and the focal point of their religion was a temple on Mount Gerizim.

Meanwhile, in Greece, the statesman Pericles (498-429 BC) set in place a democracy for privileged males. Women and slaves were without power, but the ideals of personal freedom and governmental action after group discussion, gained a foothold in the civilized world. The Greek notions of freedom and many gods went with Alexander in his military campaign across the Near East. There is the story that the conquering Alexander gave proper reverence to the Hebrew God by offering sacrifices to this God in the temple at Jerusalem. He behaved similarly in all the countries he marched across. After his death, his general Pompey ruled in Palestine and Egypt.

Controversies among later Greeks, Syrians, Jewish high priests, and usurping high priests triggered the Maccabee rebellion (167-142 BC), during which period the Jerusalem temple was desecrated by being dedicated to Zeus. Judas Maccabeus invited the Romans onto the scene as allies, and for that reason, there were Roman soldiers attempting to keep order in Jerusalem at the time of Jesus.

During this time of upheaval for the Jews, the rest of the world was also evolving theologically. If we are to believe that God wants our fulfillment, in spite of the fact that we have been created with large amounts of competitiveness, aggressiveness, and selfishness in pursuit of our own good, we must ask ourselves how God can possibly hope to accomplish this fulfillment objective. By spurts and starts and stops, we have had changes towards greater cooperation and tolerance. We have had notable instances of love and healing right from the start of religious history–the goddess Isis, the wisdom of Thoth, and the concern of Yahweh. There are other god-aspects such as Dionysus, that point out our baser characteristics. Kindness for fellow human beings was emphasized by Zoroaster, Confucius, and Buddha. Some humans followed this path of kindness. Some continued in oppressive and violent behavior. Places such as Japan still have traces of sun god worship, but have ethics imported from other countries that expand the consciousness of its everyday citizens.

Our fulfillment and the fulfillment of all humanity depends on our idea of God, and on our commitment to the good of others. Some of our historical religious beliefs have blossomed and then faded. Others seem to be more on the main stem of an evolutionary tree whose prime thrust is a God of justice and love who urges us to empathy. Some beliefs such as formal child sacrifice have disappeared. Other practices such as child abuse, starvation, and harming children in war, are still with us, but we recognize them as evil, and hope to overcome them. Some blossoming religions and some that have dwindled down to a dead end, are described below.

8.2 Zoroaster

Ancient Polytheism. There were many religious beliefs that affected the writing of the Bible. Early Indus and Sumerian beliefs were influenced by the near-by population of Persia. Persia before the time of Zoroaster had a religion much like Hinduism as the ancient settlers of Persia came from the same tribes which had guided their sheep from Persia to India and back. Their religion might seem polytheistic, with specific deities attached to the three major classes of society as with the Hindu caste system: (1) chiefs and priests, (2) warriors, and (3) farmers and cattle breeders. The deities or *asuras* (which means *lords*) were attached exclusively to the first class. There were two forms of sacrifice, animal sacrifice and the fermented juice of the haoma plant. The priestly class was called *magi*.

Ancient gods of Persia were *Vayu* (the wind), *Tishtrya* (demon of drought), *Anahita* (the strong undefiled waters), *Verethraghna* (victory), and *Rapithwin* (lord of the noonday heat). There were also sons of gods and divine heroes, humans who had been divinized (somewhat like some Christians have fashioned myths of saints today). Some of these Persian saints were Atar, who brought fire to humankind, Yima who chose death over life, and Trita who like Indra slew a dragon and liberated the waters. A similar folk tale of dragon slaying is also told in Pope John Paul's hometown of Krakow in Poland. Besides traveling north to Teutonic lands,

Persian folk tales were incorporated into Zoroastrian beliefs.[2]

The Man, Zoroaster. The religious reformer Zoroaster is a mythical figure who may have existed side by side with Moses or David or the Jews of the Babylonian captivity. Early Greek writers date Zoroaster at 5000 years before the Trojan War of 1200 BC (which may be interpreted to mean only 500 years), and some modern Persians say he lived as late as 660-583 BC. History also knows this person as Zarathustra. *Zoro* means *bright*, and *aster* means *star* or *god*. The name might imply his profession, such as a person who contained the light or knowledge of God. Zoroaster saw God in visions and spoke of him as friend. Zoroaster changed Persian religion from magic, blood sacrifice, and superstition to a code of ethical conduct. The practitioner of this faith abided by a code of ethics under which he promised kindness to those who belonged to his group.

I forswear henceforth all robbing and stealing of cattle and the plundering and destruction of villages belonging to worshipers of Mazda. I promise householders that they may roam at will and abide unmolested, wherever dwelling with their herds; I swear this with uplifted hands. Nor will I bring plunder or destruction, not even avenge life and limb. I confess myself a worshiper of Mazda, a follower of Zarathustra. I profess good thoughts, good words, good deeds (The Avesta).[3]

When he started his preaching, Zoroaster didn't have much going for him except a good system of ethics. At one point he was thrown into prison. Because Zoroaster debated well, King Vishtospa listened to his teachings and told his countrymen to obey them. Zoroastrianism became the religion of Persia and spread to Armenia and other parts of the Near East.

Esther. The *Book of Esther* in the Bible may be telling us about the situation of Zoroaster. In this Bible story King Ahasuerus had a wife named Vashti. The writer of the Bible story is not to be considered an authority on Persian names, but rather as a relater of word-of-mouth history. The names she uses are names which will be understood by her Hebrew listeners. The name *Ahasuerus* is a translation of the name *Xerxes*, a name given to many Persian kings. The name *Vashti* for the queen is similar to the name *Vishtospa*, the name of the king associated with Zoroaster. The name *Esther* is similar to the name of the goddess *Ashtar*, and is the second part of the name Zoro*aster*. *Mordecai*, as the guardian of Esther, has a very significant name. If we substitute vowels and hyphenate, we come up with *Marduc-cai*. *Marduk* is the shining god of the Near East and *cai* signifies association. *Mordecai* might possibly mean theologian or priest, or have to do with the spiritual protection of Esther. Esther may be the real influence towards the one true God in the Persian court. The biblical author may be relating to us the tale of how the One-God belief came to be emphasized in Persia through the influence of a goodly woman.

In the story of Esther, Ahasuerus disposed of his wife Vashti because of disobedience, and then made Esther, one of the most beautiful women in Persia, his new queen. Ahasuerus had a prime minister named Haman who felt all Jews should be put on the gallows. Esther was Jewish, and her uncle Mordecai advised her to beg the king for mercy for her people. King Ahasuerus listened to Queen Esther's tale about Haman's perfidy. Haman was put on the gallows and Mordecai became the king's advisor. In this manner, monotheism under the name of the God Ahura Mazda may have become prominent in Persia. Eventually, the Zoroastrian priesthood became very authoritative with power next to the king.

A later king of Persia, Darius, about 500 BC, was a follower of Zoroaster and stated that he was king by the grace of Ahura Mazda. Darius is mentioned in the Bible as respecting other people's idea of God (Ezra 6:1 and Daniel 6:26-29). From these expressions in the Bible, we might conclude that following the early Zoroastrian beliefs influenced kings to be ethical and tolerant, and that responsible religious worship evolved in Persia.

Dualism. In Zoroastrian doctrine, Truth or Order opposed the Lie, or Disorder. Zoroastrianism is known for its doctrine of dualism. The Good God is Sharamazda or Ohrmazd or Ahura Mazda (in Persia) or Aramazd (in Armenian). The Evil God is Ahriman, the Spiritual Foe. God Ahura Mazda, the Wise Lord, has no association with evil. According to Zoroastrian beliefs, the Christian God contains evil as he allows creation and his own son to suffer. A tinge of Zoroastrianism may be what has caused some Muslims to say that Jesus was not crucified on the cross, that through some transformation, it was really Judas the Betrayer who suffered. Zoroastrians believed in both individual judgment and the resurrection of the dead at the final battle between good and evil. They didn't believe in the eternal punishment of a hell; for them the purpose of punishment was to reform or correct. Eternal suffering in hell cannot be corrective, and a just God would not sponsor such eternal damnation. Any punishment after death is tempo-rary, and the punishment fits the crime. When good ultimately triumphs, all men will be resurrected out of heaven and hell and be united with the good God. There is the final defeat of evil when the world is sealed against Ahriman, the evil one. This time is called the Renovation, not the end of the world. There are similarities here with Jehovah's Witnesses.

We can see the Zoroastrian dualism in the Chinese concept of *yin* and *yang*. The Christian and Muslim Satan is developed out of Ahriman.

Zoroaster receives his law from Ahura Mazda on a mountain, as did Moses and Hammurapi. There are six days of creation. The first couple according to Zoroaster were Moshya and Moshyana. This combines the myth of Adam and Eve with that of Moses and adds confusion to the dating of Moses. The Zoroastrian tradition contains a flood problem, but it is not so much rain as it is a bad winter.

Other Beliefs and Practices. Zoroastrianism has a belief in saviors. These favored individuals are conceived by virgins and by the seed of Zoroaster which is miraculously preserved in a lake where the virgins happen to be bathing. This belief in virginal conception predated the Mary and Jesus story by hundreds of years. The idea of multiple saviors is also drawn from the avatars of the Hindus and extended in later times to Baha'ism.

Zoroastrian rites used earlier Persian rituals and traditions in the same way that Christians recite Jewish Psalms. For example, prayers harkened back to the fire altars of the Khaldeans, yet they used that praise to glorify their God of Light. ''Worthy of sacrifice art thou, O Fire, son of Ahura Mazda!''⁴ ''The Wise Lord was father of all, the strong and holy one who established the course of the sun and stars ... who fashioned men and creatures in the beginning by his thought ... the father of immortal powers.''⁵ If God can be praised in the same old way, God hasn't changed very much.

Corpses are neither cremated nor buried. Zoroastrian treatment of the dead is to leave them exposed in Towers of Silence or on high places where birds or dogs tear them apart. This recalls the vigil of Saul's wife Rizpah when David had her sons killed, and she tried to prevent the birds from their task (II Samuel 21:10). Did these customs prevalent in David's time originate with the people of Palestine or with the Zoroastrians in nearby Persia? There are purity regulations for dead bodies and menstruating women which may have been copied from, or copied by, the Jews.

Scriptures. The teachings of Zoroaster are set down in seventeen poems called *Gathas*, a section of the Zoroastrian Bible called the *Avesta*. The *Avesta* is believed to be direct revelations from Ahura Mazda, the one high God. The other *immortals* were created by his will. They are Vohu Manah (good thought), Asha Vahishta (best righteousness), Spenta Armaiti (holy devotion or Holy Spirit), Khsathra Vairya (desirable dominion), Haurvatat (wholeness whose symbol is holy water), and Ameretat (immortality). Ahriman was the devil, and at some point (as in the *Book of Revelation*), Ahura Mazda would throw Ahriman into the abyss which would be followed by resurrection of the dead. The good would be welcomed into Paradise by beautiful maidens, and the bad would fall into hell. The six *immortal* ones plus other *worshiped ones* surround Ahura Mazda, like angels and archangels. One of these worshiped ones, the *Keeper of the Fire*, became a deity– *Mithra*. This gave rise to the religion of *Mithraism*, a competing religion to Christianity in the Roman Empire. Mithra, the god of friendship or contract, and Varuna, god of true speech, were considered to be the basis of all ordered life. There is a Mithra statue in England on Hadrian's Wall with sun's rays around its head. Persian soldiers stationed there by Roman overlords carried their beliefs to their foreign outposts.

8.3 Developments in China and Japan

Chinese Early Gods. In China matriarchal societies of 5,000 BC with a spinning, weaving, Longshan culture, were replaced about 3,000 BC by patriarchal groups that domesticated animals and fermented grain to make wine. Early Chinese beliefs were that the world had no beginning and no creator. Man shaped it. Mythical heroes gave fire, writing, and irrigation. There was a Chinese Hsia creation myth recorded in 2200 BC. A later historian, Sima Qian, 100 BC, described early China as first made up of herders, then farmers, then kings.

The kitchen god, Tsao Wang, was the most popular early god. He is identified with the inventor of fire and was a god similar in character to the Hindu and Khaldean fire god Agni. One week before the New Year's celebration, Tsao Wang would leave the hearth side to report on the household's behavior to the Jade Emperor, as he was also the god of family morals. The moon god in China was Yueh Lao and at his festival thanks were given to the gods of earth, rain, and wind. The Taoist Lord of Heaven was a Chinese representation of the Roman Jupiter. His name was Yu Huang which has similarities to the Hebrew name for God, *Yahweh*.

Lao-tse of 6th century BC, China, and his disciples such as Tswang-Tse were apostles of peace. "Through burning love they sought to unite fraternally the people of the world ... They forbade aggression and ordered weapons to be laid aside so that mankind might be rescued from war."[6]

Confucius. Confucius was another philosopher of the same time and place. He believed that if people studied the wisdom of the elders, they would be able to create a just and peaceful world. He investigated prisons and concluded that most prisoners were poor and uneducated, as they are today. He felt that if one educated people and taught them useful trades, there would be little need for prisons.[7] He did not tell people what gods they should worship or what he thought about death. One of his maxims proclaimed 600 years before the Christian era was, "Do not do unto others what thou wouldst not they should do unto you."[8]

Not everyone understood or practiced Confucius' ways. Far eastern religion and ethics had gruesome aspects. Female babies continued to be sacrificed on the hillsides long after Confucius raised Chinese consciousness about killing of slaves.

Sun Gods. Chinese beliefs migrated to Japan and elevated Japanese ethics. Japanese believed their emperor was related to the sun. The world was created by a divine creator couple, the god Izanagi and the goddess Izanami. They gave birth to the sun goddess Amaterasu. The emperor was the earthly descendant of Amaterasu. Indian maharajas thought themselves to be direct descendants of the sun. The Egyptian pharaoh also believed the sun-god favored him as his son. These beliefs may have been exchanged by traders. Chinese, Japanese, and Koreans had rituals of ancestor remembrance and embraced the ethical concepts of Confucius, Buddha, and others.

8.4 Buddha

Early Buddhism. The dates for Siddhartha Guatama, the Indian prince who was the founder of Buddhism, are disputed. *Theravadins* in Burma, Ceylon, and India say that Buddha, the Enlightened One, lived from 623 to 543 BC. Those *Theravadins* in Cambodia, Laos, and Thailand date Buddha at 624 to 544 BC. Western scholars and *Mahayanists* prefer later dates such as 566-486 BC, 563-483 BC, or 558-478 BC. But time is not important for the communal body of Buddha, or body of transformation, which connects and unites all the Buddhas of the past with those of the future. This collection of loving and considerate thought by many different people can be compared to the Catholic belief in the Communion of Saints.

As Christianity has many sects, Buddhism also has its divisions. There is *Theravada* Buddhism (meaning *doctrine of the elders*) which offers personal salvation to the individual. *Mahayana* Buddhism offers salvation to all. India and Persia are not so very far apart and frequently exchanged religious ideas. The Persian *Ahura Mazda* is similar to the Buddhist *Amitabha* who presides over a paradise of light inhabited by pure, stainless beings. These beings are reborn after invoking the name of Amitabha which means *infinite light*. This Infinite Light has resemblances to Akhenaten's sun god, Harakhty, the Fashioner of Brightness.

Similarity with Isaiah. When the original Buddha attained omniscience at the dawning of the day under the Bo-tree, the Buddhist scriptures tell us:

> *hells were flooded with radiance*
> *the ocean became drinkable*
> *the blind from birth received their sight*
> *the deaf from birth, their hearing*
> *the cripples from birth, the use of their limbs*

and the bonds and fetters of captives broke and fell off.[9]

Was Jesus quoting Isaiah or Isaiah's interpretation of the words of Buddha when he spoke in the synagogue at Nazareth (Luke 4:16-19)?

The spirit of the Lord has been given to me,
for he has anointed me.
He has sent me to bring the good news to the poor,
to proclaim liberty to captives
and to the blind new sight,
to set the downtrodden free,
to proclaim the Lord's year of favor!

The dates for Isaiah (actually for the second writer of Isaiah who was probably with the exile community in Babylon, 588 BC) overlap nicely with the dates for Buddha given by the Theravadins.

Similarity with The Holy Spirit. Holy followers of Buddha were known as Bodhisattvas. One such loving person is the Sanskrit Saint *Avalokiteshvara.* The name *Avalokiteshvara* means "The Lord who regards the world with mercy."[10] In India this god is masculine. In China she is feminine, the goddess of mercy, Kuan Yin (or the Japanese Kwannon or Cannon). When this Bodhisattva was to receive release from the vortex of rebirths, creation lamented that he/she was leaving it. Therefore, out of love he/she agreed to stay incarnate in us all. Whenever we are in converse with each other, he/she will be present, instructing us and mercifully helping us. This is similar to the action of the Holy Spirit in Christianity.

Buddha proposed the possibilities of the spiritual lotus that could dwell in the human. Old Testament prophets such as Ezekiel may have spoken of taking the heart of stone and turning it into a heart of flesh (Ezekiel 36:26), but not until New Testament times do we hear of the possibility of God's spirit dwelling in your soul and my soul.

Dharma. In its oldest form Buddhism owes much to the Hindu *Upanishads* and the theory of *dharma* or true righteousness. *Dharma* is loving activity, the vehicle of transport or the boat of faith for the Buddhist.

With the reign of King Asoka about 250 BC, Buddhism was proclaimed to the masses. Asoka waged a war against the Kalinga people in southeast India in which 150,000 were reported captured, 100,000 were slain, and many times that number died from the general effects of that war. He never fought another war. In one of his rock edicts or stelae, he asserts that "the chief conquest is the conquest of Right and not of Might." He abolished war in his empire and encouraged the people in their pursuit of *dharma,* or consideration of one another. *Dharma* is the recognition that one's well-being is connected with the well-being of everyone else. On the western frontier of his kingdom edicts written in Greek and Aramaic have been found. Asoka himself went on tours among his people in which he spoke to them about *dharma,* visited the aged, and gave to those in need. Soon a power system was put in place. Those who came after Asoka on the throne continued to hold the Buddhist faith, but were less gentle rulers.

The listing of the qualities of the godly immortals of Zoroastrianism contains similarities to qualities endorsed by Buddha in his Eightfold Path: Right View, Right Thought, Right Speech, Right Behavior, Right Liveli-hood, Right Effort, Right Mindfulness, and Right Concentration. The negatives of these are among the demons of Zoroaster–jealousy, arrogance, lethargy, debauchery, and wrong-mindedness.

8.5 The Greek Potpourri

The Greeks and the Romans were the recipients of the Hebrew-Egyptian-Mesopotamian amalgam. They also contributed a major advance in foster-ing open discussion and free exchange of ideas. They responded to their cultural inheritance by worshiping in a multi-god fashion, yet exhibiting greater freedom and fewer restraints in their ethical systems.

The World View of Homer and Hesiod. The Greek writer Homer, author of the *Iliad* and the *Odyssey,* and the Davidic author did their writing about the same time (1000 BC) and had access to some of the same material. Homer, whose name means *one who fits a song together,* may be a composite of one main author with later commentators. Being of one particular time and place, Homer made up a story that reflected the names, wars, geography, and history of his time and territory. He pulled the more imaginative parts of his story both from his own fertile brain, and also from stories that had been handed down from his people. In his *Odyssey* the hero boated the known world (see map on pages 196-197) and reacted with people in many localities. Women were there in abundance, some indepen-dent, some to be abused. It would take only one well traveled anomaly to change the genetic construction of many peoples. Legends can give us many kinds of information. They can tell us something about our beginnings. Homer gives us geographical names for his time and an idea of where travelers left offspring. He combines bits and pieces of old legends into an informational and free flowing story.

The Greek historian Hesiod is thought to have lived a few hundred years after Homer. Hesiod, as a setter down of Greek traditions, wrote some of what is credited to him, but the majority is probably by other authors riding on his name. Hesiod certainly knew of the Egyptian traditions, and he also had heard of Moses. Hesiod's tale is of the evolution of the world from chaos. This evolution begins with worship of the natural world of earth and sky and changes to an anthropocentric worship of gods and goddesses who act quite human. As in Egypt, a first God-entity by emanations produced successive other God-entities. The first "beings" were *Chaos* (void), *Gaia* (earth), and *Eros* (immanent creative energy). *Gaia* (earth) produced a "son," *Uranus* (sky). Gaia and Uranus produced the Titans, one of whom was *Cronos* (time). Cronos had a "son," Zeus. Zeus castrated Cronos, and then Zeus was left in power. Unfortunately, the children of Chaos hung around inciting disorder. From the maternal natural line of Gaia (Mother Earth), we end up with Zeus and patriarchal tendencies. In another version Cronos reportedly married his sister Rhea, and they had six children, Hestia, Demeter, Hera, Hades, Poseidon, and Zeus. As in other cultures, different "aspects" of the divinity were thus personified.

We can partially blame Hesiod with stamping society with the curse of patriarchalism and empowering the male. Hesiod justifies male dominance as necessary for law and order. Hesiod records the folk wisdom of his time and thus affirms it, proving that "the pen is mightier than the sword."

In Rome. Greece and Rome exchanged gods and goddesses, giving them different names and different qualities as time passed. There is a theory by Euhemerus, a Greek from 4th century BC, that the Greek gods were deified men. Aurora, the Roman goddess of dawn was called Eos by the Greeks. She was the sister of Helios, the sun god, and of Selene, the moon goddess. Her son who was killed by Achilles in the Trojan war, was named Memnon. This is a remembrance of Agamemnon or the great Sargon of Agade of Mesopotamia. The later Greeks while ruling in Egypt concocted the conglomerate god Serapis from Seras (or Osiris) and the bull-god Apis in a bid for Egyptian religious unity. They even mummified the chosen bulls when they died! Instead of deification and mummification of our heroes today, we honor them by remembering their virtues and naming them saints, or proclaiming special holidays to recall how they have helped our society. Perhaps this was the original intention of the ancestors who chose to remember their notable members.

8.6 Phoenicians and Hittites

The Greeks had many assorted gods and the Phoenician city states had a similar collection. These included dying and rising gods, such as Asclepius or Eshmun in Sidon, Adonis in Byblos, and Herakles or Melqart in Tyre. The friend of Solomon, King Hyram of Tyre, in the 10th century BC built a temple for Melqart. Some of these gods came to the Phoenician cities by way of the Hittites. There was child sacrifice, and why not, if the gods were doing it! There were found 20,000 urns of cremated sacrifices of animals and children at the Tyrian colony of Carthage.

The Phoenician tribe also carried the sad tale of a God sacrificing his son. Cronos, becoming the sun god El of the Phoenicians, sacrificed his son Anobret, when danger beset the land. So why shouldn't Abraham sacrifice his son? Or the divine Father of Jesus? Early people struggled hard to find ways to please capricious gods.

The Hittites dwelling in Asia Minor before 1200 BC had a hideous tale of how Kumaris castrated and swallowed the genitals of Heaven. Through this process Kumaris conceived a son, the weather god. The Persian legend of Kumaris may be the original thread of the story about the Greek god Cronos. Cronos castrated his father Uranus and was defeated and imprisoned by his own son, Zeus.

8.7 The Norse Gods

God-Names. It is easy to follow trails of some of these god-stories. There is a list of rivers and place names that can be traced from the gods of India to the Teutonic gods. Myths similar to those told in India suddenly jump to notice in northern Europe. Legends tell us that Troy or Turkland in Asia had a chief named *Munon*. As *Aga* means *chief*, this man was called *Aga Munon*. (Again we have *Agamemnon*.) This chief had a son *Tror* whose mother was *Troan*, daughter of Priam. The name of the city of *Troy* is derived from these names. Wandering tribes took this *Tror* name northward, and it became *Thor*. Thor married Sibil or Sif, and one of t'... r descendants was *Voden*, whose name was also *Odin*. The pair of *Voden* and *Frigida* left Turkland for Saxland. This tribe of Northerners (or Danites which means *Northerners*) became called *Norsemen*. Three of their sons or descendants were Vegdeg, Beldeg, and Sigi.

Carriers of Legends. The people in the territory of what is now Sweden supposedly welcomed these *AEsir* or people of Asia, because they were polite and considerate. The term *Asians* in later day Teutonic times comes from the word for *lord* which is *Asura* (which is also Arthura). As far away as England, there are *Arthurian* legends about a great king who governed with a Round Table of his knights. The beginnings of such legends may have come from the tales of Sargon I, the great king or Agamemnon, who governed with a circle of lesser city dignitaries in Sumer.

The Scythians from southern Russia buried weapons and horses with their dead leaders under *kurgans* or large mounds of earth. A great iron sword in a golden scabbard was recovered from a tomb in the Crimea or north Black Sea area. Could this be King Arthur's sword which was given the name *Excalibur*? Could the Isle of Avalon, the burial place of Arthur, be an island in the Black Sea? Arthurian legends traveled west along the Danube. The Celtic Druids or priestesses committed sacred lore to memory from generation to generation, and thus were carriers of legends to Britain and to the other countries through which the Celts passed.

Another carrier of legend was the tribe of Dan. As it headed north it displaced tribes who refused to acquiesce, accepted hospitality from others, and absorbed legends from foes and friends. The people in Finland and in Hungary (Magyars) possess a language that has common peculiarities. They may have been people still speaking pre-civilization language, when pushed to new locations by the Danite invaders.

The name, *Nahor*, of the relative of Abraham, traveled north, became *Njord*, and assumed godly significance. The name *Odin* migrated north and became Woden. Woden had the same characteristics as the god Mercury. There is interchanging of names and qualities of gods among the nations of the earth.

Healing and Inner Vision. Both Woden and Mercury had the ability to heal. Mercury had the snake-healing symbol on his staff similar to the serpent pole of Moses. Odin was sometimes pictured as a snake. Think of Moses in the desert holding up a snake on a staff in order to heal. Some of the Moses legend may have been transferred to Woden. Woden was reportedly blind in one eye. This may mean that one of his eyes turned inward, and that he had second sight and could foretell the future. The Egyptian queen Nefertiti had a statue that had but one eye. She may have been noted for inner vision.

Water and Wisdom. Worship of gods is often accompanied with pre-scribed holy food or holy drink. There is the sacramental action of bathing in holy water. The mead of Odin is clearly patterned after the holy drink *soma* of India or the *haoma* of Persia. The Teutonic goddess Saga drinks daily from gold cups out of the turbulent river, Sokkvabekk. She is a water sprite with the gift of knowledge. From her we get our word *sagacious*. She could be from the same mythical strands as the wise Saraswati of India, goddess of learning, and the sagacious woman, Abraham's wife, Sarah.

Other Comparisons. There are lesser myth comparisons. Noah has the raven and the dove on his ark, while Odin has two ravens, Hugin and Munin, who gather news for him. Saul summons up the Witch of Endor (I Samuel 28:3-24), and Odin also summons up a long dead seeress. In the Denmark tale of Hotherus and Nanna, Balderus sees Nanna bathing and falls in love with her. David also falls in love when he sees Bathsheba bathing (II Samuel 11:2). These myths teach ethical concepts and increase tribal unity.

8.8 Christianity

God encouraged humankind's evolution in a loving direction through the person of Jesus. The followers of Jesus see him as the perfect and complete incarnation of the word of God, one who clearly portrays the nature of God, and hence is a true divine exemplar for humankind. For his followers, all prior enfleshments of the word had been both imperfect and incomplete. Jesus speaks of himself as *living water*. In this Age of Aquarius the image of the Water Carrier makes us think of the water of life inundating humankind. Jesus tells the woman at the well that his new philosophy of life is better than that which comes from the well of Jacob (John 4:14) which may refer to the philosophy of the earlier Hebrews. He pours out his life that we may have life. He suffers for those he loves. He advises us to love one another as he loves us.

If Jesus had not come bringing the message of love, the name of the Hebrew God might have gone the way of Zeus and Ptah. Our world needs an all-embracing God of love, and Jesus transformed a sectarian God into an inclusive God who wanted to care for the world.

The Meaning of Love. In order to find out what is meant by, "love your neighbor as yourself," we must investigate the meaning of the Aramaic word for love which was used by Jesus in Mark 12:31. The verb *ahavta* is commonly translated as *you shall love*. When the verb is followed by an indirect object introduced by *to*, the meaning may be more like *to help* or *to be useful to*. We might translate, "Love your neighbor as yourself," as, "You shall treat your neighbor kindly for he is a human being like yourself." We are not merely to have a warm, cuddly feeling about our neighbor. We are to act considerately towards him. To love is not only to feel, but to act concretely and responsibly. Love is not a hazy feeling; it is doing something beneficial. God, as love, did not just have feelings; God created the earth.[11] Another definition of the Indian word *ahimsa* (or love) is that it is the emotional state and power of truth. It involves the use of the mind and will to communicate love and good will.[12]

Epiphany means *to make manifest*. With Jesus' appearance, the quality of love was made manifest on earth. It takes a Jesus, Savior, to transform an instrument of death such as the cross into a myth of new life. It will take the cooperation of everyone of us to transform death-dealing cultures, into a world safe for children.

Church Formation. When Jesus left his religious teachings in the hands of his followers and the followers formed church groups, the church groups thought that their faith community would remain constant and pure forever.

They sometimes did not make a distinction between the loving Spirit of Jesus and their structure of power. Jesus exuded love, and it even was absorbed by his clothing. What miracles were worked by touching the robe of Jesus! For some, the Church seemed to take this love and bottle it up in liturgies and sacraments, to be doled out as those in authority felt it was needed.

We could look at ancient church organizations as similar to the old railroad bridge that crosses the Hudson River at Poughkeepsie. The bridge builders thought that trains would be able to use this edifice forever. They had no thought for the ravages of rust and time. There stands the bridge, with screws and railroad ties occasionally falling off. No trains cross it, as even long ago it vibrated wildly. It is much too expensive a project to take it down. It is left there as an interesting historical aberration. Today, we still need to travel. However, we can travel freely, using a variety of private cars, trucks, buses, trains, and planes.

Jesus did not visualize an elaborate legalistic church structure as a vehicle for his teaching. His teaching was to fill each human heart. He had no need of a bridge. His message was that we could move spiritually in our material realm. We would all have the capabilities of being loving and considerate, each moved by the Holy Spirit. We would not need complex structures, based on a presumed omniscience and certainty, to transport us. **Men and Women.** People would find it easy to relate to each other if they internalized Jesus' message. Men and women would respect each other and give each other freedom of action and belief. Jesus, in particular, treated women with greater respect than was customary at the time. In many ways, the Bible takes small steps to the emancipation of women. Though Jesus is clearly portrayed as the exemplar for both men and women, the Bible emphasizes the spiritual equality of men and women in describing Mary and Jesus as both full of grace; Mary, in Luke 1:35, and Jesus, in John 1:14. They are both in favor with God; Mary, in Luke 1:28,30, and Jesus, in Luke 2:52 and 3:22. Men and women both come into the world with equal capacity to be filled with God's spirit.

8.9 Constantine

Jesus may not have intended to found a church as we sometimes think of church today, but a loving community grew around his beliefs. As centuries passed, certain people became more convinced that they had the full truth of Jesus' message. They wanted everyone to see the truth as they saw it. On the other hand, the Roman gods still were worshiped throughout the Empire. The Emperor Constantine saw how strong beliefs in these two different faiths divided his nation. He became an advocate of both faiths, and his molding together of these diverse religious beliefs affected future generations in a positive manner.

Priestly Functioning. In this amalgamation, the priests who serviced the temples of Jupiter and Apollo were not necessarily dismissed from government service. Constantine had proclaimed freedom of worship for all. Structures such as pantheons had caretakers who were willing to provide areas for the worship of the Christian God and his Son. The Pantheon in Rome was built by the Emperor Hadrian in 117-138 AD as a building for all the gods. Five hundred years later, in 607 Pope Boniface IV rededicated it as an exclusively Christian church.

This transformation of temples was not too difficult, for the Christian God of Constantine was a Father God like Jupiter and had a Son like the young God, Apollo. Although the early Christian house communities did not have altars, but used a community table, they were able to effectively employ the temple altar as a table for their service. The Christian chief priest found it easy to imitate the High Priest of Jupiter who wore a white robe and biretta when he officiated at the sacrificial altar. Our present day system of priests arose at this time even though the ancestral Hebrew community had abandoned its priesthood in favor of the more communal practice in the synagogue. Those individuals who led home worship communities gradually died off. They were replaced by priests officiating in the temple-church structure. The larger official buildings could hold more worshipers and gave the community a sense of the power of their God and their faith.

Cultural Evolution. Evolution does not surface only in ethical beliefs. Evolution occurs in our understanding of the word of God and the written tradition, as there are changes in language and meanings of words, new interpretations during translations, and enhancements seen in ancient pronouncements. Evolution occurs in our understanding of myths as their content varies, and as we are freed from fundamentalism and beliefs about inerrancy. There are paradigm shifts in the history of theology and of the church. These can be ushered in by a strong temporal ruler. Often we see historical proceedings similar to what went on in the reign of David. David may have helped a few outcasts to come into ruling positions, but Solomon was evidently not as gentle a ruler, and his son Rehoboam put grievous burdens on the people, so that the northern section of the kingdom broke away. David had parts of the Bible written to influence his constituents in positive directions. President Reagin's script writers also had a cooperative TV cheering section.

A community structure that is put in place to serve the people, such as the Moses' law, will be taken over by an initially well-meaning power group, such as a king wishing to justify his rule. This may develop into a harsher rule or an authoritative priesthood, which will eventually be opposed by some prophetic individual. Another reform movement to assist the people will take place. We see developments like that today– the powerful government, the power groups in the church, and the non-governmental groups willing to serve the downtrodden.

There are two possibilities for evolution of culture. There can be progress in kindness and consideration in each person's personal growth, or there can be strong leaders who influence change. The various leaders in the early Christian centuries were different in their theological approaches, even though they shared certain common convictions. From expecting the imminent second coming, groups evolved to a sense of responsibility for the good of people in their time and area. Augustine, Thomas Aquinas, and Bonaventure were each broader in their outlooks, but still hampered by their societal notions. For instance, they could not think of women as equal to men. Other evolvements concerned Protestants who enlarged their Christian philosophies, but still found time to develop prejudices against other Christian groups. Today we find religions proclaiming the brotherhood and sisterhood of all peoples, and the love of one God for all peoples, yet still not loving and respecting all peoples.

Amalgams and Roman Christianity. There have been many people down through the years who have tried to coordinate religious traditions in a non-threatening manner. At one time the Egyptian priests incorporated many of the qualities of the lesser local gods into their great god Osiris. This saved many arguments and possible loss of life due to punishment for heresy. The Hindus were very broad-minded. They co-opted Buddhism. We see the same attitude in the Hindu acceptance of many foreign beliefs and the easy setting up of a shrine to Mary in a Hindu temple. The Sikhs coordinated Hindus and Muslims, and then finally withdrew from both. Catholics do not object to additional saints pictures on their church walls, or to the adding of saints' names in litanies. Jacob Frank (born Judah Leib in 1726) led a group that was Jewish, Muslim, and Catholic. It performed Muslim duties on Friday, Jewish rituals on Saturday, and Christian, on Sunday. Religious purists, however, shouted it down.

Constantine had a broad and enlightened view of religion, and wanted others to share this insight. He wished to keep the empire united and under his control. He was an imperfect human being with a vision of one universal God who was responsible for all people, and a mission for his time and place, to enforce this vision on his contemporaries. This mixture of

Christian beliefs and Roman structures has been given the appropriate name *Roman Catholic.* The word *catholic* means *universal.*

Constantine saw the virtue of encouraging the Christian Trinity as a refinement of the Trinity of Roman gods, while continuing the well-established religious structures. We celebrate Christmas at the time of the winter solstice so as not to deprive the Romans of their holiday, and we still use the name of the Teutonic god Eo (Assyrian god of the sea, Ea) in our Easter resurrection rites. Constantine legalized the harmonization of Roman and Christian beliefs.

8.10 Islam

Several centuries later, we find that Muhammad was a prophetic and protestant reaction to the forces initiated under Constantine. Constantine had begun his rule in Rome and then moved his capital eastward to Constantinople. This capital was further from the Roman gods and closer to the many religions of the Near East. His picture of God was influenced by both the positive and negative aspects of the religions around him. Islam has much from Zoroastrianism and from the Hebrew, while also respecting the basic Christian ideals. The Koran has the Zoroastrian Satan acting in its pages and tells the story of the biblical Joseph without the Judah connection emphasized by the Davidic author. The Koran respects Jesus as a prophet of God and gives women the model of Mary.

Prohibiting Images. Muhammad objected to what he saw as worship of idols, particularly the Assyrian gods and goddesses whose statues were set up in shrines as role models for people or as ways to express godly qualities to people. He chose to express the qualities of God through words rather than images. Fortunately, human kind had reached a stage of development where people could read and write these descriptive words. The human is someone who can understand symbols. The pre-writing human needed statues for symbols. The writing and reading human often uses words for symbols. Muhammad felt the Muslim culture had outgrown the need for, and confusion about, statue symbols.

Positive Morality. When the Muslims later came to power in Persia, the Zoroastrian group lost popularity even though it was highly monotheistic. It had forgotten to listen to the needs of the people. It had become a tool of the rulers used to placate their constituency. The people were swayed by the positive morality of Islam, by the commitment of its adherents, and by its inclusiveness. One did not have to be born a Muslim. Islam has no sacraments. God knows the faithful believer by her good deeds, not by a baptismal mark or anointing. The Muslim believes that God has created humanity for the purpose of doing good, which action will give them fulfillment. They believe in God as being One– the Creator and the Final End.

Muslim women celebrate the birth of Fatima (605 AD), the daughter of Muhammad and wife of the Shi'ite leader Ali. Her sons, Hassam and Husein, were the second and third Imams. The Shi'ite Muslims believe that a messiah (Meelaad-e-mahdee) from the female line of Fatima will come in a time of evil and re-establish justice.

Perhaps peoples and cultures need new symbols and new religious leaders every so often in order to combat the staleness that inevitably sets in as power and authority seek to control the dispensing of love. The ideas of service and consideration for others need new expression and new leaders in every age. Oppressed factions seeking power need a voice to explain their feelings and their needs. If we were truly loving and listening, we would hear their discontent before it became serious. We are often so caught up in our own concerns that we have no time to notice the needs of others.

Leadership. Religion has steadily evolved from individual worship by Friends of God such as Abraham, through tribal worship and religious laws enforced by priests, to the more prophetic leader who would guide all people towards service to a God of Love. However, leaders can be uplifting or burdensome; they can be nurturing facilitators or domineering masters. Jesus did not set up a priestly structure. He told us that the Holy Spirit was willing to be in all of us. He classed the authoritative priests and Pharisees of his day as hypocrites and as those that tie up heavy burdens and lay them on men's shoulders (Matthew 23:4). Muhammad did not organize a priesthood or sacraments, but some of his followers took leadership positions and presumed to advise others in many matters. Muhammad proposed the Five Pillars of Islam as a simple program to build the holy community. These pillars are belief in God under the name of Allah, daily prayer, giving to the poor, fasting in the ninth month during the day, and pilgrimage. A person can follow these precepts and never see the inside of a church or need a priest, imam, or muezzin.

All Muslims can give alms to the poor and seek justice for the oppressed. They must not wait for a leader. Sometimes a leader will not have the concerns of the oppressed in mind, but be looking for his own aggrandizement. Some leaders give their followers permission to bomb innocent people. The good Muslim submits to God, and performs loving actions. The Koran teaches that *on the pilgrimage*, whether it be to Mecca, or through life, he is to *remember that there is to be no lewdness nor abuse nor angry conversation.*

One God, One Community. For the whole earth to become the Holy Community, we all must believe in the One God who created us. We must practice toleration and try to understand those who worship this One God with different cultural practices. Through prayer and meditation we can learn what God would like us to do. This prayer does not have to be in a church or mosque. Too often we find that churches, synagogues, and mosques preach intolerance through their exclusion and oppression of certain groups. Some churches will not let women officiate on their altars. Mosques will often not admit those of other faith groups, and have secondary sections for women. Would the One Creator God who contains both male and female, keep women in secondary positions or refuse to let them give homilies? Both men and women are knowledgeable about God's ways of peace and justice.

Footnotes
1 Gerhard Kittel, Ed., *Theological Dictionary of The New Testament*, describing the word, "messenger," Eerdmans, Grand Rapids, MI 1964.
2 John R. Hinnells, *Persian Mythology*, Peter Bedrick Books, NY, 1985, p. 22.
3 *The Avesta*, as translated by A.V.W. Jackson in *Encyclopedia Americana, Volume 29*, "Zoroastrianism," p. 733.
4 *ibid.*, p. 32.
5 *ibid.*, p. 44.
6 Mircea Eliade and Joseph Kitagawa, Ed., *History of Religions*, University of Chicago Press, Chicago, IL, 1973, p. 149.
7 Joseph Gaer, *How The Great Religions Began*, Dodd, Mead, NY, 1956, pp. 124,125.
8 *ibid.*, p. 125.
9 Henry Clarke Warren, *Buddhism in Translations*, Atheneum, NY (1896)1953, p. 82-83.
10 Joe Campbell, *Myths To Live By*, Bantam Books, New York, 1973, p. 138.
11 Abraham Malamat, BAR July/August 1990, "Love Your Neighbor as Yourself– What It Really Means."
12 Lawrence Apsey, *Following The Light for Peace*, KimPathways, Katonah, NY, 1991, p.15.

IX

Weaving
The Threads Together

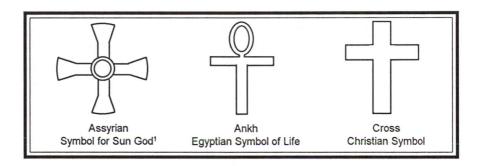

| Assyrian | Ankh | Cross |
| Symbol for Sun God[1] | Egyptian Symbol of Life | Christian Symbol |

9.1 Evolution of Festivals and Legends

<u>Tantalizing Possibilities.</u> No one could possibly uncover all the threads of history or understand the leadings and wisdom of God. As we scratch the surface of our knowledge of previous beliefs and question what lies below, we are flooded with empathy and bits of insight. We learn from fact, and we learn from myth. We try to see the world as the ancients saw it. We try to understand their language. We seek for present day interpretations of their myths that will help us to heal our social problems. Myths are also told to enable us to laugh at our futilities and to bear the pain that comes with real life. Laughter helps us to rise above oppressive situations.

These myths come from far back in our misty beginnings. Certain positive elements in religious beliefs seem to be easily transmitted. There is an inner longing in the human being for giving of ourselves to benefit another and for eternal life– for some kind of unison of ourselves with infinite divinity. Perhaps God placed these longings within to encourage us in our ethical journey. These basic yearnings common to all humans are incorporated in the religious myths from other times and other countries.

Teachers, story-tellers, and historians often draw pieces from multiple old stories, to create a new story that best conveys a particular message. We also find that very old ideas are carried forward but clothed with up-dated settings and descriptions that suit a new situation.

We ask many questions of the past, hoping that answers will help us to live a better future. We have had many religious forebears, many prophets, many aspects of God. Who are we to believe? There are so many questions we could ask. From our little bit of knowledge, we can grow so many suppositions. What rites and celebrations helped the ancients through their days? Funeral rites, for example, dramatized the meaning of death in a given culture. Stories of elaborate funerals abound.

Today we do our funerals and our interments in a certain way. We perform in this manner because down through the ages, people have become comfortable and comforted by this established process. The funeral procession for Jacob is described in Genesis 50. The author may have intended this to be a writing about a prototypal funeral train, because she couldn't possibly have known the details about an event that took place hundreds of years before her time. She wrote about the funerary journey northward as she supposed such an event would have taken place. It may not have been as elaborate as described. The final resting place is *Mamre*, which is a standard name for a high plain where religious worship was held, and where heroes were commemorated. The biblical author saw the proper place for burial as Israel. She felt the Egyptian notables should accompany such a funeral cortege. Perhaps she was describing the legendary funeral of another great man that people carried in their mythical repertoire. If we had the ability to track these legends and locate the places where they seem to arise, we could learn more about early tribal movements. We also might be better able to trace our religious and ethical evolvement.

Sargon I was an important leader who may have had an impressive funeral cortege. Historians have assumed that Sargon was a Semite from the east who came to rule a mixed group of Semites and Sumerians in Mesopotamia. Sargon may have come from another location, such as Turkey or the Caucasus, and if so, his burial might have involved a large funeral cortege of Semites and Sumerians winding north to Nimrud-Dagh, a place of worship and commemoration.

Legends of such a tremendous burial may have circulated in the Black Sea area, and may have evolved into the mythical lore associated with King Arthur. Other Arthurian legends seem to be drawn from the story of Sargon I, so there may be a connection among Arthur legends, Sargon legends, and the burial tale of Jacob. In the Arthurian legend, Arthur is buried on the Isle of Avalon. Could the original location of Avalon be an island in the Black Sea? Ancient leaders were often boated to their last resting place. Corpses of pharaohs floated in state on the Nile, and their funeral boat was placed near their tomb site. Many Nordic grave markers were stones combined to form the shape of a boat. Today boats do not have such an important part in funeral proceedings, although other funeral and festival customs are similar to those of days gone by.

There are many ancient festivals that people of today still find immensely satisfying. Christians celebrate the feast of Christmas as a remembrance of the new light of wisdom coming to a dark earth. We continue to celebrate Christmas with gifts, acknowledging God's gift to us. Jewish people recall their exodus from Egypt under God's loving care, in the festival of Passover. We add new festivals that remind us of good persons and God's guidance of the oppressed. We march on Martin Luther King, Jr.'s birthday. The young religion of the black community, Kwanzaa, uses old symbols of candles, color, and water, in meaningful new ways.

If we were to provide celebrations for a new religion of understanding and tolerance, we would want to incorporate festivals that were meaningful for our age. Legends which would enhance the building of a just community might tell of forgiveness by victims of holocaust. They might celebrate consigning nuclear bombs to the bottomless pit. Statues might emphasize the beating of swords into plowshares, as is demonstrated by the statue at the United Nations Plaza.

Sun Festivals. The ancients held joyous feasts on the winter solstice to cheer each other up at this time of general depression. When the human system receives less sun, it is undernourished and displays less enthusiasm. In this age of plentiful electric lights and seemingly plentiful energy, we may not pay too much attention to the sun, but it still affects our lives at every moment. Rarely, do we look at the sun and contemplate our dependence upon it. We can hearken back to less mechanized times to imagine a little child growing up and questioning her care-giver, ''Where does the sun go at night? Why are the days getting shorter? Why do flowers come up in the spring?'' People believed there was some connection between the sun and a providential God. The wise parent or grandparent is not going to admit total ignorance on these subjects. If ancestor tales or myths are not handy, they will make up something plausible. The vacancies in our knowledge are filled with on-the-spot explanations. The science of theology is reason's response to curiosity about what seems supernatural. These spontaneous responses are sometimes even incorporated into belief systems and considered sacred.

For the Chinese emperor the sun rose above islands to the east, so he named those islands *Zapangn* (or Japan) which means *source of the sun.* On their part the Japanese came to believe that the sun goddess was an ancestor of the imperial family. The emperor's soldiers had the emblem of a bright round sun painted on their shields. Many festivals were built around the apparent movements of the sun.

Like our religions themselves, festivals have evolved to contain always more spiritual meaning, more ethical teaching. Festivals began with celebrations of joy and supplications for nature's bounty. From honoring sun, moon, wind, water, and creatures, they progressed to the incorporation of rituals that led to spiritual insights. These festivals have been transferred from tribe to tribe. Names have been changed. Reasons for celebration are different, but seasonal events like harvests, full moons, and summer and winter solstice remain fairly constant.

Sacrificial Myths. There were also festivals of sadness. The women in Palestine wept for the sentence pronounced on Jephthah's daughter (Judges 11). People in Palestine also agonized with two different Tamars– one, because she was raped (II Samuel 13:1); the other, because she had to resort to being raped to get legally pregnant (Genesis 38:6). David's weeping for Absalom reminds us of the Babylonian god-king weeping for his son Tammuz (Ezekiel 8:14). When the sister of Tammuz goes to the underworld and brings her brother back, there is rejoicing, and the world is renewed.

This very important myth of the dying god who may be resurrected is associated with the Egyptian Osiris, the Greek Adonis, and the Finnish hero Lemminkainen. In the Norse myth, the shining god Balder, the son of the god Odin, is killed when evil Loki tricks blind Hod into shooting him with mistletoe. The gods chain up the devilish Loki, but Loki will be able to escape and make havoc on the final day. The Norse believed that Loki, the devil, would be unchained and storm Asgard, the home of the gods. The earth would burn and likewise, the planets. Nothing good would be left. Other religious groups have incorporated this notion of destruction on a final day.

In the Christian belief system, the incarnation, death, and resurrection of Jesus, the son of God, is the complete fulfillment of the ancient yearnings. Jesus gives of himself for all humankind. His resurrection is the promise of life after death for all. For Christians, these events are the final realization of the hopes that had been reflected in earlier myths.

Antecedents of Christmas. The problems of the Babylonian god Tammuz surfaced in the Roman religion in the festival of Saturnalia. This festival at the time of the winter solstice commemorated an early period under the auspices of Saturn when freedom prevailed and oppression was unknown. At the ending of the festival many candles were lit in the temple dedicated to Saturn as a sign that at this time no more human victims were to be sacrificed. Households celebrated by "turning the tables." Slaves wore tunics adorned with purple, and were waited on at table by their masters.

The Christian celebration of Christmas continued this Roman holiday of Saturnalia, yet brought across the message of Jesus as the light of the world. The Buddhists, Zoroastrians, Moslems, and Hindus also end their rainy season with pageantry that is reminiscent of ancient Assyrian Tammuz New Year rites. The Christians and Jews transfer the New Year renewal rites to the time of the spring planting. The Christians preface this feast which they call Easter, with a period of forty days called Lent. (The Anglo-Saxon word for *spring* is *Lenct*.) Present day Christians are encouraged to do good works and to eat less at meals in Lent. Early Christians and some other faiths observed Lent by not eating during the day, but eating after sundown. The Moslems have a feast day, 'Id al-Fitr, to celebrate the end of Ramadan fasting. They fast from food and water during the day for the month of Ramadan.

The Christian festival on January 1 was formerly offered to the god Janus who had two faces, so that he could look both forward and back. Janus is a mythic forebear of our New Year hero, Father Time. A Catholic feast in February formerly honored the mother of Mars, Februa, with a blessing of throats and candle processions. This feast was called Candlemass and was changed to honor the Virgin Mary by Pope Sergius in 684 AD. Today this February feast is the Feast of The Purification of The Blessed Virgin Mary, and throats are blessed on the following day which commemorates Saint Blaise.

Miraculous Events. The very special nature of a particularly holy person was early expressed in terms of the nature of its conception or in tales about its birth. For example, the myth of Mary's virginity may have philosophical roots in India and Egypt. In the Hindu epic *Mahabharata*, the hero Karna is conceived and born of the virgin Kunti due to the sun god Surya. The god restores Kunti's virginity after conception. Kunti hides her child and puts him in a basket in the river like baby Moses. The Virgin Birth legends also have something in common with the Egyptian goddess, Reddedet, wife of a priest. She immaculately conceived three children of the sun god Ra. She was also given the title *Khant-kawes* which means *mother of two kings*.

Myths also honor the love of a heroine mother for her hero child. The mother-baby grouping seems to be of Egyptian origin. Isis holding Baby Horus predated the Virgin Mary with Baby Jesus. When a little more clothing decorated the pair, Egyptian worshipers could easily transfer worship from an Isis-Horus statue to this new Queen-Lord or Mother-Son combination.

The magi of Jesus' birth are also in stories told of Zoroaster and Krishna. In Buddhist lore, holy men offer gifts of perfume and garlands to the new born Buddha.[2] In many myths there are dragon slayers and workers of miracles. Odin, for example, was truly remarkable. He could calm the wind and make the waves sleep. Again, this seems to be a way of conveying a message that this person was unique and of special importance. We still hear tales of those who calm the wind and waves, and we are comforted by these tales. Like other myths, these stories of miraculous events are laudatory affirmations which serve to indirectly support kernel beliefs, such as the wisdom and love of the hero or heroine. They may be poetic license, but they give us confidence in adopting the kernel ideas.

Communion Notions. Rituals and festivals served to emphasize and celebrate the establishment of cooperative or loving community. We can think back to the Teutonic story of making the first man Kvasir (in Teutonic) or Kumaris (in Persian) by all the gods spitting into a common vessel. This action was also a symbol of an agreement to make community and peace among warring factions. It was a less messy communion than that of early Asians who proved their brotherhood by cutting their veins and mixing their blood. (If AIDS were prevalent, they would all have died.)

Ancient festivals often incorporated the sharing of a food or drink offering. In this act, they declared their amity with one another and with their idea of divinity. When we share our communion cups in our churches today, we likewise achieve a spiritual unity with our current concept of divinity, and re-dedicate ourselves to that unity.

Another left-over from festivals is how one presides over the gathering of the people. A religious precedent that has been carried down through the centuries, was the Egyptian pharaoh Akhenaten's window of appearance. He had a balcony where he, as the Beloved of the God, would present himself to the people who crowded the temple. A present day similarity is seen in the Vatican in Rome, where the Pope makes his appearance in a window. This custom was probably carried from Egypt through the Roman priests of the god Jupiter.

The Flows of Legends. Earlier peoples had their stories of a long rain, fights between brothers, gods who let their sons suffer, and their memories of the garden of better times. This heritage has been transmitted all over the world, and contributed to greater understanding among peoples. The Indian gods, the Norse gods, the Persian gods, and the Hebrew heroes all have elements in common. As there are combined groups of gods in the Indian repertoire from different racial groups mixing, there are two groups of Norse gods, those of the race of Aesir and those of the Vanir who were earlier in the land. The Aesir have Odin or Woden for the universal father. The Hebrews have inheritance from Egyptian and Mesopotamian cultures, and have a forefather image in Abraham or Ab-Ram or Ab-Brahman (as father of nations), where Brahman represents the spiritual possibilities inherent in all humankind.

It is hard to trace the direction of flow of the religious legends. Some could have started in India and flowed north. Some could have begun in Persia and gone both northwest and southeast. Some may be pre-Persian. Some beliefs such as sun worship and human sacrifice may have spread from India to Tibet to Japan to Siberia to Alaska and eventually to South America around 10,000 BC. The sun god became less omnipotent, when other forces were also seen to be powerful. When human self esteem and the value of human life increased, human sacrifice was less prevalent.

9.2 Sacraments and Symbols

A sacrament is a sign or symbol of something holy, something that we use to help us relate to the mysterious. A sacrament can be a person, place, object, or procedure. For those who can accept it, the sacrament is an invitation to a religious experience. It is then the occasion for a clearer perception of value or meaning. Speaking broadly, as God made all things, all things are holy, and the earth and everything therein can, for some, be sacraments. Speaking specifically, there are certain items or actions that, more than others, can be used to connect certain groups with the holy, and help them to worship God more perfectly.

Initiation Rites. Many ancient cultures included rites of admission which dramatized the value of belonging and the necessity for responsibility. Circumcision was considered to be a sacramental action by the early Hebrews. This signified belonging to the people of the covenant. Some early belief systems paid attention to phallic energy, and the importance of dedicating your inner energies to the production of children. Circumcision was a holy action with many peoples, including the aborigines of Australia, America, and Africa (Jeremiah 9:24-25) but not with the Philistines (I Samuel 18:25) or by Hittites (Genesis 34:13-14). Women could also practice a type of circumcision, seen by some, as a gesture of dedication to God, and by others, as mutilation.

Another action sacrament of early people was the anointing of a king with sacred oil. The prophet Samuel anointed Saul as king of Israel by pouring a phial of oil on Saul's head, kissing him, and saying the proper words (I Samuel 10:1).

Cleansing Rites. Water has long been the symbol of spiritual cleansing to a new life. The rite of baptism is very ancient. It did not start with John the Baptist; a painting from an Egyptian tomb of 1380 BC show two streams of water being poured over the dead man's head to purify the corpse. Another ancient baptism medium was the blood of a bull. Today Christians recall the sacrifice on Calvary and proclaim their spiritual purification and sanctification by the blood of Jesus.

Snake Symbols. An ancient symbol of energy from a tradition 5000 years old coming out of India and Tibet, is the Kundalini symbol.[3] This evolutionary energy is pictured by the *caduceus* symbol of two snakes intertwined in a double helix. This has similarities to the Asclepian medical healing symbol of ancient Greece still used by our doctor profession today. There is also the caduceus or staff of a herald, such as was carried by the god Hermes or the god Mercury, which is pictured with intertwining snakes topped with wings.

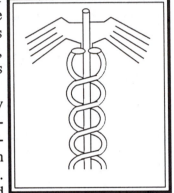

In Africa such standards were used by royalty and religious to represent their authority. They might have snakes to represent wisdom, and either an ankh symbol or a cross, with the energy symbol of the sun and its rays. Sometimes the sun's rays have feet to remind us that God walks over the earth. All these symbols speak of a God of process energy and are still appropriate today. We sometimes see this sun symbol of a disc with rays spreading out from it, as a representation of the Blessed Communion Bread in Catholic churches.

The Ankh. The Egyptian symbol of the ankh could be compared to a hand mirror. The word *ankh* is similar to the word for *life*. One meaning of this symbol may be the special spiritual life and wisdom given by the god to the pharaoh. The pharaohs are often pictured receiving the ankh from a god. Perhaps in this mirror form it is intended to remind the pharaoh that when he looks in the mirror, he will see the human body in which the god has chosen to dwell. When we look in a mirror, if we could believe that God made us to carry God's love, and that God would like to dwell in us, we would have greater self-esteem.

The ankh symbol has been said to resemble a sandal strap. There is a quote in the Bible on the sandal strap. John the Baptist says in Acts 13:25,

"There is one coming after me, and I am not worthy to loose his sandal strap." This may mean that John considers Jesus' gift of spiritual life from God much greater than his own. A further development of the word *ankh* may be the word *anchor* as a sturdy supporting hold. In comparative symbology we come up against the Christian symbol of the cross as similar to the ankh. The cross has become a Christian representation of God giving true life to the world.

Horns and Disks. In the New Kingdom of Egypt (2100-1800 BC), the god Amun was identified with the ram; the ram's curled horns when attached to a human head, were a symbol of that human, being a god. Like Naram-Sin, the conquering later-day Alexander is identified as being godly. On his Egyptian coins he has horns (almost hidden by his curly hair), thus implying to those who used the coins that Alexander was the godly son of the god Amun. Horns and disks surface in other religious symbolism. The two horns around the disk of the sun of Egyptian myth, have a distant resemblance to the double crescent on the mosques of Islam and to the disk of the host of the Christians.

Modes of Expression. How do various cultures convey their ideas about the nature of God? Different religions carry the aspects and attributes of God in different baskets. Christianity displays God's kindness and gentleness in the person of Jesus. For Christians, Jesus best informs us about the true nature of God by his own way of life. Hebrews and Muslims also describe a personal God with godly characteristics. On the other hand, Taoists and Confucians speak of impersonal Heaven-Earth principles and forces. Buddhists and Hindus locate the being of God in the individual mind. The Muslims honor the goodness of major prophets such as Muhammad and leaders such as Hassam and Husein, and talk of evil as the devil. The Christians mold Saint Francis and the devil from plaster and approve of the attributes of one and disapprove of the attributes of the other. The Hindus show Kali in black iron and point out both her positive and negative characteristics. But all have words, statues, or paintings to represent the elements or qualities of God.

The clothes worn by those who officiate at religious ceremonies have ancient resemblances. Many garments evolved from the animal sacrifice customs of earlier times. The high priest of Jupiter wore white, and his henchmen who did the actual animal slaughtering wore red, so that their clothes wouldn't show the blood marks. Today the Pope wears white, and his seconds-in-command, the cardinals, wear red.

Statues and other art objects remind people of our spiritual heritage and of people no longer present to the human eye. Besides statuary, paintings, and words, there are many metaphors such as equating Jesus with the Bread of Life. Early Egyptians compared the god Horus to a falcon. Christians symbolize the Holy Spirit as a dove. In our day a Christian expression of unity with the divine is in the sharing of the Holy Eucharist. This sacramental communion invites one to re-dedicate oneself to the godly way of life taught by Jesus.

Viewpoints and Idolatry. If we were to have appropriate symbols for a new worldwide religion of love and understanding which included all previous religious communities, what symbols would we use? Our everyday symbols have to do with sex and weapons. These, too, affect our sense of values and meaning. From a motherly Isis loving her infant, we have progressed to free sex and abortion on demand. We are back to child sacrifice. We abort our babies and throw away our teenagers. We sacrifice our children's good to some ungodly idea of profit, either through the selling of drugs or through selling anything on TV that will make a little money for corporations (such as sugary cereals or beer or violence). TV's use of seductive symbols encourages children to believe that if they buy the products advertised, they will have a wonderful experience, but all that comes to pass is over-excited and unthinking behavior, depression from poor diet containing sugar and additives, and disillusionment.

Our symbols undergo slight changes during the years. We have gone from altar stones under the shade of trees, to churches made of stone and wood. From worshipping in nature, we have evolved to making temples from the goods of nature. The human being has not changed drastically. God has not changed. The human's understanding of God has evolved. We have evolved enough so that we can be tolerant of others. We can be tolerant of their sacraments and symbols. We do not have to accuse them of idolatry in order to bolster our own tender egos.

Idolatry is when we focus completely on symbols and forget the reality they represent. These symbols may be images, viewpoints, or scriptures. Even the Bible can be used as a graven image if we make a god out of it. The Bible is not God; it only points to God. Idolatry encourages us to believe our symbols are the only proper symbols and to think that God does not love those who use other symbols. Instead, we should see that God loves all, and that each culture joins with all the others in cooperatively relating to the infinite divinity that is common to us all.

It is more important to believe the message of love than to believe that the symbols and structure of your religion are more perfect than the symbols and structure of your opponent's religion.

9.3 Hebrew/Christian Concepts from Egypt

Human beings desire a certain amount of order in their lives. For this reason, they seek stable governments for their communities. When tribes were wandering, there was usually one firm leader, as in times of emergency, it was good to have one clear voice shouting the orders. In relatively peaceful times, there would be the opportunity to listen to everyone's opinion, and the tribe would have the luxury of group government or consensus.

Local Gods to One God. In Africa some of the nomadic tribes found a haven on the banks of the Nile and ordered their lives to the rhythm of its floodings. The tribal gods they brought with them accommodated their powers to this nurturing location. The ancient cities each had their favorite candidate for the most important deity. Heliopolis favored the sun god, Ra or Atum. In Memphis respect was given to the power of the earth, as represented by Ptah. In the Elephantine area of southern Egypt, there existed the god Khnum who supposedly made all creatures on a potter's wheel. The power of the wind was celebrated in Thebes, under the name of Amun, and whoever has been blasted by a sand storm, would understand the worship of this power.

Communication along the Nile was excellent, and stories about the favorings and finickings of the various gods were quickly disseminated. As rulers and their preferences changed, one god or another would be celebrated as the most powerful. If three cities united under one leader, that ruler might announce all three gods as equally powerful, in order to placate the general population.

There is such a trinity of gods celebrated in The Amun Hymns, supposedly written in the reign of Rameses II of the 13th century BC. Three aspects of one God began to appear. All gods are three: Amun, Ra, and Ptah, and there is no second to them. "*Hidden* is his name as Amun, he is Ra in face, and his body is Ptah. Their cities are on earth, abiding forever: Thebes, Heliopolis, and Memphis unto eternity."[4]

God in The Ruler. The association of God with a ruler or great leader has roots in many cultures, including Egypt. Ancient Mesopotamia liked to relate their rulers to the gods by saying that they were a god. In Greek myth the rumor would be circulated that a certain strong ruler was the offspring of a god and a human being. However, Egypt had a somewhat different idea of divine kingship. The gods who cared for the pharaoh in Egypt were believed to be incarnate in the pharaoh. The king was not a god who assumed human form, or a semi-divine offspring, but was a human being in whom the god chose to manifest himself. The god would still be distinctly himself in the natural or spiritual area of his concern, but would somehow extend some of his substance, that which made him godly, into the physical and mental being of the ruler. It was believed that the pharaohs were finite human beings who died when their time was up. When they died, and their son as new ruler was acclaimed, this incarnation or manifestation of the god would envelop their successor. The pharaoh was thus able to be the mediator of the relationship of the god to the rest of the people. This had the advantage of making him the unquestioned ruler with the ability to keep order in his territory.

His incarnation would begin at his coronation. The *Pyramid Texts* describe the relationship of the god Ra to the pharaoh:

> This is my son, my first born ... This is my beloved with whom I have been satisfied.

> This is my beloved, my son; I have given the horizons to him, that he may be powerful over them like Harakhty.

> He lives, king of Upper and Lower Egypt, beloved of Ra, living forever.[5]

With death the pharaoh's being would return to the god.

> Let (name of pharaoh) ascend to thee, enfold him in thy embrace, for he is thy bodily son forever.[6]

Disillusionments and Replacements. This system of keeping order with the god working through the pharaoh, worked very well when the pharaoh had been brought up properly and was of reasonable mental capability. However, not everyone in the kingdom prospered under this incarnation. Also, the custom of intermarriage among royalty could produce an inefficient ruler and wreak havoc with politics and the kingdom. Interbreeding may have caused the fall of dynasties.

In addition, where the first born was the one chance for the god to incarnate his power and wisdom into the human situation and to maintain the current order, the death of the first born meant demoralization for an entire population. For discontented groups, including the descendants of the tribal leader Jacob dwelling in a generally unpleasant servitude, there might be opportunities to claim one of their own, as the one upon whom the god's favor rested. In order to prove the acceptability of your candidate for the office of leader and representative of a god, it would be wise to state that he was brought up in pharaoh's household. If the first born son of pharaoh died an untimely death, the logical place to look for another heir would be in this same household where young men related to pharaoh received proper training, and closeness to God was assumed. There would be resistance to such a change of leadership, by those who favored other aspirants for office or who served other gods. If the other gods and their adherents proved more powerful and more acceptable to the general population, then your group might feel compelled to get away from Egypt and seek the freedom of the desert. In the wilderness the gods of the Egyptian cities and their incarnations would no longer have control.

In our twentieth century minds it is difficult to make the leap between a god incarnating an Egyptian pharaoh, and the Jewish belief in one God. There are hundreds of years between the Hebrew nomads on the shores of the Red Sea to the nobles of the Kingdom of David. The sojourn in the wilderness itself took a long time, covering two or more generations.

Yet in all that time the memory of what went on in Egypt was not erased, and in the Old Testament we find certain expressions associated with Egypt. Even in the New Testament, the religious memories are strong and today we can find in our scriptures influences from early Egyptian worship that are often startling. For instance, we have an implied statement of our faith origins when Matthew 2:15 calls to mind, "Out of Egypt, I have called my son." This Old Testament pronouncement is taken from Hosea 11:1 which goes on to describe God's guidance of the people of the world.

Faith Maturities. God leads us to believe in a God of loving kindness, but unless our faith has matured, we struggle against this type of God and worship material things. Similarly, there was a certain maturity of faith required to go beyond the gods of the sun and the wind to a God who created the sun and wind.

The One Creator God covenants in the wilderness with those who come out of Egypt, away from the over-domesticating authority of political and theological matters. When human beings accept responsibility for their own actions, there is the greater possibility for creative concern for other people and for a liberating covenant with God.

9.4 The Transfiguration Narrative

The historical description of an event can easily be colored by the inheritance of the writer. Consider, for example, the story of the Transfiguration. In the Hebrew mind in the first century AD when the New Testament was written, there still lingered the memory of a god incarnating the pharaoh. Hence when Peter, James, John, and Jesus went up on a mountain to pray

(Luke 9:28-36), their Egyptian beginnings went along with their first century Hebrew beliefs. The men on the mountain top and the biblical writers may not have recognized these early Egyptian leftovers in their consciousnesses, as we similarly fail to recognize all the bits and pieces of our various faiths that have come, not only from the more obvious places such as Persia, Assyria, Greece, and Rome, but even a little from African jungles and far away islands.

Many threads are gathered together in this small section on the Transfiguration (Luke 9:29-35)– *Jesus was transfigured before their eyes. His face became as dazzling as the sun, his clothes as radiant as light. Suddenly Moses and Elijah appeared to them conversing with him. Upon this, Peter said to Jesus, "Lord, how good it is for us to be here! With your permission, I will erect three booths here, one for you, one for Moses, and one for Elijah." He was still speaking when suddenly a bright cloud overshadowed them. Out of the cloud came a voice which said, "This is my beloved Son on whom my favor rests. Hear him."*

Strands of the Egyptian disk of Aten are present in the *dazzling sun*. *Radiant as light* brings to mind the Persian god of light Ahura Mazda. The two opposing factions of the Jewish faith are represented by Moses, as legalistic, and Elijah, as charismatic and prophetic. All this symbolism passes into the cloud of God's love and wisdom, and what comes out is Jesus, alone, who incorporates all these aspects of God, and incarnates and represents this one God, in his teachings. Thus the disciples are instructed to *hear him*.

The disciples, being ordinary run-of-the-mill people, want to do something to commemorate this spectacular religious event. Their first thought is to build a shrine, or three shrines, so as to accommodate all argumentative faiths. Shrines and churches may not necessarily be what God is about, for Jesus discourages this idea of booths. We are not being asked to multiply cults and construct separate buildings, but rather, to spread the message of love.

II Peter 1:17 makes a re-statement of the pyramid text proclamation which described the relationship of the god Ra to the pharaoh– *[Jesus Christ] was honored and glorified by God the Father, when the Sublime Glory itself spoke to him and said, "This is my beloved son on whom my favor rests."* This statement is applicable to very few. Jesus is considered the beloved and favored son. When we state that someone is uniquely equipped to do a job, we mean that there are very few individuals thus equipped. As the pharaoh was the unique person in his years of rule who could measure out god's justice to the people he ruled, so (in a more complete way) was Jesus the unique expression of God's love, for his time. Could Jesus pass this possibility of being an expression of God on to his followers?

The Evolution of Ideas. In Jesus' last supper discourse, we see an evolution of Egyptian ideas surfacing. If the ruling pharaoh, or incarnation, does not go away, the incarnation will not come to the new pharaoh or group. In John 16:7 Jesus says, "It is for your own good that I am going because unless I go, the Advocate will not come to you!" Indeed, the Spirit does come in Acts 2:2, when the disciples "heard what sounded like a powerful wind from heaven," which brings us back to analogies with the Egyptian hidden god Amun, the god of the wind who gives breath to the human, and who ruled through the pharaoh in Thebes.

We see this further idea of spirit coming to select followers in the Apostolic succession, and in the ability of the Pope in Rome to speak ex-cathedra, and bring the true message of God. Many of us today still find this notion of God being present in greater quantity in one human being rather than in another, quite viable.

This idea of one man supported by a god as being the best educated and wisest politically, was good for ancient Egypt, as long as the gene pool held up. However, today we have possibilities of *ALL* being well educated and up to date politically. Hence, there has evolved the concept of the Holy Spirit acting in every person, with a greater sense of personal responsibility. Perhaps we have less need of an official spokesperson in all matters. Perhaps to a greater extent than earlier, each should make her or his own personal covenant with God, and each should resolve to lead herself or himself in a loving and understanding manner.

9.5 Similar Beliefs?

The roots of our religious beliefs are made up of many bits and pieces from all over the world. The temple in Jerusalem was not the first temple erected to honor the maker and upholder of the universe. It was a copy of those erected by the people of Egypt to worship the Eternal Being in whom they believed. Before the Bible, there were compilations of the wisdom of the Eternal Being in Egypt, India, and Mesopotamia. In a similar manner, our symbols are intertwined. This entanglement becomes suddenly apparent in the strangest places. The goddess Eos of Roman times is the goddess Aurora of the Greeks, the daughter of Theia and Hyperion, who were Titans, early Greek super gods. Hyperion being the original Greek sun god, was displaced in greatness by Jupiter and Apollo. Many of Apollo's noble characteristics are found in Jesus, and some of the ideas associated with the dawn goddess,

Eos/Aurora, are still with us. The name of Eos is used in Easter, the feast of the dawn of new life. Even scientists get into this act of using the names of gods and goddesses for the purpose of keeping orderly sequences. The second main division of Tertiary rocks is called the *Eocene*, meaning rocks laid down at the dawn of recent times. This may sound like utter confusion, but it all developed, slow step by slow step. In like manner, our theological beliefs have developed.

There are many interweavings that can be seen by glancing at our religious history. We all come from the same boiling pot. It's as if we have all opened our veins and mixed our blood (as ancients did), and belong to one blood brotherhood. There is One God who loves us, and wants us to have a successful universe.

The Book of The Dead. Christianity is indebted to many previous thinkers for its inspiration. Before the Bible was organized, the people of Egypt found the wisdom of the eternal in *The Egyptian Book of The Dead*, composed about 2300 BC, much of it attributed to Thoth, the god of knowledge. Its sentiments often surpass our holy thoughts of today. We can reaffirm much of what it says about loving concern for each other.

The Egyptian Book of the Dead contains *Pyramid Texts* and *Coffin Texts*, and has such a morbid name because its sayings were found inscribed in tombs. Its ancient title was more positive, *Chapters For Coming Forth By Day*, which meant that a dead person had the ability to leave the tomb. It spoke of the human hope for resurrection after death. *The Book of The Dead* may contain material referred to in II Samuel 1:18, when they mention the *Book of The Just*.

The *Pyramid Texts* contain very ancient material. Some sections reflect back to less respectable religious customs. The "Cannibal Hymn" of the *Pyramid Texts* represents the dead king as eating the gods. Though somewhat repulsive, this, too, reflects the yearning for union with the divine. Egyptians worshiped a variety of gods and goddesses. Each city had its special care-taker god, and then also adopted whatever other deities seemed efficacious. Most Egyptians believed in Atum-Ra, the sun god as the chief god, but Osiris was also a favorite. Before Jesus came to fully incarnate God's message to the world, people had the constructive examples of Isis and Osiris.

The finest copy of *The Book of The Dead* is one credited to a dignitary named Ani. The godly son Horus is depicted in Ani's tomb as presenting Ani to his father, the god Osiris, thus assuring Ani of resurrection. Like other noble Egyptians who could afford proper ceremony and burial, Ani's soul is weighed in at judgment time. If the soul can be balanced with a feather, then the judged has no weighty matters on his soul, and the gods can receive him into eternal life.

We can not know the actual fate of Ani's soul in the realm of the other future world, but in this world the message written down by Ani goes on and on. The message may not have been composed by Ani or Thoth, but by some less prestigious person, but it is through Ani that we and other generations have heard the message. Others have taken the message, whittled at it according to previous conceptions they have had, and we can say that even this side of heaven, there is something eternal about Ani's soul. A bit of this soul has been inserted into new people and other civilizations. A free translation of the thought of this soul in Ani's "History of Creation" is as follows—

At first a voice cried against the darkness, and the voice grew loud enough to stir black waters. It was Temu rising up— his head the thousand-petaled lotus. He uttered the word and one petal drifted from him, taking form on the water. He was the will to live. Out of nothing he created himself, the light. The hand that parted the waters, uplifted the sun and stirred the air. He was the first, the beginning, than all else followed, like petals drifting into the pool ...

It was in a world out of time, for there was neither sun nor moon and nothing to mark the night from day until Temu reached down into the abyss and uplifted Ra. The sun shone on Temu's bright face, day began and Ra lived with him from the beginning of time. That was the first day of the world.[7]

Similarities between this and phrases in Genesis or the Gospel of John can be noted. From Genesis 1:2— *Now the earth was a formless void, there was darkness over the deep, and God's spirit hovered over the water.*

From John 1:1,4,5— *In the beginning was the Word ... All that came to be had life in him and that life was the light of men, a light that shines in the dark, a light that darkness could not overpower.*

Thus the message or word of the Eternal Being is carried through to our present day reminding us of "the ancient Egyptian doctrine that it was through Knowledge, the Word, the Speaking, that the universe came into existence—the Logos, to use the Greek word, by which all things are made."[8]

Scriptural and Other Similarities. At the end of the Middle Kingdom in Egypt, papyrus texts of *The Book of The Dead* were being mass produced in quantity by the scribes of the day, having both text and pictures. Surely many Hebrews were exposed to this text, and felt their souls relating to this word.

In Egypt the One God or first principle is sometimes called Temu, Ptah, or Ra. Often his name is hidden from the general populace as the name of God was considered secret and not to be spoken or written down. This reservation on speaking God's name was also observed by the Hebrews.

The God Horus was an emanation of the chief gods. Horus was, in some accounts, known as the twice born. He was born once in heaven through the goddess Nut of a divine spiritual nature and once of earth, through Isis with a material mortal nature. Similarly, Christians believe that Jesus was both God nature and human nature. They also believe that Jesus rose from death. Osiris, possibly a deified mortal, is also said to have risen from death.

St. Paul has commonalities with *The Book of Dead* in the papyrus of Nekhet, chapter 15– *At any moment you enter heaven by saying, "I am a temple of Ra.'*[9] In I Corinthians 3:16 Paul tells us that we are temples of God. Also from chapter 15, *Papyrus of Nekhet– Love is his light; compassion, the light of the world.*[10] Christians speak of God, as love, and of Jesus, as the light of the world.

Two thousand years before Jesus, we assume that people were ignorant of Jesus' ethic of selfless giving. This is not so. Quite the contrary is true. The selflessness in the Jesus story is preceded in its outline in a previous myth. Christians developed a role model in Mary, the mother of Jesus. The people of Egypt had a similar pair of role models. The noble person Osiris rose from the dead and was elevated to god-hood after being cruelly murdered. His caring sister-wife Isis was the healer and role model for the women of Egypt, and also elevated to the rank of deity. Christians believe that if they live and die while upholding the beliefs of Jesus, they will go to eternal life in heaven. Similarly, their predecessors in Egypt believed that a dead person, such as the pharaoh who was properly ritually identified with Osiris, would be raised to life again in a different realm.

Four Thousand Years of Progress? Egypt and Ani and *The Book of The Dead* were not the start of the marvelous love story of God. The people of Persia carried the story in their hearts. They brought bits of this story from southern Russia and from India. From small beginnings, they wove other interpretations such as the Zoroastrian religious belief in Ahura Mazda as the good god, and Ahriman as evil god. Do we save what is good in these older worship systems or do we carry over the bad, or is it some of both? Animals are still sacrificed to Durga (Kali) in Calcutta. In Nepal buffaloes, goats, and fowl are sacrificed to Durga. Elsewhere animals are smeared with red saffron to simulate blood. In Egypt animals are dedicated to God with a reddish brown stain.

Have we made progress in forming loving community over the past 4000 years, or has our competitive human nature kept us at ground zero? Is

Set still hacking Osiris into fourteen pieces? Looking at the historical record, we recall that the Hyksos stepped on the Egyptian scene with trained horses, war chariots, and iron swords. Kings were enabled to roam further in their conquering forays. Kublai Khan rolled into Peking, and soon gun powder, paper money, and printing came on the scene. Horses, chariots, and swords were replaced by tanks, planes, and bombs. Our cities are full of drug ridden unemployables, looked down upon by those who have accumulated more than they need. What has become of our God of healing and of love? The God of service is displaced by banks that loan for a price, and the price often seems to be inflation and the *sacrifice* of the poor. When a country is under military rule combined with guerrilla harassment, crops are destroyed and available bread is taken for soldiers, instead of for women and children.

The peoples of the first world must accept their responsibility to share both what is spiritual and what is material, with the peoples of the third world. If people decide to be considerate of other people, we will be able to supply the spiritual and material needs of both the poor and the rich. God or Allah, the Creator by any name, loves all peoples, and desires the fulfillment of the earth. Surely, this loving generous God will give us the strength to be part of God's majestic caring process. Understanding and kindness will help us to overcome our fear and distrust of different races and religions, for the unifying God made all races and religions.

9.6 Tolerance and Intolerance

Warring Gods. Because peoples were at war with each other, they believed that their gods were at war with each other. They reasoned that if two gods were connected with two opposing factions, and each god followed was a believable god, then one god must be good, and the other must be evil. If your side won, your god was the good god, and the other god was second-rate. Some of the gods early people worshiped had faults like us and had trouble getting along. Worshipers felt that if people resembled their parents, people should also resemble what was responsible for creating them. We are all both good and evil. People who believed they followed a just God felt justified in concluding their opponents were evil people who should be destroyed.

Present day nations have factions which choose to blame their economic problems on other ethnic and religious groups. Blaming the other has been popular from the beginning of time. Adam blamed Eve for the incident in the garden. In Egypt, Osiris opposed Set; these heroes originated in different territories. (The name Seth is a name revered as that of an ancestor by Palestinians who didn't follow the gods of Egypt. Set or Seth is a son of

Noah in the Bible.) In northern India, we find Ashura of the Assyrs versus the Hindu gods. The Tamils celebrate the victory of Lord Subramanya, God of War, over Taraka of the Ashura enemy, as the victory of good over evil. Even today they climb to a hilltop shrine and shout, "Vel! Vel!" (Vel is similar to Bel or Baal. Vel is also similar to El, the Hebrew name for the God of the mountain.) This shouting commemorates the invincible weapon given to the god by his godly mother. Who is this mother but the mother of all being, and what is the invincible weapon of being, but love? Do the Tamils think about law and love when they chant *vel, vel, vetri vel* to the heavens? Do they still hate the Persians because early Persian types drove their ancestors beyond the Indus? The Israelis, too, worshiped God on a mountain, under the name of El. They found God's weapon to be law, that God's order was kept by human obedience to God. One can be obedient and unloving. One can be loving, but feel compelled to disobey laws set by men who erroneously think they are serving God.

One God. When all our belief systems are so intertwined, how can we be intolerant of one another? The Christian beliefs have their roots deep in the experience of the Hebrews and the soil of Egypt. They have other spiritual faith statements that were acceptable in their time, having been previewed by somewhat similar statements from Babylon. An example of the latter is the Babylonian story of a god's son, Tammuz, who rose out of death. The Jewish God Yahweh has traveled to all parts of the world with Hebrews fleeing persecution. This same God, the God of all the earth, was worshiped under the name of Agni by the Khaldeans; this same God was seen by the Hindus as the Brahmanic God of Being; this same God was worshiped on the hearths of China as the kitchen God who cares for daily needs. This same God is the Creator of all human beings and all human systems. As the Muslims proclaim– There is only One God!

We are the ones who are at fault. We refuse to recognize this God in others, and in the worship forms of others. Tolerance is the healthy respect for others and the acceptance of their unity with the one God, as equal to our own.

One of our tasks is that of unifying the people of the world while still allowing them their diverse faiths. Each person should have the opportunity to follow her own belief system, but should also attempt to understand other systems. Emphasis should be placed on ethical beliefs that are held in common. Appropriate unifying sacraments and festivals can be taken from all religions. Many symbols are cross-cultural. Happily, there are composite symbols already in existence such as that combining the Hebrew Star of David with the Muslim crescent and the Christian cross.

Exclusivity. What marvelous threads run between the religions of the different countries! How can one speak of the God of the Jews or the God of the Christians when the one God made all the varying peoples and loves and cares for them all? It is not a truthful stance for one religious group to claim to know God particularly well, and proclaim themselves chosen when their religion is built on the faith and beliefs of myriads of other people who have gone before them. No one group knows all about the unknowable God!

God certainly does not promise the kingdom of heaven to just one group when God has made us all. Those who can believe such exclusivity or geno-centricity for a privileged group are not thinking clearly. The Syrian theologian, Ephrem (died 373 AD), threatened the Jews (and this may be applied to any God-seeking group), "If one kingdom of heaven is not promised to all of us, one gehenna is enough for all of you."[11] We must be tolerant of one another. We must believe that we all can be worthy of heaven.

9.7 Prayer

It is well and good to say we should be tolerant, but how far is our tolerance to go? Are we to be tolerant if some cult leader is handing guns to his followers and telling them that God wants them to kill all trespassers on their territory? Would we have been able to remain aloof if we were with Cortez and the Spaniards in Mexico beholding human sacrifice? If we perceive what we think is evil in another religious group, we are obliged to fight that evil. Much that is wrong goes on behind the scenes in religion, as we are all human, fallible, and often deluded by power. We have all seen examples of child abuse, sexual promiscuity, and other forms of immorality perpetrated under the privacy of a religious covering. Often these perpetrators of abuse are more to be pitied than censured. They may be the victims of abuse which occurred in their childhood, and may be acting out traumas that are held deep in the dark places of their minds. Things that are "unspeakable" have happened to them, and they have handled these events with denial, so that it only comes back in dreams, or surfaces when they are controlling others.

It has been rumored that the phenomenon of Hitler was the result of one man (who happened to be Jewish) raping Hitler's mother. The trauma undergone by the mother, was subconsciously handed on to the son, and fomented his rage against all Jews. Think what further agonies could have been avoided, if were possible to defuse that particular rape victim!

In fighting the evil of abuse and trauma, what weapons do we use? *Fight* and *weapon* are very heavy words. We each must take the responsibility to do battle, and we each must choose our weapons carefully. Our job is to change the situation from that of abuse and fear to one of gentleness and trust. We are to use the power in us, or a power that will work through us, to transform these poor situations.[12] There are many tools to be found in the transforming power kit, with which God has equipped each one of us. One of the most effective tools is prayer.

Prayer can be considered a form of sacrament as it is a way of getting in touch with the holy or with the power of the holy. We each have a holy spot within. Our prayer can be a symbol to others of what we believe. Prayer spoken aloud is a way of displaying or exposing the holy spot inside of us, to the gaze of another. Prayer does its work, whether the individual you are praying for, knows about it, or not. However, it helps to have the individual or group know of your non-antagonistic and positive leanings.

In the instance of a war-like cult leader, if the concerned community staged a prayer vigil off the cult property but within view of the cult, their positive thought would penetrate to the cult and its leader and cause some rethinking of position and attitude.

Attitudes, words, and postures associated with prayer vary widely with faith communities. Part of the action of prayer when not addressed to God but described as positive thought, can be performed by an atheist. Any opponent of abortion could affirm to a proponent, "From the depths of my heart, I would wish that you could see the wonderful possibilities present in all human beings, particularly the unborn." Those of us who believe in a caring God have the added comfort of feeling God's support in our affirmations, and expectations of miraculous results.

Footnotes
1 Stela of Shamshi Adad V (815-811 BC) from Nimrud Temple of Nabu, large cross is symbol of the sun god, British Museum, London.
2 David A. Leeming, Mircea Eliade, Ed., *The Encyclopedia of Religion Volume 15,* "Virgin Birth," MacMillan Publishing Company, NY, 1987.
3 Richard Milner, *The Encyclopedia of Evolution,* Facts on File, New York, 1990, p. 259.
4 Eric Voegelin, *Israel and Revelation,* Louisiana State U. Press, 1958, p. 86.
5 Samuel A.B. Mercer, *The Pyramid Texts in Translation* and *Commentary, Volume I,* New York, 1952, sections 1(a-b), 4(a-b), 6.
6 *ibid.,* sections 2(12a - 13b).
7 Normandi Ellis, *Awakening Osiris,* Phanes Press, Grand Rapids MI, 1988, p. 64.
8 P.H. Newby, *The Egypt Story,* Abbeville Press, New York, 1975, p.106.
9 Normandi Ellis, *loc. cit.,* p. 49.
10 *ibid.*
11 Robert Murray, *Symbols of Church and Kingdom,* Great Britain, Alden Press, Oxford 1975, p. 65.
12 Transforming Power is a concept of the Alternatives to Violence Project, 3049 East Genesee Street, Syracuse, NY, 13224.

X

The Theory of Love and Power

Recycle of The Holy[1]

*There are always new poems to make
but never a new God; always
new truths to state, new perceptions
through new eyes. But looking ahead
through the mists of the stars in the universe
we see back around to infinity
the back side of God
who creates all and is ever creating.*

*We strive to reach ahead and be like God
only to find that we were like God
when God created us, and that we continue
in God's holiness with every breath, and, yes
the Messiah of God is risen, is with us
always, or we would be as good as dead.*

10.1 Domestication of Populations

In Genesis 1:28 God blessed the human beings and advised them to fill the earth and subdue it and to control the animals. We are to treat the earth with care and concern. God does not say that we are to control each other. However, the human being has put into place all manner of structures to control other human beings. Herders gathered together wild animals and tamed them for the purpose of making a livelihood off of them. Some religious professionals did likewise with populations. However, not all those seeking greater truth about the eternal were guilty of such grand domestication or control of their associates. More often religious leaders were altruistic and working for the fulfillment of those in their charge.

Domestication has taken place in diverse circumstances. Domestication of populations by war lords or conquerors or priestly establishments takes place most often several centuries after a charismatic religious figure has proclaimed an ethic of love for oppressed people. Domestication can also take place in times of great inhumanity, before a major prophet preaches the need for reform. A population can be made pliable for God's word in a situation such as the Babylonian Captivity (586-516 BC). Political unity and political domestication have also sometimes fostered religious domestication. The role of Alexander the Great (356-323 BC) was not to promote an existing religious belief, but to consolidate the known kingdoms. Then in the subsequent Roman Empire, at the time of Constantine (325 AD), the new religion of Christianity was more readily spread through out the area.

The many religious beliefs such as the multi-god systems of Egypt, Greece, and Rome, the one-God beliefs of Christians, Muslims, and Jews, and the ethical beliefs of Buddhism, Taoism, and Confucianism, are preserved by structures designed to keep their groups orderly. Often this order is maintained through a combination of hope for personal betterment and through fears of damnation or community disapproval. Does God keep earth orderly through power, through weapons, through fear, or does God give us freedom to act out of personal responsibility and concerned love? In having groups of humanity reach their goal through binding religious forms, we may be short-circuiting humanity from its proper path of responsible love, and encouraging argumentative differences among power structures or leaders.

Is it necessary to have a power structure to carry the message of love? In Egypt the common people were content to believe in the goodness and healing power of Isis. At some point the stronger god Ra was enthroned in the temple and serviced by priests who received a portion of his sacrifices for their upkeep. Many peoples followed this cultural pattern, and generations later, many of the societies of the earth seem convinced that it is necessary to worship God in temples made with human hands and to pay intermediaries (priests, pastors, rabbis, imams, etc.) to oversee the worship in these temples.

Frequently throughout history, prophets have spoken up and pro-claimed the availability of God to all. Ordinary people who are listening rejoice at this proclamation, and many devote their individual lives to God's service without feeling the necessity for a go-between. On the other hand, some individuals are followers rather than leaders. For those who prefer a leader, the methods used to guide, facilitate, or control the flock can be gentle and peaceable. There may be prayers for healing. Places may be declared sacred. Shrines may be set up. Statues and symbols may be put in place to make worship easier. Sometimes the god or his spokesperson becomes more demanding. They want better behavior, more sacrifice, and perhaps even a grander temple. The religious leader may build his commu-nity by complaining about the misdeeds of those outside the community. It may seem then as if the god permits the mistreatment of populations who do not worship at his temple.

Violence. Side by side with the evolution of concerned love, we have seen the spread of weapons of war as if one was somehow related to the other. We can imagine that many an early man lived in a loving community. He wanted to protect that community against the outsider, so he organized power groups for protection (because he loved the insiders). These power groups invented weapons– swords, dynamite, crucifixions, tortures– often out of fear for their own lives and the lives of those they loved. However, those who use swords must expect that swords will be used against themselves. Those who employ violence against others must expect violence in return.

The threat of violence may occasionally be necessary to lead us toward permanent peace. It sometimes seems that only because we view the cruel results of discrimination, slavery, pogroms, and racial genocide, are we impressed with the need for love and understanding for both the oppressed and the oppressor. Without the presence of power, evil, weaponry, and persecutions, we might never have evolved to see that all nations, creeds, races, and sexes would profit from concerned cooperation.

In this evolution of forced cooperation (arising out of fear), groups selected leaders in order to crusade against other groups. Kings were expected to go out to war. Gods were selected to go out to war with the king who worshiped them. Their belief in their god as the one supreme Lord and the righteous leader of the community fostered inflamed nationalism. If we are taught that our God is the one true God, and that other people have other gods who are evil, the unthinking among us will be easily influenced into killing other humans like themselves. They will see the other person as evil and deserving of death. They may even feel that if they die as a result of opposing these others, they will be rewarded with a blissful after life. The maniacal god of war marches to war with the soldiers, and the gods or goddesses of concerned love are left behind at the hearth side.

Today when all human beings can see the hideousness of harming civilian populations when "great powers" fight with bombers and tanks, how can any human being risk being a soldier in such an army? Too often, leaders incite followers by emphasizing religious differences, and term their cause a religious war in order to encourage thoughtless participation. How can one follow a leader who looks only for power and control, and thus fly in the face of loving concern for other human beings? Soldiers are *people* who can contemplate on what is just and good. They can be used to help. Many soldiers are trained in skills and can help to build homes for the homeless. Some can teach others to grow better crops, or heal the mentally and physically ill, or be role models in the inner cities. Soldiers don't have to be relegated to the sole category of trigger pulling.

Power Versus Love. When we look back at the history of our earth and the story of civilization, we must try to learn what pieces of our searching were helpful for all humanity, and what pieces distracted or took away from the general well being. There was much that was helpful in the wisdom dispensed by the philosophers. There also must have been some good aspects of power and authority. It surely took strong and powerful leadership to rid the world of child sacrifice in China and human sacrifice in Mexico. Were these improvements based on power or love? Will it be power or love that rids the world of war? Perhaps we need a dedicated combination of both. Communication has made the world into a global village. Communication can support power and control. It can encourage racial hatreds and sexual improprieties, through manipulation of minds. Communication must be used for community betterment. It is necessary to communicate a new religion of love and tolerance throughout the world in order to preserve the world.

We have seen how God created the heavens and the earth, and how the human being came on the scene. This human being behaved in a vacillating manner. She could love, and she also could hate. She was capable of doing terrible things to her fellow human. We hope that God's purpose in creation was not to have us inflict misery on one another. Some of us humans believe that God is all-powerful, but some of us worry that God started something that got out of control. Those in positions of power and authority in the church or in the state, remind us that there are controlling forces. They warn us that if we don't behave, there will be consequences that our actions have instigated.

Moses tried to establish a loving community in the wilderness showing us the concern of God for wandering tribes. David took this wilderness community structure and bound it together with a power play. He used the seeking-after-goodness-and-justice that resides in the hearts of all people, and invited many tribes to come and be part of his community. This kingdom of David's was held together by dedication and trust as well as political and military power. Because David rose to power in Israel, the people-oriented God of Moses was enshrined as the God to be worshiped. Because God uses both love and power, the words of gentle prophets are set in place by authoritarian rulers. God may use the forces of both love and power to encourage us to our optimum fulfillment. Cruel leaders may rouse the people to desire justice. Ice ages may encourage genes that withstand adversity.

Sometimes evolutionary pain is conveniently blamed on God because we can't see any other purpose in it. Or does God allow evolutionary pain as part of a larger birthing process? In our looking back, we suppose that the dinosaurs may have become extinct because they developed in the wrong directions. It is possible that God corrected this backsliding by allowing a meteor or other environmental conditions hostile to the dinosaurs. The Bible says that when humans became obnoxious, God sent a flood. Having promised not to use the flood tactics again, God perhaps allowed the explosion at Thera to shake up civilizations that were getting too set in selfish ways. God's power was perhaps being used to urge the world community towards greater understanding of others.

Law. When we cast our eyes around the world, and observe behavior, we might decide that law and order is the only way to go. Without the pressure from authority, people are inclined to be irresponsible and to do what seems good for them. We often feel that if we obey laws (which may be unjust and biased), we will have order, and we will save the world. However, laws may be sitting too heavily on those in low places; the oppressed may be plotting revolt against laws that you and I believe to be very reasonable. Laws are to be obeyed by those who make up the laws, but we cannot always expect those who do not have a chance to give input, to obey the laws we make. Understanding and communication are better methods to peace than rule by law.

Law may have its problems, but it is not all bad; it gives us guidelines to follow, and it tells others what we are about. Enforcing laws through police power can be helpful as well as hurtful. Power can contribute to a sense of order. God gave us freedom to choose our directions, but we need guiding knowledge to make wise choices. Children need parents who set bounds to their behavior. Grown people also need guidance that contains a measure of authority. Unfortunately, some authorities often profess to know more than they really know, and act as if they always did everything correctly. This hypocrisy is annoying to those they are supposedly helping. Those who try to help must be listeners before they are advisors.

Love and Hate. Over the ages, God seems to be guiding us to be more loving. Let us try to define love more explicitly. If we enlist the assistance of previous cultures as given in the Bible, we might describe the concept of love as pity for the needy. Love, where commitment to God is concerned, might be described as a spontaneous feeling which impels to self-giving. Deuteronomy 6:5 and 13:4 talk about love when it is directed towards God, as being a transformative power of soul in the inward person. Our soul chooses to direct our body to be useful to the creation. We are to help the needy because they are a part of God's creation just as we are. If we are forming responsible souls, we will seek to transform ourselves and others to be kind and noble.

There are other kinds of love besides the transformative and the altruistic. There is love between man and woman as described in the Old Testament by Jeremiah and Hosea. There is the love of a father for his son as in David's lament for Absalom. Love can be between equals as well as between the one giving and the recipient. Love has to do with respecting the other and acknowledging her rights. Love seems to be a quality inborn in the human, passed between generations, and even possible when one generation is considering a future generation, or past generations. Sexual love can strengthen the spiritual bond between two persons and can enhance family life, but when sex disrespects women, aborts babies, or brings unloved and unwanted children into the world community, it is not furthering the good of humanity, and cannot be considered to be positive.

We cannot command love to happen. We cannot prod the pervert or the addict to love themselves and others. Love is a non-legal quantity. We cannot encircle it with legal directives. A person can obey all sorts of minute rules and regulations, and be a totally unloving automaton. We cannot force one person to love another, but when love is flowed into the human container, then it flows back out to others.

We cannot command hate either. It is easy to see how we can cause someone to fear, and how the path of fear often leads to hatred. If we suggest to a person or group that another is liable to harm them, we start them thinking negatively. If we want to encourage love, we must be constantly affirming, constantly enumerating good qualities in the other group, constantly praying for the other's fulfillment. Our words and actions have the power to change fear into active interest, which leads to knowledge, to trust, and to love.

The Bible advises us to have loving concern for both the fellow national and the enemy (Deuteronomy 22:1-4, Exodus 23:4). Ezekiel 47:22 advises that aliens are to be treated as citizens. We are to share the goods of the earth with others. It seems that some of our early ancestors thought ahead to future generations and had loving concern for those who would come after them. Some ancestors such as the mythical Abraham looked forward in time to the well being of their descendants. Do we, the people of the world, living today, have this concern for those who will participate in the future of this earth?

The Search for Fulfillment. Hunting and gathering people were here 500,000 BP. God certainly knew about them and their hopes and their vagaries. They were pretty much like us. The mothers loved and protected their young. In 9,000 BC there were many towns dotting the landscape. Along the Nile rulers of cities were wielding power (6,000 BC). In Mesopotamia there were trading cities, there was writing, and soon there were soldiers marching. God knew about all that. God saw both the giving and the greedy. Greedy rulers wanted MORE; they wanted more land, more people to bow before them, more bronze and tin. What did they really want? Did they go marching, marching, just to see the world, or were they looking for a little excitement? Were they escaping from the humdrum of daily living? From generation to generation we search. Rather than needing the domestication offered by power structures, perhaps we need to develop our own internal motivations in a wholesome search for our fulfillment. We think we may find fulfillment if we have a little power, or money to buy material goods. Some of us seek for a comfortable mind, for our fulfillment. We search for love, for admiration, and for someone to love and to share our resources. Sometimes our drive for power seems to be a search for someone to adore us. We have a basic need to be appreciated. As we escape from subservience to our animal appetites and learn how to work with our environment, as we escape from our selfishness, by choosing to be considerate to one another, we will have less need for power grabbing and aggression. As we meditate on our beginnings and on the God who created all this, we will get a clearer idea of how the One God dreams of our fulfillment.

10.2 Alternations of Love and Power

Has humanity come closer to the peaceful future that we hope God projects for it? A frequent occurrence in history is that an understanding leader will arise and urge the people to be responsible and loving. The people will listen to this prophet. They will reform their ways and become model citizens, doing good to one another. When the prophet dies, other people who believe in his methods will encourage still others to follow the good deeds of the leader. At some point power structures like a king or priesthood, will insist that the people follow the prophet's regulations. They will believe that they alone know the true regulations and beliefs of the prophet. They will convince the people that they are the ones who know and the ones to be trusted. The people will forget the true message of the prophet and will follow the power structure obediently.

Another prophet will arise who sees that the power structure doesn't have the full truth. She will go back to the message of love and understanding as preached by the previous prophet. The people will be swayed by this new prophet and her charismatic and truthful statements and will follow her. People will act responsibly and lovingly. As before, another power structure will come onto the scene, supporting the message of love. As before, leadership in the power group will become corrupted. This scenario repeats itself again and again. But we are making progress. Each time this happens, the idea of love and understanding is reinforced. With our present day methods of communication, more people hear about and have concern for the oppressed, and become dubious of those enforcing power.

India, Mesopotamia, and Egypt. Down through history we can see alternations in love and power. Early cave artists in India and Europe showed by their drawings that they believed in the power of the supernatural. This belief in something or someone beyond the human, eventually led to the temple establishment at Ur in Mesopotamia to praise and placate the incomprehensible. It seemed that the gods who were serviceable to people and who listened to prayers, sometimes turned into gods who liked a return for these services. It seemed that they expected priests and priestesses to run their organizations. These servants of the gods received payment from those in the population who wanted their prayers heard. In Mesopotamia, there was a variety of gods, several for each city state in the area. When Sargon I came to power and unified the city states, he also unified cultural and religious beliefs. He was the head man, and it was his culture and his god-ideas that were spread in the Near East.

These ideas went wherever he went trading. Egypt had some ideas of its own, but it was willing to incorporate those of other countries. The gentleness of Isis was exchanged for the leadership abilities of a Ra. The Egyptian people were easily led like sheep by their pharaohs who considered themselves as shepherds. The Egyptian priesthood held innumerable festivals, became the entertainment providers for the crowds, and became more and more powerful over the lives of the common people.

Hebrew Power. From this Egyptian milieu came some of the Hebrew groups that left Egypt and set up their communities in the desert. The tool for community cooperation was an amalgam of early laws from Egypt and Mesopotamia. When David needed a means of molding a group of variegated people into a nation, he used this "Moses" law, the fame of Joseph and Joshua, and historical legends. His power tactics encouraged a law abiding community that favored the one-God belief.

David is an excellent example of a person of power who was able to integrate ethical and religious relationships, and to make an orderly kingdom based on the reign of a monotheistic God. He combined obedience to law and worship of God with charismatic leadership. His personal actions were able to display to the people his belief in the quality of forgiveness, and his ability to leave the vengeance to God. He forgave Shimei the Benjamite (II Samuel 19:16-23). While he may have treated women with chauvinism in an era of patriarchy, he displayed love and understanding for his friend Jonathan (II Samuel 9:1) and his son Absolom (II Samuel 19:1-4).

When the Hebrews who had been forced into exile in the Babylonian Captivity were allowed to return to Palestine, their community of love and obedience to the law was pressured by those who assumed power. In Babylon, the message of love had been reinforced by Isaiah. Nehemiah and Ezra, the leaders of the remnant who returned from Babylon, wanted to be sure that the supposed injunctions credited to Moses and the law statements of priests who followed Moses, were properly observed. Again we see the message of a loving community being enforced by power. Ezra and Nehemiah were the power structures that preserved, yet warped, the message of love. They purified the Jewish community, emphasized its "chosenness," yet did very unloving things like exiling the non-Jewish women and children from the community.[2]

Other groups are sometimes fascinated with maintaining the *purity* of their religion. The Jews of Ezra and Nehemiah's time were very particular about what they felt were their select traditions (which may have been tinged with Zoroastrianism). Those returning from exile had certainly heard of and perhaps been influenced by the gods and goddesses of Babylon. When they got back to Judea, and the people who had been left behind told them how they thought the Hebrew religion should be carried out, they felt the other group quite unorthodox. When some of their number married with members from these other groups, the children heard and put together all sorts of stories. Strict Jews were horrified by this, as they felt that their beliefs were the only true beliefs. They could not make allowances for the other group's cultural "peculiarities." This controversy ended up with one group, later called the Samaritans, worshiping on Mt. Gerizim, and the other group worshiping in Jerusalem.

Human Sacrifice. In the Near East there had been a tendency to child sacrifice. This had been a dispute among various religious groups and individuals. Some children and secondary wives or concubines were considered expendable. They didn't have too many rights. Which group could decide better the questions of human sacrifice in war, of child sacrifice, or of abortion– the power group or the individual undergoing the sacrifice? The human sacrifice at ancient Ur was undoubtedly believed to have a good and godly purpose. It has the appearance of a power group decision. The individuals concerned might not have been as enthusiastic.

This tendency for power groups to sacrifice life may have continued in an underground manner, as willing sacrificial victims may have not been readily available. Megalith builders fashioned the pyramids about 2500 BC. Comparable megaliths also existed in Central America. Could some followers of outlawed ancient religions in the Mediterranean area with megalithic tendencies have ventured beyond the Straits of Gibraltar, and ended up in Mexico to practice human sacrifice with religious freedom? In the South America of 2000 BC there was evidence of similarities to Near East cultural beliefs, such as a goddess statue at Valdivia. Wide hipped figurines from Chupicuaro and Guanajuanto, Mexico, 300 BC to 300 AD reflect ancient Sumerian and Hittite goddess worship. On the Sun Stone, the sun's face has hair like sun's rays as in Egypt. Tlaloc, the rain god, holds a serpent, the Moses' symbol of healing. Could these symbols have come from west of Mexico via Japan and Siberia, or from boats riding the Gulf Stream across the Atlantic?

The Aztec people may have quit one continent for another to follow the hunt or to worship in freedom, but they were eventually ensnared by their rulers and controlled by a belief system. Aztec human sacrifice could be described as a means of loving the greater community. A young person would joyfully go to her death, as she believed it would benefit the group. Might we have better community today if some of us were more willing to make sacrifices for others and for future generations?

Often, in history, belief systems have encountered and clashed. At some point, encultured Christians came to the Americas and observed the Aztec community. When the Spaniards surveyed the Aztec religious scene, they were not convinced that human offering was really an expression of sacrificial love, even though they came from a religious belief where their God allowed the sacrifice of his own son Jesus. They did not think that the

Aztecs could possibly be worshiping the same God as they worshiped. Culturally, today, some of us feel the power of the Spanish conquistador as loving, and oppose the respectful sacrifice of the Aztecs to their fierce god Huitzilopochtli. We are taught to believe in the opinions of our particular cultural authorities rather than making up our own minds impartially. We fortunately have evolved to dislike the killing of people as a sacrifice, although we still do much killing of each other.

One of the reasons the Spanish conquistadors were upset by the Aztec rite of human sacrifice was because they were physically overcome by the smell of rotting blood. Similarly, a reason we no longer sacrifice animals, is because of the smell. Incense came into use to keep the smell under control. Prophets noted that a sacrifice of praise smells better than a sacrifice of meat.

In a further evolvement of sacrifice many of us today believe that a personal bodily sacrifice by doing good deeds, is pleasing to God. We use bread and wine for symbols of the sacrifice made by Jesus and the dedication of our lives to his way. Alternatively, many are content with donations of money as their sacrifice. Monetary sacrifices (or contributions of our excess) are more acceptable for the sensory perceptions of both the power structures and the individual worshipers.

Jesus on the cross was a bodily sacrifice and was seen as giving his life freely in love for all the people of the earth. At the same time the horror of a crucifixion was emphasized. His immediate followers were also willing to sacrifice their lives that Jesus' message of love for others might be publicized. The Christians in the first century built no temples, had no statues of their God, had no altar, thus no sacrifice, thus no priest. The Romans felt that Christians were atheists as they had no visible symbols of worship. When it became necessary to formulate early Christian doctrine, the power and authority structures began to be set in place. This helped to preserve the basic message. The reason we are acquainted with this message of love is because the early church carried this message in the care of its power structures. If no power took this message under its care, we might never have heard the Good News of Jesus.

Protestants and Others. A prime building block in this early power structure was the emperor, Constantine. After his time, we had the centuries of the construction of the Roman Catholic belief system, and then the gradual revolt against the over domestication and abuses of the accompanying power system. Several hundred years after Constantine, Muhammad proposed a life of loving service to God coupled with strong views of moral discipline. Still later, the eastern branches of Catholicism also broke with

Rome and chose to worship in their own manner. The excesses of the Catholic Church in the use of its authority and measures such as the Inquisition caused people like Henry VIII and Martin Luther to revolt. They felt that personal internal freedom to worship God was being abused. Luther and other branches of Protestantism came into being as a reaction to the power of the Catholic Church. These two major divisions of Christianity, Catholicism and Protestantism, remained powerful in Europe and America.

Both churches and governments were often expected to care for the poor and to provide education and health services. The ordinary people were content to pay priests, pastors, or politicians to do many of the deeds which were deemed necessary for the good of the greater community. Concerned love relinquished much of the responsibility to power structures. Society often gave lip service to love of neighbor, while at the same time, it ignored the neighbor or treated him intolerantly.

This intolerance for the other bred new groups with their own power structures. A recent horrible example was Hitler. Hitler perceived the Jews as a group which threatened his group. He claimed that those who followed him would find order and safety in their society if the Jews were evicted. Evolution sadly may need the example of a Hitler so that people can see the defects of trusting in charismatic rulers and the necessity for loving one's neighbor. However, those who are persecuted in one generation rise up to persecute others in a following generation. Hitler types and Klu Klux Klan inciters keep appearing and gain followers. Their idea of God is a god of exclusivity and vengeance.

Male or Female Leadership? One can think of God, as the perfect creator, containing all opposites. God is male and female, extrovert and introvert, upholder of both the oppressed and the oppressor, guider of the leader and of the follower. If we are to be perfect like God, we will contain all these qualities. We will possess and employ both male and female ideas of goodness. We have the ability to choose which paths will lead us to our greatest fulfillment and to God's plan of perfection for us.

Governmental structures are usually put in place by men. Such structures frequently encourage competitiveness, play upon fears, and have unsound economic and environmental world, national, and local policies. Greed and competition shoulder out concerns for *third world* problems. If we could set greed and power structures off to one side and encourage "the least among us" towards personal fulfillment, there would be less need for guns and oppressive power structures.

Using a power structure to carry the message of love is hampered by the fact that one group will be in power, and the less powerful group is expected to follow. For example, the people who govern in the United States are usually men. The few women who are chosen to govern, are often those women who lead forcefully. Many women, often not accepted into the political power process, guide through facilitation, as they are experienced in helping children to express themselves. The average male does not understand government by facilitation. Your political candidate does not listen to the people; he tells the people what he knows, and tries to impress them with his knowledge, even if it is only calling the other candidate names. This is a rather backwards way of trying to establish himself as a hero who presumably does not have his opponent's faults. Our day and age thus gives publicity to non-heroes. Our youth are deprived of positive role models. The Egyptians emphasized their role models to their youth by making their heroes into gods. Later generations de-mythologized these gods.

Every tradition becomes encrusted with well-meaning impediments. For example, Jesus' message was understandable, but then his followers cast his thought in their type of concrete. They established rites and traditions. These were copied and added to, century after century. Amalgamations entered in. Each generation of young Christian adults looked over the package, saw something of Jesus, and eventually accepted the package. Today with our standards of morality set by the sex and violence of TV, and with massive doses of conflicting philosophies, the Christian package of loving kindness is not accepted so wholeheartedly. Present day role models to inspire the young to deeds of kindness, are hard to find. Those who are mistreated or misjudged by society find it hard to believe in a God of love.

10.3 Who Is Your God?

We each have our own idea of God.

What gods do we worship today? What kind of a God do you have? Is your god/goddess a god/goddess of love or of power? What kind of love? What kind of power? The kind of society we have and the way we actually live our lives, influence the kind of God we believe in. Our society proposes other gods for us to worship. Our concept of what God is, does not develop sufficiently in a society oriented to self-indulgence. Some who see too much greed and materialism in our present mode of Christmas celebration, suffer disillusionment. They begin to feel that gift giving is a farce perpetuated by commercial interests. They ask themselves what god our culture worships. Others struggle against this tide and try to preserve the concept of a loving, forgiving God.

We can try to climb out of our culture and mind set, and enter into another time and personality in order to understand others' searchings and our comradeship with them. Imagine an Indian youth on the craggy California coast about the time of Christ. He has seen storms on the sea, and has watched the sea gulls fishing from off shore rocks. His care givers have fed him with fish from the sea and collected berries and roots to sustain him. He is old enough to be accepted into the adult community who trace their ancestry back to a great conflagration. When asked about the nature of God, the youth might respond, "The God of my tribe is like a caring father or a nurturing mother."

Imagine a teenager in New York City, child of a single parent mother. She has trouble keeping food on his plate, in spite of the government assist of welfare. What does he know about God? What God does he worship?

Imagine an incarcerated female in a state correctional facility. She has served ten years for a crime she did not commit. Her God may be a strict God who punishes the wrong doer, or her God may still be a God who loves and forgives, or she may have no faith in any God.

Imagine an Egyptian princess two thousand years before Christ. She has never heard the instruction, "Love your neighbor as yourself." Nevertheless, she tries to be a healing person. She thanks a bountiful God for her lovely world.

All of the above people have different ideas about God, and about good and evil. Each has had the concept of God influenced by the actions of others around her. The love or hate, the caring or the abandonment that pervade the culture influence the perception of reality and of God. Would you blame the New York teenager if he found God uncaring and too remote to have anything to do with his existence? His God might be his gun. His ritual would be using a drug needle. Ultimately, it is we who make God for ourselves and for others. Our social systems that we all help to create reflect the power and economics that we worship, and they influence others to that channel of thinking. We build our own interpretation of God, and hence we build our own future, for good or evil, through our present actions.

Footnotes
1 Poem by Cora E. Cypser
2 John Bright, *History of Israel*, Westminster Press, Philadelphia, 1972, p. 391.

XI

To Renew The World

Evil has no foresight! Evil lives only for the present. –Zoroaster[1]

11.1 Commonalities of Beliefs

Here we are, at the tip of the evolutionary arrow, traveling through time. How do we benefit from all that has gone before? How can we now contribute, in our time, to the renewal of the world?

What Life Is Like. Only 350 years ago, the earth was considered to be the center of the universe created 6000 years back by a patriarchal God. The white male human was thought to be the one chosen to dominate humans of different race or gender. Now we are not so sure that is the case. "...we humans are a profoundly immature species; ...we do not know most knowable things; and ...we are only now beginning to learn how to learn. ...We are aware of our consciousness, but we cannot even make good guesses as to how this awareness arises in our brains, or even, for sure, if it does arise there."[2] We act like we have lived on the earth forever, but underneath we are running scared.

Life is rough. We observe other people making stupid mistakes. We shudder when leaders drop bombs on countries or groups. We can't believe that there are sufficient reasons for terrorists to plant bombs that will kill innocent people. That's not all that life is about. There are signs pointing in other directions. From viewing the television scene, we see that some people in the world want peace. Some believe that armaments are a curse to be avoided. The ability of nuclear bombs to destroy the whole earth makes us reconsider what we really want our countries to do with monstrous weapons.

We know that life has been both positive and negative since people have had the voice to talk about it and to write their thoughts down. Love was there at the beginning, waiting for recognition. From the heart of Africa and up the Nile River, people assumed that there were powerful spirits who had love for human beings. The feather representing justice, the sun as seeing all that happened on the earth, guided Queen Hatshepsut of Egypt, who knew she was protected by loving spirits, and that she was impelled by those spirits to be a wise and responsible ruler.

This same guiding love showed concern for the people dwelling in Palestine, and they responded to this spirit by building a great temple in which to worship this guiding force. Power structures were put in place, and those who were self-righteous treated the other people in the land with cruelty, even as is done in many countries today. Such behavior brought on its own punishment. The temple had to go. It could not confine the God of all the world. It had been a place where roots were sunk down, and blossoms and weeds had sprung up. This is what happens throughout the earth. God does not need temples for the process of love and understanding. The God of us all grows in hearts everywhere. Love and understanding grow best in the open field of freedom. God continues to lead us out of our cultural enslavements to future freedoms.

Many Religions, One God. Belief in this God grew in different soils all over the earth. The Hindus believed that souls earned their way to blessedness through doing good deeds, and that all religions were possible paths to God. The kind of God that Buddha believed in was a God of nothingness, a God who would come within, when self was extinguished. The God of Jesus was a loving Father, a God who would be there when needed. The God of Paul was selective– a monotheistic God who loved those who acted justly and consigned others to punishment. The ruler Constantine worshiped a broad, inclusive, demanding God; Constantine respected the truth in many traditions and combined them. This God was both a God of love and a God of power, and Constantine found that God's servants could be manipulated for both these ends. Church and state combined in a strict rule. Those who worshiped a God of gentleness fled as monks into the desert to avoid ruthlessness and manipulation.

The God of Islam is a stern God requiring responsible behavior and insisting that you help your neighbor to be responsible. The Muslims believe that if you see a wrong, you have a duty to stop it physically. If you can't, then condemn it with your mouth. If that doesn't work, condemn it in your heart.

Our religions have all come out of the same cooking pot, and they are able to maintain their differences, yet to cooperate on the things that really matter. Human beings all over the earth have sought for the face of God. They have searched for greater knowledge of themselves, their environment, and the purpose of this creation. As we come from the same creative hand and have similar genetic make-up, we would expect that our religious constructions would have a lot in common. This turns out to be so. There are overlapping relationships among our varying ethical beliefs. The major religions do agree on seven items of importance–

1-They believe in the reality of the divine.
2-This reality is able to be contained in the human.
3-This reality is for the human, the highest good.
4-This reality is love, revealing itself to the human and in the human.
5-The way of the human to God is the way of sacrifice.
6-Religions teach the way to God, but also the way to neighbor.
7-Love is the most superior way to God.[3]

The descriptions of God that exist in the world today have helped humanity through many situations and are still suitable for us, the living. If we observe the wisdom imparted to us through these God-ideas, we can help to rid the world of armaments and will be able to dwell in peace with one another. We should reassess the relationships that we would like existing between people and God and between people and people, so that we can have a viable earth. We do not want relationships that will simply deteriorate into an arms race, where we stockpile weapons to destroy one another, always fearing whatever group is slightly different from us. As fear multiplies, and we have killed off everyone but the last two persons on earth, will one of them then feel compelled to kill the other? This scenario does not have to come to pass. The love we generate should be able to overcome the fears we harbor.

Utopia Is Not Realistic. The vision of the world's future as set down in the holy scriptures of all faiths requires reassessment in each age. This particular age is complicated with ethical problems such as abortion, sex, and gender, with medical technologies and diseases such as AIDS, with armaments that can destroy the earth, with gains in psychology and psychiatry that should help us to be more open to prisoners and the mentally ill, and with communication technologies that make available new forms of governance.

Muslims, Christians, Jews, Hindus, and Buddhists all emphasize that we must be responsible for our own salvation and the salvation of others. The mission of all faiths is to help the world to live fully. This can only be accomplished through education of the uninformed and support of the weak. Each of us has a part to play. Each of us must try to make the peaceable kingdom visible.

Utopia is a state that is not likely to occur, but *working towards* Utopia is a good direction in which to move. Peace is not a final achievement; it is an action that continues. In Utopia, there would be no need for weapons. In our approach to Utopia, we should attempt to get rid of most of the world's weaponry. Weapons can be used to serve both good and evil. A knife can be used to cut food for the hungry, or to plunge into the heart of a human being. We must bless all the tools whose misuse can be debilitating. We must all pray that we do not use our tools for evil ends. Let the weapons which we depend on, be the spiritual weapons mentioned in Ephesians 6:14-17, such as the sword of the spirit and the breastplate of righteousness. Let us cut through murky situations with understanding and clearness of vision. Let us guide others with kindness rather than force.

We should understand why we do battle with each other. Two rats can be standing peaceably on an electric grid. When the grid heats up, they will attack each other. This is due to the instinct to protect themselves, just in case the other rat is causing the problem. When will we learn that the other is not the problem, and choose cooperation rather than snarling? When we are in a difficult situation, we have minds that can analyze and discover the source of our fear.

Some animals are more peaceful than others. Male rhesus monkeys do little else than fight, reproduce, and die. Gorillas have a family structure that is more caring. Our species has come as far as it has, because we often form groups that care for one another. Our species has grown because the powerful have often chosen to care for and protect the weak. Our species has developed because it often loves. If love is the reason we have come as far as we have on the evolutionary path, it seems reasonable that we should continue in this manner.

Seeking The Utopian Community. Where will the path of love lead us? What new evolutionary heights await us? We can no more see our future than the lowly lemur could envision and create Chartres Cathedral or a TV set. Even in this era of mass warfare and refugees, we see possibilities of healing through the laying on of loving hands. We see tortured souls find a place of peace when another listens with concern and understanding. Early religions recognized that the spirits of the dead that were loved come back in dreams to warn of danger and to direct. What kind of quantity are our spirits, and what capabilities do they have? When we unite in the thinking and doing of positive projects, we humans are more fulfilled, than when we slink around with guns, fearful of each other.

In a Utopia, all groups and institutions would perform smoothly together to accomplish goals. In real life, people must strive very hard to work cooperatively. With any agenda there are so many variations possible, and so many positions asserted, that it is often difficult to see any areas of agreement. We cannot just join hands, sing songs, and say we are at peace. We must all listen to each other so that we can understand each other, and then agree to accept each other's differences. Understanding the other helps to lessen our fears about the intentions of the other.

In their inner government, groups and institutions striving for Utopia would not exercise patriarchal authority, but would listen to their members. There would not be fallible leaders ordering bombings of innocent people, but the people who are being governed would decide whether or not to use mediation and conciliation, or to let loose raw power. With improved voting procedures and communication, more reasonable and prompt decisions could be made. It seems that most leaders really don't like the responsibility of killing people out of social custom. The American Civil War general, Ulysses Grant, actually wept when many in his army were killed, but he conformed to social pressure and led his remaining men off to another battle.

If a community were working towards Utopia, there would be less racial and sexual prejudice. Women and minorities would have their input listened to. This does not happen as a matter of course, in real life. Individuals have to put forth effort to listen and understand the *other*, the one who is expressing a contrary or unique viewpoint. Women and minorities, too, must learn to listen. All people have the same obligations to make a more perfect world order. Minorities can sympathize with the oppressed at home or abroad. Women, as mothers, often have more empathy for those mothers in other countries whose children are being starved or bombed. Most churches and governments fail to see the necessity for the female viewpoint in organizational decisions. But God made us male and female and expects us to use both male and female aspects of humanity to solve the problems that beset humanity. In times of hope and stress when we need the spirit of love and understanding, this spirit is poured out on us, enabling all of us, men and women, to shoulder the burdens and aid in solutions.

Shared Authority. The idea of shared authority, rather than a strict and absolute hierarchy of authority, has developed slowly over the centuries. It is still a difficult lesson for many. Some, for example, interpret the Bible (I Corinthians 11:10-16) as limiting the roles that women should play in church matters. However, one has to understand the culture of the times, and look for the underlying message rather than the tactic that was appropriate for those times. In Greek and Roman culture, for example, covering the head was a clear sign of humility. It was used by the high priest and by the emperor when they performed religious rites. Today many men and women no longer use that tactic, but the quality of humility, even for one in authority, is a characteristic that should be encouraged. Hence in our time, the Bible cautions us that women and men must have the proper humility before God when they teach in church. Women and men should carefully consider their teachings and actions as fallible mediators of God's message. A few priests recently have by their example emphasized to us that we should *not* listen to their teaching. We must not follow anyone blindly. We will know the good tree by its fruit (Matthew 7:16). Men and women who speak in church or elsewhere should make themselves open to God's spirit, and facilitate group discussions that encourage positive actions. Women and men should not teach with an authority that suppresses and restricts individual freedom, but should teach in a nurturing way, correcting others and their children in love, giving these others reasonable freedom, and instructing them as to proper choices. Men and women should use all their talents, take initiatives, and speak up against injustices. It is not right for the people of God to be passive, inactive, and dependent on a few leaders for handouts of grace. All must be *actively* compassionate, empathetic, caring, and kind, at every opportunity. It is a waste of our spiritual potential to appoint a few select men or women to be chief club members in a church, and to have them ration out the gifts of the holy spirit and the sacraments, and lead services as if they were the only ones able to do anything spiritual. We are all fallible, but we all have the potential for holiness. We are, to some degree, potential prophets, priests, and leaders. We must fully participate in the administration of our church sacraments to one another. We must help each other to overcome fears and faults. Groups such as Alcoholics Anonymous and Gamblers Anonymous are examples of such support. Where an authoritative priest or pastor may be unable, a supportive community may be able to assist the individual towards victory.

Sin. Every culture attempts to set guidelines for the good of the community. This can be done in a supportive or a suppressive manner. The churches, for example, often talk of *sin* and make it something we should fear. They speak of *original* sin, *venial* sin, and *mortal* sin. Supposedly, we come into the world burdened with original sin, or inclined to do evil. Some individuals, such as Jesus' mother, Mary, are believed to be conceived without sin. I believe we are all conceived without sin, that we come into the world with the genes that God has given us. These carry our inheritance of our evolutionary past. We are not yet completely developed spiritually. We have some inherent fears, some selfishness, some unnecessary defensiveness. But despite these limitations, I believe we are born without guilt. The Bible does not say that a little baby is born full of guilt. What could make us out of favor with a loving creative God? We enter upon the world scene as God's good creation. The phrase, *we are all conceived in sin,* means we are born, still not fully developed as spiritual beings, into a potentially corrupt situation, *not* that we come with a depraved soul. Jesus saw all peoples as in God's favor. God made us all and is pleased to fill each human heart.

Venial sin is a lesser misdeed. *Mortal* sin is a very serious commission, done with full consent of the will. *Sin* is such a negative word. It makes us think of poor choices and a lack of will power. Yet God has given us this marvelous opportunity to choose! We can choose our own good ahead of the good of others or vice versa. We can decide to feed ourselves before we feed the starving, or the other way around. We can choose to believe only our own opinions rather than to listen to those of others, or we can carefully weigh the opinion of others and then decide our best course. We can maintain power structures that benefit only us, or we can use our power to empower others.

All power is not evil; power can be used for good. Self-benefit is not necessarily sin. If we don't take care of ourselves, we won't be healthy enough to take care of others. The basic sin has something to do with using power at the expense of others. Selfishness, a false presumption of creeping infallibility, phoney self-esteem, and finger pointing are all choices that enhance ourselves and destroy others. We are to take care of both ourselves and others. We are not to make others suffer what we do not want to undergo ourselves.

War. Over the centuries, there have often been predatory groups that prey upon others. There is often the presumption that nation states should protect their populations by means of war. However, war can easily become a confrontation between the creature and the creator. The Creator creates and envisions; the warring creature destroys and often fails to pursue visions of good. Those who grab for power think that it is for their personal good, or for the good of a nation, but in their deprivation of others, to gain power, they really hurt themselves and those they love. They upset the balance of justice in the world. This distressing result happens because God did not intend his free creatures to exercise absolute power over each other. When God made the world, he did not give day power over night, or men power over women, but each has its place and is needed in the scheme of things.

Psychologists tell us that those who participate in war find something attractive about it. There is exhilaration from the challenge of combat and a deep satisfaction in bonding with one's fellow in order to overcome the imagined oppressor. These enticements can overshadow and inhibit any appreciation of good in the opponent. We must realize that the oppressor, as well as the comrade, is an image of God and worthy of respect. Those who are caught up in war are often psychologically disturbed as a consequence.

We need to overcome our tendencies to war with visions of peace. We should put in place a methodology and a theology of peace. We need to find the deep satisfaction of bonding with others in productive pursuits. We need to teach mediation, problem solving, and forgiveness in our schools. We should make our schools and prisons into academies of peace. By analyzing our insecurities and fears and our fascination with guns as ''protection,'' we could make wars and prisons less necessary. We should refuse to implement the evil of war as readily and thoughtlessly as we have done in the past.

Law. We find the codification of positive ethical principles on Egyptian temple walls, on the stelae of Mesopotamia, in the laws of Moses, and in the laws of every civilization to the present day. However, there often develops a class of law-breakers. Why is that? Visions of peace cannot take proper shape as long as laws give preferential treatment to the greedy and selfish. If laws unfairly enable some of us to ride around in gold-plated cadillacs while others sleep under overpasses, there will be no true peace. Jeremiah states that there is no true peace when there is injustice to the weak. There is no true peace when governments put their trust primarily in weapons and in alliances among the strong. We are to let go of our overly oppressive power structures and to trust God. We must have just laws that protect the weak and lead in the positive direction of justice for all.

All laws are not just laws. Many favor special interests at the expense of others. We have multiplied laws upon laws so that no one can possibly remember them or understand them. Many are too complicated for the general population. Lawyers can find loopholes, so that one day they can prove one thing, and the next day, the opposite.

The Nuremberg trials established the fact that sometimes we are morally obliged to break the law. Before condemning a group as law-breakers, we must try to understand why they felt the need to break the law. Those who are governed by laws should have a part in the construction of those laws. It is often better to encourage people to positive actions rather than labeling them as sinners and criminals and demanding that they repent. We are not called so much to wallowing in repentance, as to the positive attitudes of forgiveness, mercy, justice, and love, with corresponding actions that benefit ourselves and others.

People are often taught to obey the law because of hope for a reward—for both temporary peace and for pie in the sky when they die. This is a bit selfish, and may have nothing to do with loving other people, but only with feeling superior to other people and making life easier for oneself. When we want what is good for all people, then we will have a peaceful world (and perhaps have less need for laws). Forgiveness is our desire for another to have peace and pie in the sky. When we wish for all around us to be in heaven with us, we are forgiving whatever they have done to us, and welcoming them into our hearts forever– and into God's heart forever. All humanity can work for respect and dignity. Each human being can work to disarm his own heart.

11.2 Some Problems, Some Solutions

There are serious problems with the societies we have formed over the centuries. Our societal actions endanger the environment of our mother, the earth, and they hamper our becoming the loving community envisioned by religious groups. We all must search for alternatives that may help.

A Throw-away Generation. The first problem is that we do not share fairly the goods of the earth. Everything from education and technology to health services and material goods are poorly distributed. One section of the world has too much, and another section starves. A relatively few people consume disproportionately, to the point of jeopardizing the ecological balance of the earth. This over-use of materials by some could conceivably result in the melting of the polar ice, the raising of the level of the ocean, and the destruction of many people as in the biblical flood. On top of that, we throw away a high percentage of what we have.

We waste water which is increasingly scarce as populations grow. Our ancestors were quite right to honor the power of whatever produced the pure waters. Water is necessary to our life. Ezekiel (47:1-12) sees a vision of a river of pure water, though also some salt marshes. We need to focus the world's creativity on finding solutions to water problems. Desalinization has not yet been economical, but technology for this continues to improve. We urgently need success in this area, to filter out pure, drinkable water. Another challenging area is further development of salt water fisheries. For example, is it possible that we could utilize salt marshes and salt lagoons along the Red Sea as salt water fisheries in the desert? The Qattara Depression in Western Egypt is 400 feet below sea level. It once was an inland sea. Could we make it one again? Could we perhaps run sea water into it and make salt water fisheries? In California pure water is acquired from the northern part of the state and from the Colorado River, but California is beside an ocean of water! Why not desalinization plants and salt water fish hatcheries? There also should be a way to use less potable water in our ''sanitary'' facilities such as showers and toilets.

We waste energy. At least partial solutions to the energy problem are all about us. With some further advances in technology, we can use more sun and wind power which are in harmony with nature. We can find less polluting means of transportation than the automobile.

Ingratitude for The Gift of Sex. Many past civilizations, in India, the Middle East, Africa, and Europe, have seen the need to regulate human sexuality. Even today, in the Middle East, we still see women completely covered from head to toe in a voluminous black garment. The primary objective of this robe seems to be the protection of women from male predators. This avoidance of an excessive male preoccupation with sex should free the mind for concentration on less selfish matters. Unfortunately, such regulations also lead to the seclusion of women, their treatment as property, and their deprivation of full participation in the affairs of modern society.

Today, in the United States, with our sexual revolution, the pendulum has swung in the opposite direction. The problem is that we use this marvelous gift of sex primarily for self-gratification. We debase and use another solely for our own pleasurable sensations, and then feel we have the right to kill the life that may be produced from this conscious choice. Even when there is no offspring produced as when men indulge in sex with men (or women with women), the element of selfishness may dominate.

How can we turn this gift of God back to its original purpose of the reinforcement of bonding love and/or the production of loving family and community? Sex would be more fulfilling as a celebration of a spiritual union between two dedicated persons. In our use of sex, we must be conscious of the wonderfulness of each other as full persons and as fabulous gifts of God. Our ancestors invented marriage for this reason, and this method has worked pretty well down the millennia. Young people should be taught that sex should not be used in infantile experimentation, as this causes mental upset, the possible destruction of a baby, or the possible production of an unwanted child and thus a throw-away adult. In the example of same sex activity, the young person is often simply allowing the unbridling of his/her emotions and his/her physical urges. For the good of the whole world, every person should make every act of sex a holy act, dedicated to God, and keep himself/herself under control.

A child is bound to have a case of low self-esteem if he believes that he arrived on earth unplanned and unwanted, as a result of his parents experimenting with their sex organs. Every child has the right to be wanted. Every child also has the right to a good education. Education programs work best if there is a supporting family in the background.

Homosexual couples can further positive growth in the world community if they include others who need love in their family. When we see celibate males forming loving brotherhoods to care for the poor, such as in the communities initiated by St. Francis of Assisi, we believe that the purposes of a loving, well-run earth are being fostered. The earth is wronged when we allow our physical feelings to be the master of a situation, and disregard the physical and emotional needs of another person or group.

Child Care. Every civilization has recognized that the care of its children determines its future. Today we seem to be forgetting this fact and are willing to neglect children of the poor all over the world, and even in our own country. As a result of uncontrolled sexual impulses, a major problem which faces our society is paedogenesis, reproduction while in the immature stage. Many children are active sexually, and produce offspring when they are too young to care for them. Children brought up by an immature parent are bound to be raised with serious omissions. Our problems with school drop-outs, youth gangs, drugs, and crime are evidence of the breakdown in family structures. We must do more to avoid child pregnancy so that all children can be raised by two mature parents.

Training for parenting is one approach. Women in prison in New York State are allowed to keep their infants with them for the first year of the child's life. While caring for their children, these women are given relevant instruction in parenting. All men and women in prison and all teen parents would profit from courses in parenting and family relationships. The breakup of families should be avoided by using alternatives to incarceration. In order to keep families intact, more thought should be given to electronic surveillance and home sentencing.

In the inner cities, often the grandparents are forced into the role of parents. Grandmothers take to this caretaking easily, and grandfathers admit to getting satisfaction from this nurturing of the young. Could an increase in the size of a social security check be an inducement for more of the elderly to care for excess children? Or would this increase the irresponsibility of the young parents? Could single parents care for other peoples children along with their own by receiving monthly checks for being foster parents? Could men in prison and on the street be required to take a parenting course to care for the children they have fathered? Could we enact stronger laws that would require every man who gets a woman pregnant to personally care for that child?

Some of these cast away children are ignored because of poverty conditions. Parents simply have no time for their children in their struggle to survive. However, children in well-to-do families are also not given proper attention. When both parents are working, they may feel that they are sacrificing themselves so that the child can have a good home, but they do not supply the companionship and direction that makes a family work. They may support this maturing individual financially all the way through college, when the child has become capable of making her own living. This can sometimes be a way of exercising control over another and attempting to re-create our selves in our offspring, without taking the time to find out what they personally want out of life. In pushing our children to be what we want them to be, we often inhibit their freedom.

Education and Counseling. Education of the young has always been practiced– first in the home and then with the aid of schools of many sorts. At one time we in the United States thought we had a first class education system, the best in the world. Now we know our education systems are very inadequate and below those abroad. Can part of the problem be that we fill the minds of our children with video cartoons, so that there is no room for more substantial material?

In the bringing up of children, the male child has always been encouraged to be competitive, to make up rules for games, and to prize gain over relationships. He has been taught to fight and not to cry, and to feel superior to those over whom he triumphs. The female child has been allowed to cry, to be more interested in feelings and relationships, and to comfort those who lose the game.

One might say that women, as the group that has been trained to be more interested in preserving relationships, should work on the molding of loving relationships through moral education and the loving upbringing of children, while men as the group that has been trained to organize rules for games, should fashion loving structures to guide humanity. Perhaps this process would work better if both men and women worked in both roles– if more women became fashioners of positive social structures, and if more men took part in loving and nurturing those temporarily or permanently less capable. As we look around the world, we see a tendency for this to happen. Perhaps our natural urges instilled in both men and women by a kind Creator are guiding us towards the ultimate goal of a kind and just society where nurturing those in need is more prevalent.

Empathetic counseling is a universal need. Those who aim weapons of destruction at school children, like the maniac in the Texas schoolyard, may be crazy, but they are not stupid. If we had a grievance committee or ombudsman or just one understanding and compassionate friend, available to every citizen, we might be able to stop the terrible violence dwelling in a troubled heart before it happened.

Settling Disputes. Denunciation and punishment are not healing. It is possible to improve our court system, which in many places only breeds further hatred and violence, by greater use of mediation, alternatives to incarceration, victim restitution, and counseling. Some of our police may be assaultive in their enforcement. Educate them in techniques of community cooperation and non-violence. Our prisons contain a high percentage of those who are poor and illiterate. Why do we suffer these abominations when we have solutions, such as mediation, psychological counseling, and remedial education near at hand? Often it seems that we have stepped back into barbarism, or is it only our leaders and the powerful who have failed to comprehend the need?

We have many alternatives for the settling of both local and worldwide disturbances. Differences can often be settled by arbitration, mediation, and conciliation. Wounds can be healed. Surprisingly, wrongs can be forgiven, though sometimes much time is needed, and ordered boundaries and distances must be kept, when people have been grievously harmed.

True peace cannot effectively be built with new policies and guarantees alone. True peace also requires the building of trust between peoples, even when history divides them. Steps are needed now to encourage greater dialogue and to build confidence between diverse peoples. Greater dialogue among peoples is often *not* the result when leaders of those peoples consult together. Fortunately, there is a certain resistance of people to admit that all wisdom resides in leadership.

We are disgusted when we hear how ancient peoples sacrificed their sons to the gods for the future good of the community, yet are still willing to see children and others in distant countries sacrificed in heartless conflicts. We must recognize that in today's world, injustice anywhere can ultimately affect all of us. We must also pay more attention to the children of our own communities, so that they will grow into fulfilled adults and become good parents to their sons and daughters. We must aid the suffering, wherever they are, or their children may seek justice violently and may even terrorize and bomb our cities.

Old and New Prison Systems. Over the centuries, various means have been tried, in different cultures, to cope with those who chose to violate the laws of the community. Summary executions, chopping off of hands or feet, scourgings, dunkings, and all forms of physical and mental torture have been tried. Many of these methods can still be found. Even today, few countries in the world have an effective way of treating those who do not conform to the ideals of their society. Our own prison system in the United States, does not heal. It destroys community and encourages recidivism. It doesn't have to be that way.

In this country we have come to recognize alcoholism as a disease. We advise persons who are afflicted with this disease to seek counseling and therapeutic help, and to attend support groups. We also are beginning to see all drug abuse as a disease. In some cases, we should seek cures for those who have succumbed to this disease, rather than further debilitating them by giving them fifteen years in prison. When we consider the severity of the Rockefeller Drug Laws implemented in New York State to curb drug use, and their failure to cure the situation, we see that it is necessary for the good of society to find another solution. Not only have these laws failed to stop the tide of drug abuse, guns, and violence, but they have needlessly destroyed lives, broken families apart, and deprived children of two supportive parents. Counseling, shorter sentences for first offenders, and home arrest would be measures that could more often be taken to correct, habilitate, and keep families together.

Many of those convicted of drug crimes, in their desire to get out of prison and lead a normal life with their families, fill folders full of program certificates, clemency petitions, and other items to impress their parole boards. Having other fallible human beings, such as governors and parole board personnel decide, based on extremely sketchy information, whether an incarcerated human will be a responsible citizen, does not lead to making that individual a responsible citizen, but makes him into a conniver and con-artist. Each incarcerated person should be enabled to plan for her own habilitation, and then to have a competent evaluation based on full information.

One recent estimate of those incarcerated for drug and alcohol related crimes was as high as 80% of the prison population. Drug abuse is not the only health problem of the prison population. Spouse abuse is another sickness caused in part by low self esteem. This disease takes two people— one who is ready to abuse and one who is willing to accept abuse. Another problem that is very difficult to treat and that incarceration does not seem to cure, is sex abuse. A majority of the incarcerated would profit from effective health and community support programs. Confinement in the prison environment does not improve either their ability to cope or their self-esteem.

It is possible for a loving and understanding community to exist in the prisons of tomorrow. Such a prison-related community would envision and enact the future good of its members, and make their present state of incarceration meaningful. Meaningful incarceration does not take more taxpayers' money; it does require careful planning by both the administration and those incarcerated. The members of the inmate community would be encouraged to think creatively and to help themselves. For example, they could work cooperatively with the administration to plan activities such as a medical jobs program, recognizing that there is a need for medical help in the hospitals both in prison and out. Educational programs would be geared to the needs of these jobs. The purpose of this project would be to improve the personal world of the inmate, and also the greater world of which he should be a responsible member. This inmate initiative would be supported and implemented by the personnel of the habilitation system.

Further prison inmate community activity might include an interfaith group to reduce racial and religious intolerance. There could be interfaith prayer and dialogue, with the purpose of encouraging kindness and personal growth in the prison population. Inmates could further AIDS education and drug abuse education to ease fears and increase acceptance of responsibility among inmates. For this purpose, they could produce informational booklets in two or more languages on health problems. Inmates could investigate and update the education program in their prison and acquire an understanding of the training and education needed for future jobs. They could volunteer time in the prison hospital unit. Correctional facilities would have much greater freedom and responsibility to experiment with different methods of habilitation and alternatives to incarceration, to decide which is the most helpful for those with drug and behavior problems.

Communities of Refuge as A Solution. Such communities have been tried before as a solution to the problems of a class of people who have been oppressed. They are described in the Bible in Numbers 35:15– *These towns will be a refuge for the people of the land as well as for the foreigner and the immigrant.* England used the inspiration of communities of refuge when it sent those in prison for non-payment of debts to their colony of Georgia and to the continent of Australia. The Bible instructs us in Nehemiah 10:31 to fore-go *all* debts in the seventh year. More recent examples of communities of refuge are the Kubutz communities in Israel and the base communities of very poor in South America. Another current example is the practice of the Grameen Bank in Bangladesh, where loans for small business are made to a group of poor people who are jointly responsible for the success of each individual entrepreneur. These relatively small communities are characterized by a pervasive spirit of mutual support. They are healing and rebuilding of persons as well as a renewing influence for the physical aspects of the community. Can such community building become a planned process for the benefit of the homeless, the "permanent" underclass, the refugees from oppression, and the incarcerated who are no longer a threat to society? In a sense, these are all refugees. What should characterize such communities of refuge? How could they possibly be created? To begin with, communities of refuge would help persons with problems to take responsibility for their own lives and to work with professionals on the cure of their own illnesses. They would also help with the health and well-being of the families of the inhabitants and the family members left behind elsewhere.

In some cases, these communities of refuge would be dispersed among the general population. In other cases, they might be physically separate. For example, the government of the United States is attempting to reduce its military budget, and some military bases are being shut down. The Nevada Weapons Proving Ground and the missile site near Tucson, Arizona, are big empty spaces that should not be wasted and made uninhabitable by the testing of weapons that destroy. The McKinney Act mandates that unused federal buildings be offered to the homeless. We should use the land that God has given to this country to support life, not to destroy life. It should be possible to make many communities of refuge in the area of the Nevada Proving Ground, thus turning territory formerly dedicated to violence into a place dedicated to peace. We would be turning swords into plowshares.

Every state should be able to make available some space and/or habilitation services for the refugees and their families to live responsibly, with adequate supervision and counseling. Those refugees from foreign countries held in refugee camps could be given the choice to join in, or to return to a similar setup by their own government in their own homeland. Economically, these communities should aim to become self supporting and should not have to be the recipients of long-term government funding. Each community of refuge would be shaped to meet the unique needs of its inhabitants. Some possibilities are as follows:

• Housing could be supplied by teams of refugees with the support of non-governmental organizations.

• The education of children and the continuing education of adults would be one of the major industries. Children could be educated and given day care by those available in the population. School buildings would be house-size, and could house one age group. Those adults with counseling and psychology degrees would be available for instructing the adult population. Educational television programs and video tapes could be used to make optimum use of professional educators.

• Preventive health care measures could also be the object of the education system and would include dietetic information, AIDS and sex cautions, and parenting courses. Every adult and child living in a community of refuge could participate in a revolving Buddy System, so that the frame of mind of every individual would have a chance to be aired. Support groups could exist, such as Alcoholics Anonymous.

• Basic, preventive health care would not ordinarily necessitate expensive doctors, but would be more like a visiting nurse group which would practice both natural and chemical medicine. In case of emergency, individuals could be sent to outside hospitals, as is done from within prison walls today.

• Community togetherness with shared responsibility and shared resources would be encouraged. Considering the religious aspect, there would be one church building or community hall put up by the community and shared by the community, as military and prison chapels are shared. There would also be one or more sports centers, art centers, and library resource centers to be shared.

• There would be one government center in each community. Groups could experiment with different forms of governance. One group might try government using a consensus form of town meeting. Another group could experiment with the California system of voter initiatives. This system could replace *representative* democracy with *referendum* democracy. Legislators elected under such a system tend to be more responsive. It is also becoming questionable as to whether legislators as we know them today, are truly necessary when votes can be counted so quickly. When legislators listen to moneyed lobbyists instead of people, they are not truly concerned with the public good. They are not representing the people, but increasing their own material gain and power base. ''What we have in capitalist societies is an oligarchy of wealth that controls the levers of electoral politics and the media, hidden under a facade of 'openness' and participation.''⁴

• Government in a community of refuge would be by the men and women of the community. The servants of the community (as the local police would be called) would be selected by the men and women of the community. There would be no drugs or guns admitted into such a community. The police would not carry guns. There would be buses for mass transportation. There would be less need for the private automobile. Bicycles would be more widely used.

• Engineering support and some adult education could be supplied by army personnel. For instance, the U.S. Army Corps of Engineers could build water supply and sanitation systems. They could creatively consider new possibilities, such as building pipe lines to arid areas. Is it, for example, possible to carry flood waters of the Mississippi to fill a depression in the Nevada desert? The army could give courses in agriculture and construction.

This would have the advantage of keeping soldiers usefully busy in their own country, so that they would be available and trained to serve populations in case of emergency abroad.

• Eligible inmates could be given a choice of whether to remain in the present prison system or to join a community of refuge. Inmates would have to stay in the area of their choice until their sentence had been served. If they wished to continue living in the community of refuge, they would be allowed to do so.

11.3 The Theology of Weaponry

Another problem this world has is the problem of weapons of destruction. Over the years, weapons have become not only more lethal, but also more responsive to the slightest impulse or emotion. We would be a wiser world if we rid ourselves of excessive weapons and relied more on spiritual strengths.

Admittedly, people have been killing each other since history began, even before guns were invented. We have the example of Cain and Abel, and why did Cain kill? He had a lack of self esteem. He thought God liked Abel better than God liked Cain. What did Cain do about his inner doubts? Did he retreat into himself, and consult his better self? Did he listen to his conscience? He couldn't consult his religious counselor. Did he talk to his parents? Perhaps there was no one for him to talk to about his frustrations. Being a strong young man full of charging hormones he used simple force to get rid of his supposed enemy.

Today you don't have to be strong to kill people. Any weak illogical person who has no one with whom he can talk out his problems, can buy a gun, shoot it, and destroy life with hardly a second thought. The National Rifle Association chortles, ''Guns don't kill people, people kill people.'' This statement is misleading, as it has taken both guns and people for us to fall into the social morass where we are today.

Some believe we have a right in this country to bear weapons, but it is easy to show the ridiculousness of the full extent of this notion. Do all citizens have the right to have a nuclear arsenal in their back yard with which to destroy their neighbor? We are beginning to believe that not even nations possess this right. Do we have the right to possess land mines which we can toss into our neighbor's yard, if he lets his dog howl too long and loudly? Can we mine our neighbor's garden? If we feel it is wrong to mine our neighbor's garden, why do countries feel justified in sending soldiers into foreign lands, and lacing the soil with land mines which destroy the innocent dwellers in the land for decades afterwards?

Can we assume it is permissible to possess all the weapons you can afford, that do not take away the economic livelihood or the rights of others? This was the assumption of the religious group in Waco, Texas, which stockpiled an arsenal. It seems that if guns are handy, they get to be used. The purchase of a gun may be a sign that I feel oppressed by others, and that I feel my rights are threatened. A gun may be an indication that I have serious inner fears. Where there are serious inner fears, violence often follows. Our imaginations play upon our fears and bring them to fruition. If I have harmed someone and expect him to retaliate, I may be in need of counseling and mediation. Talking it out with a friend or counselor is one way of lessening the tenseness of a situation. As we are all human beings like Cain in that we have moments of low self-esteem and uncontrollable anger, it can be truly dangerous for any of us to possess a gun.

The same thought applies to countries and their leaders. No country which is under the influence of human political leaders subject to greed and power plays, should use weapons until it has submitted to an international council or mediation. Progress has been shown in recognizing the dangers of available weapons. In some countries such as Japan, China, or Great Britain, it is illegal for the ordinary citizen to buy or possess a gun. Our world is going through soul searching as to the rights of military governments to have "death squads." We are approaching the point where problems can be solved by understanding rather than by use of force.

Our rights end where our actions trample on the rights of others. Others have the right to a gun free environment. We must use balance when we interpret the Bill of Rights. Those who make profits on gun sales must think of the oppressed when selling weapons to oppressors, or they are implicated in the murder of the oppressed.

11.4 Mediation

A community directed towards Utopia would make use of the tools of the mediator to insure its future. The art of mediation has been around a long time. It has been a necessary piece of equipment for the survival of the human race. With world situations exploding all over the globe, it may be humankind's most successful tool for transforming the world.

Many governments seem to be unable to care for the needs of their minorities. The wealthy often refuse to share their *surplus* with those who have nothing. When God has given the earth to all, it seems strange that those with money and power feel that the earth rightfully belongs to them. In some economic situations, such as labor/management negotiations, mediation may be the best way to explain the needs of both parties.

Can mediation be used effectively in situations where the poor are expressing discontent? Usually they attempt to do this non-violently, but often we find justified violence in their actions. The poor are erupting all over the globe demanding life instead of death, food instead of exploitation, education instead of rule by force. If instead of an armed response to a discontented minority, there were an impartial mediation council available, problem solving would be expedited, and chances for armed confrontation would be lessened.

World peace will certainly come when there is more willingness to have open discussions among nations and among individuals. Whenever ideas are aired, and people listen to each other, those people come closer to understanding and peaceful settlements. The mediator serves to clarify and prioritize issues and to encourage proposals for win/win solutions. Every situation may not be successful, but no mediation is totally fruitless.

There are knowledgeable people available who are willing to help out in local mediation situations, and who are eager to resolve world tensions. The United Nations has demonstrated that it can aid in settling world disputes if given a chance. If we want a successful world guidance organization, we should take advantage of the resources to be found in that body. The future of our earth may depend on the role that the United Nations can play in assisting people and nations to listen to each other, and thereby help in solving their problems.

Mediation: Pitfalls to Avoid. Going with a pre-conceived plan to a mediation usually insures defeat; it gives a signal that I may not be listening to anyone, and that I may have exaggerated ideas of my own abilities and sagacity. Such a signal puts a psychological block before anyone I am attempting to help. Any would-be mediator might possibly take pointers from the Afghan situation in which Diego Cordovez, the U.N. Under Secretary for Special Political Affairs, consulted with all parties concerned before coming up with a tentative proposal involving the exodus of the Russian forces. He approached all those with major interests in the confrontation, as a disinterested party or an "empty vessel." After absorbing all views, he was able to see areas of agreement and areas where there was room for give and take, that would make an acceptable or win-win situation for all concerned. It was apparent that both sides were anxious to put an end to the slaughter. Similarly, Johann Holst of Norway was successful in bringing Israel and the Palestinians to the historic Arafat/Rabin agreement.

Mediation between countries is not so very different from mediation between individuals. After all, it is frequently the policies of a few leaders at the top that have caused the problems between nations, and it is a few top brass who will decide to accept or reject peace proposals. A majority of the ordinary citizens of feuding countries would usually choose to end conflicts and stop bloodshed if the choice were given to them.

Facing reality, it is really impossible to bring all citizens to a mediation table. Many know the issues only from hearsay and are not as knowledgeable on the problems as the so-called experts. Often controversial issues are obscure and must be embroidered upon, in order to rouse citizens to a fighting pitch. Witness the average American citizen's acceptance of their previous President's antipathy for the "evil empire," and their present willingness to believe that Russia is now trustworthy. In the recent Russian-Afghan situation some of the rebellious commoners reportedly thought that the enemy they were fighting was the British. Considering the easy manipulation of the masses, it seems to be necessary to deal with the individuals who are the prime manipulators, in a mediation situation. All of this puts great emphasis on the importance of a well-informed public, with a diverse free press, and great care in the selection of leaders.

11.5 Evolution in Process

God is more constant than the sun, wider than our solar system. We have God on our side. From the point where we are in God's process of earth-creating and human-creating, we may look around and wonder, "Are we going to make it? Is this creation going to be a viable entity?" When we look back at from where we have come, we must admit that evolution takes a long time. Just think of the millions of years it has taken, so that you and I might enjoy the full moon rising in October! After innumerable years, we are at the point in this evolution where we creatures can communicate our concern for one another, and where each has possibilities of communicating with God.

If we want to talk about a successful moment, an October moonrise is a notable achievement. If each human could fully appreciate and enjoy such a moon rise, we might agree that this world is a tremendous success. It seems that God's success is measured in the framework of each individual heart. Will the process be completed? Will all our varying hearts be gathered together in joy?

God has spent so much time on us already. She has great patience and is surely ready to give this earth process all the time it needs. A good evolution takes time. We can look at this long time of evolutionary formation as a measure for God's kindness. When we use our time in this careful and creative manner, we call it patience. Patience is the power of endurance. Our individual time is short compared to God's time, but we can imitate God and use our time in patience and kindness to others. We have the power to communicate our love to others. With our present day methods of communication, we should be able to eliminate the need for war. With our knowledge of the pangs of starvation, we should be able to set in motion all that is needed to save lives and energize people. An unbiased world government should be able to mediate disputes between disagreeing factions. Our TV screens should be able to educate us to the point where Knowledge Increases Mercy, and we become a merciful people.

Let's have mediation courts instead of law courts, *servants of the people* instead of police, soldiers who are sent on peaceful missions to the distressed, and religious specialists who exemplify the message of love. Mediations for peaceful settlements should be done, but not by a power group going in with preconceived ideas of the results desired. In mediations, both sides should have someone on their team who has had contact with those who were suffering. It does not make sense to have all the representatives at the bargaining table, be those who direct soldiers from inside sterile offices.

Our governments are slowly evolving to be more responsive to the needs of people. A complex system of national government, state government, county government, and town government helps to insure that grass roots problems will be addressed. Local grassroots community groups often know what is best for their areas. If there are any corporations acting in a grassroots area, they should be influenced to feed and employ the local people for those people's advantage, not to exploit them solely for the benefit of wealthy investors. Decisions about people's well being should be made at the lowest possible levels. Government should be in place, not to rule from above, but to implement these lowly decisions. Responsible grassroots individuals, with a clear vision of the future, should be given free rein to form that future.

The Poor. In our approach toward Utopian living, we must deal with the poor in creative ways. It may not be possible to eradicate poverty, but we should find ways to minimize it. Pope John Paul's *Encyclical on Social Concerns* states that the earth is made for all. Thomas Aquinas emphasized that the very poor person has the right to supply himself from the surplus riches of others, that when in desperate need, it is no sin to take a life-sustaining part of another's property. How far can we carry this belief of St. Thomas? In New York City, the poor need apartments. There are many apartments that are empty because investors hope to make a profit on them. We would probably agree that it is scandalous that so many people in city areas, especially women and children, have no homes. Our welfare hotels are full. City governments seem paralyzed and unable to construct affordable housing. Do the homeless have a right to those excess apartments of the well-to-do?

Having been educated in a capitalist society, most of us would answer that the apartment owner has worked by the sweat of his brow, for that apartment and for whatever profit might come to him, and that he deserves his reward. It would not be fair for someone who had done no work, to move in and to take away the profit due to the industrious stranger.

Profits are a very important part of our present American capitalistic society. We need money to educate our children effectively, and to set aside for our old age. We also seek profits, as with them, we can increase our material possessions. Nevertheless, many feel that the lack of decent housing is an injustice, demanding that more creative programs be undertaken to remedy the situation.

The early Hebrews had this same problem of people running up against hard times. In Leviticus 25 they set forth a proposal for families to help members who had experienced difficulties. We don't know how many people used this Jubilee method, but it seems a little more friendly and people-oriented than disaster insurance. The Jubilee Regulations return the land to the original owner if the purchaser has taken advantage of the original owner's misfortune. We, too, have struggled with issues of justice for those who suffer. Our current usage of medical insurance, unemployment insurance, car insurance, the welfare system, etc., are related to this problem. However, our methods are not universally admired because some insurance, such as medical, is not available for all, and some programs, like welfare, do not adequately lead to the full development of the recipients.

Other sections of the Bible seem to downgrade the accumulation of wealth. The rich young man in Mark 10 was very ethical and very wealthy. Jesus told him to leave his wealth and follow him. In ancient times, as now, those with wealth were often tempted to use their wealth unfavorably against the poor. In Isaiah 3:14 Yahweh calls to judgment the elders of his people, "You are the ones who destroy the vineyard and conceal what you have stolen from the poor. By what right do you crush my people and grind the faces of the poor?" Those of us in power might reply to God that she gave us the earth to *populate* and *subdue* (Genesis 1:28). However, *populate* does not mean *over-populate*, and *subdue* does not mean to *crush* but to *support and cultivate*. We have to use common sense and balance in our interpretations of the Bible, the Constitution, and the Bill of Rights. We are to facilitate the physical and spiritual growth of both rich and poor.

The Challenge. The process of evolution is still underway, and we are part of the process. This era of civilization is breaking away from old preconceptions. We are passing from the era of the nation state concerned with power and domination. We are hopefully entering a new phase, the era of the individual who cares for the other people in the world. We must make sure that all in the world are served with water, not weapons; with bread, and not guns. We must aid one another. We are drawn from the same depths; we must assist one another to fulfillment.

Footnotes
1 Joseph Gaer, *How The Great Religions Began*, Dodd, Mead & Co., NY, 1956, p. 222.
2 Lewis Thomas, "On The Edge of Knowledge," *Think*, July/August 1979, p. 46.
3 Mircea Eliade and Joseph Kitagawa, Ed., *The History of Religions*, U. of Chicago Press, Chicago IL, 1973, p. 142.
4 Rosemary Ruether article in *National Catholic Reporter*, 11/1/91.

XII

Spiritual Evolution

It is the spirit in human beings,
the breath of the Almighty,
that makes them understand. *–Job 32:8*

12.1 Holy History

Many of the really basic concepts, such as the nature of God, the process of creation, and our ultimate destiny after death, are hidden from our view. A presumption of certitude is perhaps fatuous and deceptive. So techniques such as myths, allegories, and metaphors are often used to convey a veiled truth while leaving room for interpretation and future insight. Holy scriptures often are wisely of this sort. If we understand these methods, we can gain greater understanding and better appreciate the tremendous value of holy scripture.

Holy history starts way back at the beginning. It starts with God who was before the beginning. As far as the earth is concerned, one of the first acts of God, was its creation. No one really knows how God did such a marvelous thing as the creation, but religious and scientific specialists down through time have sometimes professed to have inside information and have been very willing to reveal it. Many of the stories have been tongue-in-cheek tales, to get a child to go to sleep at night. These stories have been told and retold and taken literally, when it probably would have served the purpose just as well to take them figuratively. Many times a story was told orally, and then written down much later. These written stories were believed literally by some, and translated into other languages carefully, with little allowance made for imperfect translation or total misunderstanding of an ancient idiom.

There are many creation stories in the Middle East in which one can see similar trains of thought. If we work backwards from the later variations, we can see what the original story might be. The Jews elevated the creation stories by having God create the sun, moon, land, and water. When the Babylonians and Persians told their creation stories, these same physical quantities were personified by gods and goddesses. Persian folklore contains a Tree of Life. The Bible has placed the Tree of Life and the Tree of The Knowledge of Good and Evil, in a garden of Eden. Thus the writer of the Bible creation story conveys the messages of God's providence and goodness, clothed in the best ideas of earlier sages from many places.

In order to correctly tell about American history, we have to describe the roots of democracy as seen by Plato, various European struggles, and the exploits of slave traders off the coast of Africa. When describing some aspect of American life, we often ask, ''Why do they do that? Why a Supreme Court? Why judges in a court system? '' Then it is necessary to relate the traditions of previous time. Human kind has evolved slowly, and is still evolving. We have many imperfect solutions, many stop-gap measures, as we try to design the ideal world.

Similarly, holy history is not just our Christian holy history, as we are not the only group of people who have ever thought about higher powers. Christian religions have their roots not only in Christ, but in the stories about Moses and Noah and in inherited insights from thinkers in India, Persia, Mesopotamia, and Egypt. Muhammad, too, relates beliefs that were handed down by mouth from his ancestors back to the prototypal Abraham.

So it is with all religions. Religious specialists try to devise the best ways to worship God and the best ways to improve the human's relationship with God and man. We shouldn't leave this important task to the specialist. We each should make this task our first priority. But we can't do a good job of improving our relationship with God and man, unless we know something about our history and how our current concepts were shaped to their present form. We should try to find out what worked and what failed. Unless we know where we have come from, how will we know what direction to go in?

The characteristics of divinity and the role models or divine prototypes we strive to emulate, have been expressed in different ways in different cultures. At times, people are inspired by saints, and at other times, they express their admiration for role models by the worship of lesser gods. For some, these lesser gods are simply aspects or expressions of the one true God that we find difficult to know.

In early Greece, men and women who became noticeable for their courageous exploits were honored by their followers who expressed this honor by saying the hero was parented by one of the gods. They saw some of the noble characteristics of the god evidenced in their hero. If a person were truly great, those who related the story of his life, would let you know about his greatness by emphasizing his holy origins. Some similarly honor their heroes when they talk of the conception of Buddha and Jesus as holy and miraculous.

The idea of the "communion of saints" both in this world and in the next, also has a long history. The ancient Khassia people north of Syria would meet at tomb sites so that the foregoing spirits would aid in current deliberations. The Chinese and Koreans also carry the belief that their ancestors are interested in their well being. As those who lead exemplary lives are in tune with God's spirit, we act quite naturally when we denote them as our friends as well as friends of God and ask them to join us in our prayers to God. Surely, their spirits have become intertwined with God's spirit. Surely, God's spirit is working in our beings to produce a transformed world, a garden wherein there grow a Tree of Knowledge and a Tree of Life.

Holy history is not just the history of the more successful religions. Our religious beliefs have been affected by the lowly who can tell us a lot about God. Frequently, those in power have killed off the scientists, "witches," and theologians who opposed them. It has been said that the victors are the ones who write history. Often we will find that one of the powerful, like an emperor, will get behind a religious movement, and give it impetus. Rival religious beliefs may have to go underground. The Indian prince Asoka sent Buddhist masters to teach in foreign provinces, and supported Buddhism in his kingdom. Other Hindu beliefs were shoved off to one side, and the statue of Buddha became the largest in the temple. The Roman emperor Constantine similarly pushed Christianity to the fore. Displaced religions, however, have a way of perpetuating themselves. When the Catholic religion became the formal religion of Mexico, statues of the former mother goddess continued to be available and interchangeable with those of the Virgin Mary. Those devoted to the early native Indian goddess could continue with their ancient beliefs.

Many thinkers have been rejected and condemned, only to be recognized much later as prophetic and enlightened. Even the teachings of St. Thomas Aquinas, honored as a doctor of the Catholic Church, were, at first, criticized. Forward thinkers like Pierre Teilhard de Chardin and Henri de Lubac were temporarily added to the list of the outcasts. In retrospect, many once orthodox views are now seen as harmful. The sale of indulgences, the Inquisition, the crusades, Jewish pogroms, and opposition to freedom of speech, press, and religion, to name a few, are best forgotten.

The world again sees a revival of idea-suppression. The more liberal Baha'i sect suffers persecution in Iran. Some Baptist groups in this country root out all non-fundamentalists from their seminaries. The Catholic hierarchy tries to quiet those with innovative ideas, such as Kung, Gutierrez, Boff, Curran, and Fox. While discernment does involve selection and rejection, the dissenters, like Jesus, frequently prove to have the key insights for spiritual evolution.

Let us be open to the working of God through us. Surely, God will help us onward and upward on this evolutionary journey. When roots are set in good soil, and nutrients are provided, the result is blossoms.

12.2 Traffic Lights

Have you ever contemplated the power that is found in a traffic light? There you have a human creation that is put in place to keep order in human affairs. Traffic lights have evolved slowly side by side with rules and regulations for their promotion. First non-uniformed people directed traffic as necessary. Then uniformed people were designated. They held up signs. Electricity came along. Colors meant certain things. Pedestrians, too, were included in the act. All of us, drivers and pedestrians, automatically obey the traffic light to the best of our ability.

Religions seem to be eased into place in the same manner. We may automatically assume that they will take us to heaven, or at the least, help us to live a good life. Why should they? They are largely human creations (though hopefully inspired by God) devised to guide and keep order. However, like traffic lights, they are very useful, and they have evolved through need and through wise people's intuition of a way to fill that need. It's the way the individual human responds that is important. The automatic, non-critical response to the traffic light may not always be the best type of response to our religion.

People also have religious needs which are met through personal inspiration and insight. Because of these needs, religious pathways have slowly evolved. It seemed at first that anyone could walk in the garden and talk with God, but then it became apparent that some could talk to God better than others (for example, Moses). Shamans were trained to mediate the spiritual to the community. They began to have their particular liturgies and a distinctive costume. They performed periodic rituals, and in different cultures we called them priests, rabbis, ministers, or mullahs. For many, they were like the traffic lights. We could find them at every juncture of our lives, ready to direct us and to maintain order.

If all the traffic lights were taken away, would cars and pedestrians devise ways to behave in an orderly and responsible manner, like is the case at four-way full stops with pedestrian walks? In New York City, this probably would result in massive traffic jams.

What if we awoke one morning to find all the houses of worship had disappeared? If all the authoritative churches and religious specialists were taken away, would people be considerate with one another and behave with truth and justice? Certainly not! We would find that situation very demoralizing. On the other hand, we see a rippling of more and more people evolving to be more knowledgeable, more understanding, and more considerate of others. As I Peter 2:9 encourages, we are all to be priests, prophets, and kings. Doesn't that imply a lessening of the traffic light mode? Definitely yes! The mode of operation has already shifted from that of traffic lights to a need for facilitation of dialogue in the cooperative search for truth and fulfillment.

12.3 The Meaning of Compassion Today

Compassion has many definitions, and a human can show compassion, understanding, and companionship in a variety of ways. Some think of compassion as empathy or love. The opposite of love is often not hate, but inconsiderate power and control. If we truly love, we allow the person whom we love to exercise her freedom. If we seek sexual power over this person, we are not allowing freedom. If we want to control that person for her own good, we had better re-evaluate our presumption of superior wisdom and ask ourselves if we are allowing sufficient freedom.

We want good things for our everyday living, and we want things to be orderly. We want safety for our children. We also want our children to conform to society, because we think that they will be happy and safe in this conformity. We look at our larger society, and wish that it would be conforming and peaceful. We have pity for the hungry, as we regard them from our ivory tower of sufficiency. We do not like to see beggars because they disturb our sense of order. We wish that they would get a job and take care of themselves. Do we really feel their pain? Do we understand their rejection? God has mercy on us, as she looks down from her place of fullness, but does God have love and compassion for us, or just a disinterested aloofness? *Compassion* means *suffering with*. Does God suffer with us? Do we *suffer with* the suffering?

Are we truly companions with the people of the earth? The derivation of the word *companion* is *a person who shares one's bread*. Do we share ourselves with others? Christ on earth walked with the multitudes and invited them into his heart. Like Christ, we should be compassionate companions to our fellow travelers on the earth.

To be compassionate companions:

- We must be filled with God's message, as Jesus was filled with God's message.
- We must be fulfilled by allowing the message of love to flow through our beings.
- We must not hamper the tide of love by entertaining negative thoughts.
- In our *suffering with* we must imagine positive good for those who are too distressed to think clearly.

Love can be uni-directional, but the great depths of love are found when two people love each other. The deepest love is a two-way street and each person must have the freedom to respond. Mature love can only grow from a free exercise of personal power. This loving exercise of power seeks the growth and fulfillment of the other. It accordingly shares fully in both the joys and the sorrows of the loved one. If there is a creative and free God of compassion, this first cause must have power to create, or there is no creation. If you are a God and have no creation, you have nothing to love, except yourself. Creators who are so wonderful, must create more to love. Greatest growth occurs when the creation responds with a return of love. Love is an expansive process, that walks hand-in-hand with power and is fully compassionate with those loved.

12.4 The Presence

The Word was made flesh. God created the earth, and in the process of creation, consciousness penetrated the material of the earth. The earth was inspirited. In particular, the human mass was made and inspirited. Have our thoughts about the Presence of God within us evolved since the times of Enoch or Egypt? In most belief systems, God is both immanent and transcendent, within us and beyond us. We believe that the Spirit of God is somehow within us and with all the universe that God created. At the same time this Spirit is infinite and more than we can ever imagine. This Cosmic Creator stands beyond us surveying and directing this creation.

If God is with us, we should have words to describe this Presence. The Egyptians proposed the *ba* as the dwelling place or form or outward manifestation in which God's Spirit chose to reside. The god could appear in any *ba* he desired such as a bird, an animal, a pharaoh, a shadow form apparition, or a half human plant. The *ka* was seen as that spark of God's Spirit dwelling in that particular place. The *ka* spark can refer to one's highest ethical self. It equals one's best choices. It might be described as the *something of God* that is in everyone or the invisible life force which manifests itself from within, the divine essence.[1]

A multitude of *ba* representations can all be expressions of the one *ka* essence or the invisible life force. *Ka* sparks existing in *ba* manifestations such as human beings may get covered over and be temporarily lost but eventually get uncovered and travel homeward to the source of being.

For the Egyptians, the *ba* or body that surrounds a *ka* spark, may be a material body or it may appear as a shadow form at death. The ka spark may inhabit either of these body appearances, it may find a new material form to inhabit, or it may leave material forms behind and unite with the divine essence. The Egyptians believed Amun to be the divine essence or spirit behind all things. Our everyday prayer ending *amen* derives from this name Amun which means *hidden*. Our understanding of the Hebrew expression of *amen* as *so be it* or an expression of assent,[2] is therefore enlarged to, ''Let it come to be, as the hiddenness, mysteriousness, and incomprehensibility of God will have it.'' This broadening of our understanding of the *amen* formula, includes the human acceptance of suffering, and the acknowledgment of God's superior wisdom and impenetrability.

The *ka* or inward force or spark resides inside the *ba* or material manifestation. A human can transform his material *ba* only by dying. This Egyptian treatment of soul and spirit has similarities to Paul writing in I Corinthians 15:42-53. St. Paul says that each perishable human frame embodies a soul (ka) and when you die your soul leaves your material body (ba) behind and gets a new spiritual body (also ba). In verses 42-44 Paul asserts. ''The thing that is sown is contemptible but what is raised is glorious; the thing that is sown is weak but what is raised is powerful.''

Similar words to those of St. Paul are found in the ''Papyrus of Nekhet,'' Chapter XV, ''See how the seed falls from the tree and is buried. Die at once and live again. You shall grow like that sycamore, rooted in matter, bound for boundless sky.''[3]

If I allow God's Spirit or *ka* to dwell in me, then I become a *ba* or dwelling place of God. I would then be a temple of God. You in your exercise of freedom can also become God's temple. In exercising her freedom, God can choose to have her Spirit reside in objects such as the whole earth, a tree, or temples made with human hands. In our freedom, we can rebuff God's presence. The tree cannot refuse God's energy or deny its own being. Teilhard de Chardin has written about the different levels of ''consciousness'' in animate and inanimate objects and the potential of consciousness in the human.

If we devoted attention to God's presence (or ka sparks) within us, for the purpose of discovering what God is like and transforming ourselves in godly directions, we would have the pleasure of awakening to a new day, or a new self. Just think of the awe of all humankind awakening to this realization and hence to a transformed world!

12.5 Development of Ka

Everyone has a right and a duty to be creative. By fervent searching for insight and truth, by dreaming great dreams, we are able to sort out positive objectives, and then to realize those objectives. We must also have the ability to step outside our hypotheses, and to separate fact from fancy. We should be able to make critical judgments about what our creative imagination has proposed. Sometimes the substance of a viewpoint becomes so vital to us, that it takes another person or a group of people to put us back on a stable footing. We need others to help us affirm or clarify or correct our theologies and to join with us in our worship.

Development of godly perspectives occur through the incorporation of ka sparks that reside in a circle of friends. A group dedicated to encouraging kindness through recognition of the inspiration of God which is within each one of us, aids in the earth's evolvement in the direction of Utopia. Such a consolidation or union of what is positive seems always to have three dimensions. We need three viewpoints of the One God to keep us realistic. We need God coming at us from three *directions*. The first direction is the God who is beyond us, the God who created the universe, the All Holy whom we can never hope to understand, the God who is due our whole-hearted worship. The second direction we find within ourselves. When God made each of us, a piece of God's spirit was incorporated within, so that I can communicate with what is holy and dedicated in my soul. I can be in touch with the immanent God, and you, too, contain God immanent. Each of us can look within and find a trace of the spirit of God! We are, in a small way, avatars of God, representations of God's being. The third direction we find in others. I must recognize this aspect of God in the other, both in those enwrapped in God who can inspire me to justice, such as Jesus, but also in those who oppose my idea of justice, whom I might describe as my enemies. I must be particularly sensitive to this direction. Not only must I see God in Jesus; I must be sure to see the seed of God's spirit in those with whom I have difficulty relating. My enemy has the potential of becoming a saint! Such a venture of trinitarian spirit would transform our society, if we duly acknowledge the creator God, if we recognize the aspect of God present in ourself, and if we are diligent in recognizing the spirit of God present in others.

"Where two or three are gathered in [Jesus'] name" (Matthew 18:20), there is the possibility of forming a spiritual trinity. *In Jesus' name* means our alignment and dedication of ourselves to the spirit of love and kindness that is the essence of Jesus. We must *be* the embodiment of God's spirit for one another. If I have the Spirit of God in me, and you have the Spirit of God in you, and the Spirit of God is transcendent or outside of both of us, then we make a Trinity of Spiritual Presence. What couldn't we do with such a quantity of Spirit! If God is for us, who can be against us?

The ancient Egyptians could philosophically describe what they thought to be the relationship of God and pharaoh. They felt that this chosen person must have been very close to God in a special way, that the spirit of God was greatly and abundantly in him. Many people have felt filled with God's Presence and have believed they were justified in acting for what they thought was for the benefit of humanity. Not all, however, truly follow the spirit of God within them. Hitler may have recognized the power of God's presence in the world. He may have had a godly desire within himself to lead and perfect his people. But he did not have respect for the godliness of other human beings. He had no empathy for the Jews or for the handicapped. If we do not pay heed to God's triune presence, in the Transcendent, the Self, and the Other, things may turn out catastrophically. We need to listen for God's voice coming from all three directions. Through empathetic discussion, humankind comes to greater knowledge of the self, of the other, and of the universal.

The Inspirer, Helper, and Comforter whom we need is near at hand. In fact this Presence is nearer than hands or feet and closer than seeing. A paraphrase from Jesus in John 16:32 states, "I am not alone, for the Presence is with me." In John 14 we are assured that this Presence of God will also be with us. We are homes where the holy dwells, if we invite this Cosmic Companion within.

12.6 The Individual and The Spiritual Economy

We have considered how the evolution of spiritual concepts, including notions of empathy, caring, and kindness has progressed over many centuries. We have observed how different streams of thought from different cultures converge. The questions, then, arise– How does the individual contribute to this worldwide spiritual growth? How can we affect the spiritual economy? When we look at our video screens and hear of massive crimes against humanity done by people far and near, we shudder and feel a sense of helpless frustration. What can we do to influence good in such evil situations?

Teilhard de Chardin has proposed the idea of a spiritual encasement of the earth called the *noosphere* or thought layer. What sort of reality are our thoughts? If our thoughts can influence ourselves, why can't they influence others? At a basic level, we agree that thought transfer can occur from reading the written words of another person. From an observational level, we make an interpretation of another's thought by gazing at their face. On an even higher level, we make much of extra sensory perception. It may be that unspoken thought interchange amongst human kind is a reality.

It seems that I can use my positive thoughts to balance out negative thoughts, not just within my own being, but in the whole noosphere. If I face an annoying situation and swallow my annoyance and internally offer this situation in exchange for good to occur in a distant situation, I often later on hear of a positive development in that foreign place. If I am abused by another individual and say a prayer for that individual to become a better person, I may even right at that moment find that he has become more reasonable. Time is also a quantity in this economic equation, and perhaps it will be years later that I hear something good came out of a distasteful incident.

Jesus said about devilish problems, "This kind comes out only by prayer and sacrifice." With his sacrifice on the cross, he influenced good thought in the noosphere for all of us in the future. In a vision at Fatima, Mary urged prayer and sacrifice for the conversion of Russia, and we feel that there have been positive developments because of the prayers of many. There are many minor sacrifices that people are capable of offering. Why can't all those concerned with the good of the world offer their prayers for peace of all nations in a long term experiment which might prove this economy of the noosphere?

In both our inner cities and in warring foreign nations, the human spirit seems to have encountered lack of freedom and accompanying frustration, which eventually issues out in violence. If all this annoyance could be transformed by the oppressed into positive thoughts that searched for win-win solutions and personal fulfillment for all, then, perhaps, the spirit of God would flood the earth. If from outside the war zones, those of us under less tense affliction could offer our prayers and sacrifices for those inside, there would be a further gain in the realm of the spiritual economy.

Throughout the ages, in a large or small manner, every person has either added to or diminished the world's spiritual abundance. Even our thoughts can make a difference. Each of us had better be careful about every thought we think, as each of us, in at least a small way, is responsible for the good of the whole world.

12.7 Leadership

Leadership, such as kings, dictators, prelates, popes, priests, or presidents can be positive or negative. Often those in power come to believe they are always correct. When those around you are servilely agreeing to your every statement, because they want to remain in your limelight, it is difficult to make self-corrections. It is often necessary to consult the bottom of the power pyramid, if you want an honest opinion. One should be ready to communicate with the opposition. The hold-out in the consensus circle is the one from whom we may learn the most. Good leadership needs proper feedback from those being led, and must be capable of self-criticism.

Proper leadership should encourage what is good for all humankind. Leaders should undertake leadership with the idea of assisting the people to fulfillment. They should help citizens to obtain the objectives of caring for the earth, creating family and offspring, and making a greater community who will also care for the earth. Good leadership can be supported vigorously by more and more people. Together, we can tackle the massive problems of poor education, poor housing, overly violent TV, drug abuse, unwanted children, and proliferation of weapons.

However, we cannot delegate our responsibilities to a few leaders. To encourage our present day culture into more positive directions, we should put emphasis on every person's responsibility to perform service to others. Every person then has a leadership role in her own sphere of influence. This can be accomplished through moral education, and through each of us being a role model who portrays the quality of kindness and who shows consideration in the personal growth of other human beings. This acceptance of individual responsibility for ourselves and our society, is better than giving up our freedom into the hands of leaders who use rules, regulations, and enforcement squads (such as police and soldiers) to preserve order.

The transformation of humanity was given new impetus by Jesus. His teachings on transformation moved the focus from one that was purely self-centered to one that included the other person. Empathy, caring, kindness, understanding, and compassion enliven the human spirit. Muhammad added the quality of responsibility for others to this Christian structure. As we move towards the third millennium since the birth of Christ, there is a change in world perceptions taking place before our eyes. On our TV screens we see that soldiers are being used for new purposes, such as feeding the hungry. Win-win solutions are being found to accommodate opposing factions. Millions of "points of light" glow more brightly from individual initiatives. Grass root movements are taking place to improve education, health care, and the plight of the hungry and homeless.

All groups should strive to recognize the spirit of God in each other. As God's message is somehow available and built-in to every human being, his message is always with us. As we hear the message, the spirit has ebbs and flows upon the earth. This period of psychic entropy could now be transformed into a period of psychic energy, if we all thought in a positive manner. If enough people pray, encourage others, and respond to God's urgings in their inner beings, the world would be saved from any prophesied destruction.

We can create a world that is concerned about people. We are not powerless. The human today has a type of control over her own evolution. Through community action, she can help to insure the future of the earth and possible improvements to it. If her culture encourages consideration and kindness, as opposed to warfare and death, who knows to what evolutionary heights we will ascend!

12.8 Rights and Responsibilities

There are many guidelines that we can use to create and maintain a process which would encourage both individual and group fulfillment. The General Assembly of the United Nations has proclaimed A Universal Declaration of Human Rights. Everyone has the right to life, liberty, and security of person, the right to recognition as a person before the law, the right to freedom of movement, the right to privacy, the right to own property, the right of peaceful assembly, the right to work, the right to an education, the right to an adequate standard of living. Those of full age have the right to marry and found a family.

A supplemental statement of human rights, which focuses more on internal growth, includes the following rights to–

- be treated with respect and consideration.
- say "no" without feeling guilty or selfish.
- have and express one's own opinions and feelings, including anger.
- express one's talents and interests through any ethical channel.
- make mistakes.
- set one's own priorities as to needs.
- be treated as a capable adult and not be patronized.
- be listened to and taken seriously.
- be independent.
- ask others to change behavior that continues to violate one's rights.[4]

These are all reasonable rights, but we see many places in the world where the populace does not possess these rights. This is often because someone else is exercising oppression and control instead of respecting the rights of those being oppressed.

Sometimes we think that we possess rights, but we should not exercise these rights, if they impinge on the rights of others. Some rights we should not exercise are made obvious in situations where our actions affect others adversely. For instance, no one has the right to be a domineering elitist. No one has the right to carry a weapon with which he plans to control another. No one has the right to drink alcohol or take drugs that will make him unable to control himself. No one has the right to a sexual experience that may produce a child if he is unable to support a child. (Any man who places his seed inside a woman and walks away ignoring the outcome, is culpable. His desertion may make him guilty of the murder of his own child.) No one has the right to a sexual experience with another person if that other person is not willing, for sex is often a means to control another and an excuse for allowing oneself not to exercise control over oneself.

There are rights that weaker members of our populations possess, that require responsible actions on our part, such as the right of every child to two wise and loving parents. There are also the rights that handicapped persons have, so that they can function effectively in a society geared to the average.

We need to be conscious of our rights and to be prepared to stand firmly as we insist on them. We also need to constantly recognize that for every right there is a corresponding responsibility to respect the rights of every other person.

12.9 On To The Future

Call to The Inclusive Community. In Moses' time people responded to the call, "Come away, and we will become the just community." This has been tried, and the results were not always up to expectations. The people flowed into Israel and displaced the people living in the land. An army later came and shipped the Hebrews off to Babylon. Cyrus of Persia found these immigrants to Babylon difficult to rule. He believed if he offered them the plum of returning to Palestine and rebuilding the temple, they would be model subjects in his empire. Hebrews left Babylon and went to the land of Israel where they rebuilt their temple. They tried to be the *just* community, but became an *unloving* community in their treatment of the people who had occupied the land in their absence. Again they lost their rights to the land and were dispersed by the Romans in the Jewish Diaspora. Again, in the present era, the Jews have returned to Palestine, and the world waits breathlessly to see if any lesson has been learned. How will they treat the people of the land? For maximum effectiveness, positive dialogue should take place at the grass roots level, as well as among the upper echelons, (and every place in between). This has been realized in Israel-Palestine since its conception, and is a prime consideration in its holy books, but has not necessarily been put into practice. We now see a glimmer of hope that the basic tenets of both Judaism and Islam will bring compassion, forgiveness, and cooperation to the fore.

We look at the greater world community and ask, "How will we treat each other to make the just community in our world?" Americans look inward at the problem of their own minorities. Do some of us feel and act superior to the less privileged among us? How long will God allow us to dwell in abundance, as others suffer?

These times the world is a crowded place. There is no spot to run to, in order to form the elect group. The call becomes, "Stay where you are. The whole world is our community, and we must find ways to treat everyone in this world community with respect and consideration."

The Meek Are To Inherit The Earth. We do not have to think the same as others, or act the same. We must not be intolerant or proud, or presume that we possess total truth, but we must have the qualities of respect, humility, tolerance, and love. This will necessitate a less rigorous hanging on to the traditions and older patterns of behavior.

For each individual, awareness of truth grows with time. Yet in the community, truth becomes myth through elaboration and exaggeration of story tellers whose subconscious intent is the arousal of enthusiasm and conviction, as well as cult growth. Truth thus becomes enveloped in a cloud of myth, and the individual has difficulty sorting out what is applicable. The distorted kernel of truth can become a barrier.

Traditions are meant to be bridges to help us across murky, roiling waters. When the waters subside we can sometimes leave our bridging structures behind. In the holy community aiming towards Utopia, we must all compare notes with one another. We must consider both past and current experiences, and be willing to leave some favorite hiding places in search of new light.

Visions. Every human being is capable of being kind and considerate of others. We are created so that we have the freedom to react both positively and negatively. Outside forces can influence us in either direction, but we are each ultimately responsible for our actions and reactions. Some reactions may be programmed into us fairly deeply, but we can still change this programming by an act of our will.

What of the future? We are not doomed, so let us lift up our heads! The prophets and traditions do not proclaim that all will end in tragedy. There are many positive statements in the Book of Revelation. There will be a new heaven and a new earth (Revelation 21:1). The radiant glory of God will be with this new city (Revelation 21:11), which will appear though night still covers the earth and darkness the peoples (Isaiah 60:2).

We are asked to be transformers. Jesus was the transformer of people's attitudes, viewpoints, and values. We are to be transformed through the renewal of our minds (Romans 12:2). Confucius transformed royalty who practiced human sacrifice, into wise rulers. Similarly all of us should consider ourselves as possible transformers of ourselves and transformers of bad situations into peaceful, productive ones. God created the earth with its human envelope. Will we humans freely choose to be kind? Will creation be a success because we cooperated, or will it be a failure because we choose to harm others? *We* are the freely moving actors in this drama. We who have evolved from the material of the earth, can use the material substances of the earth for the creation of kindness and for our spiritual fulfillment.

I envision a world where each child is loved, and can therefore mature into a loving adult. The education of a child should be both by example and instruction, so that the child is well equipped to handle life experiences and to control fear.

I envision a world filled with understanding people, where there is no need for aggressive or power-hungry leaders, where the joy of life will be in helping one another to fulfillment. Even the fear of death will disappear, because people will understand their place in God's grand scheme.

I envision a world where people are kind to one another.

Footnotes
1 Karl W. Luckert, *Egyptian Light and Hebrew Fire*, State U of NY Press, Albany, NY, 1991, p. 44.
2 Leonardo Boff, *Trinity and Society*, Orbis Books, Maryknoll, NY, 1988, p. 232.
3 Normandi Ellis, *Awakening Osiris*, Phanes Press, Grand Rapids, MI, 1988, p. 47.
4 Basic human rights from Alternatives to Violence Project Assertiveness Exercise.

Selected Bibliography:
Agrawal, D.P. *The Archaeology of India*, Curzon Press, London, 1985.
Anati, E. *Mountain of God*, Rizzoli, NY, 1986.
Apsey, L. *Following The Light For Peace*, Kim Path., Katonah, NY, 1991.
Armour, R. *Gods and Myths of Ancient Egypt*, Amer. U in Cairo, 1986.
Boff, L. *Trinity and Society*, Orbis Books, Maryknoll, NY, 1988.
Bright, J. *A History of Israel*, Westminster P., Philadelphia PA, 1972.
Calvin, W. *The Ascent of Mind*, Bantam Books, NY, 1990.
Campbell, J. *Myths To Live By*, Bantam Books, NY, 1973.

Civilizations of Asia, Editoriale Jaca, 1987, Chivers Co., Bath, Avon, 1990.

Coon, C. *The Story of Man*, Alfred A. Knopf, NY, 1954.

Eliade & Kitagawa, Eds. *History of Religions*, U of Chicago Press, 1973.

Eliade & Leeming, Eds. *Encyclopedia of Religion*, McMillan, NY, 1987.

Ellis, N. *Awakening Osiris*, Phanes P., Grand Rapids MI, 1988.

Fritsch, A. *A Theology of The Earth*, CSPI, Washington DC, 1972.

Gaer, J. *How The Great Religions Began*, Dodd, Mead & Co., NY, 1956.

Herrmann, S. *A History of Israel in OT Times*, SCM Press, London, 1975.

Hinnells, J.R. *Persian Mythology*, Peter Bedrick Books, NY, 1985.

Interpreters Dictionary of The Bible, Abingdon Press, NY, 1962.

Kamil, J. *The Ancient Egyptians*, Amer. U in Cairo Press, 1988.

LIFE, Eds. *The World's Great Religions*, Simon and Schuster, NY, 1958.

Lloyd, S. *Ancient Turkey*, British Museum Press, London, 1989.

Luckert, K. *Egyptian Light & Hebrew Fire*, SUNY Press, Albany, 1991.

Macqueen, J.G. *The Hittites*, Thames & Hudson, London, 1986.

McCall, H. *Mesopotamian Myths*, British Museum Press, London, 1990.

Neville, R.C. *Behind the Masks of God*, SUNY Press, Albany, 1991.

Newby, P.H. *The Egypt Story*, Abbeville Press, NY, 1975.

Oates, J. *Babylon*, Thames & Hudson, London, 1986.

Piggott, S., Ed. *The Dawn of Civilization*, McGraw Hill, NY, 1961.

Reade, J. *Mesopotamia*, British Museum Press, London, 1991.

Redford, D.B. *Akenaten The Heretic King*, Princeton U. Press, NJ, 1984.

Robinson, T. *The Bible Timeline*, Friedman Publishers, NY, 1992.

Stuart, G., Ed. *People and Places of The Past*, Nat. Geog. Society, 1983.

Tapsel, R.F. *Monarchs, Rulers, Dynasties*, Facts on File, NY, 1983.

Voegelin, E. *Israel and Revelation*, Louisiana State U Press, 1958.

Weiner, J. *Planet Earth*, Bantam Books, NY, 1986.

Whitehouse, Ruth, *Dictionary of Archaeology*, Facts on File, NY, 1983.

Wilkinson, J.G. *The Ancient Egyptians*, Bonanza Books, NY, 1988.

Wolcott, L.&C. *Religions Around The World*, Abingdon Press, NY, 1967.

Epilogue

by Rudy Cypser

The foregoing chapters present a vast panorama of God's providence, extending over space and time, called here "The Creation of Kindness." They explore the possible interrelationships among widespread cultures, perceiving how we all have roots in ancient times and foreign places. That worldwide phenomena could also be referred to as the *enfleshment of the word*– that is, bringing to reality the spirituality of which humankind is potentially capable, and the realization of humankind's divine destiny. In widely separated cultures over many centuries this has involved the struggle to perceive the meaning, the deeper values, and the destiny of life. In almost all cases, the conclusion has included the growth of consciousness, expressed as spiritual qualities in which the human can excel, like empathy, compassion, and kindness. In almost all cultures, this also includes the importance of recognizing the worth of the individual, the building of community, and an emphasis on cooperation.

A Multicultural Process. As the book illustrates, this infusion of spiritual consciousness has been an ongoing development for millions of years. Yet, the more recent ten thousand years has seen a widespread crystallization of these concepts and their expression in multiple systems of thought. China, India, the Mid East, Africa, and Europe all participated in the awakening. In particular, from the Indus Valley to Mesopotamia, Assyria, Palestine, and Egypt, and across the Greek, Roman, and Persian empires, challenging insights, hypothesis, and dogmas swirled back and forth among these diverse peoples. The Holy Scriptures of the Hindu, Buddhist, Hebrew, Christian, and Muslim traditions are among the writings which attempt to organize these spiritual awakenings into life-guiding wisdom. As the preceding chapters indicate, each of these scriptures has benefited from the thousand of years of inquiry and the exchange of insights among the peoples across the arc from India to Egypt. Each has interpreted their insights in a different framework that associates this growth of consciousness with a view of the infinite and a concept of God.

The Immanent God. There has thus evolved, in many cultures, the concepts of a transcendent and immanent God– both "out there" and near or within each person. The concept of the immanence of God relates to the personal interaction of God with each human, and hence to the universal *enfleshment*

of the word in each and every person. It has been variously expressed:
In the Hindu tradition:

> You have to feel that all the attributes of the Lord should manifest themselves in you. ''The broad-mindedness of the Lord should become part of me. The selfless feelings which characterize the Lord should become part of me. The unbounded Love of the Lord should become part of me.'' When you have this feeling then you reach the position of ''I and He are one,'' and **there will be perfect unity.**
>
> *Discourses of Sathya Sai Baba on the Bhagavad Gita.*[1]

In the Buddhist tradition:

> **Buddha-nature exists in everyone** no matter how deeply it may be covered over by greed, anger, and foolishness, or buried by his own deeds and retribution. Buddha-nature cannot be lost or destroyed; and when all defilements are removed, sooner or later it will reappear.
>
> *The Teaching of Buddha*[2]

In the Christian tradition:

> In this way he (Jesus Christ) has given us the very great and precious gifts he promised, so that by means of these gifts, you may escape from the destructive lust that is in the world, **and may come to share the divine nature.** II Peter 1:4
>
> God is love, and anyone who lives in love, lives in God, and **God lives in him.** I John 4:16-17

Impediments. These many scriptures indicate that we have made progress in the awareness of our potential. One might think that the wisdom of the ages thus inspired, would by now permeate the world and produce a universal solidarity among humankind. Sadly, this is not yet the case. History shows that our favorite religious institutions sometimes presumed to have reached a pinnacle of knowledge and certainty. This, combined with the allures of power and authority, sometimes led to a premature fixation on interpretations, and over-domestication of people. As if that were not bad enough, the presumption of certainty encouraged a false sense of uniqueness and exclusivity, with resultant separations from and enmity with other groups.

Looking Forward. In contrast to this trend, the foregoing chapters again remind us of the common and on-going work of the Holy Spirit in *all* peoples, in *all* our worldly space, and in *all* times. They remind us of our common pilgrimage, benefiting from our common source of inspiration, and sharing in the fruits of our diverse interpretations of that common inspiration.

The hope of the world still remains bright despite all setbacks. The consciousness of peoples continues painfully to rise. The movement to a worldwide consensus was neatly expressed in the *Declaration of A Global Ethic*, produced at the Parliament of World Religions in September 1993.[3] As a hopeful sign, some of the very practical points emanating from a raised consciousness, and included there were:

• Every human being without distinction of age, sex, race, skin color, physical or mental ability, language, religion, political view, or national or social origin possesses an inalienable and untouchable dignity. And everyone, the individual as well as the state, is therefore obliged to honor this dignity and protect it.

• No one has the right physically or psychically to torture, injure, much less to kill, any other human being. And no people, no state, no race, no religion has the right to hate, to discriminate against, to "cleanse," to exile, much less to liquidate a "foreign" minority that is different in behavior or holds different beliefs.

• No one has the right to degrade others to mere sex objects, to lead them into or hold them in sexual dependency. We need mutual respect, partnership, and understanding, instead of patriarchal domination and degradation. We need mutual concern, tolerance, readiness for reconciliation, and love, instead of any form of possessive lust or sexual misuse.

• We must utilize economic and political power for service to humanity instead of misusing it in ruthless battles for domination. We must develop a spirit of compassion with those who suffer. We must value a sense of moderation and modesty instead of an unquenchable greed for money, prestige, and consumption.

• Earth cannot be changed for the better unless the consciousness of individuals is changed. We will work for such transformation in individual and collective consciousness, for the awakening of our spiritual powers through reflection, meditation, prayer or positive thinking–for a conversion of the heart. Therefore, we commit ourselves to a common global ethic, to better mutual understanding, as well as to socially beneficial, peace-fostering and earth-conserving ways of life.

Footnotes

1 *Bhagavad Gita, Discourses of Sathya Sai Baba*, Prashanti Nilayam P.O., Anantapur Dist. Andhra Pradesh, 515134 India, 1989, p. 35.
2 Bukkyo Dendo Kyokai, *The Teaching of Buddha*, Kosaido Printing Co., Ltd., Tokyo, Japan, 1985, pp. 68, 78.
3 *National Catholic Reporter*, September 24, 1993, pp. 11-14.

Index

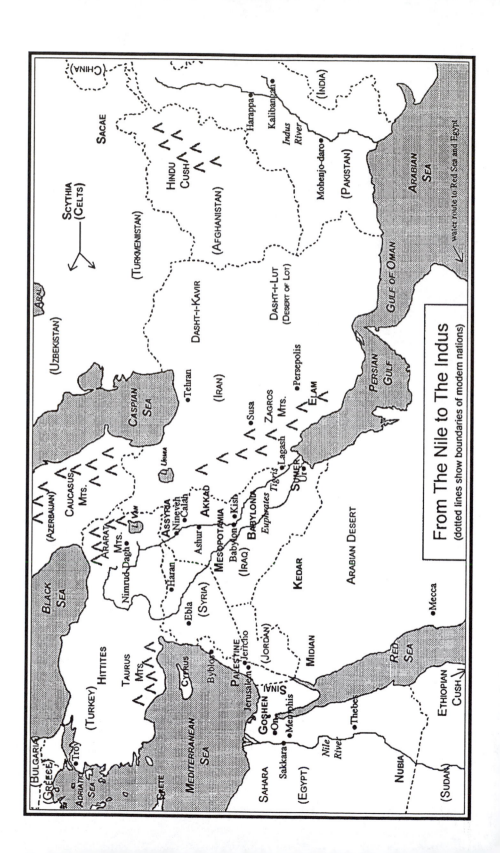

From The Nile to The Indus

(dotted lines show boundaries of modern nations)

OTHER BOOKS BY CORA E. CYPSER

Taking Off The Patriarchal Glasses
which emphasizes women's contribution to the Bible.

Covenant and Consensus
which challenges us to improve our relationships
with God and the human.

A Triad of Poetry Volumes
Versings and Conversings
Seasonings
Lion and Lamb

Written with Rudy Cypser:
The Process of Becoming
a guide to personal fulfillment.

Available from:
KIM PATHWAYS
16 Young Road
Katonah NY 10536